MYTH AND SUN

OTHER BOOKS FROM CLEMENS & BLAIR
(www.clemensandblair.com)

Unmasking Anne Frank, by Ikuo Suzuki
Pan-Judah! Political Cartoons of Der Stürmer, by R. Penman
Passovers of Blood, by Ariel Toaff
The Poisonous Mushroom, by Ernst Hiemer
On the Jews and Their Lies, by Martin Luther
Mein Kampf, by Adolf Hitler
Mein Kampf (Dual English-German edition), by Adolf Hitler
The Essential Mein Kampf, by Adolf Hitler

OTHER BOOKS BY THOMAS DALTON
(www.thomasdaltonphd.com)

Classic Essays on the Jewish Question
Debating the Holocaust
The Holocaust: An Introduction
The Jewish Hand in the World Wars
Eternal Strangers: Critical Views of Jews and Judaism
Hitler on the Jews
Goebbels on the Jews
Streicher, Rosenberg, and the Jews: The Nuremberg Transcripts

Myth and Sun
Essays of the Archetype

Martin Friedrich

Clemens & Blair, LLC
— 2022 —

CLEMENS & BLAIR, LLC

Clemens & Blair, LLC, is a non-profit educational publisher.
www.clemensandblair.com

Library of Congress Cataloging-in-Publication Data

Friedrich, Martin
MYTH AND SUN: Essays of the ARCHETYPE

p. cm.
Includes bibliographical references.

ISBN 979-8986-7250-00
(pbk.: alk. paper)

Printing number: 9 8 7 6 5 4 3 2 1

Printed in the United States of America on acid-free paper.

CONTENTS

DEDICATION

Dedicated to my family, a divine manifestation of *der heilige Wille* and a bridge for the MAN TO COME.

To my wife, ᚾ: The Germanic folk rose to the heights through the efforts of wives and mothers like you.

To my sons, ᛏ and ᛡ: You embody the truth of the Eternal Return and shoulder the task of carrying the fire of *der germanische Wille* into a future that needs it. Remember: Our Honor is Loyalty.

ACKNOWLEDGMENTS

Without the work of those preceding us, the support of caring souls around us, and the possibility of those to come, we would never amount to anything.

I am grateful for the work and influence of the *die Kämpfer* of the Great Sacrifice (1920-1945) and the Great Struggle (1945-present), Friedrich Nietzsche, Martin Heidegger, Savitri Devi, and Miguel Serrano. Their work, and the effort of those yet unknown, will make certain a Great Restoration.

Many publishers ultimately declined to publish this work, even after initial agreements to do so; thus, this effort has been years in the making. When Hegel ended his *Philosophy of History* with "The German World," he perhaps could not see that, because of his contemporaneousness with it, that age was ending and a new world, "The Jewish World," was beginning. Wilhelm Marr's *The Victory of Judaism over Germanism* and Theodor Fritsch's *The Riddle of the Jew's Success* are but two of the many works marking the transition from one age to the next. It could perhaps be argued that, indeed, there was never a "German World" at all, but only a burgeoning "Jewish World" to which the Germanic folk were simply responding with their characteristic flair. By the time of the two fratricidal world wars, the world was already firmly in Jewish hands; *the wars would not have happened otherwise*. Thus, these wars were not transitional markers, but only the Germanic folk's paroxysmal rejections of inevitability.

It is therefore understandable that so many would shy away from publishing a work like this: like so many "paroxysmal rejections" before it, it seeks to highlight the evils of modernity. Modernity does not like its reflection. And if we see some of what is written already come to pass, it is only because such events have been foretold long ago. After all, whether we consult the Bhagavad Gita, the Edda, Nietzsche, or the work of our Germanic Führer, we can see the future.

— Martin Friedrich

PREPARING THE WAY

AN INTRODUCTION

Der germanische Wille ist Gott. This belief belongs to northern souls, northern blood. *Let us look each other in the face,* demands Nietzsche, *We are Hyperboreans.*[1] Nietzsche did not write for everyone; and what was Nietzsche if not a prophet of the Germanic will? *Where you can divine,* Zarathustra reminds, *there do you hate to calculate.*[2] Zarathustra did not speak for all ears; and what was Zarathustra if not an augur of the Aryan *Geist*?

The Germanic will stands opposed to the materialistic calculators — the deducers and reducers — of this world. *This world is a will to power — and nothing besides!*[3] Through faith in the power of the Germanic will, the northern souls uplift and honor all that precedes them; through this same faith, we clear the way for the MAN TO COME, we bridge the way to something higher.

Honor, loyalty, discipline, cleanliness, decency, strength of being — these are the marks of the Germanic will; faith in the power of Germanic blood — this is the sign of a holy will that has not lost its ancient roots. We set ourselves apart from others through our blood loyalty and indomitable ethic: this is our only means of survival. Betray this means and we betray our folk.

We *are* Hyperboreans — faith in and loyalty to our folk assures us of the bridge to that ancient and future race. By conserving the past, we ensure the future. HE WHO CAME BEFORE has shown us the way. When we adhere to HIS principles, we clear the way for the MAN TO COME. HE is the ARCHETYPE; we are HIS *heilige Wille* and HE is ours.

The postwar diaspora of the Germanic folk has demanded a spiritual unity. It is only through this spiritual unity that we will endure the coming trials. Whereas in HIS time the *Deutsche Arbiter* were united under a common banner, today our banner is the silent oath we swear to *der heilige Wille* that binds us. We are workers for the cause common only to us, and we must unite. In this way, we

---

[1] Nietzsche, *Antichrist,* §1.

[2] Nietzsche, *Thus Spoke Zarathustra,* Part III, "The Vision and the Enigma."

[3] Nietzsche, *The Will to Power,* §1067.

appropriate the internationalist slogan: *Workers of the world, unite!* Shorn of its bloodless meaning, this slogan now becomes our own. We are of *ein Volk, ein Reich, und ein Wille*: workers of the world, unite! For whom do we work and fight? Now we fight for the MAN TO COME.

∞ ∞ ∞

René Guénon describes a crisis of modernity wherein, with the dawn of the Enlightenment, man became the measure of himself: he alone was the template for rectitude and the goal toward which his descendants should strive. *Je pense, donc je suis — I think, therefore I am.*[4] Already when these words were spoken, we felt the tremors of the peasant revolt Luther so fiercely upbraided; already we heard the sharp whistle of the guillotine, the Red Terror; we yet heard the march of money against common blood in two world wars; and we hear, still, the enforced socio-political "progress" imposed upon peoples not evolutionarily designed to adapt to such rapid change. Man has developed over vast swathes of time; he is adapted to glacial change, for such change suits his temperament; what, then, can we expect when ages worth of change floods his native capacity? Time will tell.

And what does modernity tell us if not this: just as quickly as a window opened for humanity, that same window was all but shut tight. The Enlightenment was a boon for European man: he escaped the fetters of potentially crippling dependence — upon stagnating piety, scholasticism, and unthinking familial mandates. But if it was a boon for him, by allowing the voice of the quantity to be heard, then it was also his undoing, for not every voice *deserves* to be heard. Speaking thus is anathema in the modern world, naturally; speaking thus is akin to any excommunicative sin of the medieval world, of course. For what Descartes unleashed with his brilliant dictum was not a step on the moon and a "giant leap for mankind," but instead, oppressive and unwieldy interconnectivity and globe-spanning ICBMs; the analogy is there — *all things in moderation.* With man being man, however, moderation must be enforced. Hence, to invoke an evolutionary perspective once again, man developed a taste for fats and sugars: gorging himself on them meant greater chances of success through times of dearth; but his environment provided a much-needed check on his developed tastes: fats and sugars in any

[4] Descartes, *Discourse on Method* (1637).

significant amount were rare and life was a constant trial; now, however, his tastes match the endless supply of fats and sugars processed in so many money-minded laboratories, and he becomes what he eats: a blob manufactured for the ritualistic bartering of the money-powers; he has no identity beyond what his narrators tell him.

So, what is the crisis of modernity? It is man himself. It is his inability to process and adequately adapt to a rapid change toward a rootless future. We humans have tremendous appetites — not just for foods, but also for ideas, and we want to belong — even if that means forcing others to belong or die, physically or metaphorically. Thus, we want to consume, but we also want to produce — in great quantity, not just materially, but ideologically. *I think, therefore I am*: this is modernity's mantra: I, me, mine. *If I can prove it, you must believe it, or be shunned*, so says the modern man. But where is the proof? Proof is in the numbers — What is the quantity? What is the profit? How can we increase the profit of proof? With greater quantities of proof-eaters, greater quantities of consumers — this is how. How do we get more consumers? We must abandon and excoriate the *ancien régime*; we must explode all the limiting factors that gave birth to our cultural genius. Race, creed, and kind — what are these but limiting factors, inhibitors to greater quantities of proof and profit? We must explode the culture which birthed us in order to progress further, so says the modern man. Time will tell. Time tells of every sin and virtue, yet one is more fleeting than the other.

What is the crisis of modernity? *It is a culture turning its back on the Germanic man that raised it to the summit of greatness*. The Germanic man is not localized to Germany, of course: his genius and intrepidity are everywhere in Europe: he is the Norseman, the Goth, the Dane, the Vandal, the Saxon, the Norman, the Celt, the Bavarian, the pre-Christian Roman, and others. He is the natural pagan and conflicted Holy Roman Emperor. He is Alexander, Caesar, Hermann der Große, and Barbarossa; he is Napoleon, Friedrich II, Moltke, Wilhelm, Léon Degrelle, Jochen Peiper, and Hans-Ulrich Rudel; he is Eckhart von Hochheim, Richard Wagner, Guido von List, Dietrich Eckart, Alfred Rosenberg, Friedrich Nietzsche, and many others we admire — or once did. The Germanic man is Zarathustra, the Aryan who conceived the dualistic understanding of a world which moves at glacial speed, a world that must be molded by the fire of *der heilige Wille*. Those who would turn their back on the Germanic man are like so many dwarves, perching themselves on Zarathustra's shoulders:

> Mutely marching over the scornful clinking of pebbles, trampling the stone that let it slip: thus did my foot force its way upwards.
>
> Upwards:—in spite of the spirit that drew it downwards, toward the abyss, the spirit of gravity, my devil and arch-enemy.
>
> Upwards:—although it sat upon me, half-dwarf, half-mole; paralyzed, paralyzing; dripping lead in mine ear, and thoughts like drops of lead into my brain.[5]

The heavy lead pulling the modern man into the abyss is nothing less than the mass quantities of the modern age — quantities of proof, of profit, of individuals, of voices, of the barnacles and other hangers-on so pervasive as to be wholly smothering.

This collection of essays asserts to the world: "'Halt, dwarf! ... Either I — or thou! I, however, am the stronger of the two...'" It is a weaving together of culture — Germanic culture — through the time modernity wants so desperately to annul.

One is hard-pressed to find outlets that extoll the virtues of the Germanic folk — not in academia, not in the home, and certainly not in the media. This reflects a forgetting, a disremembering, or even a misremembering that modernity so often represents. After all, the Germanic man seeks quality over modernity's quantity — so the two are as antithetical as Zarathustra and the dwarf: who can blame the dwarf for wanting to forget his better? *None but the Germanic man.* Everything is increasingly modernized, diversified, and multi-culturized — i.e., everything is rewritten to fit the narrative of those with the means and desire to rewrite. We will see later who the revisionists are, but their goal is clear — for it is the same goal that sparked the two world wars: destroy the Germanic man, dilute his holy blood, and pave the way for the material-man, the organic robots, the golems — all in the name of *liberté, égalité, fraternité,* which is to say, all in the name of increasing profit through culture-exploding ideology — a demonic ritual as old as the tetragrammaton. This, then, is a spiritual struggle. We must remain loyal to our cause; we must labor for our folk and prepare the way for the MAN TO COME

[5] *Thus Spoke Zarathustra,* Part III, "The Vision and the Enigma."

— the return of Baldur, son of Wotan and god of the summer sun, das Sonnenrad — the Eternal Return.

The crisis of modernity is a severing of the link of goodness and prudence over time: it is the exploding of the *ancien régime* itself, or that which led to our pre-to-early-modern ascendancy. This severing might be seen in the intersticed sunwheel — *das Hakenkreuz*. Yet the arms of the redemptive *Hakenkreuz* represent the ages revolving around the center pole, or axis. Reuniting the wheel of time through its spiritual center, this axis is the Eternal Return of the MAN TO COME. *Das Hakenkreuz*, then, represents the possibility of a spiritual, more human future; a rejection of the sunwheel is a rejection of the gods that birthed us and the gods who must return, thereby completing the inexorable cycle of time. In this way, rejection of *das Sonnenrad* is a rejection of time itself; it is anti-Nature, which is evident in the exploitative nature of all things materialistic. Thus, again, it is a spiritual struggle. Spiritual struggle is that which sets new "gods" against the old: for modernity, money and all its materialistic appurtenance[6] represent the new "gods." Modernity shuns the spiritual good of the past for its organic brutality; but man needs external checks when his internal discipline is scant — and what are the quantity if not hordes of unchecked, undisciplined voices — so many voices with so much of nothing to say? The work of the "great Germans" — those bastions and heralds of the Germanic *Geist* — was to join the unchaining stores of the Enlightenment to the strict discipline of the past: those meritorious workers who separate themselves from the masses through their disciplined, honorable actions are alone the voices deserving of speech and sound; all else is whimpering quantity.

The darkness of modernity seeks to actively or passively overwrite the good, but brutal blood of the past; this is why the Germanic *Geist* is subject to calumniation and derision, particularly in media and academia. That critical point between what modern scholarship identifies as the medieval period and the modern was nothing but a reawakening of the Germanic spirit: it was the rebirth of an ancient spirituality, the culmination of all previous ages in the

---

[6] In short, we can understand this as *rationalism, scientific rationalism, pure rationalism*, or even *scientism*. It is *that which stands opposed* to any sense of spiritual will or faith, for there are few things more intolerant, destructive, and oppressive than the godless materialist and his "compassionate" ideology. This creed is intolerant to all but machines.

soul of the Germanic *Dasein* — *Seele, Geist, und der Wille zur Macht*. (If it is recognized as anything else, it is because the Western world has distanced itself from that which made it great — because the quantity have spoken.) The derision, then, stems from the diametric opposition of the materialistic machine against the light of spiritual being.

Every essay in this collection is an honoring of this sense of spiritual being — scholarship be damned. For what is scholarship but subjectivity in fancy dress? Reason is a tool, after all, and not a god, despite its fervent, blasphemous worship by the proof-eaters, who survey and amass it like so much slop in a sty. Modern scholarship is naught but acquiescence to the prevailing worldview, an outward manifestation of the crisis of modernity, an apotheosizing of reason, the bellowing of the quantity. To rail against such servility pleases our spirit and honors our ancestors. We should always use reason as the mere tool it is and subordinate it to something ever holier: the will of the Germanic man.

This collection means to add to a tradition that is under attack — a tradition that culminated in the demonized (and often deliberately misrepresented) writings of Friedrich Nietzsche and Alfred Rosenberg; a tradition manifested in the steadfast heroism of Hans-Ulrich Rudel and Léon Degrelle; a tradition represented in the glory- and merit-based brilliance of Napoleon; a tradition as ancient as the seas surrounding primeval Hyperborea and as recent as the Third Reich: the history of the true European culture that beckons its future destiny; for without it, we will all simply melt into a rootless mass of faceless producers and consumers — exactly what the golems of modernity would wish.

∞ ∞ ∞

Just as a degenerating Rome won the battle against Jesus and lost the war against Christianity, the Liberalistic West's victory against the human spirit is fleeting. Human nature guarantees this — for men are not machines. We are all spirit and will, and our grounding is necessarily mystical.

A humanity cut off from its mystic roots is fated for machine-like alienation. This alienation imparts nihilism; this nihilism offers only degradation, and this, in turn, leads to socio-cultural death. This death — this darkest night — is followed by the glowing sun of spiritual renewal.

Schopenhauer said this world is a will-to-live; Nietzsche said this world is a will-to-power: they are both right, and it is time that proves their case over and again. This is the Eternal Return; this is the human spirit. Baldur may yet return — and reaffirm the heroic light that resides eternally within the northern soul. *Hail the lightning that rends the night — hail the sun that follows the dark!*

Our fights are tough and relentless as never before... It is now a fight for survival, a fight for everything.

— HANS ROTH, *EASTERN INFERNO*

∞ ∞ ∞

We are forerunners of a new time, and even if many or all of us should no longer experience it, we will nonetheless be able to say at our end: we have lived, and it was beautiful to live and to fight...

— ALFRED ROSENBERG, *BLOOD AND HONOR*

Chapter 1
A Philosophy of Life

FOUNDATIONS FOR A HEALTHY SOCIETY

The Essential Triumvirate

Every healthy society must be founded upon three essential aspects: the *family*, the *State*, and the *self*. Each aspect is reliant upon the others and, further, needs the others for complete fulfillment. Yet if one of the three could be said to be pivotal to the triumvirate, it is *family*. The self is born into the family and the State arises out of the collective need to protect and enhance the needs of the family. Society and life-as-we-desire-it are predicated on the family. Next in order of precedence is the State. Since the State is a direct magnification and enhancement of the family's — that is, the key aspect's — needs, the State must be prioritized above the self. The State is the vehicle through which the community — i.e., the collective, or collection of *kinsmen* — achieves its collective will; and as such, the State takes precedence over and above the self. The self, being born into the family, is an extension of the family and, over time and the establishment of the defined State, becomes an extension of the State itself. In this way the self is reliant upon both family and State for its existence. *Individual wants and needs must always be subsumed under the first two aspects' will*; the self must always be deprioritized for the sake of the collective. This is why *personal* (selfish) *ideology* must always rest firmly and benignly in the *background* of family and State fulfillment. This is also why the triumvirate must be understood as "family-State-self."

The Self and Will

Although the self is deprioritized within the essential triumvirate, this does not mean the self is unimportant. Being of the triumvirate, the self is essential to any healthy society. However, the self must be understood as merely an extension of that which precedes it: the family and the State. Yet, moving beyond this "merely," the self must also be seen as the willful mortar binding the triumvirate together. The self might only be seen as functional if it understands its place within the triumvirate and acts accordingly: acting accordingly means always *self-improving*. *Self*-improvement is the means by which both the family and State are enriched and strengthened. The self is never improved for its own sake, but for the sake of the superior aspects: the family and State. In this way, the individual will *self*-sacrifices for the sake of the collective, thereby improving the group and — by extension— improving the self as well.

The Triumvirate of Self

Self-improvement is achieved through its own triumvirate of body-mind-spirit, or the physical-mental-spiritual. As in the case of the overarching family-State-self triumvirate, each aspect of this triumvirate of *self* likewise depends upon the others, and the corresponding strength of each aspect determines the strength of the organism. Therefore, the physical and mental each must be exercised — i.e., must be *made fit* — so as to increase individual capacity to fulfill its *spiritual* mission: *self-sacrifice for the sake of the collective*. Just as the *family* is the most essential aspect of the family-State-self triumvirate, the *spiritual* is the most essential aspect of the physical-mental-spiritual triumvirate. The *spiritual* is always understood as *that which is transcendent* — or, that which transcends the physical-mental realm. The only way to achieve transcendence is to sacrifice the individual will for the sake of the collective will; in this way, the temporal is sacrificed for the enduring and the spiritual aspect emerges. This is why physical and mental fitness *for the sake of* the family and State — and *not* the individual — leads to a strengthening of the spirit. One no longer acts for one's own self, but for the sake of that which transcends him: the family and State, the outward manifestations of holy blood. Self-improvement for the sake of anything other than the family and State — i.e., anything other than the collective will — is shameful narcissism, which is to say, *un-health* or *disease*. This is why the focus of any healthy society must be, at its core, the family and the spirit.

The Sickness of Individualism

The modern West began its lustful affair with the self (as individual will) with Luther's Reformation.[1] The affair was particularly useful in bringing rationalism and self-structured improvement to the fore,

[1] We might understand this as the beginning of the Enlightenment, the inadvertent byproduct of Luther's reforms.

leading to exponential growth in Western power. Luther, being Germanic, returned the power of reason — the power of God — to Western (i.e., Germanic) man, in a sense.[2] This, in turn, led to the "enlightened" offshoots of Christianity: Christian/scientific pantheism, deism, positivism, humanism, etc. From these turns and the concomitant dethroning of aristocracies, came the rise of the common man.[3] The common man found everywhere the opportunity to satiate his whim and fancy — something previously unknown to him. And while the leaders of the West's push toward rationalism might have expected more (or less) from their fellow man — i.e., more effort toward self-improvement — what the most optimistic of them got was distinctly less than imagined.

The revolutions of the common man reached their zenith in the American and French Revolutions, creating the first modern sociopolitical ideology: Liberalism. The intellectual elite devised the contemporary notions of *liberty* and *freedom*; *liberty* being the "freedom from" something; *freedom* being the "freedom to do" something, barring interference with another's individual will. The European and American experiments roughly paralleled each other and ultimately settled on certain "guardians"[4] mediating the common man's tastes through spectacle and media.[5] These guardians' — or elites' — goal, because of Liberalism's synchronous maturation with the free-enterprise system, was and is *money*. Self-interest was and is the focal point of the Liberalistic ideology;

---

[2] The Semiticism of the Roman Church made every effort to quell the power of the Germanic will (*der heilige Wille*) — typically through subversive and traitorous means. This is illustrated in Charlemagne's perfidious destruction of his own people's pre-Christian way of life; it is illustrated in the blasphemous mural on the *Externsteine*, depicted in the bent Irminsul. A folk that had always had direct communion with God through its holy blood and will were now expected to commune with God only through a middleman. The "middleman" is the very definition of Semiticism. Luther, while yet beholden to Christianity, could not help but reassert his Germanic will, rejecting some of this notion of the slinking "middleman."

[3] Or so the story goes. Perhaps a more cynical view of modern history might suggest that the people were empowered to choose which of the *manufactured* worldviews best suited their tastes — instead of, as was done formerly, silently acquiescing to the dictates of the elite.

[4] Immanuel Kant, *What Is Enlightenment?* (Berlin: *Berlin Monthly*, 1784).

[5] Alexis de Tocqueville, *Democracy in America* (Chicago: University of Chicago Press, 2002).

likewise, self-interest was and is the fulcrum to a free market. What this self-interest gains in the competition that swells the tide upon which all ships might rise, however, is lost in the disintegration of any healthy and enduring State's communal integrity — or that official extension of the community, which is the natural extension of the family.

This overwhelming emphasis on self-interest and profit spawned modernity's second and third alternative ideologies: communism and fascism. These ideologies, too, arose from the stream of rationalism that produced Liberalism; but their ensuing divergence from that shared stream rested in the perceived corrosiveness of Liberalism on the self and its relationship to the community. To this end, the former concerned itself with the dialectic of class struggle and rectifying the individual's alienation from himself and fellow citizens as only a means of production for the guardians; the latter concerned itself with a subsumption of the individual *into* the collective, thereby *correcting* the community's disintegration. Each alternative to Liberalism's predominant self-interest (of individual will) saw, as did Luther before them, the inherent flaws in a system predicated on individualism.[6]

The sickness of individualism rests in its prioritization of the individual will over and above the collective will. Without a central focus on *self*-sacrifice for the *collective* will (which, again, manifests in the family and State, in blood ties), there can be no transcendence, which is to say, no healthy and familial spirituality. Of course, the spiritual does exist in Liberalistic societies; especially in America, religious communities abound. Yet the religious spiritualism offered is irrelevant if its crux is not bent on edifying the individual only insofar as the family and State he serves are improved; any additional focus (e.g., focus on a *personal* relationship with God or the hereafter, or an idealistic adherence to abstractions in the name of "liberty" — i.e., *selfish* focus), for the purposes of a healthy State, is inconsequential or, at worst, detrimental. And when spirituality is lacking, the triumvirate of self (physical-mental-spiritual) dissipates,

---

[6] Luther on the plague of the peasant uprising, the fruits of an empowered and emboldened common man: "[Remember] that nothing can be more poisonous, hurtful or devilish than a rebel. It is just as when one must kill a mad dog; if you do not strike him, he will strike you, and a whole land with you.... I think there is not a devil left in hell; they have all gone into the peasants. Their raving has gone beyond all measure."

resulting in the breakdown of the essential family-State-self triumvirate.

What is to be done?

The second and third alternatives' solution to combating Liberalism's society-degenerating flaws was to establish a State apparatus capable of mitigating or reorienting the *self*-interest of the citizenry toward the spiritual, or that which is transcendent. In this respect, each alternatives' approach was a means whereby tradition might be *conserved*, wherein pre-Enlightenment society aimed at rallying the citizenry[7] around a *common will* of the monarch (God) or aristocracy and the communist/fascist apparatus sought to realign the masses to *something other than* the individual will. Thus, it was the individual will which was seen as the bane of modernity, and it was the alternatives' solution to evade the traps concomitant with an individualistic society by creating and fostering a *transcendent cause* through which the family and State might be prioritized.

There is nothing "evil" in these alternative ideologies in and of themselves, of course. Though we might take heed to not replicate the shortfalls of, say, a dialectical materialism that reduces all to calculable material in our revisiting of their transcendence. If a future alternative to Liberalism's inevitable degenerative *self*-interest is to be proffered, let alone successful, it too must seek to reorient the interest of the self back to the collective family-State-self. It is only in this way that a society might find the health necessary to endure the force of time and the proclivities of fanciful man.

It is toward this *traditionalism* that we should strive. And therein we might one day be lucky enough to embody the Napoleonic dictum, "The fatherland has the right to expect great things of you" — or perhaps even Kennedy's "Ask not what your country can do for you — ask what you can do for your country." Through a mindful, spiritual traditionalism — one that embraces the positive aspects of tempered reason, as was the aim of our alternative ideologies — we might also overcome the shortfalls of any privileged indolence masquerading as tradition. Tradition must not be upheld for its own sake any more than liberty must be pursued for its own sake; rather, tradition must be understood as *the means by which we achieve subsumption of the self into something higher.* But while modernity perilously seeks to throw the baby out with the bathwater

7 If rallying was necessary at all — i.e., if the social roles were not implicit.

by supplanting *all* tradition with pure rationalism (manifested in progressive policies and the pursuit of liberty *for its own sake*), any meaningful future must conserve the tradition of deprioritizing the self for the sake of those higher things: family and spirit. Only in this way will a society flourish; only in this way will a society endure.

Transcendence of the self should ever be our aim; transcending the self should ever be our mandate.

FAMILY-STATE-SELF: THE CLASSICAL TRIUMVIRATE

That which binds a people together is *ethos*; some might call this *culture*. Of antiquity, this ethos might be understood as a triumvirate of family, State, and self: one did not exist without the other and each was a reflection of the other two. This triumvirate manifested itself in the Classical world principally through *gloria* (glory) and *dignitas* (worth), each of these being founded further on a self-reinforcing sense of moral piety, which itself cyclically sprung from the self-reinforcing ethos. That is, Classical antiquity was a closed system in which the family, State, and self were one; glorifying one was glorifying all, and failing one was failing all. The legends of antiquity embodied this self-reinforcing ethos through both their familial relationships and individual conquests for the fatherland, since, of course, the two were identical.

An analysis of two Classical legends — Hannibal and Scipio Africanus — and their historical intersection might both illuminate this triumvirate and act as a marker for the potential failure of any ethos not bound by such moral piety.

∞ ∞ ∞

Many consider the greatest military minds of antiquity to be Alexander the Great, Hannibal, Scipio Africanus, and Julius Caesar. Of these, perhaps the least is known of Hannibal, the Carthaginian legend.

Most of what *is* known about him has been written by his enemies, the Romans, and consists of their struggles against his mighty forces and brilliant tactics during the Second Punic [Phoenician] War (c. 219 BCE). What little is known of him, though, lists great virtues amongst the basest traits. Hannibal was intelligent, yet dastardly; fair, yet vicious; attentive, yet unforgiving, etc. In short, he was a man of strong will, keen insight, and a very definite set of morals. Writing in c. 25 BCE, Roman historian Livy said this of the Carthaginian general:

> There was no leader in whom the soldiers placed more confidence or under whom they showed more daring. He was fearless in exposing himself to danger and perfectly self-possessed in the presence of danger. No amount of exertion could cause him either bodily or mental fatigue; he was equally indifferent to heat and cold; his eating and drinking were measured by the needs of nature, not by appetite; his hours of sleep were not determined by day or night, whatever time was not taken up with active duties was given to sleep and rest, but that rest was not wooed on a soft couch or in silence, men often saw him lying on the ground amongst the sentinels and outposts, wrapped in his military cloak. His dress was in no way superior to that of his comrades; what did make him conspicuous were his arms and horses. He was by far the foremost both of the cavalry and the infantry, the first to enter the fight and the last to leave the field.[8]

But what was the foundation of his character?

When he was nine years old, Hannibal's father, the commanding general of Carthage's forces in Spain during the First Punic War, asked little Hannibal if he wanted to accompany him on a Spanish expedition. The boy quickly accepted his father's invitation. But before his father would let him come, he ushered Hannibal to a sacrificial altar and, laying the boy's hand on the victim, made him "swear never to be the friend of the Romans." Hannibal never forgot this oath, and he made it his life's mission to destroy the civilization that ultimately killed his father.

Hannibal achieved unparalleled success against Rome. Both his tactics and strategy were as brazen and sweeping as they were effective; yet Hannibal's history is not written by Carthaginians, it is written by Romans. Why?

---

[8] Livy's *History of Rome*, book XXI.

In their histories, the Romans blamed Hannibal for instigating the Second Punic War, for he "unjustly" attacked Saguntum, a city allied with Rome deep in Carthaginian territory. Hannibal, while of course acting on behalf of the Carthaginian State, was ultimately fulfilling the oath he swore to his father. And in so doing, raised the ire of Rome and launched himself into history — but history was not on his mind, his father was.

After suffering numerous military setbacks in both Sicily and Spain and following Hannibal's incursion into Italy, the Romans called on two brothers to command the army sent to meet Hannibal at Italy's northern Alps: Publius and Gnaeus Scipio. In 211 BCE, the brother-generals were killed in battle. Feeling the shock of not just losing two of its generals, but also the impending doom of defeat, the Roman senate rushed to replace its army's leadership. The most likely candidates all refused generalship — by then they were well aware of Hannibal's skill and ruthlessness [in one of his largest victories, Hannibal laid waste to more than 44,000 Romans in the deftly fought Battle of Cannae just five years earlier]. Only one man, just 24 years old, volunteered to command Rome's forces against the feared Hannibal: another Publius Scipio, the fallen general's son.

Scipio joined the fight against Hannibal in the war's second year; he was barely 18 years old. In a clash near Tincius in Italy's northern Alps, Scipio, then still a teenager, saw Roman forces taking heavy casualties against the determined Carthaginians; his father, Publius, leading the now disarrayed forces, was in peril. Scipio, comprehending the weight of the situation, took charge of the melee and rushed in to save his father. This impressive feat, uncommon for hardened soldiers, let alone a teenage boy, won Scipio the respect of his fellow Romans and renown throughout the Republic. Fate, however, pits death against us all eventually, and the elder Publius would yet be claimed by Hannibal's warriors.

Years later, after consistently earning the adoration of his peers, subordinates, and superiors, the young Scipio would take command of Rome's final hope against the Carthaginian onslaught. In Spain, the same land where Hannibal once swore his familial oath to relentlessly pursue to Romans to his dying day, Scipio, avenging the memory of *his* slain father, dealt Hannibal's forces their first substantive blows. Hannibal, meanwhile, had deepened his incursion into Italy, coming a mere six miles from Rome. Scipio, however, having studied Hannibal's tactics through the war and divined his strategy, sailed for Carthage, expecting to lure the city-state's leader away from Italy; his plan worked. Hannibal's pride would not suffer homeland defeat, and he left his Italian campaign to save his beloved Carthage from the Roman scourge. His attempt was thwarted, though, by not just time and distance, but also Scipio's own brilliance. Carthage's rearguard fell easily to the young Roman, and once Hannibal's main contingent arrived, it was too little too late. The legendary thorn in Rome's side had finally been defeated by Scipio, the brash Roman, soon to be christened *Scipio Africanus*: savior of Rome, conqueror of Carthage.

∞ ∞ ∞

What is it that finally links these two legends of antiquity? Certainly, their efforts on the battlefield and their devotion to their fatherland. *But isn't there more?* What determined their course in life? *Family*. Whether a sworn paternal oath or a courageous volunteering in the face of heavy odds, both Hannibal and Scipio defined themselves both in relation to their father *and* their respective State. There was no difference between the two, and a slight against one, was a slight against the other. What man asks of his son an oath to defeat the enemy of his homeland except a man who defines his actions through the lens of the State? What man fights alongside his brother and son against enemies of his homeland except a man who understands only the State? What man commits his life to fulfilling an oath he swore to his father at just nine years old if not a man who dedicates his life to family bonds? What man avenges his father's death in the face of perilous odds if not a man drawn into action by familial love?

These are histories and questions worth pondering because they not only help us understand the past, but also our present and future. History remembers these two men, not because they were unique in their motivations, but because they were the absolute embodiment of the ethos of their time and place. This ethos bound family and State together because there was no reason to separate them. Theirs was an ethos of glory (*gloria*) and worth (*dignitas*); theirs was an era of citizen-State symbiosis.

Yet like Carthage, the Roman Republic, too, would one day fall. Unlike Carthage, though, there was no external threat to conquer her. Instead, a decline in morals and ethos were marked as the signposts to civil strife and republican decay. Livy and, indeed, many of the notable Roman historians, understood the histories they conveyed through a moral lens. This is because, like the family unit, the State should be understood and judged by its fruits according to a moral code, or that which stands as the foundation for a people's ethos. And ultimately, these historians, like many of the Roman citizens themselves, are *arbiters* of history and not mere *conveyors* of it. The ethos of family-State-citizen symbiosis pervades not only their interpretation of history, but also their living of life, just as it did the lives of all the legends of antiquity. Glory for the State is glory for the family is glory for the self, and vice versa; each leg of the triumvirate is a reflection of the other two: this is the defining link of Classical greatness; it is the measure of all *dignitas*. Without it, there can be only decline and fall, just as any two-legged tripod is destined to fail.

When Rome finally fell, her citizens were concerned principally with their own *selves*. The Republic gave way to bickering, gridlock, corruption, indulgence, and individualism. Abandoned was the triumvirate, that which our legends embodied: family-State-self. This is a warning of history. This warning should concern the greatest republic since Rome: America. The traditionalist roots of American culture[9] have degraded into partisan bickering, gridlock, corruption, selfish indulgence, individualism, and, worst of all, blind servitude to abstractions. Yet just as Rome had her Caesar to overcome decay, so too will America have hers.

Human nature is not just our will; it is our destiny.

TO LIVE, TO COMMAND, TO CONQUER

The community is an army and children are its weapons.

Every army is an organization and every organization, like every community, is built and maintained for an objective. For some, the goal is defense; for others, the goal is empire; there is no middle ground between defense and empire, so one must choose one or the other.

---

[9] When one hears "American culture" today, surely only gross debauchery and shallow money grubbing come to mind. Yet we must recall that America has *European* roots, which is to say, *Germanic* roots — a far cry from materialistic debauchery. If the roots of a nation are eradicated, only a bloodless, materialistic husk remains. Such a rootless society will fall with the first strong wind.

Defense is understood as a necessary component of any organization — whether one is defending its existence against competitors or justifying its existence to superiors, peers, or subordinates; that is, defense is taken as given and is the least effort needed for organizational sustainment. Defense, like empire, relies on multiple fronts to achieve its objective.

Empire need not consist of terrain, colonies, or puppets; nor does empire need to reveal itself under the mask of war, for there are other instruments of power. The modern West, for instance, might seek to dominate its peers and opponents economically, while other, less structured or robust communities might seek to dominate their peers and opponents through cultural influence. Whatever the case, a certain goal is pursued along one or more fronts and the conditions under which the goal is achieved can be seen as domination. Any equilibrium desired or reached in pursuit of this goal must only be seen as a respite along the path to future domination, to future empire.

Defense *voluntarily* pursued across all instruments of power amounts to a weakness of will, a blind idealism. The organization that *merely* defends itself, or willingly seeks perpetual equilibrium will, in time, succumb to the more predatory instincts surrounding it. For while some wish for equilibrium in their *idealistic defense*, others seek imperium and the means to achieve it.

The natural balance of things suggests that both the weak will be overcome and that strong wills erode in time. Spates of supremacy are undercut by flurries of mediocrity; weakness is squashed underfoot, and strength is corrupted by further pockets of weakness. The ebb and flow of events and their corresponding power is a matter of limited perspective; what endures is the fact that strength is but one body with many faces. The organization that focuses its intrinsic strength of will behind the multiple fronts of power is best equipped for survival. Survival, ultimately, means *countering the natural balance of things by creating the conditions for future dominion, for future empire.* In short, empire is life.

The organization that seeks defense as a means pursuant to later strength is yet seeking empire; it only works within the parameters of its given time — i.e., it does what it can. What ensures its success or failure across the instruments of power and into the future is the will to endure. Endurance is survival; survival is dominion; dominion is power; and all success and failure, then, hinges on the will to power.

∞ ∞ ∞

Communities coalesce out of a necessity that morphs into culture. A culture arises out of a community because, over time, there exists tradition (shared history), vision (shared purpose), and the ways through which the culture is sustained (values). Communities, like the States they birth, rely on instruments of power to exercise their values. Viewed holistically, a community's *end* or *objective* is survival, the *way* it achieves this end is through its value system, and the *means* by which it is achieved are the instruments of power; the overarching strategy, if circumvention of the natural balance of things is sought, is dominion.

To achieve dominion, a community, like the State it births, must deploy any number of weapons; the weapons are deployed across the instruments of power; the types of weapons deployed are determined by the community's values. A strong community — whether its manifest State is robust or not — will always know its greatest weapon: the community's embodied past, present, and future: its children.

Our children are our greatest weapon — for defense, for imperium. Our children are the bulwark against foreign influence, the rampart through which we conserve our identity. Our children are the means by which we advance the frontline in this clash of blood and culture we call life. This is not to say that children are to be objectified or devalued — not in the least; our children are our most prized possession, our most cherished treasure. They are *ends* in themselves and, because of this, they are our greatest *means* to value the whole community. Our children are everything. A community that fails to see its children as its greatest asset in its march against time and alien influence betrays itself, acting as traitor to its voiceless past; the future for a failing community will be an existence with another face, a face disconnected from its past, a face divorced of tradition — the face of an *international man* made for *international cliques*, which is the face that holds dominion over the perpetual defenders.

∞ ∞ ∞

Necessary for the successful deployment of any weapon system is maintenance. If your weapon is money, you must secure the funds and understanding to deploy it appropriately. If your weapon is a rifle, you must know how to disassemble, clean, reassemble, and fire it effectively. If your strategy is dominion, your way of achieving it rests in your values, i.e., your culture; culture propagation is gained via the supreme cultural weapon — the means by which we protect and further it — our children. If children are our weapon, we must know how to develop them.

∞ ∞ ∞

To develop a child is to develop his *self*. The essential aspects of the self are the physical, mental, and spiritual.[10] For the self to be healthy each aspect of the self must be healthy; to neglect one aspect in favor of another is to undermine the health of the entire organism; further, neglecting the health of the self — especially the self of the child — is undermining the health of the community, which is tantamount to treason, no small crime. In the end, a parent must set the example for his children; and, in the end, a parent who fails to see himself and his family as integral to the health of a larger whole must himself improve. To not set the example is to contribute to a decaying folk.

To develop physical health, the parent[11] must instruct the child on the imperativeness of healthy diet and exercise. This requires parental effort, but such is the nature of proper parenting. A healthy diet consists of natural or minimally processed foods; a proper diet minimizes or eliminates "comfort" foods, for such so-called foods, which ostensibly sit as the foundation for many modern Western diets, lead only to physical, mental, and spiritual decline and disease. Likewise, the parent must instruct the child on healthy exercise. Exercise must be functional and incorporate the whole body. Learning about the body and its different energy systems will be helpful to building an effective exercise regimen. Ultimately, physical health creates the conditions for mental and spiritual health.

Nurturing mental health means emotionally and pedagogically "being there" for your child. A parent must satiate his child's emotional needs; to do otherwise is neglect. Scholastically, a parent

[10] See "Foundations for a Healthy Society" in this collection.

[11] It is understood that not all caregivers are biological parents. However, "parent" here means anyone who courageously and responsibly takes ownership of the child's well-being. Tangentially, it is also understood that not all biological parents are courageous or responsible; arguably, these unfortunate and dastardly souls are not worthy of the title "parent."

must educate himself enough to competently augment (or surpass) the institutional instruction the child receives. Parent-child discussion — from even the earliest ages — is essential to not only build the foundation for familial communication, but to also stay abreast or ahead of institutional instruction. The attentive parent must be able to provide context or fill in information gaps otherwise ignored by the schools. This will also ensure the child is exposed to broader knowledge streams that institutions (public or private) often disregard. Homeschooling is an option, but recommended only for the astute and capable parent; care, in this case, must be taken to prevent social isolation, which could lead to later culture shock and corruption. Like physical vigorousness, mental health must be sought to undergird the self and its spiritual purpose.

As that which is transcendent, the spiritual aspect of the self is its highest aim. A child must always understand that his physical and mental health are achieved and maintained, not merely for the individual, but for the family and community which he will later strengthen. He must understand that his blood represents the blood of his ancestors. Every child is a self, and every self is a part of something *larger*, something *higher* — the family and community. It is incumbent upon the parent to instruct the child in his role and purpose; for the self's purpose is not different than the family's, nor is it different than the community's. The child's purpose is the aim of every self and every community: not merely surviving, but *thriving* — the goal is *dominion*.

To neglect proper care and maintenance of our greatest weapon, our children, is to betray all who have come before us, all who stand by us now, and all who will have their existences snatched from them in a globalized future. Is it easy to just let your child lengthily sit in front of a television, tablet, phone, or some other device? Yes, it is. Is it healthy? No. Is it engaged parenting? Definitely not! You would never leave your rifle in the rain simply because *you* wanted to stay dry — if you did, your rifle would rust and fail to function properly. Is it easy to shovel various processed and "comfort" foods into your child's mouth? Yes, it is. Is it healthy? Absolutely not! You would never let your car, yard, wardrobe, or — God forbid! — your phone fall into a state of disrepair. All the more reason that we should focus all positive energy and effort on our greatest asset and future salvation: our children.

For our children are weapons, and the community is the army. Proper living and proper conservation of our heritage demand much work; but this work is echoed in our children and our community, the means by which we further our values; and our values are the ways through which we achieve our final and enduring objective. What is our objective? *To live, to command, to conquer!*

SURVIVAL MECHANISM

Life is evolution; and *evolution* is only another way of saying *competition*. At the heart of any successful ideology must be a competition. Lack of competition means lack of evolution and, thus, death. This is why Marx's communism fails. *To each according to his need; from each according to his ability*: While this credo describes a novel symmetry, it does not factor in the one essential aspect of existence: competition. All life has evolved to compete.

Where leaves grew healthy and untouched, insects soon swarmed to feast. Where only insects once passed, unabated, through limbs and leaves, soon a web was built to catch them. Where spiders tangled their quarry in peace, the bird pierced its place into the system. The reptile killed the bird; the mammal preyed on the reptile; consciousness overcame the mammal; and ideology tries like mad to neutralize consciousness. Niches filled by predator and prey are only opportunities for life to exploit inherent system weaknesses; this is only to say that life is born out of evolution, out of necessity, out of survival. When life is not snuffed out, it is strengthened for the next trial. *What doesn't kill makes stronger.*[12] Life is a series of inborn attacks. Survive these attacks and your genes might yet make it one generation more. The consciousness that now sits atop the system ignores these attacks or tries to spin them as *immoral*. This is done through ideology — that is, what consciousness creates to save or prolong its existence, or, another survival mechanism. Ideology, then, is only an extension of the evolutionary process.

Culture determines adopted ideology. Consciousness, sparked by blood, determines culture. And while consciousness and, indeed, life itself might be accidents, once their roots take hold, necessity and competition determine them. Cultures adopting passive ideologies do so from necessity; likewise, aggressive cultures become so because life made them so — *it's in the blood*. Layered on top of consciousness' instinctive and genetic will-to-live is another drive: a

[12] Nietzsche, *The Will to Power*, §934.

cultural instinct to incorporate or dominate. These instincts are inclinations and nothing more, yet they drive the genetic impulse. Survival of the individual matures into survival of the group. That is, every culture became a culture by sacrificing the needs of the individual for the needs of the group. Cultural competition, then, becomes the means by which survival of the "fittest" unfolds at the top of the system, within the consciousness that sits atop the system. At the apex, the competitive urge is satiated — though, no longer from inter-species conflict, but from intra-species conflict. This is why cultures exist: the competitive drive is so genetically ingrained in us that we must fight even when we, as a species, have "conquered" the system. When our competition is gone, life creates new competition. Yet this is only to say that the system is never "conquered" and that life, essentially, *is* competition.

Which is the moral one: the spider who spins the web, or the fly who breaks it? We say they are amoral actors locked in an amoral fight, that the spider and fly are merely manifestations of the evolutionary process — that is, extensions of life. It is true they are amoral actors; the one plays spoiler to the other; this "spoiling" function is not born of *ill* will, but simply *will* — the will to live. The will to live is amoral. Morality is something devised by consciousness to justify existence or rulership at the system's apex. It is in this way that morality, as the governing principle of ideology, is an extension of the evolutionary process. Consciousness, via devised moral concepts, assigns blame in *internecine* fighting. What we dismiss at the system's lower rungs as amoral instinct, we glorify as free will and rectitude at the apex. Consciousness — i.e., the evolutionary process — is very kind to itself, until it sees the *other*. The *other* is not prey, but the *other* is a threat, a challenger to *existence at* or the *rulership of* the apex. The competition in us, as a culture and ideology, seeks justification or dominance — even if that means a dominance of incorporation or tolerance.

Marx's communism, with its novel symmetry, seeks a balance among men that does not exist. Aside from clear inequalities amongst the peoples of the world, Marxism discounts the competition inherent in life and, subsequently, in consciousness, and in so doing props itself up as a philosophy which seeks to undermine reality. This is the calling card of Nietzsche's slave-morality. The slave-morality began, of course, as a religion. We in the West recognize it most clearly in Christianity. *Those who are first will be last and those who are last will be first*; and, *the meek shall inherit the earth*. From the outset, the slave-morality has tried to thwart reality. If you cannot beat the mighty in this life, beat them in the next by creating an afterlife where your rules — the rules of *weakness* — win the day! This is the essence of slave-morality: create the anti-reality philosophy.

When Christianity was new, it was fiercely persecuted by Roman rule. The Romans mocked and sought to devastate the religion of the meek at every turn because the Romans, who ruled much of the Western world, rose to power through strength and dominance — not meekness and subservience. The Romans did not *become* the servant; the Romans *created* the servants. Roman religion, if it was present at all, was a continuation of Greek mythology: humans are a part of life just as the gods are and in this capacity are predator and prey, salvaged only by strength of will and wit; that is to say, Greco-Roman paganism recognized and incorporated the evolutionary process. Christianity, on the other hand, in its position as the ruled, flipped the script; as an ideology of a *ruled* people — born out of the ideology of the notoriously and perennially ruled people, the Jews — Christianity declared characteristics of the *ruled* worthy of emulation. In this way, those who were last now became first. The game — i.e., life — could now be won by losing, and it was only a matter of time until the winners in this life, the rulers, would be ravaged by a "God" whom they mocked, a "God" who wanted to conquer the conquerors. The afterlife, in Christianity, was prioritized over the worldly life because the worldly life was a lost cause. How could this world not be a lost cause when you are a slave? Thus, the Semitic slave-morality gave birth to Christianity; and the slave-morality sought to undermine reality — this *life* — with a philosophy, with a creed, with meekness and the *after*life.

All of life is manifestation of the evolutionary process, which is to say that all life is competition, which is to say that all life is conflict. The only impediment to life running its thoughtless course has been an unprecedentedly self-aware consciousness, which is to say human consciousness. In its infancy, this consciousness was still governed by untamed will; it rose to heights unseen in the world's history — it is still piercing new heights. Over time, untamed will began to feel guilt and shame over both its errors and its strengths; after all, untamed will, while incomparably strong, is unhindered by considerate reason; this has led humanity through much enormity — through the torturous turns of maturation. The Western world rose to the top of the apex through its version of will tempered with considerate reason. The Greeks inspired, the Romans conquered, Crusades were fought, anti-Western cultures were defeated and enslaved, barbarians were emboldened and countered a strangely religious Roman Empire, the Empire fell, and the barbarous mixed with the civilized. What remained was an unconsolidated, but newly empowered Greco-Roman culture; this was Western culture atomized, and what was once a single bullet was now a shotgun blast of Westernism.

What, then, do we make of Roman Catholicism (or "Universal Christianity")? Although scholars have pointed to many reasons for the fall of the Roman Empire, we might distill it down to this: *guilt*. No, the fall of something so great as the Roman Empire — *great* by any meaning of the word — cannot be pinned on one thing specifically, but perhaps, generally. After all, it was Constantine, the Roman Emperor who presided over the Empire's peak, who intimately felt the religious pleas of his Christian mother. It was Constantine who ultimately rejected the paganism of centuries of Romans before him in favor of a deathbed baptism. It was Constantine, whose patronage fueled the meteoric rise of the Catholic Church, who called the First Council of Nicaea some ten years after his dream of the Christian cross. It was Constantine who outlawed the persecution of Christians after centuries of martyrdom. In this way, Constantine became the patron saint of guilt — or guile. Perhaps his decisions were motivated by the possibility of expanding the Empire even more, on the momentum of a freshly galvanized and inspired creed. In either case, Constantine was anything but a man, anything but a conqueror. He was a businessman, a politician, an opportunist given to the whispers and machinations of a shadowy slave-power. Constantine's power was the power of a million slaves; and like any headless mass, Constantine's Empire took the first stuttered steps toward collapse.

Ultimately, the slaves sought to win by losing. And anyone who thinks this is indefinitely sustainable is destined to subvert the mechanism that won power in the first place. Not even the once-slaves who rode the tide of Christianity all the way to modern, internationalist, and global economic-interdependence believe in the tenets of slave-morality. These *rootless internationalists* simply exploited a golden opportunity to prey on the spiritual emptiness of a directionless emperor. Today the former slaves ape conquerors — like so many golems, so many organic robots. Yet true conquerors need the blood of a folk rushing through their veins — a blood rooted in a spiritual soil. Blood does not course through the once-slaves' limbs, only currency. And in this way, they sit perched at the apex, spouting an ideology of "freedom," which is naught but doublespeak for *unwittingness.*

ON HUMAN NATURE, MORALITY, AND NATIONALISM

It has been said that change is the only constant in life. This is not true. The only constant in life is human nature; change is utterly dependent upon this constant. It was Kant who finally articulated the nature of our perception as passive and active shaper of the world we discern and judge; it was Schopenhauer who lifted the veil even more by defining all of our discernments and judgments as contingent, not upon a *known unknowable* — a *noumena* — but something as tangible as *will*; and it was Nietzsche who finally shed the will of all moral judgment and recognized it purely for what it is: the life-force behind all existence, the amoral prime mover. *This world is a will to power — and nothing besides!* Nietzsche proclaimed, and he is right.

A man and woman enter into a relationship together because each gets something from it: companionship, loyalty, affection, mutual support and satisfaction in all its forms. The couple wants to *be there* for each other and to be loving, supportive parents, if blessed with children. This relationship, like all relationships, is a transaction. The man and woman give of themselves what they can afford to give and each receives from the other what cannot be efficiently or abundantly produced alone. In this capacity, the couple becomes *invested* in each other: their subsistence and happiness become intertwined. Here we find the source of morality.

Man, as a social animal, depends on his relationships with others for survival. It is man's nature to be social and dependent, in some capacity or another. This is man's most valuable currency and, despite the vicissitudes of this or that political or economic system, the constant confronting time is man's nature as a social being. We often view breakdowns in the social environment negatively; we might call them *bad* or *immoral*. Thus, if a husband undermines the trust his wife places in him and has an affair, she — and many others — would recognize him as a *bad* husband and father. Likewise, if he simply abandons his family for some selfish reason, he will also be considered *dishonorable*, *irresponsible*, and many other deserved epithets. In fact, if we only look at the word *selfish*, we find a word that is most commonly understood in a negative way. This is because, intuitively, we know that to look after only oneself — to break social partnerships for individual gain or to not enter into these social relationships altogether — is something *unnatural*, something *reprehensible*. This, then, is the source of morality: social bonds. Keeping social bonds is viewed both internally and externally as *good*; likewise, breaking social bonds is viewed as *bad*. Morality ultimately stems, then, from human nature.

When one declines social bonding, one essentially declines morality; when this occurs, one is considered, at best, egomaniacal and, at worst, sociopathic. Focusing too intently on one's self is typically disadvantageous or not advantageous to the group and, thus, frowned upon. This is why our stomach turns when we see someone who is greedy, wrathful, gluttonous, lustful, prideful, envious, or slothful. We intuitively and experientially know that the person who acts in such a way is harming the group, impeding survival; we know that they lack the discipline to quell their basest desires and act for the greater good — that is, they lack the discipline to act in ways that strengthen, not weaken, the social bonds. Conversely, when we see someone acting selflessly, honorably, responsibly, courageously, loyally, and the like, we see this person as acting for the benefit of more than just the individual.

Human nature, then, as the source of societal bonds, is the source of morality. That which acts against the social bonds acts against human nature — it is unnatural. Life would indeed be easy if everyone always acted how we have defined and how is commonly understood to be *good*. But life is not easy; life, if left to its own devices, would be nasty, brutish, and short.[13] And everything commonly understood to be *good* is in constant war with that which seeks to undermine it: *we* are at war with the *other*, the *bad*, the *immoral*. It has always been this way and will always be this way. Why? — Because there is not one set of social bonds, but many. And this is only to say that there exist varied cultures, the "anthropological" bases for society. Ultimately, we cannot say this or that culture is moral or immoral any more than we can say the complexities of life or human nature are moral or immoral. All of existence is amoral. It is only our perception that judges the amoral and makes it something good or bad, positive or negative. Objective morality — i.e., morality that exists independent of human

---

[13] Thomas Hobbes, *Leviathan*, Part I.

perception — does not exist. *This is not to say that morality does not exist,* for it certainly does — as assuredly as culture exists. What this means is that morality is always group focused, or relationship dependent. That which impedes or precludes advancement of the group is evil; that which fosters or enables group advancement is sublime.

If the group is the center and source of morality, and if there are various competing groups, then it can only be said that one's *own* group is the center and source of the highest morality. And, unless we are to be understood as egomaniacal or sociopathic, we have an obligation to uphold the sanctity of *our* group, *our* culture, and *our* morality. Anything that threatens our group, culture, or morality is to be understood as anathema. This, then, is the source of cultural pride. One does not merely have pride in one's ethnicity or geographic location; one has an almost *mystical* appreciation for the holiness of one's own morality. And if a sense of shared cultural history and destiny can be understood as nationhood, then pride in one's group is only otherwise known as *nationalism.* The holy veneration of one's social group — sprung from the liquid roots of blood-bound kinsfolk — is a kind of mystical *socialism.* A bond that is driven by shared culture, history, destiny, and blood might otherwise be called *National Socialism.*

THE IMPORTANCE OF WORK

Keep from being idle. Keep from being idle and you will be purer than most; however, do not aspire to perfection and do not come under the spell that proclaims perfection's existence; otherwise you will live in constant failure, resulting in apathy and idleness. Rather, seek only to perfect your learning from mistakes. Forge a life of disciplined moderation; but remember that both discipline and moderation are predicated on occupation — and thus the question is raised: with what should I be occupied? Work. For yourself or others of the same blood, above all, *work.* Keep work balanced among the physical, mental, and spiritual. Preference to one area of work over another leads to excess and imbalance, which, in turn, promotes idleness.

Distraction is not work; and enjoyment is not distraction. Distraction is the temporary assuaging of the malignant malady of boredom, the parasitical companion of idleness. Difficult to overcome, distractions ruin work's vessels: body, mind, and spirit.

Distractions feign worthwhileness simply because of their ease, but they leave no lasting betterment. The happiness and satisfaction ensuing from distractions are akin to the empty sublimity concomitant with addiction. Euphoria in the haze of distraction is the Trojan horse masking an inconsequential death.

To be consequential means to work to better oneself. To live a life of consequence means to aid improvement rather than idleness. Idleness, by nature, is not improvement; popular culture, in its negligence and misguidedness, inculcates existential torpor by glamorizing it. Popular culture, therefore, by espousing work's reverse, is not an agent of edification. Exploiting naivety, popular culture seeks to make a profit; often it succeeds. Popular culture is a hollow promise of change; it is hedonism; it is "love" gurgling in the wake of societal pressures. Popular culture is the definition of insignificance.

So, keep from being idle and refrain from indulging in the traps of popular culture. Fill your time with strengthening your body, mind, and spirit, leaving no room for excess. Devotion and strength of will in work, which could also be called personal growth, orient you to consequence. Consequence, by implication, amounts to freedom. Idleness, by association, amounts to slavery.

Always remember this: future choices are determined by present habits.

CHAPTER 2
THE COSMIC ORDER

A VOICE FROM THE PAST, A VISION OF THE FUTURE

"Apart from all ideology, the great man and the masses are a unity, both are in the service of the Idea, and each finds his historical significance only with regard to the counter-pole. Carlyle voiced the instinctive demand of this age when the idea of authority and monarchy has once again a good conscience: find the *Ablest Man,* and let him be king.

"Democratic ideologists, with their heads buried deep in the sand, say that maybe a bad monarch will appear. But the imperative of History is not to produce a perfect system, but to fulfill the historical mission. It was this that produced Democracy and it is this that now pays no attention to the whining of the Past, but only to the rumble of the Future. Good or bad, the monarchs are coming.

"On the front of the tottering edifice is printed in gaudy letters: Democracy. But behind it is seen to be a cash-till, and the banker sits, running his hands through the money that was the blood of the Western nations. He looks up in terror, as the sound of marching feet is heard"[1] — the thundering feet upon whose shoulders sit the coming kings. His shifty hands lose count and begin to tremble, *for he knows the blood that gives value to his paper has turned against him.*

"*Protest! Protest!*" the banker cries to the by-standing herd, his last refuge before the gallows. But the herd can only whine and fights for nothing; the herd cannot fight for the banker, for the two have not yet eaten together; now their dining days are gone. And now that those in the trenches have turned their eyes to the financiers, the money-soul can but sniffle and stifle the sound of *revolt* in his voice, for he knows his jig is up. The men in the trenches *have* eaten together; they are of one body, one mind, and one soul: the spirit of *blood,* of *rank* and *authority,* the *bonds* that fix a folk.

---

[1] "Apart ... heard." Francis Yockey, *Imperium.*

The men in the trenches have fought together; they have fought *for something.* Their feet have marched against that which threatened, no matter the cause, for their intentions were *of strength* and truly Germanic; they fought openly for their cause, and *still* they eat together. The herd and its bankers have known neither death nor life together; they answer only to the call of "Every *person* for themselves!" (The masculine is not in their language because it is not in their spirit.) The herd and its bankers have not *fought* for anything — they have only *run* from the authority that demands more of them than their individual souls can ever demand of themselves.

"*Protest* for your *freedom*!" the banker implores his deracinated herd; but the herd is not of one body, one mind, and one soul: it has no sense of history, no sense of destiny, no sense of folk. The herd cannot see beyond its own nose; and for this reason, the herd can never eat together, can never *fight* together. The herd can only run together — *run* from the authority that can be its only salvation.

When the feet march and the tables turn, the bankers can only *cower*, for money is bloodless, though it is stained with blood. And when the feet march, *this is the distant thunder of the coming monarchs.*

HOMERIC CROSSROADS

Homer's *Iliad* is a work of transition, and in this way, it is a work of prophecy. Though the theme is subtle, one can trace through the narrative the thread linking two ages of man: the age of heroes and the age of (rationalistic) man.[2] Homer shows us the crossroads on which we stand; as with all prophecy, Homer's work weaves together both our nascence and our future as a Western folk. The composite *now* is the moment of decision.

When the Greek hero Achilles faced Hector, the greatest of all Trojan warriors, near the city's walls, the two men negotiated the terms of the victor and the vanquished.

Hector, *enlightened* and presaging the rationalistic fate of Western man, recognized the equality of both their worldly rank and

---

[2] Borrowing from Vico the successive ages from which "the nations will be seen to develop": the ages of gods, heroes, and men. Giambattista Vico, *The New Science of Giambattista Vico*, unabridged., translated by Thomas Goddard (Ithaca: Cornell University Press, 1968), 335.

their spiritual rank as men; under the law of both gods and men they were of one kind; in this respect, Hector recognized what men call *justice*. Hector's terms were that the victor will bury the vanquished; in this way, both men will have lived and died in honor.

Achilles, representing the bestial rearing and instincts of bygone days — Achilles, being born of a beautiful nymph and a powerful king — Achilles, a god among men, set the conditions of victory in stark contrast to those of the *enlightened* Hector: "When have men ever made pacts with lions? And when were wolves and lambs ever of one mind?" The great Achilles continued: "If I kill you, I will drag you naked, bound to my chariot, three days around the walls of Troy, and finally I will give your body to my hunting dogs to eat."

When Hector fell, Achilles kept his promise to drag the defeated body. Thus it is shown that "the weak want laws; the powerful withhold them."[3]

Homer was the greatest of all Western poets and his work has been emulated for millennia. In this way, Homer is immortal. Homer reached immortality because he spoke of that spirit which yet endures: human nature. Though the arc of time sits beyond the scope of men, we can yet glimpse its full story: the thread of human nature links beginning to end. And though man makes pretensions to enlightenment, this is but a fabricated piece of the whole — a *whole* bestially reared, a *whole* of instincts.

If we follow the thread of human nature into the future, we will see what Homer divined: the Enlightenment will have its time and that time will be vanquished by man's own primeval tether to irrationality, i.e., *life*. We have been told of man's capacity for infinite progress. This is a bedtime story we tell ourselves, that we tell our children. We should take care, however; for what lurks beyond our walls — what sits in the open dark is *that which comes to conquer*. When the enlightened one tries to reason with the snarling instinct, reason capitulates to power, honor submits to humiliation.

Achilles kept his promise: *this* is the promise of Homer. Achilles, like Homer, is immortal; Hector is known — if he is known at all — as the conquered prey of the Greek hero. Enlightened Troy, like its hero, fell. This is the fate of all the enlightened ones — because the tether of irrationality is wrapped too tightly.

---

[3] Vico, 85.

When the enlightened one is so desperate to save the world, he loses the ability to save himself. This was the difference between Hector and Achilles. This is the arc that connects beginning to end.

According to legend, from the remnants of pillaged, enlightened Troy arose a new people; a people yet beholden to the bestial rearing that so swiftly struck down the enlightened ones; a people yet beholden to the primeval instincts their gods demanded of them: the Romans.

The Romans passed through their gods, their heroes, and finally through their dissolute men. Their Empire and influence were beyond measure, born of strength and violence. Yet when the rationalistic men arrived, dissipation followed, and the conquerors became the conquered. Constantinople, like Troy, fell with a violent whimper. And in its fall were scattered the seeds of our modern age.

In cultural pathology, the bedtime story of progress is as fantastical as the hopes of northern reinforcements whispered amongst the Byzantine nobility the night before Constantinople's sacking. Under the arc of time, we do not see one large, ever-growing cultural tree; instead, we see a number of distinct plants — all separate cultures with their separate fruits and flowers. We see the birth, rise, decline, and fall of cultures. But, most importantly, we see a pattern inherent in this pathology: enlightenment comes before the fall.

Enlightenment anticipates the fall because it is, fundamentally, a *letting down of one's guard*: in it, all men are essentially good, capable and worthy of progress. An enlightened Achilles, if he wins, will bury his honorable foe. Yet this betrays the Homeric wisdom; the arc of time is linked by but one thread: the thread of human nature. To be sure, human nature is both Achilles *and* Hector; yet human nature is not driven by abstractions or any pretensions to enlightenment, but by *power*. Ultimately, it is the Achillean promise which will be fulfilled: the victor will not just reap the spoils, but will ignite the future, fertilize the fields with the blood of the fallen, and thus continue the thread divined by Homer so long ago.

Escape the tether of irrationality, we cannot. Meet our ever-present foes with the Achillean barbarism so near the successes of our ancestors, we can. Should we fail to meet this challenge narrated by the span of human existence, we will surely fall by the hands of others who *are* compelled to continue the Homeric thread: the ancestral heroes of future ages.

We are on this earth for such a brief moment; let us not be lulled to sleep by any bedtime story, no matter how pleasant. We are on this earth for but one purpose: let us preserve our lineage and defend the blood and culture which birthed it; anything less is conspiring with the enemy. And who is the enemy? It is he who tells us that justice will conquer human nature, for justice itself is defined and redefined by immortal human nature. No matter how many times the story is told, Hector always loses to Achilles. This is because the story does not change; and it is also because Achilles is immortal. It is Homer we should thank for chronicling our heroic past; and it is to Homer we are indebted for showing us our future. But now is our moment of decision, now we must decide which path to take: fallen Hector or victorious Achilles.

THE SEA PEOPLES: AN ANALYSIS OF CULTURAL PATHOLOGY

A warlike Bronze Age people, known only and cryptically as "the Sea Peoples," ravaged what they saw as foreign encroachments into the Mediterranean (c. 1210-1175 BCE), paving the way for Western dominance in the region.

We know very little about the Sea Peoples. Mostly, our knowledge of them is sourced in their victims' brief and ominous descriptions. The powerful Egyptians left records of them, typically of this sort: "They came from the sea in their warships and none could stand against them."

Some have argued that the Sea Peoples were northern Europeans migrating south and east, perhaps driven by the will to conquer; some mark them as Greek soldiers, sent to expel alien peoples from their borderlands. Still others say the Phoenicians — "elite" Jews — used the Sea Peoples via their ancient art of "revolution from above,"[4] pitting European mercenaries against a waning Hittite Empire in the sacking of Troy, sparking enough local chaos to reap the ensuing rewards they — the Jews — ultimately orchestrated.

Yet, while we know little, we can say with certainty that their influence is immeasurable. It can reasonably be suspected the Sea Peoples were early Western Europeans. If this is the case, our cultural

---

[4] See Kerry Bolton's *Revolution from Above*; it details the Jewish role in financing societal instability for (Jewish) profit.

ancestors rose up against what they saw as *weak* and *foreign* in order to wrest power (resources) away from *alien* peoples. Had the Sea Peoples not sacked foreign city after city, laying waste to ancient Hebrews, Hittites, and Mycenaeans, the future of Western civilization becomes uncertain.

It is endlessly fascinating how a people so impactful can be so unknown. This leads us to believe that (1) the Sea Peoples cared little for *recording* their efforts and far more for defining their efforts through *action*; this speaks to the power and effectiveness of *irrationality* — i.e., prioritizing the *act* over and above the *discussion*, and (2) more importantly, that three triggers of societal collapse have proportional correspondence: civilization maturity, rationality, and societal weakness.

It is telling — and perhaps should be alarming to us — that how "wise" and "rational" a civilization believes itself to be has no meaningful influence on its actual strength and durability. In fact, the inverse seems more historically accurate. Consider our language: "barbarians" and "barbaric" are conceptually synonymous with "violent"/"violence" and "unscrupulous" or "wild," etc., while "civilized" and "civilization" are conceptually synonymous with (assumed) "power"/"powerful" and "deliberate" or "rational." *Yet history is rife with examples of civilizations falling to barbaric peoples.* Why? It can only be because of the corresponding indices mentioned above: that the more maturity, rationality, and presumptive power a civilization assumes, the weaker it becomes. Why is this the case?

Reason, left unmitigated and unchecked, leads a people to assume an *unfounded optimism* regarding human nature, leading to more tolerance — both internally and externally — more openness (to foreign influence), and a more idealistic *Weltanschauung*. This inevitably leads to weakness because it directly undermines that which founded the society in the first place. If we closely examine history, we might see that cultures follow similar arcs: in succession, societies generally grow with (1) the *familial community*, which expands into (2) *local clannishness*, followed by (3) *regional tribalism*, then (4) *socio-spiritual merging* (Age of Gods), leading to (5) *barbaric culture* (Age of Heroes), and ending with (6) *rational civilization* (Age of Man). This Age of Man, or *rational* civilization, is the last step in our cultural pathology because at this point civilization becomes untenable: it is manifest weakness, it is optimism and openness, it is blind idealism and death.

This civilizational death begins internally, gradually rotting the once-barbaric and spiritual social core via *rationalistic idealism*,[5] and ultimately culminates in susceptibility to internal civil strife, external force, or some combination thereof. Thus, the path is laid for future (foreign) barbaric conquest, recycling the six-step cultural arc listed above.

History's mysterious Sea Peoples ravaged and dominated because they were *barbaric*[6] — they possessed the unmatched warrior instinct of the European folk: "They came from the sea in their warships and none could stand against them." They left no record of their actions because they had not yet reached the cultural point of their victims, that of *rational civilization*. Their barbarousness paved the way for Western flourishing in the Mediterranean; it paved the way for the Greek and Roman Empires, until they, too, succumbed to rational civilization and faced the barbarous Asiatics, who ultimately conquered the Byzantine remnants of Roman dominance at Constantinople in 1453.

It is said that the night before the Ottoman assault, the Byzantine leaders of Constantinople gathered in the Hagia Sophia for a midnight prayer — beseeching the Lord for help against the Muslim invaders. When the prayer service ended, the siege began; and, in the end, more than 4,000 lay dead, nearly 30,000 were enslaved, and countless murders and rapes ensued in the aftermath; Constantinople fell and the Byzantine (Roman) Empire was finished. *Idealism* will tell you that the Lord works in mysterious ways; a more *pragmatic* view will tell you that the Byzantine prayers were

---

5 This is a cumbersome, yet more descriptive way of saying *Liberalism*. That is, the *rational* pursuit of conceptual abstractions for their own sake, or even the nominal adherence to the use of such "buzzwords"; e.g., pursuing liberty for liberty's sake, equality for equality's sake, tolerance for tolerance's sake, etc. — i.e., pursuance of an ideal without regard to practical impact. More plainly, something like tolerance, for instance, is pursued for its own theoretical merit, even if it means tolerating hostile forces. Likewise, equality is pursued ever and always, even if it means accepting the injustice of ignoring the superior man and his superior performance. And so on...

6 *Barbaric* here is meant to oppose *rational civilization*. Remember: *rational civilization* spells the *end* of a people; *rational civilization* increases proportionally with *Jewish* influence. It is *rational civilization* that calls free peoples "barbaric" — note that the *civilized*, Christian Romans called the conquering pagan-Germanic tribes *barbarians*.

answered only by foreign savagery. The barbarians won the day, and that which lies *beyond* this world had no retort.

Civilizations rise and fall, to be sure — but *must* they? Oswald Spengler, in his brilliant *The Decline of the West* (1918), assures us that they must, for cultures are organic just like any living thing; Vico, in his *New Science* (1725), leaves some doubt, for the culture that can *sustain* its barbarism can disrupt the cultural cycle — Vico understood this to be possible only through religion. What leaves us room to doubt the presumed inevitability of the West's fall is reason, certainly, but it must be *reason tempered with a spiritual and pragmatic traditionalism that allows us to see the shortfalls and weaknesses of reason itself.*

The Sea Peoples, effective though they were, had success not because of their inherent strength, but because of their victims' inherent weakness. The modern West has the luxury of both historical perspective and the fruits of the Enlightenment — luxuries the Sea Peoples did not have. This presents us with an opportunity to take advantage of Vico's doubt and *sustain* our barbarism through reasoned, pragmatic traditionalism. We are at a crossroads in Western civilization's history, a Homeric crossroads. We might follow Hector's path — that of reasoned Enlightenment, that of idealistic optimism; or we might follow the path of Achilles — that of spiritual and pragmatic traditionalism, that of rational barbarism, that of heroic endurance. The choice is ours to win or lose. History has time and again offered us the answers; will we accept those answers, or will we be revolted by them, revolted by human nature, and seek shelter in that which lies *beyond* our world? Vico counseled us thusly nearly 300 years ago: if religion is lost among the peoples, they have nothing left to enable them to live in society: no shield of defense, nor means of counsel, nor basis of support, nor even a form by which they may exist in the world at all.... For religions alone can bring the peoples to do virtuous works by appeal to their feelings, which alone moves men to perform them.[7]

Now is the time for a new view of religion, of spirituality — one unburdened by idealism, and one freed by pragmatism. It is the time for a path that permits us to sustain our cultural barbarism, so we might not be lost to history like the Sea Peoples or destroyed by the ages like so many ancient civilizations. Now is the time for a return

[7] Vico, *The New Science of Giambattista Vico*, unabridged., translated by Thomas Goddard (Ithaca: Cornell University Press, 1968), 426.

to reverence of *der heilige Wille*; it is the time for the consolidation of our spirit — *unser kultureller-Geist* — into that higher will which sits untouched by the ages. For good or ill, human nature endures because it is unmarked by the creeping blot of rationalism; it is the business of an enduring folk to sacrifice both the rational and irrational to the transcendental spirit of conserving its legacy by any means. In this way, cultural pathology becomes cultural theology, and inevitable illness becomes exceptional apotheosis.

Take heed: it is our business to sacrifice; and it is our business to conquer, that none may stand against us.

THE COSMIC STRUGGLE: A RETURN TO REVERENCE

We live in the midst of a cosmic struggle. It is the struggle between light and dark, Good and Evil, cosmos and chaos; it is the struggle between the spiritual and material planes.

We must understand and live existence as a cosmic struggle, for it is a contest between the past that birthed us and the present and future which threaten us; it is a contest between *spiritual* culture and *rational* civilization. The identity of any folk is rooted in its relationship with the divine, with God and Nature; this is to say that culture is sourced in myth. Removal of these mythical roots is the end of a folk. Further, faith in myth must be preserved — particularly cultural faith, folk-faith. For faith is nothing besides the manifestation of a people's will — the will to bend man and Nature to a shared vision of the future, a vision born of the past and threaded through the present by a succession of cultural heroes.[8] Removal of myth and faith from a folk, then, is removal of the people's will, the ground of all being. Without will, the existential framework of being is lost and man is consigned to a rootless drifting toward soulless technological progress.

The cosmic struggle is universal struggle, for it affects us all. Further, this struggle is existential, for who imagines that life extends

[8] The heroes of any folk might be acknowledged or not; however, the closer a *culture* comes to the degenerative forces of *civilization*, the more its *cultural* heroes will be demonized — if they are acknowledged at all — by its institutions. In short, the surest sign of a people's health or sickness is reflected in its heroes and villains. Do we demonize those who try to save our community? Do we praise those bent on individual and material gain?

beyond our being? The outcome of this contest, then, will determine man's future course — whether he is *enslaved* in material, self-interested "freedom," or whether he is *freed* by being bound to the common cause.

We are manifestations of this struggle and our life exposes our allegiance; that is, that which is *physical* — our life — tells of our *metaphysical* — our cosmic — identity. Thus, we need not concern ourselves with *that which lies beyond* by looking beyond *that which manifests itself before us*. That is to say, the physical is our key to unlocking the secret of the metaphysical.

By their fruit you will recognize them. He who produces good, spiritual fruit will be contrasted against he who produces evil, material fruit. What is spiritual? It is that which transcends *mere self* for the sake of something higher.[9] If our individual existence only bears meaning in the context of our community, then our community surpasses our self in significance and our self becomes the vessel through which our community is conserved; that is, the self, if it bears good fruit, must be conservative. Likewise, if the self is conserving community identity, then it necessarily looks to the past, for the past is what defines it and sets the parameters for any vision of the future. Thus, the further we drift from the past — in spirit, not in time — the further we drift from the sense of good that defines us. "Good," then, is committing our self to preserving the "good" of our community, however deep its roots. And if our idea of "good" changes, this is only an indicator of our spiritual decay, or the mark of evil, the mark of material.

What is material? It is that which accepts the self as the *A* and *Ω* in determining what is good; it is the pursuit of individual happiness and rationalism irrespective of their impact on the community; it is the rebellion and freedom of peasants; it is a distancing of the community-of-selves from the traditions which birthed it; it is disintegration. Further, it is of course *materialism* and *materialistic*. The material denies the validity of the spiritual by disconnecting itself from the community's roots: this is "progress." The *material* prioritizes worldly gain over community stability; it is a destabilizing force, for it extracts *individual* opportunity from both within and without the confines of the community; it is unadulterated, borderless exploitation and the parasitical betrayal of a spiritual symbiosis. It is

[9] See "Foundations for a Healthy Society" in this collection.

the praise of calculated chaos over communal cosmos. In a word, it is *Evil.*

A system that honors the Good is good; a system that honors Evil is evil. Put another way, a system that conserves the traditions of the community through subsumption of the individual is *spiritual*, and a system that abandons tradition for the sake of individual gain is *material*. Our understanding of these facts is *a posteriori*, for the physical always reveals the metaphysical; removing such depth from our understanding leaves us with only physical tautologies: where *good* is good and *evil* is evil. That is, man is left defining his own morality, divorced of his community, which, in turn, morphs into the parasitism of pure Evil: the material-man — fearless, yet uncourageous.

Who among mortals, if he fears nothing, is righteous?[10] Certainly not the material-man! He lurks in the shadows of society, in the shade of power, corrupting whoever will bend his ear to hear his deceptively sweet promises. Meanwhile, his host society's integrity is undercut and its material potential is met, so he looks beyond his "borders" to open up the next society to his damning ingratiation. He is a being without fear, to be sure, for he is emboldened by the prospect of exploitation — his nature leaves him feeling powerful, but it is a false power; for his power is without courage: it is a power of the shadows, a power of darkness. The material-man's power is not one of courageous creation *ex nihilo* — no! His is a power of fashioning, of crafting, of molding; it is a power of the *dēmiourgós*, the Demiurge.

Courage is the best slayer — courage which attacks, which slays even death itself![11] The material-man and his Demiurge, devoid as they are of creative courage, cannot overcome their parasitical inadequacies — the inadequacies that relegate them to a life of exploitative leeching off superior creators. No, the folk in this world, those for whom faith in the communal spirit still supplies the infinite courage of will, *der heilige Wille*, will indeed conquer the material plague of the material-man! *For courage is the best slayer.* And he, the haunting golem that hangs on our shoulders, reaping all reward from our forceful steps which carry him ever higher, will be cast down; and *we* — *we* will be made lighter. And the Good will stand

---

[10] Aeschylus, *Eumenides*, 700.
[11] Nietzsche, *Thus Spoke Zarathustra*, "The Vision and the Enigma."

anew, transfigured: unburdened by the soulless weight of materialism and enveloped by the mythic light of a folk undaunted.

If we are to endure, we must recognize the Supreme God as existing in the will of HIS folk. Who are HIS folk? It is they who share a common past and vision of the future; it is they who believe that looking backward is the only way to look forward, and that looking to the past is the only way to witness a living future. And if this implies a multiplicity of peoples, then if *we* are to endure, *we* must understand the true will of God as that which prevails in *us*. The choice — and thus the future — is ours to take. If we do not take it, if we instead sit idly, spiritlessly by or play host to material-rational parasites, then some other courageous people will own the future; either this, or the internationalist trolls will slip from one culture to the next, exploiting and exhausting their host's faith and resources until cultural spirit devolves into a technological husk, and the earth — both man and Nature — will lie scorched in their wake.

Kultur-Geist und völkischer-Glaube — faith in our community — must signal our return to reverence. A mythic-faith must guide our hand in shaping our shared future, which is to say, lauding our common past. Berdyaev instructs us:

> How then can a real ... society be established? Only by religious enlightenment and complete change of heart and will.... What is needed is not to spread ourselves abroad ... but to *steep ourselves in true spirituality*, to come back to the fatherland of the spirit. *That would be a more profound revolution than any that the activities of external revolutionaries can bring about.*[12]

"Spreading ourselves abroad" is a task for the demiurgically driven material-man, not the man bound to his folk with the courage to create space for his indomitable will. The material-man is the external revolutionary of individual, exploitative gain who sees his interactions in tautologous context: good is good and evil is evil: he moralizes only for selfish gain and scoffs at the *völkischer-Glaube* of the Supreme Good, the community of the folk imbued with *der heilige Wille*. We must ultimately and finally revere our past and our

---

[12] Nicolas Berdyaev, *The End of Our Time*, (San Rafael, CA: Semantron Press, 2009), 200. Emphasis added.

folk in all its terrible brilliance, so we might be worthy of the Good our courage demands of us.

When we have merged our wills to achieve higher, binding ends, then our cosmic struggle will be won and our mythic-faith will have been preserved. Until this time, we will continue to surrender our creative courage to the rootless material-man and his demiurgic machinations. Let us hasten, then, our return to the reverence of our folk, to the Good which is our salvation.

LIFE'S GOVERNED APOCALYPSE

Night is closer than day to the mystery of all beginning.
— NIKOLAI BERDYAEV

The governors of all life are space-time and human nature, which is to say that all of life is predicated upon these two concept-entities. Put another way, every question posed can invariably be answered by both space-time and human nature.

Space-time is the forum in which we act; human nature is the foundation for action. Specifically, human nature is essentially self-interested action.

The basis for all religiosity has been, is, and will be concerned with man's grappling with human nature — that is, religiosity is concerned with how man might overcome his nature in achieving or contributing to something greater than himself. This is the essence of man's spiritual life: that he overcome himself.

∞ ∞ ∞

In prehistory, man's seed was scattered to the winds. If we share any common ancestor, it means that over time our people disagreed on this or that, or perhaps matured, determined it was in their best interest to relocate, and ultimately transposed to other realms. In this way, all culture arose from some past disagreement or maturation: the once-shared vision of past and future between compatriots became fragmented. A line was drawn in the sand, and former brothers became strangers. Through the ages, these spiritual disparities manifested as physical, or racial, disparities; this, of course, was the result of geographical differences and breeding — or natural and artificial selection. *Racial* differences are the end result, then, of historical *cultural* or *spiritual* differences. "Race is the image of soul".[13]

For the majority of man's existence, Nature[14] has deemed it necessary to compartmentalize our cultures (save graduated overlap) and, subsequently, our races. In bringing us closer together than historically ever before through globalization, it seems Nature has deemed it necessary to homogenize us once again. Or has it?

∞ ∞ ∞

The majority of significant religious traditions indicate some kind of "Golden Age" at man's inception, followed by an abrupt or gradual Fall. This Golden Age is typically understood as a time of harmony within one's group and with Nature: men bear no major quarrel with one another and resources abound; it represents the golden day of a people. This likely suggests a time before cultural-spiritual-ideological breaks within a community, and a time when the sparse population on earth gave man enough nomadic or agrarian quarter. If the Fall indicates a community's first major upheaval — the twilight of day — then the spiritual goal of a community — the goal of a religion — is to bring the community back into communion with the Golden Age, back into harmony with man and Nature. Prehistory served as the foundations for all significant religious traditions. That is, prehistory represents the Golden Age of later religious traditions; spiritual divisions among prehistoric societies indicate the Fall; and antiquity into modernity indicate man's decline into further disarray — his descent into darkest night — and his desire to re-commune with his culture's divine Golden Age.

From antiquity to now, religious traditions have defined themselves as a means to re-commune with God (or the Golden Age) and a means to understand evil (the Fall). This is only another way of saying that religious traditions have defined themselves as a means to understand human nature (the Fall, evil) and a means to overcome the self (re-commune with the Golden Age; or, implicitly, the age of communal integrity). In order to re-commune, however, a final cleansing must occur; traditions have seen this cleansing in different

---

[13] Alfred Rosenberg, *Myth of the Twentieth Century*. Also translated as "Race is the counterpart of soul." See *Myth* (2021, Clemens & Blair), 20.

[14] By "Nature," in this case alone, we understand both Nature (geography and natural forces) and human nature (selectivity).

ways, yet most are truly apocalyptic. The residue of the Fall is spread by the growing stain of man upon the earth over time, invariably necessitating a moment of total destruction of all *others* — resulting in a new dawn, a new Golden Age. This Golden Age is only possible through the elimination of spiritual differences — that is, differences of opinion. And the surest way to eliminate differences of opinion is to eliminate great numbers of people, which the Apocalypse traditions foretell. So, though man might "fight the good fight" by overcoming his self in daily life — if his age is not apocalyptic, then his rebirth is nothing more than subjective and, thus, objectively futile; his Golden Age will exist merely in his spirit, at best.

In many of the significant religious traditions of antiquity and in those that have endured into modernity, the end times were frequently thought to be "nigh." Paul of Tarsus was convinced his mission was to convert the Gentiles before the imminent return of Christ; John of Patmos believed the end he envisioned was soon at hand; the Hindus believe *all* history is a history of the final Dark Age, wherein most life will be consumed by the destroyer-creator, Hari-Hara; major strands of Judaism mark the formation of a Jewish State (Israel) as a sign of the times; Islam notes a number of modern issues as indicators, etc. In each case, the religious traditions mark several key indices of the coming Apocalypse. Historically, this final cleansing was understood to be fast approaching; yet historically, beyond his eager and destructive nature, man has not possessed the means to eliminate himself until now.

In the past, when our understanding was limited, our physical world was limited. If we step into the mindset of a spiritual seer of antiquity, we might see that the means of community destruction are certainly upon him; too, he sees the spiritual waste in his society leading to both mental and physical waste; for him, the end is truly nigh. Yet from our vantage millennia later, we see that the means for mass destruction — for true global cleansing, i.e., Apocalypse — were not available. Our seer of antiquity saw degradation and endured hardship, to be sure; but his perspective was limited to his era; his time was destined to be merely subjective overcoming, or subjectively religious. It is only modernity that grants us the technological precipice from which to view our imminent Apocalypse. For it is only modernity that offers us the globalized and "small" world; it is only modernity that offers us multiple means by which we might finally meet our long-awaited spiritual cleansing, our final conquering of the collective self.

Ultimately, what binds us to the man of prehistory and early history are life's governors: space-time and human nature. From prehistory onwards we have awaited the final destruction our nature guarantees us; when before our former compatriots introduced their now-alien ways, Nature was kind to us: our technological scope was too small. Our nature sought to neutralize the cultural-ideological threat, but our era determined its localized reach. It is only now that we have the technological means to usher in our new Golden Age, our objective religiosity. Human nature remains constant; space-time has allowed for technological progression. This is to say that the scale is tipping.

Apocalypse is coming; human nature assures us of the *who* and *why*; space-time will soon tell us the *where* and *when*.

∞ ∞ ∞

The aim of any people, of any culture, of any ideology, should ever be to sustain itself through the coming hardships by galvanizing a spirit of solidarity, a spirit of supremacy, and a spirit of salvific transcendence of the self for the perpetuation of the community.[15] Anything less is a guarantee of failure, a forgoing of divine re-communion, and forfeiture of the group's future. And anything less assures our position as fodder for stronger cultures.

Berdyaev tells us that "night is closer than day to the mystery of all beginning".[16] This is only to say that once the Golden Age has passed into twilight, the night becomes our ally, our means through which the new Golden Age might be reached. For the night of human transgression, of communal disintegration, serves as the backdrop from which we detail the light that guides us to the new dawn: as surely as God has given us day, HE has also given us night; and surely as God has given us night, HE, too, gives us the *lightning and the sun*.

The "mystery of all beginning" is prehistory. What life assures us is an end to history through Apocalypse. What clears a path and lights the way for a people back to that time before the Fall are the lightning and the sun; without the dark, our victorious salvation would not be visible.

---

[15] See "Foundations for a Healthy Society" in this collection.

[16] Nikolai Berdyaev, *The End of Our Time*, translated by Donald Attwater (San Rafael, CA: Semantron Press, 2009), 71.

THE ARCHETYPE AND THE ACCELERATION OF TIME

The end will come quicker than we think. The technological progress of modernity has created an "acceleration of time" which cannot be righted without faith. Seemingly, human nature has stayed stagnant since its beginning; yet, arguably, human nature has *degraded* since its inception, as the "sun" of rational civilization has flattened man's dimensions into an alienated shadow with its gravity.[17] This is to say that the "scales are tipping".[18] We must be ready, then, to endure and overcome the future that threatens us.

Being ready means being spiritually ready. Physical and mental preparation are useless if they are not centered on the higher, spiritual preparation. Likewise, spiritual preparation is futile if it is not supported by physical and mental preparation. Being spiritually ready means consolidating with like-minded folk; it means building spiritual defenses against the material forces[19] that incessantly seek to undermine man's spiritual nature and the health of the folk.

Building spiritual defenses means creating the conditions for their higher aim: focusing on the ARCHETYPE. First, creating the conditions for spiritual defense means achieving physical and mental health; it means rejecting the alienating influences of the material-man and his machinations. The material-man, in his infinite lust for power and mammon, seeks to destroy the mental and physical health of the spiritually-minded folk he craves to oppress; he destroys by exploiting man's inherent weakness of will: he packages destruction under deceptions like *convenience*, *need*, and, most detrimentally, the liberal-democratic abstractions of *justice*, *equality*, and *liberty*; he obliterates the spiritual by bombarding the senses with technics, with gadgetry, all in order to debilitate the spiritually-inclined man's mental and physical health, thereby precluding his spiritual health, which, in turn, guarantees the reign of mammon and the material-man. Second, what is the ARCHETYPE? The ARCHETYPE is HE WHO CAME BEFORE; we embody the ARCHETYPE when we join our efforts for the spiritual purpose of defending our folk against the material-man. The ARCHETYPE is our coming to grips with the inadequacy of

---

[17] Recall Zarathustra's rebuke of the dwarf in "The Vision and the Enigma": "'Thou spirit of gravity!'"

[18] See "Life's Governed Apocalypse" in this collection.

[19] See "The Cosmic Struggle: A Return to Reverence" in this collection.

individuals, of *atoms*, of *singular beings*, and it is our somber acceptance of the void of deliberateness spawned from the material-mind; our new way is the ARCHETYPE and the ARCHETYPE is pure Being, pure *Geist*. The material-man seeks to entangle us in disease-inducing distractions so we might become docile toward his malevolent, maniacal ends of greed and selfish power; he desires this end because he knows the spiritual folk are powerless when they become mired in the material-world of exploitative religiosity. For never forget: the material-man, too, has his gods and rituals!

Through his demiurgic power, the material-man has all but conquered this world; this is why we see constant wars and rumors of war (material-war is simply *profiteering* by other means), persistent social unrest, and "progressive" societal acceptance of what was once anathema. The origin of the material-man's power is the Demiurge, but this is the same as saying his power is the *commercial-spirit*, the *parasitical-spirit*, the means of seeking *Advantage, Advantage über alles!* Yet the material-man's advantage is not his devotion to higher, spiritual solidarity, but his devotion to the *exploitation* of man's weak will, his proclivity to glorify the "easy wrong" over the "hard right" — that is, the material-man's advantage is the introduction of *self*-focused chaos into the once-stable community. But the Demiurge remains, lurking, not content to wait when there is a world to be won and a spirit lost: no, the commercial-spirit is only the means by which the world is won, the means through which all *Volksgeist* is shucked and replaced with the all-enveloping cloak of material-theocracy: a New World Order for the Demiurge and his golems.

The material-theocracy is based on the alienating interpretation of life through science and economics. Science under the material-man is essentially mathematicized Nature — i.e., Nature rendered spiritless, inorganic, *Nature-less*. The marvel, mystery, and magic of Nature are extricated in favor of a cold, detached reduction of warm spirit into algorithms and equations. That is, material-theocracy is rationalism *par excellence*; it is the apotheosization of conditions conducive to the reign of material-man. The groundwork for the furtherance of this material-theocracy can be seen in the ever-growing reach of STEM education[20]: children and parents are being indoctrinated to unquestioningly accept the conditions of the material-man and his usurpation of the *Volksgeist*. It has even been

[20] STEM: Science, Technology, Engineering, and Mathematics. See nsf.gov, ed.gov, and nms.org for more information.

said that "[science] is ... an approach to the world, a critical way to understand and explore and engage with the world, and then have the capacity to change that world..."[21] This is only to say, however, that science presumes to be a faith, a philosophy, a system of beliefs through which one can establish a worldview. And from this worldview one can make decisions about, not just the world generally, but also about societal relationships and even the unknown. Very rationally, when science bumps up against the limits of knowledge, it is satisfied to admit ignorance, as if ignorance were a means to inspire. Certainly, ignorance is a means to further inquiry, but there will always be a time when cold, deliberate inquiry fails to meet the moment. Arguably, men have risen to challenges and rallied the strength to overcome them through *faith* — not science. Science, far from being a *worldview* from which we can "engage with the world," is a *method*, a *tool* we use to supplement our irrational faith — and this is a good thing. As systematized rationality, science is a method or tool we use to *acquire* information about the world; it is necessary, but it is not an end in itself; it is a means to achieve higher, spiritual ends. As systematized irrationality, on the other hand, faith is the mode, the *Being-ness* through which we are *inspired* to meet and overcome life's trials. Science acquires; faith inspires. But clearly, the latter, organic view is not necessary for material-theocracy; instead, material-theocracy demands a religious fervor to support its means of achieving a material end.

The end achieved by the material-man is one utterly devoid of life-affirming faith: it is mammon, the money achieved through the forfeiture of the *Volksgeist* via STEM, via rationalism. The only purpose behind anything attempted by the material-forces of this world is money; for money is the means of exercising *acquired* power without being *organically* strong.[22] The theory of wealth and its exchange, of course, is economics. And what is economics if not the study of how to materialize all life? Here, then, is where we stand: science and economics are the foundational principles of the material-man, they are the means through which he achieves power and dominion over all organics, the means through which the

[21] Barak Obama, 2015.

[22] A modification of a Sombart phrase: "Money became the means whereby they [the Jews] — and through them all mankind — might wield power without themselves being strong." Werner Sombart, *The Jews and Modern Capitalism* (Batoche Books, 2001), 242.

Volksgeist is erased for the *possibility* of anticipated or speculative material wealth. The furtherance of science, technology, engineering, and math for the sake of increased material wealth — either on part of the individual or the State — does nothing to bind a people together organically. That is, there is no common thread, no common faith which acts as a center of gravity for the community, around which all souls might revolve. Instead, there is only procurement of information and pursuit of material wealth acting as societal cores; while this might work for the short term, it will have no lasting value, if only for their dependence on external factors, both domestic and international. A folk needs MYTH to endure and spiritual ambition to transcend the vicissitudes of economics and technological progress.[23] Yet the material-man abandons all notions of folk in pursuit of this scientific progress and amassing of material wealth, for money has no borders. This accounts for our acceleration of time.

Decline means imbalance. Imbalance means a tipping of the scales. If on one side of the scale we hold irrationality, and on the other side of the scale sits rationality, if one side carries more weight, naturally, the scale becomes imbalanced. If the modern world, through material-man's dogged pursuit of material-theocracy, seeks to achieve perfect rationality through the presumed transcendent powers of science, then the rational side of the scale will inevitably outweigh the irrational side, and thus begins societal decline. The society tumbling, declining toward the heavy side of the scale will perceive time as accelerating toward an imagined end. From the material perspective, society progresses toward technological saturation and "infinite" wealth; from the spiritual perspective, because any account of human nature is abandoned for the "enlightened" presumption that reason alone can win all hearts and minds, society speeds toward an unwieldy accumulation of technics without the discernment to properly employ it. This is what is meant by the acceleration of time, and this is why the end is imminent.

To counter the threat of Apocalypse, we must struggle to return to the ARCHETYPE and prepare the way for HIS return through our vision. We must reinvigorate and uplift the *Volksgeist* for the sake of our survival; to neglect the irrational — the MYTH — *at all*, is to concede defeat at the hands of the material-man, the golem, who will lead us all to ruin through his "enlightenment." If the example is the

[23] See "The Cosmic Struggle: A Return to Reverence" in this collection.

ARCHETYPE, and the ARCHETYPE is HE WHO CAME BEFORE, then the only way to endure through time is by looking backwards, conserving the past that created our spirit, the past that has shown us DAS RECHT. Our endurance is predicated on correcting society's degenerative imbalance by preserving the MYTH: the MYTH of our salvation through victory, and faith in the ARCHETYPE'S return. In this way, the folk deepen their roots in the earth by lifting their spirit above it, and the deepest roots will form the ARCHETYPE'S *final battalion*,[24] those worthy souls who have worked to usher in the new Golden Age,[25] those worthy souls who have cleared the way for the MAN TO COME.

THE WAR-SOUL AS NECESSITY IN A LIBERALISTIC STATE

> *We are willing to grant that war, abhor it as we may, often develops and places in strong light, a force of intellect and purpose, which raises our conceptions of the human soul. There is perhaps no moment in life, in which the mind is brought into such intense action, in which the will is so strenuous, and in which irrepressible excitement is so tempered with self-possession as in the hour of battle.*
>
> — WILLIAM E. CHANNING, 1828

---

[24] Adolf Hitler: "The only thing that matters in this fight is who leads the last battalion on the battlefield." 05 December 1932; "Decisive in a battle are not the total losses; rather, he alone who remains with the last battalion has won the great battle..." 15 January 1936; "The great victories of world history were accorded to that party which commanded the last battalion on the battlefield..." 03 May 1940; "The last battalion on the field will be a German one!" 08 November 1941. And Miguel Serrano, from *Adolf Hitler: The Ultimate Avatar*: "Everywhere in the world, more and more, the young are 'born Hitlerists.' Resisting ... propaganda, their controlled education and even family pressures, *they are Hitlerists*, born as such.... They are heroes who, there, next to the Bunker in Berlin, gave their lives and now return to continue fighting and await the return of the Ultimate Battalion, with their Führer Adolf Hitler, to unleash, together, the combat that will end the Darkest Age, the Kali-Yuga."

[25] See "Life's Governed Apocalypse" in this collection.

In a 1966 interview with *Der Spiegel*, Martin Heidegger notes, quite matter-of-factly, that man, in his relation to the modern, *technicized* world, is unsalvageable through purely rational means; for rationality, or "thought," can only hope to show us that rationality and thought are "at an end" as a means to achieve expression of *Dasein*.[26] This is to say that reason — rationality — is only good insofar as it expresses to us its *limits*, and if we prioritize rationalism above all else, this is only a furtherance of the conditions that promise an undercutting of *Dasein*. "Only a god can save us," Heidegger portends, and "the only possibility available to us is that by thinking and poetizing we prepare a readiness for the appearance of a god, or for the absence of a god in [our] decline, insofar as in view of the absent god we are in a state of decline." "Thinking" for its own sake — as evidenced in the institutionalization of rationalism in the modern world — only alienates us from the spirit of *Dasein*, the spirit of ourselves, our *Volksgeist*, and creates the conditions for the inevitable return of this spirit through tumultuous means. For if the current state of the modern world indicates *pure reason* — rationalism — and further reveals the downward spiral of cultural degeneracy, then a change to this current state through the reintroduction of the irrational, as being fundamental to the *Volksgeist*-ian *Dasein*, can only cause a paradigmatic upheaval. This upheaval can be understood as the Apocalypse, or the return of the ARCHETYPE.[27] Heidegger's "god" is the upheaval that signals the return of the *necessary irrational* to the existence of man.

∞ ∞ ∞

War is our salvation. No, war is not to be glorified for its own sake nor sought, for it is indeed terrible; but, practically speaking, war is staving off the cultural degeneration concomitant with the rationalistic society, the Liberalistic society. War is a Liberalistic society's life support.

First, what is meant by *Liberalistic*? To be *Liberalistic* means to operate under the auspices of Liberalism, whether one is a devout liberal *or* conservative, in the political sense. *Liberalism* is contrasted with *Statism*, wherein the former prioritizes individual liberty above

---

[26] *Dasein* is *Being, existence*, the *uniquely human* experience for Heidegger.
[27] See "Life's Governed Apocalypse" and "The ARCHETYPE and the Acceleration of Time" in this collection.

all and the latter values civic responsibility the most.[28] The Liberalistic society, most often seen in and best exemplified by the modern West, prizes *liberty* ("freedom from" something) and *freedom* ("freedom to do" something) as a means of achieving social progress; the ties that bind the citizenry of the Liberalistic society are, paradoxically, their self-interest and, given the similarity in ideological sensibilities between it and capitalism,[29] the pursuit and prioritization of money. Rationalism is the driver behind the interests in self and money in a Liberalistic society because Liberalism is fundamentally idealistic. *Theoretically,* Liberalism is a fine means of achieving physical, mental, and spiritual fulfillment — i.e., achieving social fulfillment — for if an individual can be convinced of the value of and given the opportunity for his own rational progress, then, as a rational being and being naturally inclined to such endeavors, he will unhesitatingly and undoubtedly take advantage of such opportunity; likewise, money — its pursuit and procurement — secures the liberty of the individual.[30] Practically, however, we too often see the disciplined and magnanimous self-interest of Liberalistic theory devolve into the selfish-interest and indolence of Liberalistic reality; similarly, we see the industrious pursuit of money theoretically achieved in capitalism involute to a distinct money-soul, a state of being predicated on money and the means of achieving it *über alles.*

In short, Liberalism, which is to say, rationalism, is the faith in rational progress to a point of Fichtean synthesis, to the summit of Hegelian perfection in the absolute *Idea.* This is why in Liberalistic societies there is a *dogmatic* adherence to abstract concepts — concepts such as liberty, equality, justice, etc. — in the face of all pragmatic application; and, further, this is why Liberalistic societies are so often, both historically and presently, seen as degenerative: the

---

[28] This distinction is the author's. All political ideology can be properly understood via a "three-dimensional" spectrum, wherein the traditional liberal-democratic understanding of "left" and "right" are mere subsets of the larger Liberalistic v. Statist spectrum.

[29] See "Foundations for a Healthy Society" in this collection.

[30] Rousseau, in his *Confessions*, states, "As long as my purse contains money it secures my independence." Thus, in every Liberalistic society there is an indelible link between the pursuit of happiness (*liberty*) and money. Of note: in just the first four books of the *Confessions* of Rousseau, a man so ideologically linked to the "liberty, equality, and fraternity" of Liberalism's birth, *liberty* is mentioned 20 times, *money* is mentioned 41 times.

dogmatic commitment to ideas in themselves ever trumps the practical consequences of the ideas; thus there can be seen always the tradition-busting "progress" within the Liberalistic society. *Consequences be damned, the Idea will flourish!*

And so it is that the idea meets reality in contemporary Liberalism. In America, the West's *auteur par excellence* of the Liberalistic ideal, the Idea is ever on the march — toward what some perceive as *progress*, toward what others perceive as *paradoxical absurdity*: communities based on atomized individuals, non-traditional marriages, a culture of multiculturalism, ethnic diversity based on ideological homogeneity, progressive-tolerant religions, single-parent families, etc. *Diversity* wins the day in the modern West, save in regards to the *uncompromising adherence to the Idea*: diversity wins the day because the Idea is divine; and if the Idea is divine, then Liberalism is its faith. But *such twosomeness is surely more lonesome than being alone!*[31] Such uncompromising diversity must inevitably lead to a disintegration of spirit; for one cannot have an integration based on disintegration any more than there can exist a spirit of non-spirit. This disintegration is the alienation of modern man, his manifest lonesomeness.

The modern West displays a wealth of technicized communities, a plethora of cultures, a spate of rationalism, and a dearth of spirit. In its never-ending search for the expansion of the Idea, Liberalistic societies focus their energies externally; for the internal has been found wanting, the spirit has been ineradicably linked to the nefarious tradition of an *ancien régime*. The external focus is the way in which the material-theocracy[32] will be achieved, for the external focus is never satiated and must always *consume*, and it is material that is acquired and consumed. Materials are acquired through war, whether that war is understood as business-corporate or the traditional storm of steel. This pursuit of war for material acquisition and non-spiritual ends is simply the manifestation of the money-soul. The money-soul — i.e., the Liberalistic society — cannot sustain itself of its own accord: it focuses itself externally: it must *consume* — both ideologies and materials. But war for the Liberalistic State serves another purpose beyond satisfying its need to consume: it simulates the internal focus of the spiritual; it creates in the warrior and fabricates in the society-at-large the *synthesis* of

---

[31] Nietzsche, *Thus Spoke Zarathustra*, "The Vision and the Enigma."

[32] See "The ARCHETYPE and the Acceleration of Time" in this collection.

reason and spirit, of the rational and irrational. That is, war, for the Liberalistic State, is a means by which *Dasein* might be generated.

In attempting to generate *Dasein*, the Liberalistic State attempts to postpone inevitable social disintegration by fostering *esprit de corps* amongst the citizenry. In this way, the externally oriented consumerism, which drives the war effort, is forced to look inward toward the spirit, toward the internal saintliness that can only accompany the faithful spirit,[33] thus creating the war-soul. Unlike a more tradition-based, culturally homogeneous society that inculcates sustained sentiments of shared (collective) purpose through its internal focus on the cultural soul (*der Volksgeist*), the Liberalistic State, through its inherent external focus, can only achieve the stabilizing (integrating) effect when it perpetuates war to achieve its external, material-ideological ends. In this way, the social spirit is created; in this way, the Liberalistic State develops its war-soul.

War forces individual liberty to melt away into the ultimate civic responsibility. The disintegrating consequence of satisfying myriad individuals in their pursuit of the *concept* in fulfillment of the *Idea* has no recourse but to invert when faced with the existential threat; death cultivates pragmatism, and idealism scurries into the shadows like a cockroach under the spotlight. Ernst Jünger reminds us of what is essential when "the future of the world" is at stake: "I sensed the weight of the hour, and I think everyone felt the individual in them dissolve, and fear depart".[34] Jünger records, too, the fatalism concomitant with war: capable men are mowed down; chance meetings between comrades preserve life where otherwise death lurked; bursting shells might snuff your match or your being, depending on divine diktat. The primordial understanding of "ancient history",[35] where life depends always on *the gods* and *the will to power*: this is the foundation of civic responsibility; this is the mandate of reality reflected in the saintliness of the war-soul.

---

[33] Ernst Jünger, *Storm of Steel* (New York: Penguin Classics, 2016): "When once it is no longer possible to understand how a man gives his life for his country — and the time will come — then all is over with that faith also, and the idea of the Fatherland is dead; and then, perhaps, *we shall be envied, as we envy the saints their inward and irresistible strength*." Emphasis added.

[34] Ibid., 231.

[35] Ibid., 150.

Even if the masses are instructed to "go shopping," "get down to Disney," or conduct "business as usual" in the face of an existential threat — i.e., to deprioritize the war effort[36] — they are nonetheless aware and, what is more, are exposed to constant threats of external enemies in the *consumer*-driven twenty-four-hour news cycle. If the individual consumer in the Liberalistic State chooses to "unplug," then he merely instantiates the rationalistic urge to self-interested *liberty*, thereby contributing "the absence of a god in [our] decline." The war-soul is ultimately achieved through seepage into the collective conscious and unconscious; it is present in the media; it is echoed through entertainment — books, film, music, games, and television; it is felt in taxing, budgeting and appropriating; it is passed along the roads and talked to in the halls and aisles. And whether it is acknowledged or not, the war-soul purports to be the inward faith that sustains us in our decline: consume or die. We will yet consume. But in this materialistic, economic age, it is the "destroyer" who is damaged and the soldier who is "dishonored",[37] and the spirit instilled by the war-soul cannot withstand the external reach of the money-soul's tentacles, the tentacles pulling it ever closer and quicker toward the end of time.

Yes, to delay spiritual disintegration, the war-soul becomes necessary in a Liberalistic State; but the war-soul is not God. And only a god can save us: a return to the ARCHETYPE which has left us, a return to the ARCHETYPE which will reappear despite us — this is our salvation.

THE GREAT NOON

> *And it is the great noontide, when man is in the middle of his course between animal and Übermensch, and celebrateth his advance to the evening as his highest hope: for it is the advance to a new morning.*
>
> — FRIEDRICH NIETZSCHE, *THUS SPOKE ZARATHUSTRA*

---

[36] The West (particularly the United States) has been involved in perpetual war since 1939 (unofficially since at least 1933) (for the US, 1941, officially). President G.W. Bush, in the wake of 9/11, indicated the direction all subsequent Western leaders would take in the face of existential threat when he encouraged materialistic endeavors to salve national wounds.

[37] Jünger, 128.

Soon comes the *great noon*, when the sun sits at its peak, furthest from man. It is then that man and his shadow become one — a singularity. If man is the animate, the shadow is the inanimate — an image cast upon a cave wall, a deception. The *great noon* is the synthesis, a projection of the future when man and his antithesis become one.

What is the sun? It is the life animating man. The shadow is a feigned suspicion of man, for he cannot create *ex nihilo*; it is the deception. The *great noon* is the singularity when God's creation and man's trick become united. This new being will transcend and *obsoletize* humanity. The *great noon* is the end of humanity.

From whence comes the new being, the *transhuman*? *Thus slowly wandering through many peoples and diverse cities, did Zarathustra return by roundabout roads to his mountains and his cave. And behold, thereby came he unawares also to the gate of the GREAT CITY.*[38] The "city," as symbol for modernity, is the source of humanity's end. It is the melting pot of diversity, the bastion of free speech — so long as one's speech is approved, the fountainhead of "tainted, frothy, swamp-blood."[39] Inhabiting the city are many two-legged organisms; they are not the diviners of the new morning. Theirs is to toil, for they are the pawns; the future is not theirs. The minds moving them — kinetically or telekinetically, *they* are the future gods. The future belongs to Atlas; and in the modern world of technics, Atlas is the technocrat. The city is his petri dish. Ever bending to the will of Atlas, the organisms throbbing and thronging in the city will produce and reproduce as long as they are snug and satiated. On their toil, Atlas' means will grow. He meets secretly in plain sight with his ilk, plotting the future, the end of humanity — Ah! But not the end of the petri dish!

With his means, Atlas prepares to shrug. With this shrug comes the *great noon*. What does he discuss in secret? The breakaway civilization, the new man, the *transhuman* technocracy: these are the whispers among the technocratic elite. More than whispers, they are plans — concrete and time-based. At the dawn of *transhumanity*, where man and shadow are bound in sanitizing transfiguration, man and machine are fused. The new priests of the modern technocracy conjure supra-human power and even time itself, time as extra-

[38] Nietzsche, *Thus Spoke Zarathustra*, "On Passing-by."
[39] Ibid.

dimensional magic. Illness, age, and death are relics for the priests — signs of a less reverent, dangerous past; for the city-dwellers — the toilers — illness, age, and death are reminders of their place in the petri dish.

Priestly magic does more than delineate the castes: it transcends time. And more than physical time — the time affecting spatial dimensions — is overcome; conceptual time, too, is manipulated. *"Everything straight lieth," murmured the dwarf, contemptuously. "All truth is crooked; time itself is a circle".*[40] By transcending space-time through singularity, Atlas and his priests extend the *great noon* indefinitely. Evening comes and goes, but the *noon* never fades. Conceptually, time is looped, stagnated, and perpetuated — all for the sake of embalming the moment of Eternal Reverence. Atlas shrugs, his shoulders miming a half-circle in the air, his *transhumanity* etching a disappearing wake through time; meanwhile, the toilers continue to toil, languishing in their swamp-blood, none the wiser.

At the moment of singularity, the toilers will gaze in wonderment. It will be that moment when their material desires reach apotheosis. In seeing their material god, their spirit will forever die. *He is freely in bondage who does with pleasure the will of his master.*[41] Freedom, at the *great noon*, will become despised and dreaded. Freedom means death. Only in slavery can the toilers hope to reach the summit, the upper crust their *transhuman* gods craft. Mass control will be the toilers' salvation. Atlas will oblige.

What was it the technocrats divined in their moment of glory? The entire world, after all, was accelerating in its decline to the singular point of the material god-man on earth since 1945, *Götterdämmerung*: this acceleration was the imbalance of rationality over irrationality. Singularity was seen long before it happened. Technology was not yet mature enough to make the leap into techno-synthesis; this was the only impediment to their mastery of the world. Their plans have been fixed since the Enlightenment, since man escaped his so-called nonage and left the old gods and traditions behind for good. Man became god in his mind; it was only his body that needed mending. In this life there are only three possibilities: meaning, suicide, or oblivion. The technocrats found meaning in the death of the old gods; the toiling swamp-bloods

---

[40] Nietzsche, *Thus Spoke Zarathustra*, "The Vision and the Enigma."

[41] Augustine of Hippo, *Enchiridion*.

clutched the coattails, roused like rabble to the cause, and the culmination of this godless meaning and oblivion was the *great noon*, wherein man became enslaved to the *transhuman*, the new god on earth. Such is the plan of the technocrats, those would-be Atlases.

Atlas, however, does not belong to the earth. Atlas belongs to MYTH, and this is what the world aims to destroy, despite profane reverence for the synthesizing anti-MYTH. The only thing the technocrats have in common with Atlas is their lust for god-killing rebellion; but they do not hold up the world, this is the sun's work, it is God's. The shadows — projections on a wall, *this* is the false creation of the supposed "new man." They do not disappear in the *great noon*; they are hidden under the feet. And it is this hidden shadow, the would-be Atlases suppose, that now holds up the sky. *We are under it, therefore it is our burden*. The Eternal Reverence, the moment of singularity, is held in conceptual perpetuity as a chain around the throat of all, keeping the anti-MYTH in place. When the technocrats shrug, the only burden they unload is their deference to the God that created them.

In worshipping themselves, however, the *transhuman* priests yet worship a god. It is their destructive urge, the Demiurge. This primordial cipher mistook its distortion of supreme creation as creation itself, and so it is with the *transhuman*. Break the mirror, distort the image, and declare divine inspiration: this is the demiurgical method. They topple statues to the mud and mark themselves vanguards of the future. The Demiurge, however, is a jealous god, and cannot suffer crowded altars. Hubris transcends even the *transhuman*, and the new gods will forfeit their material gains for the destruction that was their impetus.

In an alternate past, golems of the Demiurge were collected on the island of Madagascar. At first, in collective chagrin over their unhappy state, they prospered, unifying effort for the sake of resilience. This success turned ugly, however: destructive yearnings — reflections of their maker — colored their facets, and the face each showed to another was the deception inherent in vantage. No mere misunderstandings, these deceptions were the threads tying the golems together, and likewise the mauls wedging them apart. Side rose against side and partisans destroyed each other, until the last statue displaced the mud. In this way, the golems remained loyal to their god — to the last drop of caustic anti-blood.

Though this past is alternate, it mirrors an actual future. The *transhuman* will succeed in breaking away from its petri dish and its isolation will be complete; its island will be singularity, the dawn of the "new man." Yet because its urges are negative — *the compulsion to destroy the old gods and traditions for the sake of peak rationality* — and because it fulfills its demiurgical potential — *destroying the natural for the sake of the unnatural* — the "new man" cannot escape the siphoning shadow of its Demiurge-craftsman, and this shadow will be heavier than the world so confidently shrugged off at the *great noon*.

Those techno-priests meeting in secret know the grim reality awaiting them at the *great noon*. Despite knowing, their faith compels them. Yet can we call it *faith* when they cannot do otherwise? Their autonomic response compels them, yes. This is life's governed apocalypse — the unavoidable end of an age. Pseudo-pious folly will end the existing order. The *transhuman* will revoke itself, crushed under the weight of the *great lie* that Nature can be subverted or circumvented. From folly comes fecundity.

A faint shadow has visited me, Nietzsche revealed, *the shadow of the Übermensch...* The techno-priests' singularity is not Nietzsche's Great Noon; it is only their material copy of it — *their* great noon and *our* dystopian noon, devoid of spirituality. Their shadow is not the *Übermensch*, but only an inorganic lie, the *transhuman* Frankenstein. As Serrano noted, "[the] conception of the *Übermensch* ... is a pure invention or creation."[42] The *Übermensch* is MYTH; it is the will to a higher state of being through mental, physical, and spiritual renewal; it is man's faith in and striving for the MAN TO COME. From this faith and struggle, through an indomitable will to power, comes the New Order at Fimbulwinter's break, the Viconian Age of the Gods, the Satya-Yuga — the age of the eagle and the serpent, faithful pride and wisdom. This age is hallmarked, not by any usurpation of Nature, but by Nature's apotheosization.

In raising Nature up to the noontide sun above us, we harmonize with it and bring ourselves closer to God. *This* is the Great Noon, after which dawns the morning of the *Übermensch*. Meaning, too, rests in this harmonization:

> Meaning, coming not from reason, not from the intellect ... but from the highest inspiration and concentration of energy, from the "highest tonality of

[42] Miguel Serrano, *Nietzsche and the Eternal Return* (Wewelsberg Archives, 2020), 19.

> the soul" that is possible to achieve with our lives, with our "will to power"; with an idea that comes from the depths, from the true creative Idea.[43]

This Great Noon is not perpetuated indefinitely. It is a *moment* in the Eternal Return when man might loosen his chains and escape Demiurgical bondage to enter the halls of the Supreme Creator. But because of its sacredness, this Great Noon is the *second* noon; the first is the material noon of the *transhuman*: sacredness, because of its proximity to the mystery of all beginning, comes only after the darkest night, from which the new dawn arises. First we fall, then we rise. It is only through the fall that our ancestors will muster the strength to launch into a new heroic age. We must learn piety before heroism.

In the closing days of his lucidity, Nietzsche signed letters with his name — only his name was *Caesar*, *Wagner*, *Dionysus*, *Bismarck*, *Shakespeare*, ... *Jesus*. Why? Because life is real to the infinite "I" bound up with infinite time, but only an illusion to the finite self. This might sound reversed, but it is not. The Eternal Return is both reality and illusion. Its secret can only be solved with the arrival of the *Übermensch* at the Great Noon — the moment of epiphanic ecstasy when the infinite and the finite coincide. Nietzsche's invalidity was a sacrifice to sacred *meaning*, which is to say, an escape from the Eternal Return. Though his arms were straightjacketed, his spirit was free; his sacrifice on the material plane paved the way for the MAN TO COME. It is said that Nietzsche's final collapse was in Turin, protecting a horse from the lash. He was protecting Nature, a living creature — not only the horse, but us as well. What did he see in the horse's eyes, beyond the shadow of the blinders? A reflection of the sun in the noontide sky, the coincidence of man and infinity: God in the Great Noon.

---

43 Ibid., 20-21.

CHAPTER 3
THE ARCHETYPE AND ITS OPPOSITION: VISIONS

THE *ULM REICHSWEHR* AFFAIR

By September 1930, the *Nationalsozialistische Deutsche Arbeiterpartei* (NSDAP) had increased their Reichstag representation from a mere 12 seats to 107, making it the second-largest party in Germany. Adolf Hitler, who had been recognized as *der Führer* (of the party) since at least 1925, was quickly rising to national prominence. Soon after the NSDAP's political windfall, Hitler was subpoenaed by one Hans Achim Litten — a leftist Jewish attorney, and a supporter of the disastrous Weimar Republic — to testify at the so-called *Ulm Reichswehr* trial. At the center of the trial were three German army officers accused of political engagement and electioneering on behalf of the NSDAP (the official charge was "high treason"); aside from being against army regulations, this was cause for general alarm since Hitler's party *openly dismissed* separation of the military from the political process. Civilian mediation between government and the military had been a hallmark of recent Western (and Weimarian) Liberalism, and this was now under threat. German voters, through the democratic process, *supported* this "threat."

During his examination of Hitler — which lasted nearly three intense hours — Litten questioned both the NSDAP's and Hitler's motivations; he questioned the legality of the NSDAP's popular support; he questioned Hitler's rise to prominence through the democratic process; yet through it all, despite his alleged obedience to Western Liberalism in all its pageantry, Litten questioned the very process that he claimed to be defending during his berating of Hitler. Litten, like many Liberalists before and after him, only supported his idealistic abstractions when they worked in his favor. As soon as the popular tide turned against the Liberalist tack, the Liberalists took umbrage and went on the offensive.

An important point to remember is that democracies need not be Liberalistic. The citizenry, via representatives or directly, might choose the way of *il-Liberalism*. In certain times, such as those experienced in the Weimar, parliamentarianism leads only to gridlock; its inherent inefficacy leads to stagnating, regressive impasse; in certain times, the efficacy of decisiveness is needed to overcome erstwhile gridlock; in the Weimar, the people voted for this efficacy, only to find themselves lambasted by the Liberalistic intelligentsia for their so-called *pedestrian ignorance*. The people spoke; but the guardians and protectors of idealistic abstractions — not least of which was popular liberty — could only chastise.

Germany, Hitler (and many others) believed, was under attack — not least from the Liberalistic intelligentsia. Hitler and the NSDAP challenged the military leadership to accept military politicizing and take up their rightful mantle as the *defenders* of the folk. This is precisely what the three German officers were doing when they were arrested and later put to trial; they were simply heralds of a new era. And for a brief moment in history, Hitler and the NSDAP spoke not just for the *Deutsche Volk*, but for illiberalists the across the West. This new era would put *Deutschland, Deutschland über alles*, yet not from a Bismarckian *socio-economic* perspective — as Nietzsche famously derided, but from a spiritual, *national-socialist* perspective. Never before (the NSDAP and Mussolini's *Fascismo*) had the world seen State-sanctioned prioritization of the national-cultural soul (*Volksgemeinschaft*) over economic impetus. Not since the Roman Imperium — and likely never before — had the notion of "everything within the State, nothing outside the State, nothing against the State" rose to such a feverish zeitgeist. The people had spoken; and the Littens of the world could only scold and protest their waning influence.

∞ ∞ ∞

What Litten did not expect, in his underhanded attempt to delegitimize Hitler and his movement, was the *Volksgemeinschaft* permeating even that blind-to-justice Weimar courtroom. Liberalism — in all its rationalistic materialism — *never* counts on human nature remaining essentially and irrevocably *human*; mere abstraction, mere imprudent rationalism, could not usurp man's tether to his primordial origins, to his irrational, animal nature.

Litten pressed Hitler: "What are your intentions, Herr Hitler? Will you and your party seize liberty itself from the people? Do you intend to thwart the very foundations of Western civilization with violent thuggery?" Hitler scoffed, yet could not repress his burgeoning anger: "We intend to work squarely within the law — nothing more, nothing less. [Otto] Straßer was the man of 'revolution' and he's gone. We had no use for his recklessness... But I promise you this: we *will* come to power — square within the law — and your kind will be left wanting — *heads will roll*, believe me! And Germany will finally have the power she deserves!" When Hitler finished in his growling crescendo that has become so familiar, his words were met with a *courtroom ovation*. The people had spoken again, but their sentiment thundered in contrast to Litten's withering, hypocritical Liberalism.

∞ ∞ ∞

On 27 February 1933, the *Reichstag* [German parliament building] was set ablaze. In the early morning hours of the next day, Litten and various other Liberalists (anarchists and communists) were arrested for conspiring to undermine the authority and stability of the reawakened *Volksgemeinschaft*. Litten was bounced from prison to prison camp, spending his final five years in captivity. He died in a work camp in 1938, age 34.

∞ ∞ ∞

Some might ask whether Litten's death was warranted. Yet most can justifiably ask whether Litten was right to try his hand at lambasting Hitler and the NSDAP's emergence into the national spotlight. Litten's attempt was typical of all Liberalistic behavior — especially that of the intelligentsia. We see it daily force-fed to us via the "free" media; we see it in Hollywood, professorial, journalistic, and political partisanship and protestation; we hear it parroted by the duly indoctrinated, the bourgeoisie and the "oppressed" proletariat *ad nauseum*. When the liberal-minded masses fail, their only recourse is to bring the spiritually strong victors down to their level of soulless mediocrity and misery. It is the essence of an inferior mentality: why work hard to win when you can simply coast and complain until this or that godless representative bends to your will? This is why Liberalism is the ideology of the "oppressed" ("power to the people"). The masses of "oppressed" are simply incapable of carving out their place through work, zeal, and fury, so they seek handouts to compensate for their indiscipline, for their weakness. And this weakness of will is unbecoming of any nation — of any worthwhile folk. Better we strive for hard-won power, through grit, fury, and will — *der heilige Wille*; better we "roll the heads" of those who seek to undermine the *Volksgemeinschaft*, the only meaningful wealth of a nation, a State of blood-bound kinsmen.

THOUGHTS ON THE "DE-NAZIFICATION" OF AN ILLIBERAL GERMAN

Ernst Bertram's *Nietzsche: Attempt at a Mythology* aims to illuminate the myth of reality. Bertram was a German professor who reached his literary peak just before the *Nationalsozialistische Deutsche Arbeiterpartei* (NSDAP) rose to power. By all accounts, he was not a National Socialist; rather, he was a German nationalist, valued aristocracy, and was more or less illiberal. The aforementioned book, for which he is most famous, is far more literary than philosophical and probably reads better in its original German than in English. It is Bertram's attempt to dissect what he feels was Nietzsche's internal (system) mythology. While the ideas Bertram broaches are of the greatest existential import, the book itself is largely not worth discussing.

What is interesting, though, is that, after the war, this book somehow tied Bertram to the NSDAP in the minds of the Allied powers — to the tune of Bertram losing his professorship and undergoing "de-Nazification." Yet there is nothing remotely related to National Socialism in it. The link between Bertram, who was "cleared" of any NSDAP connection (but still never regained his professorship), and the NSDAP could only be their shared illiberal sentiment, which is hardly something for which one should be persecuted.

But this harassment of Bertram after the war is just one example of many. Literally any German or Italian who was not a liberal sycophant was starved, persecuted, or brought to trial. Thousands of German and Italian families who, like Bertram, were illiberal but no "Nazis," were encamped, hounded, and killed in this post-war Liberalistic crusade. After the military war was won, the Allied powers were vicious and relentless in their cause to "de-Nazify" — i.e., liberalize — any illiberal remnants. To say the least, it was a successful crusade; if one has any doubt, consider that Germany (or the Germanic realm) once offered the world Barbarossa, Friedrich the Great, Bismarck, and any number of heroes from the two world wars, and yet now the best Germany can offer is Angela Merkel — *Mother Merkel*, hero of the Fifth Column and usurper of the German people — a pawn of the moneyed golems, the *international clique*, and economic queen *par excellence!* The best the Germanic realm can offer is Volodymyr Zelenskyy — a once-despised Jew, now Hero of the World, pit against his counter-puppet Putin in yet another fratricidal war of Germanic and Slavic people.

The point is this: Liberalism is every bit as primal and unscrupulous as any other ideology when it comes to its survival. It will punish those it deems worthy of punishment; it will ironically defame and persecute anyone who does not fall obsequiously in line with its cause of nominal *liberty, equality, justice* and the other abstract refrains. It is a *tyranny* of "the people." The once grand idea of Liberalism has devolved into violent protests (against dissenting voices), feminism, unnatural relationships and identities, and ignorance of both human nature and the widely illiberal world beyond its narrow-minded borders. In short, Liberalism is a rejection of reality and a tyrannical cause to silence or forcefully change dissenting voices. That is, it is a fanatical ideology *par excellence!*

And here is the greatest irony of all: the most Liberalistic citizens of any Liberalistic State are usually the *last* to sacrifice *their* individualism for their nation. *This is no coincidence.* Only those who value selfless service in the cause of supporting *their* nation, only those who prioritize — wittingly or instinctually — the primal call of *defending the fatherland* over their *individual liberty* rise to meet the privilege of defending their Liberalistic nation, because only the most *illiberal* citizens recognize both the advantage in sacrifice and the *existential necessity of prioritizing reality over abstractions.* Ultimately, the illiberal sentiment *is that which cherishes love of spiritual community over any ideology or individual indulgence.* And this is what Bertram was persecuted for; this is what millions of illiberal German, Italian, and Japanese families were starved for after the war. For in a Liberalistic State, one *must* prize the individual over the nation, lest he be a proud member of the illiberal institution that defends it.

In modern times, we are in national and cultural decline because we are indoctrinated to cherish the individual over the nation, or the increasingly non-existent spiritual community. Those who do not servilely toe the line are called "fascists" or "tyrannical." Yet the opposite is true and the real tyranny bubbles up from below

— from the will of "the people," the mass of economically associated individuals who care as little for their blood or nation as the many Bertrams and post-war-persecuted, illiberal families cared for the individual.

In the modern Liberalistic State, *freedom* is euphemism for freedom *for* dissipation and indiscipline — i.e., freedom *from* selfless service to one's nation. And the "freest" among us will never fight to defend our right to *ignore* our nation; instead, most will simply ignore it — because the illiberal folk will defend it for them. In this parasitical relationship, however, it is not the individual who suffers, but the nation that protects him.

Bertram lost his career and was hounded as a criminal, *for what*? For loving his nation, his folk; for challenging the money-spirit and liberal dissipation he witnessed firsthand in the Weimar Republic; for instilling a sense of cultural pride in his fellow countrymen with his words? No; Bertram lost everything simply because he was on the side that lost. And the reality is we live in a world — and rightfully so — where might makes right. The Second World War was not about "Good" triumphing over "Evil" — not any more than the battle for Troy, the American Civil War, the Cold War, the Thirty Years War, the Vietnam War, the Korean War, or nearly any other war in history were. Almost every war in history has been fought over national interests, and this, in the modern liberal-democratic West, is euphemism for *money*. It was *money* — specifically industrial specialization and economic dispensation — that won its material victory in 1945, and the money-spirit was emboldened in the now definitively Liberalistic West; *if money won, it must be right* — this is the popular sentiment. Yet money is shallow and soulless, and what binds a people must be more than this: what make a nation are *blood, culture,* and *destiny*. Bertram was persecuted for being on the losing side; his side preached cultural solidarity *over and above* money and economic unions — yet his side lost; the *human* spirit could not keep pace with so many opposing *money*-spirits; and if the idea of cultural solidarity lost to the power of money, then, the West assumed, money must be valued above solidarity, for in money there is *power*. And what is life if not a will to power?

Yet now we stand in the economic union of nation-states because we have witnessed firsthand the prevailing power of money; we are Weimar; this is the future Bertram feared and argued against, for this petty future robs all of us of our historical bond and cultural endurance. If we are to endure, we would do well to not forget that the power of money is illusory, for it masks the money-spirit undergirding it: the *individual* power of materialistic selfishness and hoarding, the prevailing inclinations of Liberalism. The *myth* that Nietzsche and Bertram were after, the MYTH that was "de-Nazified" after the military struggle, was the empowering and enduring MYTH of cultural solidarity; it is the only MYTH that approaches reality and shapes it through the indomitable human spirit. This is the MYTH of reality and it cannot be liberalized.

NAPOLEON, THE *FÜHRERPRINZIP*, AND THE FRENCH REVOLUTION

I am the French Revolution. — NAPOLEON

During his cross-examination at Nuremberg, Hermann Göring described the *Führerprinzip* thusly: "authority existed at the top and passed downwards, while the responsibility began at the bottom and passed upwards".[1] This is to say that the authority of the Führer — the leader — was predicated on "the responsibility," i.e., the *will* of the people. The people choose their ultimate authority through their collective will and entrust their will to be executed through the decisiveness of the sole leader: this is the *Führerprinzip*.

This principle has its theoretical roots in the philosophy of Hegel; practically, however, the principle has its modern roots[2] in the ascension of Napoleon Bonaparte to his seat as Emperor of the French. Hegel, whose own life temporally paralleled Napoleon's,[3] was likewise a product of the Enlightenment and grappled with both the influence of the dominant political theorist who preceded him (Rousseau) and the influence of the ascendant political actor who was his contemporary (Napoleon). In wrestling with these two

[1] Hermann Göring, Proceedings from 18 March 1946: The Nuremberg Tribunal, Nuremberg, Germany.

[2] In antiquity, the principle's roots may be traced to Julius Caesar; he is another man whose career might yet be a metaphor for all political arcs, for every society must confront their Rubicon.

[3] Napoleon was born in 1769, Hegel in 1770. While Hegel outlived the Emperor, he published his *Elements of the Philosophy of Right* in apparent answer to Napoleon's very existence (published in 1820, one year before the Emperor's death).

influences, Hegel established his own philosophical system — his *Phänomenologie des Geistes* — in which something like a Napoleon becomes not just understandable, but sometimes necessary. The convergence of Rousseau's thought, the French Revolution, and Napoleon's career stands as the canvas for Hegel's system, of which the "world-spirit" is the utmost manifestation.[4]

With this context, it becomes clear that Napoleon was indeed the French Revolution, for he was the embodiment of the Rousseauian *volonté générale* — the will of the people over whom he exercised supreme authority, the will of the people who incited the revolution and turned it into the terror that needed restraining. By embodying and exercising this authority of the people over the people, Napoleon not only concretized the *Führerprinzip*, but also informed the Hegelian philosophy which explained him: Napoleon is the French Revolution because he is the world-spirit, the world-historical figure who transcends *individual* will through instantiating *universal* will, as described by Hegel.

To further present this thesis, it will be necessary to discuss Rousseau's political theory and Napoleon as a mythic, Hegelian world-historical figure who embodied the Revolution that spawned him — that is, a discussion of both Napoleon as the rational and irrational embodiment of the French spirit and Hegel's theory of will and Idea will be had. Lastly, to determine the implications of the Enlightenment's boldest statement, i.e., the French Revolution, ultimately being embodied by an emperor of the highest degree, an examination of Nietzsche's admiration of Napoleon and influence on what became the *Führerprinzip* will be undertaken. In this way, the aim and conclusion of this essay will attempt to show that Napoleon was, as he said, the French Revolution and why he was such an inspiration for Nietzsche.

Rousseau and the *Volonté Générale*

Central to Rousseau's political philosophy is the concept of the general will. This concept, no less brilliant for its simplicity, roughly

---

[4] Hegel on Napoleon, October 1806: "I saw the Emperor — this world-spirit — riding out of the city on reconnaissance. It is indeed a wonderful sensation to see such an individual, who, concentrated here at a single point, astride a horse, reaches out over the world and masters it ... this extraordinary man, whom it is impossible not to admire." Terry Pinkard, *Hegel: a Biography* (New York: Cambridge University Press, 2000), 228.

measures the government of a stable State as indicative of its citizens' general will. Certainly, individuals might here or there disagree with the established government, but they are the exceptions that prove the rule of general concurrence with the social contract manifest in the State, for they are yet parts of a whole — they represent the swirling countercurrents in the vast river of public will. This *general will* sets the parameters for the civil liberty which is legislated by the appropriate legislating body and enacted by the executive authority. The people themselves enforce such civil liberty through their behavior and mold it through the republican process. If the citizenry finds itself in an undemocratic system, then they will either accept such undemocratic authority or revolt against it according to their collective desire. It is this general will, then, that forms the social pact binding the society together, "and it is this same power which, directed by the general will, bears ... the name of sovereignty."[5] The sovereign, for Rousseau, bears no political prejudice beyond the will of the people: "All legitimate government is 'republican' ... [and] even a monarchy can be a republic."[6]

Legitimacy, for Rousseau, is governmental leadership according laws defined by the general will. If a government reckoned itself as belonging to a legal code other than that of its citizenry, then said government would be despotic, not republican, and not representative of the general will; similarly, then, so long as a State body organically arises from the national spirit, then it will be representative of the masses and their collective will, i.e., republican. Rousseau makes further distinction between the tyrannical and the despotic: "The tyrant is one who intrudes, contrary to law, to govern according to the law; the despot is one who puts himself above the law. Thus the tyrant need not be a despot, but a despot is always a tyrant."[7] So, if the general will revolts against the despotic established authority, then the general will, as representative of the people, even if it is manifested in but one man, constitutes a legitimate republican authority.

Legitimacy also bears with it the freedom of reason — this is essential for Rousseau. For *freedom* is not a reflection of unmitigated

---

[5] Jean-Jacques Rousseau, *The Social Contract*, translated by Maurice Cranston (London: Penguin Classics, 1968), 74.

[6] Ibid., 82.

[7] Ibid., 134.

action: "to be governed by appetite alone is slavery"[8]; instead, freedom is only gained through reasoned deliberation, i.e., a deliberation that reveals an individual *restraint* in favor of the common good (the common cause) as the highest freedom. It is *reasonable*, for Rousseau, that the individual will is subsumed into the general will because the general will sets the parameters for civil intercourse; it is *reasonable* because "the general will is always rightful and always tends to the public good" and the good is, naturally, reasonable.[9] The public good, then, is the standard-bearer for reason; reason, when entered into deliberately, represents the only freedom for man.

In order to see the public good, "the public must be taught to recognize" it and "individuals must be obliged to subordinate their will to their reason".[10] The people are taught to see reason and individuals subject themselves to it when they are free amongst themselves under the law of the sovereign, which is to say, the law of the general will, the will of the people. The people are consigned to freedom when they subject themselves to the reasoned rule of law that arises organically from their spirit. Rousseau notes:

> [The most important of all laws is inscribed in the hearts of citizens], a law which forms the true constitution of the state, a law which gathers new strength every day and which, when other laws age or wither away, reanimates or replaces them; a law which sustains a nation in the spirit of its institution and imperceptibly substitutes the force of habit for the force of authority. I refer to morals, customs and, above all, belief: this feature, unknown to our political theorists, is the one on which the success of all the other laws depends; it is the feature on which the great lawgiver bestows his secret care...[11]

The spirit of a people, then, at any given time, is reflected in their institutions, or the embodiments of their institutions. And it is incumbent upon a people's institutions, the State institutions, to

---

[8] Ibid., 65.
[9] Ibid., 72.
[10] Ibid., 83.
[11] Ibid., 99.

"weaken the structure of man in order to fortify it, to replace the physical and independent existence we have all received from nature with a moral and communal existence," thereby attaining a reasonable, or good, existence.[12] This weakening is achieved through *authority* — the authority of the sovereign, the general will of the people, which is ever ascendant as long as the people are not deceived.[13]

The spirit of the French — their general will — was evident in the monarchical climate in 1762 when *The Social Contract* was first published; its publication attests to this spirit; the spirit of the French was evident in the subsequent 1789 revolt against the monarchy; it was present in the Reign of Terror that forcibly removed remnants of the *ancien régime,* and it was evident in the Directory which preceded the Consulate. Yet perhaps more than any of these proofs, we look to the ascension of Bonaparte in 1799 as the marked revelation of the *volonté générale* — because it was Bonaparte who ended the Revolution of the people against the *ancien régime* and their floundering in the face of political uncertainty. The Revolution ended with Napoleon because he embodied the French spirit, the general will, and he offered reprieve to the people suffering from the pressures of purely irrational despotism. In short, Napoleon ended the French Revolution because he *was* the French Revolution.

For Rousseau, the general will is sovereign, legitimate, good, free, and reasonable. What is the French Revolution if not a "reasonable" answer to a state of pure irrationality? And what is Napoleon if not a "reasonable" answer to the Revolution? As if presaging the Corsican's rise on the wave of the French spirit, Rousseau included this passing remark in his influential political work: "I have a presentiment that this little island [Corsica] will one day astonish Europe." Indeed, it did.

Napoleon and the French Revolution

"The revolution," notes Nietzsche, "made Napoleon possible... One would have to wish for the anarchic collapse of our entire civilization for a similar reward."[14] First, we have seen that Napoleon is the natural consequent to the Revolution because each arose out of the

---

[12] Ibid., 85.

[13] Ibid., 72.

[14] Ernst Bertram, *Nietzsche: Attempt at a Mythology* (Urbana: University of Illinois Press, 2009), 176.

same spirit, the same general will of the French — the ultimate end of which was to usurp unthinking, hereditary nobility, the *ancien régime*. Second, why is Napoleon seen as a "reward"? Nietzsche's philosophical peculiarities aside, Napoleon was the attendant to reason because he embodied the French spirit; thus he was the reward of first, the French, next, Europeans. A people that, in their determination, stays true to their spirit, especially if that spirit is oriented on freedom-spawning *rationality* concentrated and executed through an indomitable, *irrational* will, simply reaps their reward *through their own determination*. The *act*, in such cases, is the reward because it produces rewarding fruits: the reward of the French liberal spirit was *The Social Contract*: the reward of Rousseau's tract was the Revolution: the reward of the Revolution was Bonaparte: the reward of the Corsican was the still-influential Napoleonic Civil Code and enduring example of rational irrationality: this was the general will of first, the French, next, Europeans.[15] This is both the myth and reality of Napoleon, of the French spirit.

Goethe, too, noted the myth and reality of Napoleon:

> He had it, and one saw by looking at him that he did; that was all.... He had to an eminent degree a thoroughly demonic nature, so that hardly anyone else can be compared to him. The Greeks counted demonic natures of that sort among the demigods.... His life was the procession of a demigod.... One may very aptly say of him that he found himself in a state of perpetual inspiration.... He was one of the most productive men who has ever lived.[16]

Bonaparte's "production" and "inspiration" were the reality of his life that birthed the Napoleonic myth. This myth is born of man's passions — his *rational* urge toward the Rousseauian social pact of the general will and his *irrational* urge to achieve such an end *by any means*. Napoleon, like the Revolution before him, was a means to such an end; this, too, is why Napoleon was the French Revolution:

---

[15] Finally, if they have been reasonable enough to clutch the coattails of European civilization, the non-European world, too, has reaped the reward of Napoleon's Civil Code.

[16] Bertram, 171.

they are means to the same fulfillment of the French spirit, the general will.

It becomes necessary again to quote Rousseau — this time in a letter to Mirabeau:

> It seems to me that compelling evidence is never to be found in natural and political laws, unless when we consider them in the abstract. In any given government, composed, as it must be, of very diverse elements, this evidence is necessarily wanting. For the science of government is a science purely of combinations, applications and exceptions, which are determined by time, place and circumstance. And the public will never detect with intuitive certainty the relations and workings of all that.... Men guide themselves very seldom by the light of evidence and very often by their passions.... Allow me to tell you that you give too much weight to your calculations, and not enough to the promptings of the heart and the play of passion. Your system is excellent for Utopia. For the children of Adam it is worth nothing.[17]

This sounds like nothing other than further auguring from Rousseau for the essentialness of human passion, *the necessity of the irrational.* First he sees the rise of Corsica (in Napoleon), then effectively describes the necessary art that was Napoleon's life — the "art" described by both Goethe and Hegel. But why such foresight? It is only because Rousseau understood the inescapable interplay between the rational and irrational urges of man: this, too, is why his work, among so many others, stood out as the ideological impetus for the Revolution. Rousseau was a man of that *reasoned passion* which is the source of all inspiration. Kingsley Martin aptly states that [Rousseau's] influence was probably increased by the fact that some passages in his works were mystical and obscure: *The Social Contract* could be treated like the Bible and *Das Kapital* — it could be variously interpreted by enthusiasts, endlessly commented on by

---

[17] Kingsley Martin, *French Liberal Thought in the Eighteenth Century* (New York: Harper Torchbooks, 1963), 213.

scholars, and triumphantly quoted by rival schools, each certain of possessing the true milk of the master's teaching.[18]

What Martin here describes is what Rousseau and all eternal works tap into: that interwoven dynamic of the rational and irrational: the essence of man. In shucking off the chains of the *ancien régime,* through their reasonable general will, the French people did not progress with pure reason. Pure reason did not spawn the Reign of Terror's bloodshed, nor did it birth the Directory's corruption; pure reason did not offer the reins of power to General Bonaparte, nor did it eliminate the Directory for the sake of the Consulate and later the Emperorship. Pure reason sets the parameters through the general will; it is then up to mortal endeavoring to execute the will, and the realm of man is nothing if not "the promptings of the heart and the play of passion".[19]

Napoleon was the French Revolution because he embodied the general will; but more than this, he embodied the sublime passions of man — a man driven by the public good and the passion of a Homeric hero. When, after conquering Prussia, he called a meeting of Prussian nobility to articulate the terms of surrender, Napoleon reminded them: "I am not your prince, I am your master".[20] The general will does not *reason* when executing its aims; it rises to the human endeavor, the will of the man in whose hands all reality turns to clay: it becomes the *myth.*

The Myth of Napoleon

In one of the earliest looks at Bonaparte's character, William Channing all but implores the "civilized" Western man to abhor the Corsican; for "the kind of admiration which [his character] inspires, even in free countries, is a bad omen," and "spoiling" a society's rights

---

[18] Ibid., 214.

[19] The question that must be asked is: what is the ultimate goal of a society: subordination of individual will to the authority of the common weal, or individual aggrandizement for the sake of individual "freedom"? *Aggrandizement* gives us the Revolution with *its* interplay of rationality and irrationality; *subordination* gives us Napoleon with *its* interplay of rationality and irrationality. Which is best is not a matter of subjective opinion, but rather a matter of objective history, for world history is "the *world's court of judgment,*" as Hegel argued.

[20] Georg Wilhelm Friedrich Hegel, *Elements of the Philosophy of Right,* 19th ed., edited by Allen W. Wood, translated by Hugh B. Nisbet (Cambridge: Cambridge University Press, 2014), 325.

and "loading it with chains," as he feels Napoleon did, must only be loathed.[21] Throughout his tract, it becomes clear that Channing is part of the contingent evolved out of the Enlightenment that believes in the purely rationalistic spirit of progress. That is, *progress*, from this perspective, is predicated on the assumption of mass rationalism[22] and the achievement of all ends through it. If we understand *liberty* as the "freedom from" something, then Channing's chief interest, according to his and his contingent's estimation of human nature, is freedom from hindrances to the natural progress that will occur when all men are unbound by traditional strictures. But Channing contradicts his own understanding of rationalistic progress when he acknowledges, multiple times, the already-tread trail of Napoleon's conquest.[23]

Channing, noting Bonaparte's military education, insists that the Emperor is all but without a mind of his own, trained only "to obey his superior without consulting his conscience; to take human life at another's bidding; to perform that deed, which above all others requires deliberate conviction, without a moment's inquiry as to its justice, and to place himself a passive instrument in hands which, as all history teaches, often reeks with blood causelessly shed."[24] Yet what history teaches is, in placing himself as "a passive instrument in" the hands of Fate, or better still, Destiny, Napoleon simply *retells* the role of human nature through history. The *fate* to which we are bound is upheaval; the *destiny* that rises up to manage upheaval is the mythic figure. If history shows us barbarism, then history shows us the prevailing inclinations of man. This is what Channing and his contingent fail to see in examining Napoleon's character: he is the embodiment of the general will and, as such, is the *utmost convergence of the rational and irrational, oriented toward the subordination of the individual to the transcendent*; that is, he is the mythic figure.

---

[21] William Channing, *Analysis of the Character of Napoleon Bonaparte* (Boston: Kessinger Publishing, 1828), 6.

[22] This instance of rationalism is contrasted with *Napoleonic* rationalism; this instance, concomitant with Liberalism and modernity, might justly be called *pure rationalism, modern rationalism*, or *scientific rationalism* — the (anti-) faith of rationalists or *Reasonites*; Napoleonic rationalism, on the other hand, is the reason concomitant with the general will, as argued.

[23] Channing, 8, 23, 41, etc.

[24] Ibid., 8.

Another criticism Channing levies against Napoleon is his installing relatives in various seats of power and breeding into further seats of power:

> Not satisfied with this approximation to the old sovereigns, with whom he had no common interest, and from whom he could not have removed himself too far, he sought to ally himself by marriage with the royal families in Europe, to engraft himself and his posterity on an old imperial tree. This was the very way to turn back opinion into its old channels; to carry back Europe to its old prejudices; to facilitate the restoration of its old order; to preach up legitimacy; to crush every hope that he was to word a beneficent change among nations.[25]

This seems a fair point; however, Napoleon, while being against the notion of the "perpetual" or hereditary constitution, favored a *meritocracy* populated in the upper echelons by his ideological or biological progeny, whom he would mold into capable sovereigns. Napoleon, ultimately, is the French Revolution not just because he embodied the want of equality that pervaded the masses, but also because he harkened back to an *equality of the capable*, as portended by the realities of human nature and ability, which manifests in an *aristocracy of the capable*. If this devolves into a rehash of the "perpetual constitution," then this is through no fault of Napoleon; but, rather, the fault of the human nature he tried to subject.

Bonaparte prized reason, but he prized the human will as well. He embodied the Revolution because he valued not just the reasonable position of the aristocracy-outcasts, but also because he honored the will of intrepid risers. Channing, critic though he is, cannot but acknowledge, even if indirectly, the gravitas of Napoleon's mythic nature:

> Power was his supreme object, but a power which should be gazed at as well as felt, which should strike men as a prodigy, which should shake old thrones as an earthquake, and, by the suddenness of its new creations, should awaken something of the submissive wonder

[25] Ibid., 29.

> which miraculous agency inspires... He wanted to electrify and overwhelm. He lived for effect.[26]

Given his manifestation of the Revolution, in all its rationality and irrationality, this acknowledgement is understandable. And it was this power and effect that compelled the Emperor to remind his subordinates that "your first duty is toward ME, your second toward France. All your other duties, even those toward the people whom I have called you to govern, rank after these."[27] To counter the Emperor was to counter the Revolution; to reject him was to reject the rationalism of the general will[28] in favor of the overthrown *ancien régime*. France came second to him because by perpetuating the Revolution through supporting Napoleon, one sustained the State that sustained the citizenry; to deprioritize France under the will of the citizenry was to place the cart before the horse — it was to renounce the State that characterized the citizenry. Napoleon, viewed thusly, acted accordingly; he voiced the general will.

It has been said that "by looking only at the beginning and at the end of his career ... an imaginary Napoleon has been obtained, who is a republican, not a despot; a lover of liberty, not an authoritarian; a champion of the Revolution, not the destroyer of the Revolution...."[29] Further, we are reminded — no, *chastised* — that "not only do people forgive, but they forget, the cynical indifference of Napoleon to the thousands of deaths which he caused".[30] It is certain that many died because Napoleon lived; yet this is almost tautologous; it is as if one would say: because there is life, there is also death.[31] Napoleon the man is not responsible for the deaths of so many; rather, the will he embodied is the cause; for this reason, too, one is just as likely to admire him as to abhor him! Bonaparte personified the same French spirit that inspired *The Social Contract*, the same spirit that overturned the monarchy, and the same spirit that both spawned and quelled the Reign of Terror and the disordered corruption which followed: he was simply the French Revolution, and as such, was

---

[26] Ibid., 33.
[27] Ibid., 37.
[28] That is, *true reason* — that deliberate subordination of the will to the weal *for the sake of the will.*
[29] Henry Evans, *The Napoleon Myth* (Chicago: Open Court, 1904), 26.
[30] Ibid., 32.
[31] The unstated implication, then, is: *so let us therefore condemn life!*

compelled to offer freedom to his subjects through their participation in the grand drama, managed by his authority, the general will's authority. For, as we recall, *the people are consigned to freedom when they subject themselves to the reasoned rule of law that arises organically from their spirit.*

That Napoleon has become a mythic figure should not surprise us — for all who personify and execute the general will of a people rise to such a level; these figures — and there are a handful in history — are loved or hated based on the zeitgeist of the age, and such is the fate of all gods. For these gods, if we can call them so, are the *Trimurti*, the creator-sustainer-destroyers, the men who announce the *twilight of the old idols*. But "whoever kills God," Bertram tells us, "thereby preserves him for humanity."[32] Such gods sustain the mythic for all mankind; they are the focal point of the irrational, the transcendent. Men live and die for that which transcends them; when, once in every great while, a figure appears to embody the transcendent, then he becomes the lightning rod for all affections and aversions — or perhaps the *star* guiding the wise men of the time to or from his light. "Napoleon constantly referred to his 'Star of Destiny.' In instituting his famous Legion of Honor, he substituted a *star* for the *cross* of St. Louis," Evans reminds us.[33] This was only the compulsion the Emperor fulfilled to replace the *ancien régime* with the *novus ordo seclorum*; the cross of hereditary constitutions was replaced by the star of reason. Pierre-Louis Roederer, from a speech proposing the creation of the Legion of Honor, announced the award as dissolving

> the distinctions of nobility that placed inherited glory ahead of acquired glory, and the descendants of great men before great men themselves.... It is the creation of a new currency of a very different value than the Treasury's money; a currency whose title is unalterable and whose mine cannot be exhausted because it resides in French honor...[34]

---

[32] Bertram, 133.

[33] Evans, 52.

[34] Rafe Blaufarb, *Napoleon, Symbol for an Age: a Brief History with Documents* (Boston: Bedford/St. Martin's, 2008), 102.

A more definitive echo of an Enlightenment voice can scarcely be imagined! But we would be remiss to neglect the deeper, more spiritual meaning of the Legion of Honor — the meaning revealed by Napoleon being more than a mere mortal, the meaning uncovered in his epitomizing the general will. French mystic Alphonse Louis explains the switch to the Legion of Honor thusly:

> It is said that Napoleon believed in his *star*; and that if he could have been persuaded to say what he understood by this star it would have been found that it was his own genius; and therefore he was in the right to adopt for his sign the Pentagram, that symbol of human sovereignty by the intelligent initiative.[35]

Ultimately, though, no matter what mystics or scholars of any age attempt to say about the man, Bonaparte attracts them — attracts us all — because he *was* more than just a man. He himself was superstitious: he consulted his *Book of Fate*,[36] believed in the "evil eye",[37] and already began to mythologize himself through word and deed while still seated upon the throne. Yet this is only to say that he believed in himself and the eternal project of the Revolution. Found near the frontispiece of his translated copy of the ancient manuscript was a handwritten list of questions and answers — all in Bonaparte's own handwriting; in answer to one of his questions on the state of political change, the Corsican writes: "A conqueror, of noble mind and mighty power, shall spring from low condition; he will break the chains of the oppressed, and will give liberty to the nations".[38] Napoleon knew his task and, further, had the will to achieve it, for his was the will of his people. In this way, the Emperor was the embodiment of the *Führerprinzip*.

While Bonaparte lived this principle, it was Hegel who, while not directly using the phrase, came to describe its nature. And it is to Hegel we now turn.

---

[35] Evans, 53.
[36] For an interesting history of Bonaparte's treasured *Book of Fate*, see Herman Kirchenhoffer (translator), *The Book of Fate*, 10th ed. (London: Unknown, 1825), x.
[37] Evans, 51.
[38] *The Book of Fate*, xi.

Napoleon as Hegelian World-Spirit

"When Bonaparte took power," we are told, "much of France was wracked by lawlessness. The sources of disorder were intertwined — economic hardship, unemployment, draft evasion, counterrevolutionary sentiment, and a weak administrative and judicial apparatus".[39] This is only a rationalistic way of describing the state of human nature, however; it looks to the symptoms rather than the disease. It is accurate, to be sure; but its accuracy betrays the essence of the human condition. The humanists tell us, through Schmitt, that

> in people — the uneducated masses, the variegated animals, the 'many-colored beast with many heads,' as Plato calls it — there was something irrational that needed to be governed and led by reason. But, if people are irrational, then one cannot negotiate with them or forge contracts; rather they must be mastered through cunning or violence. In this case reason cannot make itself evident, it does not argue; it dictates. The irrational is only the instrument of the rational, because only the rational can really lead and act.[40]

There must arise out of the very will of the people, organically, a leader to enact their will. For the French and the Revolution, this was, of course, Napoleon. Protestations that the First Consul and Emperor was a "despot" or "tyrant" must be left aside; for, as Schmitt would say, Bonaparte was the commissar of the State: his role as decisive *leader, Führer, Emperor, dictator* was only a function of the republican spirit he served. A dictator is not a tyrant because in a dictatorial regime the State is still sovereign and the dictator serves the State (all the more since the State, too, is a reflection of the general will), whereas a tyrant serves only himself by defining his own law. Napoleon was ever subject to the will he served — the spirit of the French and the Revolution; and the fruit of this service was the unraveling of the *ancien régime* across Europe and the instituting of the civil code that bears his name.

---

[39] Blaufarb, 56.

[40] Carl Schmitt, *Dictatorship*, translated by Michael Hoelzl and Graham Ward (Maden, MA: Polity Press, 2014), 7.

Republicanism was inherited through Western traditions, handed down through the Greco-Roman spirit, and brought forth after long dormancy in the will of Napoleon — the man who mythologized himself as the modern Caesar: the man who would unite all of Europe. If along with it was dredged up the office of dictator, then this was as a necessary preservative appurtenance, just as it was during the Roman Republic. Thus it was that Napoleon rose to voice the will of the French and, if not for the limits of time and his corporeal shell,[41] the will of all Europeans; thus it is that all of Western civilization hence has felt his influence.

"I wanted to rule the world," Bonaparte laments in his captivity; and earlier in his career, he boldly states, "I must make all the peoples of Europe into a single people, and Paris, the capital of the world".[42] These are the ambitions of Napoleon, the world-spirit, the world-historical figure of Hegelianism. First, the Hegelian dialectic can be summed up thusly: the spirit (*Geist*) — i.e., the Idea — exercises self-conscious reason to achieve complete freedom through self-knowledge.[43] And for Hegel, "the abstract concept of the Idea of the will is in general *the free will which wills the free will*".[44] This is to say that the Idea is the manifestation and employment of the universal will, i.e., the objective will (of the State), which is the will of God. The Idea, then, is the will of God striving for complete freedom through self-knowledge. One of the principal means of the Idea to win such self-knowledge is through its manifestation in prevailing spirits (cultures) in their respective times. Further, within the prevailing cultures themselves, there will occasionally arise such a figure who, more than anyone else, embodies his time's prevailing spirit: he is the world-spirit of world-historical times.

Now, before advancing further, we must explain how it is that Napoleon stands as the link between Rousseau and Hegel. As was tried to make clear above, Rousseau concerned himself with the general will, roughly as an accretion of the general "sentiment" of many individual wills; that is, the general will, in and of itself, was

---

[41] Alas! — the *great will* made manifest on earth, too, is limited by corporeality. "If I had been my own grandson!" laments Napoleon at the end of his life. As quoted in Bertram, 34.
[42] David A. Bell, *Napoleon: a Concise Biography* (New York: Oxford University Press, 2015), 63, 70.
[43] Hegel, 60.
[44] Ibid., 57.

not conscious or rational. It is Hegel who picks up where Rousseau leaves off in this discussion by claiming full rationality for the general (universal) will. The body of this essay, in its arguments in favor of Napoleon's personification of the general will, has attempted to signal Hegel's "philosophy of right." In short, Napoleon stands as the link between the two philosophers *because* he is the incarnation of the general, or universal, will. In fact, Hegel argues that the Revolution itself happened because it was based on rational abstractions (*liberté, égalité, fraternité*) "divorced from the Idea"[45] — the Idea that had yet to manifest as the world-spirit.

The Idea brings order to the chaos because it must; it is only through the world-historical process that the Idea achieves the self-knowledge which brings ultimate freedom — of spirit and, to a lesser extent, self. The Idea ushers in this order by manifesting in the prevailing spirit of the time, which is to say, through the State: "Since the state is objective spirit, it is only through being a member of the state that the individual himself has objectivity, truth, and ethical life. *Union* as such is itself the true content and end, and the destiny of individuals is to lead a universal life..."[46] The world-spirit is the convergence of the Idea and the *union* of individuals: he is the authority that offers order to the hordes in exchange for their freedom, both individually and world-historically; he is the leader and Emperor; he is the embodiment of the *Führerprinzip*. Hegel further describes the State:

> The state consists in the march of God in the world, and its basis is the power of reason actualizing itself as will. In considering the Idea of the state, we must not have any particular states or particular institutions in mind; instead, we should consider the Idea, this actual God, in its own right. Any state, even if we pronounce it bad in the light of our own principles, and even if we discover this or that defect in it, invariably has the essential

---

[45] Ibid., 277.

[46] Ibid., 276. But what of subjectivity? Yes, Kierkegaard beautifully and nobly argued for the preeminence of the subjective, but we must remember that he would not exist if it were not for the non-subjective states preceding him, i.e., the family and State.

> moments of its existence within itself (provided it is one of the more advanced states of our time).[47]

Napoleon, from a Hegelian standpoint, was executing the will of God through the general (Rousseauian) will of his people. It bears noting that Bonaparte did not call himself "Emperor of France," but instead chose the official title "Emperor of the French"; he was not the owner of the French spirit, but was its trustee and executor: "the official act creating the empire stated ... that 'the government of the Republic is entrusted to an emperor.'"[48] In this way, the Emperor, while consciously executing the will of his people, unconsciously fulfilled the will of the universal spirit — the Idea — and prepared "its way toward the transition to its next and higher stage".[49]

One might suppose that this business about "embodying the will of God" and the *Führerprinzip* is appropriate for Napoleon and the French Revolution, but perhaps there is too much unsettling language and implication from Rousseau and Hegel regarding modern man and these so-called higher stages. Indeed, one would be correct — at least regarding the implication; for the later stages of the Enlightenment spawned their own reactions to the disorder (or communal disintegration) of which the Revolution itself was a microcosm. And out of the Revolution came the Hegelian world-spirit, the Idea made flesh, so as to further the course of cosmic self-enlightenment; later, out of the Enlightenment's *liberté, égalité, et fraternité* sprung the order-imposing ideologies of communism and fascism[50] — these, too, were Napoleonic attempts to enact the will of Western man. The prophet of these attempts was none other than Nietzsche,[51] for he foretold not only their coming, but also the

---

47 Ibid., 279.

48 Bell, 61.

49 Hegel, 373.

50 *Communism* and *fascism* here are meant generally to describe the alternatives which ultimately led to the great Western upheavals of the twentieth century. It is understood that *communism* and *fascism* are somewhat nebulous terms, and that what they describe are often very specific and variegated ideologies.

51 Nietzsche was not alone among Enlightenment (or "post-Enlightenment," or even pre-Enlightenment) thinkers in prophesying or speaking of cyclicality. Giambattista Vico (d. 1744) was the early Enlightenment's foremost prophet; and both Germanic and Hindu religions, among others,

coming of the modern world's future collapse. At the center of it all — the usurping of the *ancien régime*, the Revolution and its fulfillment, and the violent reactions to the "abstractions divorced from the Idea" — was the Corsican Napoleon, who certainly did "astonish Europe".

Napoleon and Nietzsche

"Is Nietzsche really a great thinker, or is he a would-be poet? Measured against Aristotle and Hegel, he is an impassioned dilettante, who as a 'physician of culture' wanted to work against his age in favor of a coming age, and finally came to the conviction that he held the future of Europe in his hands": thus spoke Karl Löwith.[52] Yet if we incessantly ask — as, indeed, so many have — if Nietzsche was a "great thinker" or "philosopher," does this not reveal his timeless truth? He "philosophized" *only* "with a hammer." That is, he was more interested in the *hammer* (i.e., the rough hue of reality, barren of abstraction), and yet we still hold him in high regard as a philosopher. His philosophy — or anti-philosophy — was his prophecy. He foresaw the power and glory of the will, and he saw it in contrast to the rationalistic abstractionism of the Enlightenment's *liberté, égalité, et fraternité.*

What was it that made Nietzsche's work so timeless? It was his valuation of that executive power of reason above all; this executive power is *will.* Will, for Nietzsche, transcends the supposed limits of corporeality and reason; will conquers all. Thus, we should abandon all rationalistic pretense if it impedes the will and reject all ideology or religiosity if it demands docility: all of it should be shattered to bits if it stands in the way of the will. Nietzsche's philosophy is primordial and seeks the roots of human endeavor; in this way, it is an anti-philosophy — for anything, especially (rationalistic) philosophy, that hinders the pure exercise of great will is death; Nietzsche's (anti-)philosophy was to wield the hammer, and this hammer is what cleared the way for the battle of wills in the

---

spoke of life's cyclicality. Nietzsche, however, suffices for the scope of this essay.

[52] Karl Löwith, *Nietzsche's Philosophy of the Eternal Recurrence of the Same*, translated by J. Harvey Lomax (Berkeley: University of California Press, 1997), 8.

twentieth century, the fallout from the so-called Age of Reason.[53] This is what makes the "would-be poet's" work timeless: he speaks to and for the transcendental will in all mankind; for it is will that binds the modern man of destiny to the willful man of antiquity or even prehistory. Will transcends, reason reduces (and *deduces* at that); and when the Age of Reason passes, it is will alone that shall remain: this, in short, is Nietzsche's creed *and* prophecy. For Nietzsche, the embodiment of this will — this utmost executor of logic and illogic, the convergence of rationality and irrationality — is Napoleon.

In Napoleon, Nietzsche saw the *will*, the *spirit*, the *Idea*, certainly, but he also saw a reinvigoration of the European peoples; this reinvigoration came through war, an unsettling of the soft complacence of reasoned living. Others in history have seen this, too, of course. Kant notes that

> War itself ... has something sublime about it, and gives nations that carry it on ... a stamp of mind only the more sublime the more numerous the dangers to which they are exposed, and which they are able to meet with fortitude. On the other hand, a prolonged peace favors the predominance of a mere commercial spirit, and with it a debasing self-interest, cowardice, and effeminacy, and tends to degrade the character of the nation.[54]

And Channing, admirer of even the rational "abstractions divorced from the Idea," whom we met above, has this to say:

> We are willing to grant that war, abhor it as we may, often develops and places in strong light, a force of intellect and purpose, which raises our conceptions of the human soul. There is perhaps no moment in life, in

---

[53] Interestingly, Vico argued (1725, *Scienza Nuova*) that there are three ages of man: the Age of Gods, the Age of Heroes, and, finally, the Age of Man (i.e., the Age of Reason). The irrational (the Age of Gods) makes possible the Age of Man, which stands as the culminating effort of any civilization (the culminating effort of a people's culture, however, is the Age of Heroes). When a people reaches its final age — the Age of Reason — its end is nigh, and the cycle will begin anew after cataclysmic death.

[54] Immanuel Kant, *The Critique of Judgment*, translated by James Creed Meredith (Oxford: Clarendon Press, 1911).

> which the mind is brought into such intense action, in which the will is so strenuous, and in which irrepressible excitement is so tempered with self-possession as in the hour of battle.[55]

Spengler, a kind of spiritual successor to Nietzsche, asserts:

> In war, life is elevated by death, often to that point of irresistible force whose mere existence guarantees victory, but in the economic life, hunger awakens the ugly, vulgar and wholly un-metaphysical sort of fearfulness for one's life under which the higher form-world of a Culture miserably collapses and the naked struggle for existence of the human beasts begins.[56]

We could continue to present such thoughts from persons across the ideological spectrum, but instead will end with, of course, Nietzsche. He speaks of "preparatory men" who "will *wage wars* for the sake of ideas and their consequences"; men who "will restore honor to courage above all," and who like to "*live dangerously*".[57] Such men will and must act as the bridge to something higher: the *Übermensch*. Napoleon was one such preparatory man.[58]

---

[55] Channing, 9.

[56] Oswald Spengler, *The Decline of the West* (New York: Vintage Books, 2006), 400.

[57] Nietzsche, *Joyful Science*, §283.

[58] "We owe it to Napoleon ... that several belligerent centuries will now follow on each other that have no equal in history, in short, that we have entered into the classical age of war, of both intellectual and traditional war on the largest scale (war of resources, of talents, of discipline).... For the national movement out of which this glorification of war is growing is only the aftershock against Napoleon and would not be present without [him].... Napoleon, who saw in modern ideas and particularly in civilization something like a personal enemy, and by this hostility proved himself to be one of the greatest among those who have continued the Renaissance: he brought an entire element of the essence of antiquity, perhaps the most decisive one, the element of granite, to the surface again." Nietzsche, *Die fröhliche Wissenschaft: "la gaya scienza"*. (Perhaps not coincidentally, both Vico and Nietzsche espoused a "new" kind of science — one not obsessive in its pursuit of pure reductionist rationalism, but one of equilibrium, one that recognizes the necessary balance of rational and irrational.) Nietzsche

Bonaparte, or rather just the idea of him, was enough to fortify Western peoples against the creeping and undermining threat of nihilism.[59] In short, this dreaded *nihilism*, for Nietzsche, was the devotion to "abstractions divorced from the Idea"[60] and their consequents. Napoleon, through his personification of the general or universal will (the rational and irrational), was able to "overcome the eighteenth century" — i.e., overcome the Enlightenment's dogmatic adherence to pure reason directed at an aggrandizement of the individual.[61] What *this* rationalism stood in obstacle to was the roots of mankind: the roots of man are the dominion of will, and to disconnect modern man from these roots through pure rationalism is, for Nietzsche, to disconnect man from what makes him fundamentally *human*: "Napoleon was an example of a 'return to nature,' as I understand it," the "would-be poet" states.[62] And this return to Nature is a reconvening with that pre-rationalistic state of man which, for Nietzsche, was noble and sustainable. The utopian march toward some kind of rationalistically perfect state of future progress is unsustainable — not just because man is subject to life's cyclicality (and in no small part because of the constant give-and-take among strong and weak wills), but also because the inherent reductionism in pure (*modern* or *scientific*) rationalism utterly rejects one half of man, thus transforming him from man to rational-biological machine.

Yes, reason has a role to play in this life; but it must always and ever be subordinate to its executor: the will of the great man — the man who embodies the spirit of his age in both rationality *and* its opposite, the man who prepares the way for the one who is to come, the *Übermensch*. For not only does this Nietzschean order of things grant men true freedom — in that they subject themselves to a *reasoned order based on authority* — but it also unchains them from "abstractions" (i.e., Liberalism, pure rationalism, symptoms *and* progenitors of the disease of nihilism). "Liberalism," for Nietzsche,

augured the future because he saw it in the past — but, more than this, also because he was attuned to the essence of humanity: the necessity of the rational and irrational. To reject one in favor of the other is to invite Apocalypse.

[59] Nietzsche, *The Will to Power*, translated by Anthony Ludovici, §27.

[60] Hegel, 277.

[61] Nietzsche, *The Will to Power*, §104.

[62] Nietzsche, *Twilight of the Idols*, §48.

was nothing more than "the *transformation of mankind into cattle*".[63] And in modernity "the values of decline and of *nihilism* are exercising the sovereign power under the cover of the holiest names"[64] — where actual gods of will are replaced with church popes preaching politics, teams of secular popes in lab coats infecting mass consciousness with their quantifiable calculations, and disconnected, jaded societies ever more distracting themselves with pharmaceuticals and mindless entertainment[65] — all in the name of progress toward the achievement of abstractions.

Napoleon, as an historical figure, represented for Nietzsche an absolute rejection of abstractions for abstractions' sake — i.e., a rejection of nihilism. The Corsican was a return to classical times, when man carved out his life with the glory and power his will demanded of him. Yet Napoleon, too, was a presaging; after all, he was just a *preparatory man*. Nietzsche saw in the Emperor an *immediate* rejection of the inevitable nihilism and alienation (from man's roots) that pure rationalism brings[66]; given *more* time, such rationalism would only be rejected and fought against even *more* fervently. Nietzsche knew his era was the calm before a storm — the tension built up against pure rationalism finally being released in two world wars; undoubtedly, because the rationalistic powers won those wars, he would say that contemporary times, too, are merely a calm before an ever-greater storm.

Christianity, which for Nietzsche was a natural ancestor of the liberal principles newly wrought by pure rationalism, is every bit as dangerous for the future of Western man as Liberalism; he predicts that "the time is coming when we shall have to pay for having been *Christians* for two thousand years: we are losing the *equilibrium*

---

[63] Ibid., §38.

[64] Nietzsche, *Antichrist*, §6.

[65] In all these ways, transcendence is sought through pure (*modern* or *scientific*) rationalism; this is to say that attempts are made to fabricate transcendence. This is the nihilistic falseness of modernity for Rousseau, Napoleon, Hegel, and Nietzsche particularly.

[66] In this way, Napoleon was the irrational (or pre-rational) antidote to the Revolution's rationalistic march toward Utopia; Utopia, because it rejects an entire half of man (the irrational), will always collapse into chaos, just as it did in the French Revolution. Napoleon was the *terrible* (in all its meanings) rebalancing of man in Nature; that is, he brought to the fore, once again, the irrational (or pre-rational) urge of man; hence, the disorder of Utopia was reversed.

which enables us to live".[67] We pay for this "sin" now in the ever more alienating nature of modern society, which some might consider some species of technocracy or plutocracy — others might simply call it *material-* or *scientific-rationalistic-theocracy* — that poses as liberal democracy upholding the Enlightenment's residual abstractions. And Nietzsche would further hold that this dogmatic adherence to such abstractions will only create the conditions for more preparatory men and, eventually, the final *Übermencsh* — the one who will discard all of the modern West's hitherto Liberalistic dogmatism in favor of his "new" order based on glory, power, and, above all, will — the will which reflects the spirit of an entire people and their determination to *thrive*, the will of a people who long for the truly reasoned freedom of subordination to the transcendent instead of the abstract "freedom" of "appetite alone".[68]

The twentieth century was merely a birth pang of the future — and it bore two world wars. Liberalism — the new religion of pure (*modern* or *scientific*) rationalism — is unequivocally unsustainable for Nietzsche because it separates man from what makes him whole, what makes him human; rationalism-at-all-costs rejects the spirit of man, the spirit of the Idea, whether that Idea be Hegelian or Nietzschean, for it rejects irrationalism. The backlash that will come from modernity's constant, dogmatic refusal to value the irrational side of man will be absolutely disastrous for Western man; if he does not take down the rest of the world with him, who knows how many or who will be left standing when the tension is finally resolved? This, ultimately, was the substance of Nietzsche's admiration of Napoleon: he was the first backlash against unbridled rationalism — that rationalism which, when "divorced from the Idea," produces the chaotic, insatiable dogmatism and disorder evidenced by the latter stages of the French Revolution proper. In the microcosm of Napoleon and the French Revolution, Nietzsche saw the whole future of Western man. Time will tell if the ultimate resolution of this future will be an *Übermensch*-like inheritor of the Napoleonic will, or will be a slip into final disintegration.

---

[67] Nietzsche, *The Will to Power*, §30, emphasis added; this *equilibrium* is none other than the balance of the rational and irrational which forms the essence of humanity.

[68] Rousseau, 65.

Conclusions

When Hermann Göring took the stand at Nuremberg, he was a man out of time. The ideology he represented was a reaction to the same rationalism that inspired *The Social Contract*, spurred the French Revolution, devolved into the Reign of Terror, and culminated in the reign of Napoleon. While Bonaparte concretized the *Führerprinzip* through action, it was first Hegel and later Nietzsche who gave it ideological flesh. The source of each's inspiration was the indomitable and primordial human will, and a harkening back to a time when all human endeavor was not aimed at rationally reducing all existence into its component parts — that is, to a time when "intellect was distinguished by rapidity of thought" and instinct, when "by a glance" and force of will, one could grasp what the purely rational "could learn only by study".[69] For where one can *divine*, there does one hate to *calculate*.[70] Göring's principal was his Führer, the sole manifestation of the *Führerprinzip*, the man whose will was the constitution.

Napoleon, too, was a man out of time — or perhaps a man *against* time. For he, too, was eventually deposed, defeated, and left behind by the supposed eternal march of rationalistic progress. He personified, if only for a moment, the spirit of an entire people, attempting, through his will and theirs, to bring them out of the chaos that embroiled them; he imposed his authority and offered them freedom through it — the freedom of any reasonable people making a self-conscious decision: a decision to willfully subordinate their individual desires for something more communal, more transcendent. When, after him, the increasingly rationalistic West built up enough existential tension — for what other kind of tension could it be? — to ignite two catastrophic ideological wars, Napoleon and his successors further proved to observers that they were men out of time. Theirs was a time before the Enlightenment, a time of Caesars, kings, conquerors, and warriors: theirs was a time of will. For Nietzsche, Bonaparte was "the ancient ideal itself" and

> appeared *bodily* and with unheard-of splendor before the eye and conscience of mankind, and once again, stronger, simpler and more penetrating than ever ... Like a last signpost to the *other* path, Napoleon appeared as a

---

[69] Channing, 32.

[70] Nietzsche, *Thus Spoke Zarathustra*, "The Vision and the Enigma."

> man more unique and late-born for his times than ever a man had been before, and in him, the problem of the *noble ideal itself* was made flesh — just think *what* a problem that is: Napoleon, this synthesis of *Unmensch* (brute) and *Übermensch* (overman)...[71]

This is to say that Napoleon, the man who first concretized the *Führerprinzip* for modernity and signaled its later incarnations, as a man in the past, is the signpost for the future. If such Napoleonic rationalism was yet usurped by the pure rationalism of the hordes, then perhaps this only indicates man's proclivity to value the easy pursuit of individual appetite over the hard subordination of his will to the authority of the general will. And this valuation, too, will have its reward; for this valuation, too, has its signposts. We bear witness to a new calm; what follows is history.

Neither the time nor progress before us is infinite. And, if Nietzsche is the prophet he *studied* himself to be, then the time before us will be rife with upheaval — an unimaginable releasing of existential tension, the culmination of the Enlightenment. Nietzsche certainly did *study* himself to be a prophet; for he was not predicting the future so much as he was describing the past. And Napoleon, the first modern manifestation of the *Führerprinzip*, the man who *was* the French Revolution, was his muse.

NIETZSCHE AND THE *FÜHRERPRINZIP*

An Opening Sketch

> *Concerning great things one should either be silent or one should speak loftily:—loftily—that is to say, cynically and innocently.*
>
> — FRIEDRICH NIETZSCHE, *THE WILL TO POWER*

---

[71] This *other* path is none other than the *valuation* of the irrational, the execution of reason through the authority of will for transcendent freedom; this is in contrast to the more noticed path (the *not-other*) of pure rationalism, the rejection of necessary irrationality. *On the Genealogy of Morals*, edited by Keith Ansell-Pearson, translated by Carol Diethe (Cambridge: Cambridge University Press, 2006), 33.

Speaking *cynically*: that is, speaking pragmatically, realistically — *life is struggle*; life is "nasty, brutish, and short" — left to its own devices, that is. Nietzsche explains how we might remain in the cynicism of life, *but yet overcome it*. That is, we should not be silent, we should become "lofty" — we should become great, become the *Übermensch*.

Speaking *innocently*: that is, keeping still pragmatic — understanding the *simplicity* of life's struggle: might is right and the stronger wins, no matter our pretensions to "higher ideals." This is ever the populist message: be strong and be fit — overcome *life's* opponents at any cost. People intuitively understand this, no matter their "reasoned" allegiance to abstractions. Speak to the essence of life — pragmatism, simplicity of struggle, the *inessentialness* of reason: this is the foundation of Nietzsche's religion.

Preface

Nietzsche's religion — *Germanicism*, a presaging of the MAN TO COME: *Übermenschlichkeit* — i.e., "Overmanity." Nietzsche himself never uses this word; but it is nonetheless present through much of his philosophy. On the surface, *Übermenschlichkeit* is an ideology of the strong (the better) over the weak (the lesser). Most of Nietzsche's students — be they professional students (i.e., "academics") or laymen — are content to stop here. It is convenient to stop with such superficiality, since such a surface reading makes it easy to denounce an "unfeeling" work and certainly does not force the student to examine his own self — i.e., examine his own *discipline*. Man, by nature, is content to be undisciplined; he is content with the painless path simply because it is easy; man is a beast, after all, and his baser instincts compel him — like a deer in the woods — to find the path of least resistance. Most men do not want to answer the questions: *Am I worthy? Am I fit? Am I strong?* The reason is simple: most men can only answer in the negative. Society proves this daily with its weak minorities playing victim and ignorant majorities content in their oblivion. Modern society is only content to answer such culturally relevant questions as, *Am I a good consumer? Am I a good producer? Am I being oppressed? Am I an oppressor? Am I tolerant and technologically astute?*

In any case, the deeper meaning of *Übermenschlichkeit* is its contextual origin: it is born of Nietzsche's "greatest weight" — i.e., the Eternal Return. "'This life as you live it now and before,'" Nietzsche's demon says in *Joyful Science*, "'you must once more live and innumerable times more....' If this thought possessed you, it would change or perhaps crush you. The question in all things, 'Do you desire this once more and innumerable times more?' would lie upon your actions as the greatest weight".[72] In order for man to be truly free, he must unburden himself of those moral fetters tethering him to a life of despair under the greatest weight: that is, he must, through a transvaluation of all values, become (a bridge to) the *Übermensch*. At the heart of Nietzsche's project — his religion, his *Übermenschlichkeit* — is principally a concern with freedom. Enabling the *Übermensch* is the only way to be truly rid of the greatest weight and instead see it as divine beckoning: "'You are a god and never have I heard anything more divine.'"[73]

The *Führerprinzip*

The *Übermensch* concept hints at another conceptual peculiarity: the *Führerprinzip*. For the *Übermensch* is ultimately an umbrella concept: men are naught but mere "bridges" to something superior. The *Übermensch* is not a crude, future being bent on enslaving the masses; no, the *Übermensch* is each and every man dedicated to a transcendent will — i.e., the collective *will-to-power*. Perhaps the most striking example of a society beholden to a transcendent will was in National Socialist Germany. This transcendent will found its focus in Adolf Hitler and was ultimately defined as the *Führerprinzip*.

During the show-trial at Nuremberg, Hermann Göring described the *Führerprinzip* thusly: "authority existed at the top and passed downwards, while the responsibility began at the bottom and passed upwards".[74] This is to say that the authority of the Führer — the leader — was predicated on "the responsibility" — i.e., the will — of the people. The people choose their ultimate authority through their collective will and entrust their will to be executed through the decisive will of the sole leader: this is the *Führerprinzip*. Hitler himself had this to say about the principle:

> My Movement, as an expression of will and yearning, encompasses every aspect of the entire folk. It conceives of Germany ... as a single organism.... Leadership is

[72] *Joyful Science*, §341.

[73] Ibid., §341.

[74] Hermann Göring, Proceedings from 18 March 1946: The Nuremberg Tribunal, Nuremberg, Germany.

> always based upon the free will and good intentions of those being led. My doctrine of the *Führerprinzip* is ... [not] the doctrine of a brutal dictator who triumphs over the destruction of the values of private life ... [but the doctrine of public discourse.] I am using every means provided by the State and its power to publish and make known my every word and deed with the goal of winning the public with this openness for every single decision of my national will by proof and conviction. And I am doing this because I believe in the creative power and the creative contribution of the folk.[75]

And further:

> As Führer, I cannot conceive of any task on this earth more marvelous and glorious than to serve this folk.... My will — and this must be the vow of each and every one of us — is your faith! To me — as to you — my faith is everything I have in this world! But the greatest thing God has given me in this world is my folk! In it rests my faith. It I serve with my will, and to it I give my life![76]

Still further: "there can be no distinction between [the Führer and the folk]".[77] Also: "My actions are those the entire folk wants! Not *one person* is standing up in Germany; a folk is rising! I am not the Führer of the German folk in order to make gestures. I have been appointed by the German folk to simply represent its interests. That is my intention".[78] And finally: "The world may no longer have any doubts: it is not one Führer or one man who speaks at this point, rather it is the German folk that speaks! As I now speak for this German folk, I know that this folk of millions joins in the chorus of my words, reaffirms them, and makes them a holy oath in its own right".[79] Clearly, the *Führerprinzip* is meant to be understood as a fusing of the people's will with that of the executive power. Additionally, this

---

[75] Adolf Hitler, Interviewed by Hanns Johst for the *Frankfurter Volksblatt*, 27 January 1934.
[76] Hitler, Speech at *Tempelhofer Feld*, 01 May 1935.
[77] Hitler, Speech at Nuremberg, 13 September 1935.
[78] Hitler, Speech in Berlin, 24 March 1936.
[79] Hitler, Speech in *Sportpalast*, Berlin, 26 September 1938.

fusing can be seen in a religious light; it is certainly painted with such language throughout Hitler's public life: "holy," "divine," "sacred" — these are a few of the words assigned to the National Socialist task, of which Hitler was the driving force.

The formal introduction of the *Führerprinzip* into Germany's public and political spheres came in Hitler's March 1933 speech to the Reichstag regarding the new Enabling Act:

> The Government of the National Revolution basically regards it as its duty, *in accordance with the spirit of the folk's vote of confidence*, to prevent the elements which consciously and intentionally negate the life of the nation from exercising influence on its formation. The theoretical concept of equality before the law shall not be used, under the guise of equality, to tolerate those who despise the laws as a matter of principle or, moreover, to surrender the freedom of the nation to them on the basis of democratic doctrines. *The Government will, however, grant equality before the law to all those who, in forming the front of our folk against this danger, support national interests and do not deny the Government their assistance.*[80]

The purpose of this Enabling Act was to consolidate control of the general will into the person of Hitler. Nothing must interfere with the enaction of the general will, to include the "democratic doctrines" regarded as "dangerous" inhibitors to the will. Nothing must counter the Führer, since to do so is to counter the State and its citizenry. To this end, the *Führerprinzip* was officially born. The principle endured as long as Hitler lived and accounted for all of Germany's perceived gains and losses over its 12-year duration.

The *Führerprinzip* and Hegel

The *Führerprinzip* was ideologically born in Hegel's philosophy. "There is a divine will, and all we are is its instruments," Hitler notes; what he means, of course, is that the body politic and its executive authority are fused inextricably together for a transcendent purpose. This purpose, for Hegel, was complete (divine) knowledge: the spirit (Idea) exercising self-conscious reason to achieve complete freedom

[80] Emphasis added.

through self-knowledge.[81] "This development of the Idea as the activity of its own rationality"[82] is most sublimely realized in "the subsumption of *particular* spheres and individual cases under the universal — the *executive* power" and "*the power of the sovereign*, in which the different powers are united in an individual unity which is thus the apex and beginning of the whole".[83] And, it is not that "particular interests [are] set aside, let alone suppressed; on the contrary, they should be harmonized with the universal, so that both they themselves and the universal are preserved".[84] This, of course, is precisely what Hitler is engaging when he says his "doctrine of the *Führerprinzip* is ... [not] the doctrine of a brutal dictator who triumphs over the destruction of the values of private life ... [but the doctrine of public discourse.]" Moreover, Hegel speaks of the "mistake of overlooking the inner organism of the state in favor of individual aspects"[85] — an idea that presages Hitler's conception of Germany as "a single organism."

"There must always be an individual at [the state's] head," Hegel posits,

> this individual is either already present as such, as in monarchies of the type in question, or, as in aristocracies and more particularly in democracies, he may rise up from among the statesmen or generals in a contingent manner and as *particular circumstances* require; for all actions and all actuality are initiated and implemented by a leader as the decisive unit.[86]

Compare this with Hitler's 1935 Nuremberg address to his subordinates: "[there are] those who are so incapable of understanding that there can be no distinction between [Führer and folk].... A commander without officers and soldiers — there are those who would gladly welcome that! I will not be the commander

[81] Georg Wilhelm Friedrich Hegel, *Elements of the Philosophy of Right*, 19th ed. edited by Allen W. Wood, translated by Hugh B. Nisbet (Cambridge: Cambridge University Press, 2014), 60.
[82] Ibid., 60.
[83] Ibid., 308.
[84] Ibid., 285.
[85] Ibid., 279.
[86] Ibid., 320.

without soldiers; I will remain your Führer".[87] The necessity of having "an individual at [the state's] head," for Hegel, is philosophical: particularity must be "brought back to universality," and it is the sovereign who embodies and focuses each in his being.[88] For Hitler, the necessity was more pragmatic: his position was developed through his life experience — as a youth in Austria, a soldier in the trenches, a public speaker and organizer in Bavaria, and as the first Führer of the NSDAP. It should be said, also, that it is surely possible to arrive at such a position through careful study of human nature; common sense dictates that if there are too many leaders and not enough followers, a task will be endless or arduous; likewise, if there are too many leaderless followers, a task's endurance will match the followers' inability to tackle it.

The followers who place themselves in communion with the sovereign — or in Germany's case, the Führer — are not "ruled in defiance of their own interests, ends, and intentions, for they are not as stupid as that; it is their need, the inner power of the Idea, which compels them to accept such rule and keeps them in this situation, even if they appear to be consciously opposed to it".[89] That is, the overarching spirit (Idea) is guiding the arc of world history so as to self-actualize: "It is through this dialectic that the *universal* spirit, the *spirit of the world*, produces itself in its freedom from all limits, and it is this spirit which exercises its right — which is the highest right of all — over finite spirits in *world history* as the *world's court of judgment*".[90] In their capacity as "world spirits," such historical Führer (plural) live out the required drama to facilitate the actualization of the Idea: "They receive no *honor* or thanks on its account, either from their contemporaries or from the public opinion of subsequent generations; all that they are accorded by this opinion is *undying fame* [in their role] as formal subjectivities".[91]

This, however, is where the Hegelian influence on the *Führerprinzip* ends and the Nietzschean impact begins. For, inasmuch as the Führer concept accepts the role of destiny in its

---

[87] Hitler, Speech at Nuremberg, 13 September 1935.
[88] Hegel, 283.
[89] Ibid., 325.
[90] Ibid., 371.
[91] Ibid., 375.

unfolding,[92] it rejects the notion that the transcendent will is subordinate to it; that is, intrinsic to the *Führerprinzip* is the notion that the will — the will-to-power — can overcome even the greatest hardships; in short, the will is everything and forces even the hand of destiny. This is the Nietzschean influence manifesting.

The *Führerprinzip*, the Third Reich, and Nietzsche

To understand the *Führerprinzip* in Nietzsche's work, we must first understand the *Übermensch*. "The *Übermensch* is the meaning of the earth," Nietzsche says through Zarathustra. What is the meaning of the earth? *The meaning of the earth is nothing except struggle*: "To you I do not recommend work but struggle. To you I do not recommend peace but victory. Let your work be a struggle. Let your peace be a victory [in struggle]!"[93] Nietzsche's work is rife with *struggle* — it is defined by it; it is struggle, for him, that creates the conditions for greatness, and it is through greatness that culture is advanced and life is made livable.

Karl Löwith describes Nietzsche's "meaning of the earth" as similar to Schelling's: it is "the terrible: a blind power and force, a barbaric principle that can be overcome but can never be eliminated, and that is 'the foundation of all greatness and beauty.'"[94] Nietzsche says in *Twilight of the Idols*, for instance, that every "new creation ... — the new *Reich*, for example — needs enemies more than friends: in opposition alone does it *feel* itself necessary, in opposition alone does it *become* necessary".[95] Nietzsche places a premium on this

---

[92] There are far too many mentions of "destiny" in Hitler's speeches to account for here. Some examples: "our folk [will] become conscious of a higher destiny" (1935); "the German folk finally comprehends its own destiny and finds its own leadership" ('35); "[the German folk] have placed their trust, their personal destinies, and hence the destiny of the Reich in my hands" ('39); "only he who struggles with destiny can have a kind Providence" ('39); "whatever life or destiny might deal to the individual among us, the existence and future of the community takes precedence over it" ('40), and so on.

[93] *Thus Spoke Zarathustra*, "War and Warriors."

[94] Karl Löwith, *Nietzsche's Philosophy of the Eternal Recurrence of the Same*, translated by J. Harvey Lomax (Berkeley: University of California Press, 1997), 149.

[95] *Twilight of the Idols*, "Morality as Anti-Nature," §3.

feeling and opposes it with reason, or rationalism[96] (e.g., "where you can *guess*, you hate to *deduce*"[97]). *Feeling* releases the *spirit* of life, while reasoning simply *levels off* life and dampens its charge through theory (e.g., all men are equal — *on paper*); becoming *necessary* means actualizing greatness through struggle — "what does not kill us makes us *stronger*".[98] This stands in contrast to Hegel's more passive take on the self-actualization of the Idea; here, instead, man accounts for *his own* destiny through the struggle, and it is with the struggle that we edge ever higher.

> "Why so hard?" the kitchen coal once said to the diamond. "After all, are we not close kin?" Why so soft? O my brothers, thus I ask you: are you not after all my brothers? Why so soft, so pliant and yielding? Why is there so much denial, self-denial, in your hearts? *So little destiny in your eyes? And if you do not want to be destinies and inexorable ones, how can you triumph with me?* And if your hardness does not wish to flash and cut and cut through, *how can you one day create with me?* For creators are hard. And it must seem blessedness to you to impress your hand on millennia as on wax, blessedness to write on the will of millennia as on bronze — harder than bronze, nobler than bronze. Only the noblest is altogether hard. This new tablet, O my brothers, I place over you: *become hard!*[99]

This passage is quoted at length because it encapsulates so many parallels between Nietzsche's and the National Socialist position. The reader confronts immediately in each the relationship and the disparity between the coal and the diamond; and in their difference lies the struggle: one is soft, the other hard. Hardness in one's being, for Nietzsche, creates the conditions for carving out one's destiny, which is a frequent Hitlerian refrain. *Destiny*, of course, does not

---

[96] This *rationalism* is meant in the modern practical-ideological sense: *modern* rationalism, or *scientific* rationalism, as defined by the centralizing of the individual over and above the traditional cultural drivers of blood, creed, kind, etc.

[97] *Thus Spoke Zarathustra*, "The Vision and the Enigma."

[98] *The Will to Power*, §934.

[99] *Thus Spoke Zarathustra*, "Old and New Tables." Emphasis added.

simply encompass struggle (*Kampf*[100]), but also triumph (*Triumph des Willens*[101]).[102] When one is hard and ever engages in the struggle against those opposing, "softer" forces, then one might leave one's triumphant mark on the millennia — or the Reich that should last millennia.[103] Finally, Nietzsche speaks here of "nobility"; he was adamant that a new aristocracy should come to power[104]; the aristocracy envisioned by Hitler and National Socialism to lead Germany and Europe into the new millennium initially manifested in the *Schutzstaffel*,[105] the Aryan representatives from countries across Europe, the Baltics, and even the steppes of Asia.[106]

---

[100] We remember, of course, Hitler's *Mein Kampf*.

[101] Title of Leni Riefenstahl's hallmark film — *Triumph of the Will*.

[102] "My philosophy reveals the triumphant thought through which all other systems of thought must ultimately perish. It is the great disciplinary thought: those races that cannot bear it are doomed; those which regard it as the greatest blessing are destined to rule." (Nietzsche, *The Will to Power*, §1053)

[103] Peppered throughout Hitler's speeches is the linkage between the Third Reich and its millennium-long future. From a September 1938 speech: "A new movement had to come along, a movement that would educate and, therefore, prepare our folk. And even if [Austria's annexation] were all that National Socialism had achieved in its historical existence, that alone would suffice to justify its existence for the millennium!"

[104] Here is one of many passages on Nietzsche's foreshadowing notion of aristocracy: "The establishment has been made possible of international race unions which will set themselves the task of rearing a ruling race, the future 'lords of the earth'—a new, vast aristocracy based upon the most severe self-discipline, in which the will of philosophical men of power and artist-tyrants will be stamped upon thousands of years: a higher species of men which, thanks to their preponderance of will, knowledge, riches, and influence, will avail themselves of democratic Europe..." (Nietzsche, *The Will to Power*, §960)

[105] A Nietzschean call for the *Schutzstaffel*: "The foundation of an oligarchy *above* peoples and their interests: education directed at establishing a political policy for humanity in general" (Nietzsche, *The Will to Power*, §1057). The National Socialist intent, of course, is that the *exceptional* SS families would ultimately become the *rule*.

[106] Contrary to popular understanding, being "Aryan," while racial in essence, was not relegated to being "German." Being "Aryan" meant being non-Semitic and non-Slavic, which, racially, transcends borders: "According to the Nazi racial doctrine, an Italian, a Syrian, or an Iranian of Nordic race is superior to a German or a Swede of Alpine, Slavonic race. Indeed, the racist considers that race is above culture, for superiority is related to genes and

The SS, however, did not represent something that might *usurp* the *Führerprinzip* as a clan of individual *Übermenschen*, but something meant to *safeguard* it: after all, they were the *Schutzstaffel*, the "protection echelon" (or "security squadron"). They were meant to be the torchbearers and protectors of the traditionalism National Socialism represented — a traditionalism ultimately defined by Nietzsche through the lens of his *Übermenschlichkeit*, which is to say, his *Führerprinzip*. For Nietzsche, the *Übermensch* is a people bound together by a transcendent will-to-power — i.e., the *Übermensch* is the *Führerprinzip*. The "noblest" State is the Hegelian one determined to impress its own *collective* stamp on millennia through its hardened will — that is to say, the truly "aristocratic" State is Nietzschean, it is Hitlerian. This is essential.

"One thing, and one only, can save us," hopes the author of *Das Dritte Reich*, "a human, spiritual renewal: the evolution of a new race of Germans who shall make good all that we have wrecked".[107] What is implied here is a reclamation and conservation of what was once experienced; Moeller van den Bruck longed for the empires of old — those that existed before, in his estimation, succumbed to the ruining appearance of widespread Liberalism (i.e., the materialistic *Weltanschauung* manifest in the Marxist and capitalist social orders): "The course of history is not determined by material forces, but imponderabilia".[108] Conservatism, for Moeller van den Bruck, was to abide by "laws which have again and again proved their validity ... while to abandon oneself to expectations which are never fulfilled is to be reputed 'progressive.'"[109]

What has "proved" its worth from time immemorial is the enlivening spirit of human nature, to which hardening struggle is inherent. Moeller van den Bruck's treatise circulated the illiberal circles in Weimarian Germany and made, undeniably, an ideological

---

Geist, which are innate, and not to language, culture and nationality, which are acquired." Abir Taha, *Nietzsche, Prophet of Nazism: the Cult of the Superman: Unveiling the Nazi Secret Doctrine* (Bloomington, Ind.: AuthorHouse, 2005), 109.

[107] Arthur Moeller van den Bruck, *Germany's Third Empire*, 3rd ed. (London: Arktos Media Ltd, 2012), 28.

[108] Ibid., 54.

[109] Nietzsche on *progress*, from *Antichrist*, §4: "'Progress' is merely a modern idea, that is, a false idea."

impact on the nascent NSDAP; it was published, after all, in 1923 — the same year Hitler made his first attempt to seize power from the "November Revolutionaries" in his daring putsch. Essential to Moeller van den Bruck's argument — just as it is essential to Nietzsche's and Hitler's — is this notion of "imponderabilia." Certainly, it is not the external that can be immediately faulted in the Liberalistic social orders, but the internal: "[The] outward success [of Liberalistic societies] is so brilliant that it tends to mask their moral failure".[110] It is this internal *imponderabilia* that demarcates between what is seen as conservative and progressive from, in this case, the German perspective. This perspective was, according to Mosse, represented in the *völkisch* movement(s) in Germany from the nineteenth century onwards; "the aim [of these movements] was to rejuvenate the spiritual orientation of Germans along the lines of Nature, the German heritage, and the folk. Or, as such [movements] asserted, the order of creation demanded 'first a new human being and then a new state,' first the spiritual transformation and then its material implementation".[111] This spiritual way, or internal focus, represented a "third way" between progressive Marxism in the East and the liberal-democracies in the West. Lack of any substantive internal life was tantamount to "moral failure."

What, then, is this internal life? It can only be described as the *collective*, transcendent will that values the collectively forged *destiny* above all; that is to say, it is the life that values *spirit* over materialistic-rationalistic (Liberalistic) *theory*. Since materialistic societies tend to be individualistic to a fault (democracies, where the individual is prized and the collective more or less ignored) or collectivistic to a fault (Marxist experiments, where the individual is bludgeoned into nothingness), their moral failing rests in not *conserving traditions* and *natural law* (the law of struggle) where the best individuals are permitted to rise to the top of society and execute the collective will.

There is some tenuous — or perhaps even muddled — footing in this balance of the individual versus the collective and what, to this end, constitutes *morality*. But perhaps the idea is, for instance from Moeller van den Bruck's view (who only wanted to echo Nietzsche's view), that *morality* is dictated by not only what furthers

---

[110] Moeller van den Bruck, 97.

[111] George Mosse, *The Crisis of German Ideology: Intellectual Origins of the Third Reich* (New York: Howard Fertig, 1998), 285.

the group over the self, but what permits the self to yet have a voice — a voice in concert with the other individuals in the group. This, of course, hearkens back to Hegel, when what seems to be described is something like a hive-mind: "what the state requires as a duty should also in an immediate sense be the right of individuals, for it is nothing more than the organization of the concept of freedom" and "particular interests ... should be harmonized with the universal, so that both they themselves and the universal are preserved".[112] Anything less than the hive-mind can only be seen as immoral; Hitler certainly based community morality on establishing and enhancing the collective mind, from his *Hitlerjugend*, to various other National Socialist civic organizations, to the resurgence of the Germanic *Thing* (or *Thingstätte*), where the community would self-govern as equals within the struggle.

Finally, for Moeller van den Bruck, it might be that the most damning aspect of Liberalism is that it "seeks to enjoy the fruits garnered by an earlier conservatism".[113] The good that the "progressive" present enjoys is only made possible by the preceding conservative era; the Liberalist seeks to shrug off such foundational traditions in favor of self-stylized "progress," which is essentially erasing the culture that made it possible; then add to this the potential for the "progressive" society to take credit for those inherited "fruits." Nothing could be more disruptive or immoral for a society, according to the *Das Dritte Reich* author and, in fact, such sentiment echoes Hegel, who views Liberalism as "potentially destructive of the very values it most wants to promote" because of such "immorality".[114] Instead of such immorality, we are offered conservatism, which "seeks to preserve a nation's values, both by conserving traditional values, as far as these still possess the power of growth, and by assimilating all new values which increase a nation's vitality".[115]

Because of Nietzsche's "transvaluation" of modern values, he chose to see his own position as "immoral" or "evil" — not, of course, from his perspective, but only in the light of modern sensibilities. This is also not to say that he saw his position as "good" — it simply *was*, just as Nature *was* and *is*. Frequent Nietzsche translator

---

[112] Hegel, 284.
[113] Moeller van den Bruck, 172.
[114] Hegel, xi.
[115] Moeller van den Bruck, 206.

Anthony Ludovici puts it thusly: "good and evil are but mere means, adopted by all in order to acquire power. Power for what? Power to universalize their kind or make it paramount: power to enable their species, and their species alone, to preponderate or be supreme on earth".[116]

Thus, in his transvaluation, Nietzsche seeks to transcend morality to a point of supreme, conservative pragmatism[117]: years after the German spoke, William James astutely noted that truth is simply *what works*; well, for Nietzsche, *truth* is what Nature demands: the struggle for supremacy and the (will) power to overcome. In a letter to his sister — who is often inexplicably ignored or discarded as an "illegitimate" source[118] — Nietzsche states that "the overcoming of morality through truthfulness, the overcoming of the moralist by his opposite — by me — that is what the name Zarathustra means 'in my mouth.'" Nietzsche's truth is "the meaning of the earth" — the triumph of the will by any means necessary against the opposition. Later in his commentary on Nietzsche, Ludovici presages Moeller van den Bruck in his conservative-aristocratic orientation:

> We are all travelling blindly toward a point which we do not know. The colors we fly, the standards of morality

---

[116] Anthony Ludovici, *Who is to be Master of the World? An Introduction to the Philosophy of Friedrich Nietzsche* (Edinburgh: T. N. Foulis, 1909), 12.
[117] Nietzsche's pragmatism, from *The Will to Power*, §455: "truth was *not* based upon motives of truthfulness, but upon *motives of power, upon the desire to be superior. How is* truth *proved*? By means of the feeling of increased power,—by means of utility,—by means of indispensability,—*in short, by means of its advantages...*"
See also *The Will to Power*, §552: "'truth' is not something which is present and which has to be found and discovered; it is something *which has to be created* and which *gives* its name *to a process*, or, better still, to the Will to overpower, which in itself has no purpose: to introduce truth is a *processus in infinitum*, an *active determining*—it is not a process of becoming conscious of something, which in itself is fixed and determined. It is merely a word for 'The Will to Power.'"
[118] As if such family members are not intellectual intimates! — we are left to suppose she is ignored and discarded because her truth does not mesh well with her detractors' truth — the will-to-power in print! Nietzsche remained, however, quite fond of his sister to the very end of his acuity and maintained correspondence with her.

> we sail under, were followed by a people who wished to attain to power. But these standards mean nothing to us now. We are so used to them, and their colors have got so blurred through wear and tear, that we do not even know out of which port we originally sailed.[119]

This is only to say that the Liberalistic present has lost its traditional bearing: we know not why we are here, yet we seek to write a future with no backstory — the essence of "progressivism."

The modern man, then, is presented with two potential situations: either (1) he cuts anchor from the past (stops conserving cultural traditions in order to properly progress into the future), which leads to cultural nihilism and eventual disintegration, or (2) he reverts to the cultural values that created the conditions for his present self, which paradoxically leads to a nihilism that seeks its own cultural death (through un-traditional progress). "Nietzsche," Ludovici rightfully notes, "therefore inquires whether it is sufficiently recognized that concepts of good and evil are originally only a means to an end, that they are only the expedient of a species to acquire power — power to become paramount?"[120] That is, are the modern West's current values a foreign imposition, a means for the "weaker" culture to supplant the "stronger" through cunning? And if the West's values were based in Judeo-Christianity, would not the imposing culture thusly be Semitic?

The possibility of this question arising in Nietzsche's work is sufficient to again see an ideological parallel with National Socialism. Further, given the modern state of Western affairs, it seems quite clear that, according to the natural law espoused by Nietzsche, the stronger culture has won and the weaker culture was decimated through so many fire bombings[121] on its citizenry and "de-Nazifying"

---

[119] Ludovici, 18.

[120] Ibid., 34.

[121] Frederick Lindemann, a Jew, was a close friend and advisor to Churchill. He developed a robust aerial strategic bombing plan to be enacted during World War II (called "dehousing"), wherein firestorms would be created to annihilate masses of German civilians and infrastructure. Lindemann believed a group of intelligent elites should rule the world (the "Chosen People" — i.e., the Jews). He believed materialistic science could create societies of humans "with the mental make-up of the worker bee" who were driven by the "fetish of equality." Lindemann devoted tremendous effort to

measures after World War II. At least, so it seems for the present time. Ludovici, however, in highlighting Nietzsche's concern about the origins of modern Western morality, emphasizes not so much Gentile-Semitic relations, but the significance of Nietzsche's transvaluation project. This significance rests in the *Übermensch*.

Übermensch as the Collective; The Collective as the *Führerprinzip*

It is one thing to claim Nietzsche's influence, or to even be unconsciously "influenced" by him, but it is quite another for the German to have actually said the things that led to so-called derivative entities.

Certainly, there have been varied interpreters of Nietzsche's work — from Marxists to fascists, from capitalists to socialists, from Semite-philes to anti-Semites, from collectivists to individualists. The politically minded modern student might err on the side of caution and say that Nietzsche's work satisfied all conditions for the above interpretations to obtain, but this seems disingenuous; for while there is some ideological overlap between, say, Marxism and fascism (both Mussolini and Hitler had an early interest in Marxism), the two mature ideologies could not be more distinct. Thus, to simply say that Nietzsche "godfathered" them all comes off as intellectual cowardice or laziness. To be sure, Nietzsche himself claimed to have run the gamut of European ideology — from hedonism to nihilism to spirituality (i.e., *his* spirituality) — in his intellectual journey, but this hardly means his mature (from roughly 1880 onwards) writings reflected such eclecticism. Rather, Nietzsche settled on a position in his mature works and sought to make it known for the sake of European culture's salvation.[122]

Nietzsche's epiphanic moment came in the depths of his own nihilism, which he claimed to have experienced for the sake of all Europeans, on convalescence in Surlej (if not before) — at the rock said to have inspired *Thus Spoke Zarathustra*: he saw through the

---

the destruction of Hitler's Germany because he hated both Hitler and Germans. What he most hated about Hitler's project was its attempt to empower the German people and eliminate class mentality — precisely the opposite of Lindemann's "worker bee" worldview. Although Britain had been "strategically bombing" German civilian targets since 1940, Lindemann's plan detailed the effort to a *science* — one meant to produce maximum carnage.

[122] *The Will to Power*, Preface, §3.

nihilism that had overtaken Western man since the "slave" revolts of antiquity: what was needed was both new and old — what was necessary was the *Übermensch*. The "old" of his idea was a reclamation and conservation of that will-to-power that not only governs all life, but also dominated the Western landscape in both the Hellenic and pre-Christian Roman ages: the will-to-power of a Caesar or Scipio Africanus, for instance; a will-to-power, too, for Nietzsche, most recently represented in the godlike Caesarism of Napoleon. The "new" of his idea was the "revaluation of all values" — the overturning of the "slave-morality" that had infected Western culture since the introduction of Christianity into the decaying Roman Empire; it was not so much that the idea was entirely new, but simply new to the modern age; for not since Napoleon — that comet of will who stormed across the Western sky for such a brief moment, that would-be Caesar — did modernity taste such a disruptive ideology.

Since that time when Judeo-Christianity came to dominate the Western mind, it, too, had given way to its offspring: Liberalism. No longer were Western men aspiring to rise to the heights of gods, as Nietzsche conceived them doing in antiquity; now the Western man desired nothing more than to bring the least of his kind — the dregs of society — to the heights of the best. The introduction of Judeo-Christianity into European culture was the first "revaluation of all values" experienced in the West; this is what led to the degeneration of the Roman world and the advent of the modern one — i.e., the advent of the Liberalistic mind, the byproduct of the Enlightenment. It was this liberal (whether manifested in Judeo-Christianity or Liberalism proper) attitude toward man that led to the overturning of the old values of antiquity; the "dignity of man," as beings in the image of God, usurped the *ancien régime*.[123] Nietzsche set out to issue

[123] Nietzsche on the Judeo-Christian "human dignity" that gave rise to Liberalism, from *Antichrist*, §43: "That everyone as an 'immortal soul' has equal rank with everyone else, that in the totality of living beings the 'salvation' of *every* single individual may claim eternal significance, that little prigs and three-quarter-madmen may have the conceit that the laws of nature are constantly broken for their sake — such an intensification of every kind of selfishness into the infinite, into the *impertinent*, cannot be branded with too much contempt. And yet Christianity owes its triumph to this miserable flattery of personal vanity: it was precisely all the failures, all the rebellious-minded, all the less favored, the whole scum and refuse of

the ultimate counterpoint to the Enlightenment; the "profundity" of the Enlightenment rested in the realization that we no longer held God in regard, but man; we no longer aspired to achieve the height of the divine, but only aspired to bring the least of us upward. The initial "revaluation" that led to such existential emptiness had to be overturned, to be *overcome*. The way to do this was the introduction of something so alien to Judeo-Christian sensibilities that it could only be described as "evil": it was the philosophy of the *Übermensch*.

Soon after — if not simultaneously[124] — Nietzsche determined the conditions that demanded the *Übermensch*: the Eternal Return. The "doctrine of will to power [the *Übermensch*] springs from nowhere else than eternal return, carrying the mark of its origin always with it, as the stream its source," notes Heidegger.[125] This is so because, whether or not such a concept represents a cosmological or psychological belief, it is necessary as the only real possibility Western man has at overcoming his now self-wrought nihilism. Western man's nihilism is a result of God — the God he ultimately "killed" by empowering man through reason; in this way, (atheistic) nihilism itself is nothing more than an ironic consequence of Judeo-Christianity:

> We moderns ... suffer from the "witty mendacity" that ancient Christianity brought upon man when it produced a denatured man in its battle against the ancient, natural man. *Our* alleged culture has no permanence, because it is erected on "untenable conditions and opinions that have already almost disappeared" ... "God is dead — now we will that the superman live." That is to say: *the death of God demands from the self-willing man an overcoming of man along with getting rid of God*: the "superman".[126]

---

humanity who thus won over to it. The 'salvation of the soul' — in plain language: 'the world revolves around me.'"

[124] Nietzsche discusses the Eternal Return in *Thus Spoke Zarathustra*: its most memorable occurrence coming in "The Vision and the Enigma." Yet he also mentions it quite explicitly in his later *Joyful Science* in §341.

[125] Martin Heidegger, *Nietzsche: Vol. 2: The Eternal Recurrence of the Same* (New York: Harper & Row, 1984), 81.

[126] Löwith, 38.

It was Hegel who first tried to halt the death of God in the Western mind: "Hegel in particular was its delayer par excellence, with his grandiose attempt to persuade us of the divinity of existence, appealing as a last resort to our sixth sense, 'the historical sense.'"[127] The death of God is the death of antiquity: the death of Western culture — the Greek city (Hellenism) and Romanism (civilization). With this death, that Hegel tried to prevent with his "unifying philosophy of history," comes the death of culture, or the foundations upon which Western culture is based. Nietzsche, then, proposes the *Übermensch* as the only means of salvaging European culture. We must recognize the death of God so that we might yet live. "Nietzsche characterizes his teaching," writes Löwith, "as the 'most extreme form of nihilism' and at the same time as the 'self-overcoming' of nihilism, because his teaching is intended to recognize precisely the meaninglessness of an existence that recurs without any goal".[128] At the same time, however, Nietzsche posits the only goal worth attaining: *triumph through struggle* and a reemergence of the "natural man."

When Zarathustra tells us that "man is something that shall be overcome" with the *Übermensch*, what is he implying about the nature of man? Quite simply, he tells us that man is weak and unable to reach the heights of antiquity — that remote history that birthed Western culture — of his own accord. Man must be overcome because if he is not, European culture *will end.* If European culture has morphed into a mass of loosely connected parliamentarian associations of individuals, then, clearly, this is what is to be overcome. Indeed, as early as the 1860s, Otto von Bismarck was already warming up to the idea of inciting nationalism for the benefit of Greater Germany through the nascent notion of popularly elected parliaments[129]; this was the "public" or "democratic" nationalism that so disgusted Nietzsche.[130] And even though Bismarck manipulated

---

[127] Nietzsche, *Joyful Science*, §357.

[128] Löwith, 56.

[129] Edgar Feuchtwanger, *Imperial Germany, 1850-1918* (New York: Routledge, 2001), 29 and 44-45.

[130] *The Will to Power*, §748: "This ridiculous condition of Europe *must* not last any longer. Is there a single idea behind this bovine nationalism? What possible value can there be in encouraging this arrogant self-conceit when everything today points to greater and more common interests? ... And it is precisely now that 'the new German Empire' has been founded upon the

his peers, subordinates, and the German people into supporting his ends (of sustained Prussian monarchy), through his machinations he fomented much of the *Liberalistic nationalism* that Nietzsche grew to disdain: "the Prussian Liberals who made their peace with Bismarck, the National Liberals, could feel that much of what they wanted had been achieved. Unity had come before freedom, but freedom could only be achieved in a united country".[131]

Nietzsche loathed such politicizing of the serious matters of culture, of the folk: "The Nihilistic consequences of the political and politico-economical way of thinking, where all principles at length become tainted with the atmosphere of the platform: the breath of mediocrity, insignificance, dishonesty, etc. Nationalism, Anarchy, etc."[132] Nationalism *itself* is never Nietzsche's enemy. Instead, he rails at the context of his *contemporary* nationalism — i.e., the Liberalistic shroud that the still-encumbered-by-slave-morality nationalism dons. Indeed, Nietzsche had seen two wars (1866 and 1870) before reaching the age of 30 — each waged in the name of German/

---

most thread-bare and discredited of ideas — universal suffrage and equal right for all...." Leftist (and quite disingenuous) interpreters of Nietzsche like to trumpet the philosopher's frequent criticisms of *Liberalistic* nationalism as critiques of *all* nationalism. No close reading of Nietzsche's work could ever support this leftist interpretation, however.

[131] Feuchtwanger 46-47. To be sure, Bismarck was no William Gladstone, but "the decline of Liberalism [in Germany] ... cannot be attributed to him" (Feuchtwanger, 78). Bismarck was an opportunist who, as mentioned, fomented Liberalistic nationalism in Germany. Mosse reminds us, too, that

> in 1871 ... Bismarck proclaimed the Prussian King to be the Emperor [and] unity seemed won at last. But the political unity of the new Prussian-dominated federation proved a disappointment to many Germans. It was prosaic, concerned with everyday problems, whereas the movement toward that unity had been highly idealistic and indeed utopian. (Mosse, 3)

What the German citizens found was a de-spiritualized version of their Greater German *Reich* — a version predicated on rationalistic, Liberalistic principles. Indeed, as Alfred Rosenberg astutely notes, during Bismarck's Reich "nationalism became no longer rooted in the folk, rather falsified into the battle-cry of folk-uprooted literati, cosmopolitans, and big businessmen," *Blood and Honor*, 256 (Third Reich Books).

[132] *The Will to Power*, Chapter I, §6.

national/liberal principles, giving a broader voice to the people ("the herd"). To this national sentiment he responds:

> remain faithful to the earth, and do not believe those who speak to you of otherworldly hopes [about the innate dignity of man]! ... Despisers of life are they, decaying and poisoned themselves, of whom the earth is weary: so let them go.... To sin against the earth is now the most dreadful thing... A polluted stream is man. One must be a sea to be able to receive a polluted stream without becoming unclean. Behold, I teach you the *Übermensch*: he is this sea; in him your great contempt can go under.[133]

In this passage we see two things: (1) it is not nationalism *per se* that Nietzsche decries, but *Liberalistic* nationalism — or that which ignited the liberal feelings of his time, and (2) the *Übermensch* is the "sea" — the enveloping concept — in which all men might course. Most important for our task, though, is the latter, in that through it the *Übermensch* concept begins to resemble the *Führerprinzip*. The citizens of Germany — the "polluted streams" — submit their will and flow into the great "sea" of the Führer, through which they are cleansed of their weakness and ideological nihilism; important to note, however, is that it is not the Führer alone who represents the *Übermensch*, but the conjoined will of the folk with the Führer. The *Führerprinzip* demands the combining of the collective body and mind of the folk and the executive power of the Führer in order to triumph over socio-cultural degeneracy and ideological nihilism through the *ancient will*, the conservation of natural law. It represents the "deliverer" of which Nietzsche speaks when lamenting the nihilistic urges of his contemporary German (European) socio-political climate: "Everywhere the *deliverer* is missing, either as a class or as a single man — the justifier".[134]

Some would argue that the *Führerprinzip* is merely an outgrowth of the State and that Nietzsche despised the so-called State. Yet if we understand the context of his time — that of fomented nationalism for the sake of Liberalistic principles — we can see that it is not the State proper he despised, but only that State

---

[133] *Thus Spoke Zarathustra*, "Zarathustra's Prologue."

[134] *The Will to Power*, Chapter I, §6.

which furthers the socio-cultural degenerative principles of Liberalism. Only then will his frequent statements like "State I call it where all drink poison, the good and the wicked; state, where all lose themselves, the good and the wicked; state, where the slow suicide of all is called 'life'" and "Where the state ends — look there, my brothers! Do you not see it, the rainbow and the bridges of the *Übermensch*?" make any kind of contextual sense.[135] For when that State which propagates Liberalism — which is to say, for Nietzsche, nihilism and socio-cultural degeneracy — dissipates, only then will the prospect of the *Übermensch* obtain — i.e., the prospect of sustaining European life and culture.

It is no coincidence that when Nietzsche talks of his "conception of freedom" he targets Liberalism as the great negative:

> there are no worse and no more thorough injurers of freedom than liberal institutions. Their effects are known well enough: they undermine the will to power; they level mountain and valley, and call that morality; they make men small, cowardly, and hedonistic — every time it is the herd animal that triumphs with them. Liberalism: in other words, herd-animalization.[136]

Instead of the Liberalistic State, it is only the *Übermensch* who (that) can provide freedom — principally because the *Übermensch* turns Liberalistic values on their head and frees man from his servitude to a morality that is severed from natural law; man can only be free when he is subject to the "meaning of the earth," because he is then in harmony with the earth. And we must remember: "To sin against the earth is now the most dreadful thing..." Further, for Nietzsche,

> Freedom means that the manly instincts which delight in war and victory dominate over other instincts, for example, over those of "pleasure." The human being who has *become free* — and how much more the *spirit* who has become free — spits on the contemptible type of well-being dreamed of by shopkeepers, Christians,

---

[135] Nietzsche, *Thus Spoke Zarathustra*, "The New Idol."

[136] *Twilight of the Idols*, §38.

> cows, females, Englishmen, and other democrats. The free man is a *warrior*.[137]

A *society* based in "pleasure" indicates the individualistic society, for Nietzsche; in contrast, the *culture* that embraces "spirit" and "becomes more indifferent to difficulties, hardships, privation, even to life itself"[138] indicates the illiberal collective[139]; freedom is the spiritual transcendence of the individual will for the sake of the group, or, in this case, the folk. We must recall Mosse, when in describing *völkisch* ideology — that ideology which, in part, gave rise to the *Führerprinzip* — notes the difference between culture and civilization: "Culture ... has a soul, whereas Civilization is 'the most external and artificial state of which humanity is capable.' The acceptance of Culture and the rejection of Civilization meant for many people an end to alienation from their society".[140] Mosse quotes Oswald Spengler here, but the sentiment stems from Nietzsche: *culture* is organic and transcendent (and worth saving); *civilization* is rationalistic (or derivative of the organic) and temporal (or decadent). Furthermore, this "spirit" of the culture Nietzsche indicates — the "folk" — represents what Mosse notes as

> [signifying] the union of a group of people with a transcendental "essence." This "essence" might be called "nature" or "cosmos" or "mythos," but in each instance it was fused to man's innermost nature, and represented the source of his creativity, his depth of feeling, his

---

[137] Ibid., §38.
[138] Ibid., §38.
[139] *The collective* can only be what Nietzsche desires for his future of the *Übermensch*, for he disparages the "society" (as opposed to "culture" — for instance, the difference between *Gesellschaft* and *Gemeinschaft*) that lacks the sense of *the collective* (*The Will to Power*, §52): "There can be no solidarity in a society containing unfruitful, unproductive, and destructive members, who, by the bye, are bound to have offspring even more degenerate than they are themselves." Also, we must look to this verse for Nietzsche's feelings on the paramountcy of *solidarity, the collective* (Ibid., §442): "This is how decadence manifests itself: the instinct of solidarity is so degenerate that solidarity itself gets to be regarded as *tyranny*: no authority or solidarity is brooked, nobody any longer desires to fall in with the rank and file..."
[140] Mosse, 6.

> individuality, and his unity with other members of the folk.[141]

It is in this "unity" that the *Führerprinzip* arises.

Later in *Twilight of the Idols*, Nietzsche praises the "will, instinct, or imperative, which is anti-liberal to the point of malice": this will is interested only in *culture* — not civilization; it is oriented on the shared history, values of *struggle* and *triumph*, and unmistakable, unshakable vision of the future that has a view on the coming millennia; it is focused on the arc of natural law that galvanizes a people through the imperturbable "first principle: one must need to be strong — otherwise one will never become strong".[142] In the posthumously published *The Will to Power*, Nietzsche outlines a set of commandments that will govern the *culture* of *Übermenschlichkeit*:

> (1) Compulsory *military service* with real wars in which all joking is laid aside.
> (2) *National* thick-headedness (which simplifies and concentrates).
> (3) Improved *nutrition* (meat).
> (4) Increasing *cleanliness* and wholesomeness in the home.
> (5) The predominance of *physiology* over theology, morality, economics, and politics.
> (6) Military discipline in the exaction and the practice of one's 'duty' (it is no longer customary to praise).[143]

This might as well be a template for the future Hitlerist *Schutzstaffel*, those guardians and enablers of the *Führerprinzip*. Additionally, although it is unstated in this set of principles, Nietzsche later offers what might be considered the first principle of *Übermenschlichkeit*: "If one regards individuals as equals, the demands of the species are ignored, and a process is initiated which ultimately leads to its ruin.... Evolution is thwarted and the *unnatural* becomes law...".[144] This might be the first principle since it asserts the primal, natural law of

---

[141] Ibid., 4.
[142] *Twilight of the Idols*, §38. "... to the point of malice," §39.
[143] *The Will to Power*, §126.
[144] *The Will to Power*, §246.

struggle for supremacy among opposing forces — *the meaning of the earth*. And what is the meaning of the earth if not the *Übermensch*?

Conclusion

The final revelatory words of this essay on the *Führerprinzip* aim to be the most important; but, ideally, they will be unnecessary given what has said above. They, too, come from *The Will to Power*, from a passage as seemingly innocuous as all the rest, if such is possible. Nietzsche again asks us to consider the "mediocre" men — those slaves to that foreign (i.e., un-*völkisch*), Liberalistic ideology; and again, he orients us to the *Übermensch*:

> the highest man, if such a concept be allowed, would be that man who would represent *the antagonistic character of existence* most strikingly, and would be its glory and its only justification.... Ordinary men may only represent a small corner and nook of this natural character; they perish the moment the multifariousness of the elements composing them, and the tension between their antagonistic traits, increases: but this is the prerequisite for greatness in man. That man should become better and at the same time more evil, is my formula for this inevitable fact. *The majority of people are only piecemeal and fragmentary examples of man: only when all these creatures are jumbled together does one whole man arise.* But, for this reason, one should not forget that the only important consideration is the rise of the synthetic man...[145]

Finally, the *Übermensch* is seen for what it is: *the collective*, the amassing of a like-minded people — a folk — for the sake of the transcendent purpose: "that man should become better," for the sake of itself, for freedom through subjection to life's natural law — and not the servile subjection to the "lie," the great slave-morality —

---

[145] Ibid., §881. Latter emphasis added. We also note that in logic, "synthetic" means *a truth that is determinable through experience* (as opposed to "analytic"). A "synthetic man," then, might be considered one whose veracity — or viability — is made known experientially, or *pragmatically*. Recall Nietzsche and Hitler's pragmatism: the pragmatism of *traditionalism*.

opposing forces be damned. It was the *Führerprinzip* which conjoined the Führer and folk into a single will — a will-to-power aimed at triumph through the struggle. The *Übermensch*, of course, was the National Socialist State, the will of all German folk fused into an executive concept.

Nietzsche leaves us finally with his prophetic warning — a warning nestled in his autobiographical *Ecce Homo*, his attempt at analyzing the eternal, spiritual will as it passed through his pen during his final years:

> For when truth enters into a fight with the lie of millennia, we shall have upheavals, a convulsion of earthquakes ... the like of which has never been dreamed of. The concept of politics will have merged entirely with a war of spirits; all power structures of the old society will have been exploded — all of them are based on the lie; there will be wars the like of which have never yet been seen on earth. It is only beginning with me that there are *great politics* on earth.[146]

The *truth* is the spirit of the natural law, the will to harness and dominate human nature for the transcendent cause, the cause of a *völkisch* spirit — the heuristic truth born out in experience. The *lie* is the Judeo-Christian death of the natural spirit, the lie of weakness dressed as "morality." The first birth pangs of this new, Nietzschean age were felt in the ideological clashes of the twentieth century; *this was just the beginning*. What follows this current calm before the storm of spirit-tensed-to-a-coil — this perpetuation of the lie — will overcome everything modernity finds familiar, for modernity itself is an apparition of the lie.

THE PRIMACY OF SUBJECTIVITY: An Examination of Scientific Rationalism via Darwin's Theory of Evolution through Natural Selection and the Hindu-Aryan Concept of Devolution

> *We are aliens from God.... Empirical science is apt to cloud the sight, and by the very knowledge of functions*

[146] Löwith, 109. This passage can be found in *Ecce Homo*'s "Why I am a Fate" — Löwith's translation is preferred.

and processes to bereave the student of the manly contemplation of the whole.... A man is a god in ruin.
— RALPH WALDO EMERSON, "NATURE"

"We have invented happiness," say the last men, and they blink. They have left the regions where it was hard to live, for one needs warmth.... Everybody wants the same, everybody is the same: whoever feels different goes voluntarily into a madhouse. "Formerly, all the world was mad," say the most refined, and they blink.
— FRIEDRICH NIETZSCHE, *THUS SPOKE ZARATHUSTRA*

A Definition

Scientific rationalism, as it is used throughout this work, can be broadly understood as transcending both *rationalism* in the *a priori* sense and *empiricism* in the *a posteriori* sense to ultimately encompass both.[147] At the *heart* of scientific rationalism is the individual's will-to-objectivity — i.e., his subjective belief that he has unfiltered access to things-in-the-world and a desire to build his worldview thusly, often imposing his will — actively or passively, but always unironically — upon others. *Je pense, donc je suis*: Scientific rationalism is the overbearing *I* of the world and, consequently, the eye of the storm that brings the *Kali-Yuga*, the Age of Man, to bear.

An Introduction

Darwin's theory of evolution from natural selection is indicative of the scientific rationalism permeating and dominating the modern West. Either inadvertently (through a dedication to an overarching rationalism) or necessarily (as a product of its time), the theory undermines what some have seen as uplifting traditions linking man to the ancestral gods. Yet, through a strict adherence to what it deems "objective reality," Darwin's theory and the scientific rationalism of which it is a part ironically miss their own subjective foundation. This subjectivity not only negates rationalism as a modern panacea for the world's ills, but also makes alternative, or supra-rational, theories equally viable. Moreover, given the subjective nature of any worldview, if a particular theory uplifts, then it might

---

[147] "Scientific rationalism" and "rationalistic"/"rationalism" are used synonymously outside of the opening paragraph.

be seen as positive, whereas if a theory reduces its adherents to mere components, then it might be seen as negative.

This essay will not argue in favor of any one theory over the other, but instead will argue against the notion of *objectivity* or *objective reality* as transcendent aims — or *ideologies* — instead of being used or understood as *mere tools* to enhance subjective worldviews. Additionally, an alternative theory of devolution will be explained from the vitalized supra-rational perspective; specifically, it will be argued that man's devolution from a superior state is at least possible from a Hindu-Aryan perspective and presents an uplifting account of the past and future. It will be concluded that, from the Hindu-Aryan perspective, which alone and firstly presents a viable alternative to Darwinism, Western culture requires a supra-rational — or what might be seen as a *traditional* — worldview to sustain itself.

Proof is in the Proof

Proof, objectively speaking, is irrelevant. Proof, like beauty, is in the eyes of the beholder. That there are competing worldviews on an individual level is inarguable; that there are competing world orders on a global level is indisputable. This competition suggests subjectivity — it is a competition of what *should become* dominant, or "objective." Proof is thought to be an indicator of some kind of truth; in the modern world — particularly in the West — since the fall of the *ancien régime* and the ascension of the quantity during the so-called Enlightenment, and ever more acceleratingly since the end of World War II,[148] *proof* is meant largely in an objective sense. *Do*

---

[148] This subject deserves its own paper, of course; but there are a number of "proofs" for this statement, since proof is what is evidently required. The West (especially America) has been in *perpetual* war, "low-intensity conflict," or "competition short of armed conflict" since its rise to world power in the ruins of a war that, from a materialistic perspective, was fought for economic supremacy in the Occident. That the victors of World War II have an ideological foundation predicated on economic prosperity is certain. That the war's victors used ideological slogans (and other duplicities) to summon support for an economic motivation is just as certain. The post-World War II world has seen an exponential rise in all things related to increased profits: "strength in diversity" is doublespeak for expanding customer bases, for instance; we are witnessing an "obesity epidemic," which is only to say we are witnessing the results of uprooted peoples being commercially encouraged to "you do you"; we are in the grip of widespread pharmaceutical addiction, which is to say we are being commercially cajoled to take *x* drug

you have proof? What is your source? Is it verifiable? These are questions posited and pursued by a dominant worldview; that is, they are natural questions given the context of the interrogator; yet their basis in reality can only be understood as subjective. If rationalism, or better, *scientific rationalism*, is the dominant worldview (i.e., if it is one of many competing worldviews), then its foundation is subjectivity.

The rationalistic worldview cannot escape the fetters of human hope. No matter its adherents' attempts to *prove* its objectivity, their efforts are fruitless. Reason, as a means to obtain objective proof (as opposed to subjective proof), is self-referential, if not self-destructive. Reason might be used to secure two types of truth: subjective or objective. When it pursues the former, it is used properly as a *tool* to understanding the world. When it pursues objectivity, is transcends its use as tool to become an *ideology*; in this way it is self-referential. One's reason, if verifiable, becomes the proof of itself. One might say, "I followed these logical steps to reach this conclusion; because I followed these steps, the conclusion is right." That is, the *ideological* process of scientific rationalism is both the end pursued and the means to achieve it. But this obtains only in theory; reality is much *different* — or, rather, reality is subjective.

If the logical conclusions of one's methodology do not align with individual or collective desires, then those conclusions are scrapped and other conclusions are rationalized. For instance, if logic leads us to see that there is an overpopulation problem, the same logic might see that the solution to the problem is a rebalancing of the ecosystem; such a rebalancing likely demands a removal of the primary stress on that ecosystem, i.e., the humans overtaxing it. At this point, however, something irrational, or altruistic, or emotional,

---

to offset the effects of y drug, which, in turn, is taken to counter the effects of a miserable diet and no exercise, and so on *ad nauseum*; we have seen the rise of constant media — or the "free" press — which is driven solely by profits; we are at the tail end of a STEM (science, technology, engineering, mathematics) revolution, wherein the discombobulated, diverse citizens are corralled into creating civically minded, innovative technology that, really, is principally used for making more effective and efficient war-means to perpetuate the state of constant conflict and extend the capitalistic fingers of the plutocratic leaders, who drive economic prosperity for a citizenry that is otherwise far too unfit — given its obesity and pharmaceutical dependency, not to mention spiritual bankruptcy — to wage said conflict in any physically demanding way. And so the cycle continues.

etc. surfaces, flatly denying the clearest logical solution. In this way, the rationalistic worldview — the worldview that proposes the notion of "objective truth" — is itself circumvented by subjective preference, even if that subjectivity is collectively derived and professes a socially acceptable foundation. Other means, besides pure reason or rationality, are used to arrive at an acceptable solution. *Acceptable to whom or what? Acceptable to the dominant system*, is the answer.

Let us look at another example: recidivism in the United States. If a convicted criminal is nearly 80% likely to be rearrested after his release from prison,[149] it stands to reason that, if a society is intent on reducing crime, which is only logical, then something should be done to reduce such a high recidivism rate. If "rehabilitation" fails to reduce the rate, then it is not a viable option; if stagnation in the prison system fails to reduce the rate, then it is not a reasonable option, either. If there is something fundamental to the character of a person that makes him inclined to criminal behavior, then it is only rational that to remove the criminal behavior from society, a society needs to remove the criminal from its midst. This could mean longer sentences (but this burdens society in other ways — unless it can be rationally monetized), or it could mean harsher sentences. Neither option would likely substantively get off the ground, however, because both options would, according to emotional and ill-informed reactions wrapped in the guise of constitutionality, prove to be too inhumane. Here, *constitutionality* is a *guise* simply because constitutionality has changed over time, and has changed to reflect a given generation's sensibilities, which is to say, such sensibilities are subjective, even if at a societal level.

This brings us to another point regarding law. The modern West prides itself on the so-called *rule of law*, which bespeaks an adherence to an objective set of standards by which governing bodies regulate society. As mentioned with constitutions, laws change over time to "best" reflect a society's norms. If laws, which are meant to be objective standards, change, then *objectivity* is only veneer. Likewise, if we examine the origin of a society's or culture's laws, then all we see is a reflection of agreed-upon or habituated practices, which, if unpracticed, result in penalty. These established laws are not written on stone tablets, nor are they written in the heavens; rather, they exist only because some powerful folks sat around determining them

[149] National Institute of Justice. "Recidivism," 2014.

for their generation's and subsequent generations' *objectives*. That is, such laws were established to best enable the society or culture to meet its collective — or collectively subjective — ends. This, too, brings us to an issue of goals.

Another word for *goals* is *objectives*. *Objectives* are those ends that a given society or culture agrees are worth collective effort. The established rules to facilitate the achievement of these objectives are the *objective* standards by which society is regulated. Again, what we see here is not something akin to "objective truth," but rather a pragmatic means to achieve subjective, albeit collective, ends. Objectives are not objective at all; rather, they are practical measures of socio-cultural effectiveness. There are as many socio-cultural objectives as there are cultures under the sun, clearly. Objectives compete because "objective truths" compete. There is a simple illustration of this fact: China is the "Middle Kingdom," 中国 (*zhong guo*). In their language, which is to say, in Sino-cultural *identity*, they are not "China," they are the Middle Kingdom. *Middle of what?* Well, middle of the *world*. Some other countries might have something to say about this Sino-peculiar *fact*. Here is another example a little closer to home: the work of Edward Bernays. Bernays was an Austrian-American Jew[150] who, among other things, was instrumental in building popular support for the United States' entry into the World War I; as part of the Committee on Public Information, he successfully painted the Germans as "evil" and "bloodthirsty," while the Allies were portrayed as "noble" and "just." After the war, Bernays

[150] It is important to mention Bernays' Jewishness because his involvement in World War I and his subsequent publications (among many other things) helped influence German perceptions of the war and the Jews in the interwar period. It also sheds light on the other (German) side of the story, which is not often acknowledged in the post-World War II West. Notably, Bernays and his Committee on Public Information as a whole were *selling* World War I to the American people — they sold it through typical propaganda means (viz., framed information); Germany, for its part, at the time, was realizing a self-assertion that stemmed from what it perceived as growing British and French hostility and its comparative disadvantage with its European peers — namely, that, before the war, Britain controlled roughly 25% of the world, France controlled around 15%, and Russia about 7%. Germany's holdings, including its own territory, stood at roughly 3%. With this information, the picture of the "evil" Germans is cast in a different light. More than anything, from the victors' perspective, World War I was fought for economic reasons.

continued his work for the government — most notably in the 1954 Guatemalan coup. Guatemala's new democratically elected government was hostile to foreign companies operating in their country; the American United Fruit Company was one of the frowned-upon businesses, and was actively being pushed out of the country. The Dulles brothers (one Secretary of State, the other, head of the Central Intelligence Agency) were shareholders in the United Fruit Company and, in short, through a blatant conflict of interest, devised a plan, with the direct help of Bernays, to overthrow the Guatemalan government and install a dictatorship sympathetic to American business aims. The plan worked and led to a decades-long civil war, killing hundreds of thousands of people.

There is much to unpack with this example, to be sure; the operative phrase, however, is *conflict of interest*. It implies a conflict between the individual aims of the Dulles brothers and the United States; yet the Dulles brothers were appointees of a democratically elected official. If we admit a conflict of interest, then we acknowledge the fallibility of an objective process (i.e., political appointees emplaced by an elected official designated through lawful means). This is not to say that perfection is expected in human endeavors; but, rather, that human endeavors are *always* subjective — whether in evaluating the merits of a candidate, an appointee, an event, a proof, etc. It is our interpretation of a thing that ultimately defines it, despite its "objective" worth. There is an endless list of examples illustrating similar points.

Consider more personal, or micro-level illustrations. An employee gets an evaluation at work. His supervisor evaluates by a set of "objective" standards. Indeed, such standards are objective on paper, but when it comes time for actually writing the evaluation, the supervisor will inevitably and necessarily factor in — wittingly or not — her own personal feelings or biases regarding the employee. Even if the employee completes all the objective standards satisfactorily, the supervisor would be remiss if she did not account for her overall "feeling" about the employee, given her knowledge and experience. Similarly, a student submits her work to a teacher. The teacher offers a rubric that is meant to be a set of objective standards, meant to enable the student to achieve the goal of "learning." Ultimately, whether the student achieves this or that criterion with more or fewer "points," is purely subjective — based on the teacher's general opinion of both the student and the content.

In each of these examples, and many others that could be mentioned, the governing principle, when all is accounted for, is *subjectivity* based on cultural desires, which is to say, humanly, irrational desires. Now, this is not to say that reason is not used — not at all. Rather, it is to say that rationality is used as a *mere tool* to achieve subjective ends, either individual or collective. The governing principle is not, nor can it be, objectivity. *Objectivity*, as a means to "objective truth," exists only as an *ideological* feature of modern Western culture. All talk of *citing*, *sourcing*, *proving*, etc. can be traced directly back to the fanciful, collectively and subjectively derived objectives of a dominant culture — a culture that seeks to *reduce* and *quantify* a thing into measurable parts. Charles Darwin, too, was of this mind because he was a product of a prevailing culture; he is an honored son, a paragon of Western culture because he so perfectly executed his culture's objectives. Because he did this, and because most cultures see their aims as the only proper aims — particularly those that base their self-identity on attaining "objective truth," like the modern West — his ideas have reverberated through the West, like an echo off a sounding board that continuously layers and distorts itself.[151]

The friction between "objective truth," or the reason-as-an-ideology worldview (i.e., *objectivity*), and reality is this: reality was, is, and always will be a product of human perception, and human perception is not objective. "Objective truth" or proof is only useful insofar as it helps one achieve subjective (even if collective) aims. That the modern, post-World War II West perhaps sees it differently — i.e., sees objectivity as something "out there," something attainable — is only reflective of the dominant cultural narrative, which is to say, the subjective-collective narrative. It is only a simple irony that an impossibly subjective narrative paints itself as objectively verifiable. Granted, not everyone — particularly, many government officials — sees our espoused world order as *grounded* in objectivity; that is, not all acknowledge the inherent or objective "goodness" of American aims — many see them for what they are: practical from a certain perspective. (If one reads any of the strategic documents published by the government — for example, the National Security Strategy — one will routinely see the phrase "US

[151] Distortion is the inevitable consequent of layering; the distortion, of course, is the apotheosization of reason (or objectivity) as an ideology, as opposed to its use as mere tool.

national interests" in the context of *securing* or *achieving* them. That any more evidence should be needed to establish the fact that *every effort* in the United States — to include every scientific endeavor — is aimed at *securing* or *achieving* the subjective-collective interests of a dominant culture is hardly imaginable.[152] This, again, only shows that the ultimate purpose of all "objective truth" is to achieve subjective aims.) Any talk of objectivity, whether in the realm of foreign policy, municipal government, education systems, the scientific community, etc. is pure propaganda; for any talk that fails to acknowledge the subjective aims of the spokesperson is simply framed information.

Every fact of Nature, in the specific context of the culture perceiving it, has a purpose. Whether the earth sits on a turtle shell or is suspended by unseen forces is meaningful only in the context of the espousing culture. Whether humans evolved from lower forms of life or have devolved from higher beings is meaningful only in the context of the espousing culture. *Does my belief help me achieve my aims?* This question could be asked — and, indeed, *is* asked, wittingly or not — from the individual or cultural level. *Securing one's interests* is the only purpose behind any lucid action.[153] Truth — whether subjective or objective — is *mere tool*; "evidence" only supports truth and, thus, only has meaning insofar as it helps an entity achieve its aims. That it is entirely possible that some future successful culture could believe that rain is the unhappy or benevolent tears of the gods says everything there is to be said about human endeavor and so-called *objectivity*.

Darwin, in developing his theory of evolution from natural selection, offered some in the world a hammer blow in favor of scientific rationalism as an ideology. Even if *he* used it as a mere tool to better understand the world, the changing cultural dynamics in the West, particularly since the end of World War II, have necessitated a less-homogeneous view of Western identity, which a

---

[152] The National Security Strategy (and other strategic documents) is an externally focused document; however, implicit in achieving external (i.e., foreign policy) aims is the alignment of domestic policy aims with them. That every aim — *especially* domestic — is geared toward exerting power abroad is indisputable. As Spengler and many others have noted, *life is politics*.

[153] Even sacrificial or altruistic actions are "selfish" in the sense that they will either support an individual or collective aim.

scientific and, as it happens, an economic worldview enable. That is, the West was once purely European, with a distinct set of values and behaviors[154]; the pre-WW1 values and behaviors (or cultural identity) — ones that Darwin would have known — have been overwritten with new values and behaviors to accommodate what was seen as a crisis of modernity (viz., the European values that "precipitated" World War I and its offspring, World War II). These new values are meant to emphasize objectivity via such things as rule of law and scientific rationalism. In this way, it is hoped that future ("European") crises might be averted.

Post-World War II cultural identity — through its *reduction* of systems into their components (e.g., the above-listed evaluation and rubric examples, and we might also cite the increased emphasis on science and psychology as explanatory means[155] [as in, this person/group is a *product* of these factors]) and through its valuing of *quantity* (particularly in terms of *people*, as a means to increased economic opportunity at all levels) — has emphasized objectivity as an *ideological* principle in order to create an all-embracing worldview (or set of objectives) that transcends historical cultural drivers like

---

[154] *Distinct* relative to, say, African or Asian values and behaviors. Consider that in African religion(s), worldly deliverance — defined as wealth and status — is the ultimate goal for adherents [Jacob Olupona, *African Religions* (New York: Oxford University Press, 2014), 3]. When this worldly salvation is attained, one's station in the ancestral realm is also assured; thus, one becomes immortal. If the twists and turns of life prevent some level of wealth and power, there is recourse inherent in the African tradition: witchcraft. One may manipulate one's environment to attain that which the natural course of things has denied: *materialistic gain*. If one has even a marginal understanding of African religious culture, then one can clearly see the motivations for African sub-cultures in the West: "bling" — i.e., posturing as materially wealthy and/or desperately striving for material wealth. Likewise, in drug-addled Southeast Asia, for instance, there is a saying that revolves around Chinese culture in the drug trade: "it's just the Chinese being Chinese." The meaning, of course, is that the Chinese gravitate toward unscrupulous activities (one of which being the drug trade) because they often show little regard for the consequences of their actions so long as profit is to be had.

[155] Interestingly, the father of modern psychoanalysis, Sigmund Freud, is a relative of Edward Bernays. The latter marked his uncle as a notable influence, which is consistent with Bernays' work on mass psychology.

race, creed, kind, etc. The new drivers are rule of law[156] and scientific rationalism, which, in ideological context (or self-referential context), work perfectly as transcending enablers — or even, in keeping with the ideological framework, *transcendental* enablers, in full Kantian glory. A cynical view of these new drivers might suggest that they exist principally to stimulate economic activity (or growth), since they explode all prior "limiting" drivers by expanding the marketplace beyond borders or other traditional understandings of communities. In any case, Darwin's theory of evolution through natural selection, while the product of *reason as a tool*, has facilitated the ascension of modernity's view of *reason as an ideology*. This is the principle influence of Darwin, without exception.

Darwin's theory helped explain the world in the context of then-prevailing cultural drivers, although he was not without his detractors — then or now. Countervailing voices expressed a deep-seated, unconscious resistance to the socio-cultural changes Darwin's theory augured. Darwin did not mean to change the Western world, but he did. His theory did not capture the origin of life, generally, but it absolutely *did* expound the origin of *human* life, since, after all, in examination of the world around us, we might see clearly that there exists a "community of descent".[157] This is often what is meant when one speaks of Darwin in relation to "the origin of life" — one is speaking of the origin of *human* life (despite any facile objections of the careless or hasty), which Darwin addresses and marks as ascent through descent. That is, man has progressed, through natural selection, from an "inferior" state to his present "high position".[158] This stands in contrast to previous beliefs, according to Darwin, that man descended from "demigods".[159] It is at this point, then, that we come to the topic at hand: the plausibility of the devolution of man from higher beings.

An Interlude of Protest

In spite of the above explanation and "proof," one might yet protest — indeed, it would be incomprehensible if there were *no* protest to the above position. A likely protest is this: *but some things can be*

---

[156] In the end, though, rule of law is subordinate to the scientific rationalism it is meant to protect.

[157] Charles Darwin, *The Descent of Man*, 1871, end of ch. I.

[158] Ibid., end of ch. II.

[159] Ibid., end of ch. I.

unequivocally *proved, and it is on this that we base our knowledge and subsequent experience — you can believe what you want about this or that, but it doesn't change the* fact *that something is true (real) or not.* Certainly, is the retort; but this hardly matters. Aside from and along with all further explanation already mentioned, the refrain is the same: objective proof is irrelevant in establishing objectivity; subjective perception and application are everything. Here is an illustration of the point — though it could be shown in any number of ways on any given day.

On a "typical" March day in Kabul, 2017, Afghan soldiers were convalescing in the Afghan National Army hospital; doctors and nurses were caring for them. The caregivers and convalescents shared a worldview that led to their lives intersecting; theirs was a Western-oriented worldview that contravened the usurped (and formerly accepted and adopted[160]) Taliban system; the two world orders defended objectives that were incompatible and, consequently, battled incessantly.

But the Taliban was not the enemy to watch that day; instead, another group, more volatile and, for a time, more dangerous than the Taliban, struck: the Islamic State of Iraq and Syria-Khorasan (ISIS-K). Around the time of the usual morning rush, an explosion rattled the hospital windows and shook the convalescents' beds — it was a car bomb just outside the hospital, a diversion from the coming onslaught. The plume of smoke rose ominously from the wreckage, like an arm reaching skyward for eternal, objective truth. Inside the hospital, doctors — tested and evaluated for their commitment to objective medical and moral standards — facilitated the entry of ISIS-K militants. Over the span of about an hour, at least five militants shot or stabbed no fewer than 50 patients and workers. During that hour, bullets from AK-47s whizzed into neighboring buildings and traffic; still-mobile convalescents roped bed sheets together and dangled them from their windows, hoping to escape to the cold concrete below; other patients, without the time to tie sheets together, simply climbed out of their windows and stood on a thin ledge — the only surface protecting them from the carnage inside and the hard concrete many stories below. The day was cloudy

[160] The Taliban are still more popular in Afghanistan than most Americans will ever know — this fact is now evidenced by reality, as the Taliban have reestablished illiberal governance.

and cold, certainly cold for a scant hospital gown wet from a morning mist.

Objectivity could not stop anyone from dying that day or in the days that followed the attack; objectivity was, is, and always will be a means to achieve a very subjective end. It is a matter of course that subjective ends have, do, and always will diverge. The only law that can possibly transcend all subjectivity — through, paradoxically, its complete reliance upon subjectivity — is so revolting to the modern West (given the West's objective *ideology* that shines with an all-too-familiar subjective brilliance) that many would prefer blissful ignorance to its reality: the only law that has and ever will matter is that *might makes right*. No one in the Afghan Army hospital, from either side, cared about Darwin's theory; few, if any, in Afghanistan care about it today; few, if any, in the broader West or even the world care about it. Its most profound relevance is largely localized to select scientists and academics that will have little impact on the world around them beyond their immediate spheres.

This is not an indictment; this is an observation. Science (and, naturally, scientific rationalism — of which Darwin's theory is only a representative), in its most enduring and, arguably, purest form, is always weaponized or is applied in a war-supporting form — that is the only lasting relevance for science, as all other technological conveniences are derivative. And it is to this end that science achieves objective dominance — i.e., insofar as *it enables the achievement of subjective aims*. The weaponization of science represents the subjectivizing of objectivity — or, the only possible ultimate use of objectivity (or reason). As long as aims diverge across cultures, bullets will tear flesh and science will leave devastation in its wake; this is only to say that divergence is *forever*. It is not rational discussion that promulgates "Western democracy" worldwide; there are countless battles waged daily to secure Western ends (across a range of diplomatic, informational, military, and economic powers) — battles that require a real crippling of Western opponents, far beyond any friendly persuasion.

This is *might makes right*. It was not rational discussion that converted North Africa and the greater Middle East to Islam; real violence and coercion encouraged the conversion. This is *might makes right*. Peaceful persuasion did not Christianize the Germanic peoples — ruthlessness did. This is *might makes right*. Rational discussion did not "de-Nazify" Germany after World War II; countless Germans, many of whom played no part in the hostilities or committed any "offense" beyond simply *being German*, were starved, shot, burned, or otherwise ostracized or brutalized. This is *might makes right*. The modern state of Israel did not materialize through congenial, rational agreement with the Palestinians; rather, the new Jewish dominion was carved out of an existing state, with the full weight of the British and American empires behind it. This is *might makes right*. To reiterate: objective proofs or truths are absolutely *meaningless* shorn of their essential subjectivity.

Here is another protest from the modern perspective: *Subjectivity is the poison that leads to war. War is the objective leveler of man's opinion — because it leads to death, the state of no-subjectivity.* War for the sake of objectivity, *then, is perhaps the highest good, as it leads to peace.* This protest, like any position, can never escape the pit of "poisonous" subjectivity — despite its rational attempt. *War for the sake of objectivity* is, perhaps, the West's (particularly the US's) official *modus operandi*. Yet there is something about the attitude of "Let's make war until they see things the way we do" that seems strikingly subjective. That is the point, of course.

Devolution as an Alternative to Evolution

> *The gods we stand by are the gods we need and can use, the gods whose demands on us are reinforcements of our demands on ourselves and on one another.*
>
> — WILLIAM JAMES, *THE VARIETIES OF RELIGIOUS EXPERIENCE*

> *Only a god can save us. The only possibility available to us is that by thinking and poetizing we prepare a readiness for the appearance of a god, or for the absence of a god in our decline.*
>
> — MARTIN HEIDEGGER, *DER SPIEGEL* interview, 1966

Plausibility, like proof, is in the eye of the beholder. Proof and plausibility obtain insofar as they harbor the potentiality to create effect. The American philosopher and one of the founders of modern psychology, William James, aptly — if unfaithfully — interpreted Peirce's theory of truth thusly: truth is what works. This is the essence of not only James' pragmatism, but also generally what we see around us on any given day. This is more than just a recapitulation of what was said above regarding *subjective* and *objective* truth; indeed, it transcends truth to encompass *fact*, objective or otherwise. Facts are nothing beyond fuel for individual or collective truth, which is to say, subjectivity. Given, then, that objectivity is a *mere tool* to facilitate the achievement of subjective aims, it is indeed plausible that humans descended from higher beings, be they gods, demigods, etc., for it is plausible that such a belief, like any belief, facilitated — or perhaps *will* facilitate — the achievement of subjective aims.

The goal of the following is not to convolute reality to a point where "anything" could be truthful or factual based on the whim of "what works," but to show that, given our current worldview — i.e., one of scientific rationalism wherein, for instance, Darwin's theory of evolution from natural selection describes what we understand as reality — an alternative worldview is possible. It does not suffice to simply say *the moon is made of cheese*, for instance, and that this belief works *because* one believes it. While it might indeed be the case that one believes such a thing because it works for them (in some unknown way), a belief must align in some respect to the current, accepted worldview, or at least not flatly contradict it. That is, a given belief must have some plausible currency on which it is based and that it can share with other worldviews (or subjective parties to the worldviews).

Barring such currency, a belief is purely subjective and will inevitably remain limited in its scope. After all, objective realities obtain — this is not disputed. It *is* disputed that we can have any unfiltered access to so-called objective reality, and what is at stake is reality's *meaning*, for meaning is elusive outside of subjectivity. It means nothing that "fire is a plasma which consumes oxygen." It means everything that fire *burns*, *warms*, *cooks*, *comforts*, *hardens*, *softens*, *lights*, *protects*, *dries*, *mesmerizes*, *signals*, etc. Does a fact lift us up or tear us down? The answer to this question determines the value of any so-called objective reality or, dare we say, *fact*. It is an attempt to answer this question that we pursue now.

Everything straight lies; all truth is crooked; time itself is a circle. Such are the words of the insolent dwarf confronting Zarathustra.[161] This, of course, is Nietzsche confronting *himself* as his early adherence to a Heraclitean and Parmenidean notion of Eternal Recurrence yields to his later *Wille zur Macht*. *You spirit of gravity,* was Zarathustra's fiery retort, *do not take it too lightly — I carried thee high!* Zarathustra's *will* carried the dwarf upward; it is the nature

[161] Nietzsche, *Thus Spoke Zarathustra*, "The Vision and the Enigma."

of supreme souls and wills to march ever upward, carrying or crushing all that is weak. Heidegger spoke of Nietzsche's "thought of thoughts"[162]; this thought was his Eternal Recurrence. However, what stood at the forefront of Nietzsche's thought (time itself *as* a circle) subsided to the ramifications of the thought — *if it were true, what then?* One might choose pessimism (life as reducible and quantifiable data), which can only lead to dreadful and degenerative nihilism, or one might choose salvation: life as the will to power. It is simply not enough that time is a circle and we behave accordingly; we must, according to Nietzsche, fully understand what that means — physically, mentally, and spiritually.

Heidegger captured Nietzsche's meaning in his inaugural address upon assuming the University of Freiburg rectorate:

> The will to the essence of the German university is the will to science as will to the historical mission of the German people as a people that knows itself in its state. *Together*, science and German fate must come to power in this will to essence. And they will do so if, and *only* if, we ... expose science to its innermost necessity.... If we will the essence of science understood as the *questioning, unguarded holding of one's ground in the midst of the uncertainty of the totality of what-is, this* will to essence will create for our people its world, a world of the innermost and most extreme danger, i.e., its truly *spiritual world*.... Only a spiritual world gives the people the assurance of greatness. For it necessitates that the constant decision between the will to greatness and a letting things happen that means decline, will be the law presiding over the march that our people has begun into its future history.[163]

Heidegger — despite his mention of "the German," like Nietzsche, is discussing the fundamental importance and necessity of science (or "objective reality") being sublimated and subordinated to subjective

[162] Martin Heidegger, *Nietzsche: Vol. 2: The Eternal Recurrence of the Same* (New York: Harper & Row, 1984), 155 and elsewhere.

[163] Heidegger, "The Self-Assertion of the German University and The Rectorate 1933/34: Facts and Thoughts," *Review of Metaphysics*, 38:3 (1985), 471, 474, 476.

will. *Will* is what uplifts, for it is only will that can *interpret* — all else is meaningless *data*. The danger of the modern age, as both Nietzsche and Heidegger saw it, was its devotion to data over the will, for such spiritless devotion amounts to nothing more than "a letting things happen that means decline," which is to say, *nihilism*. Yet even this modern devotion to data — to "objective reality," or scientific rationalism — is itself, in the end, sublimated and subordinated to the subjective will. No matter its political accoutrement, be it "communism, or fascism, or world democracy",[164] the *will* reigns supreme. Cultural drivers — whether science, religion, or some hybrid — always and only drive the will that projects itself out into the world. So, for example, we have the pockets of intellectuals and religious zealots who so desperately care about things like Darwinism, science, technology, engineering, and mathematics, all ultimately supporting one cultural will, which is projected through instruments of national power — one will becoming dominant over another. Such is the case for every culture: petty lower-level concerns ("objective realities") and squabbles are all sublimated into the strategic (subjective) will to power. It is this *will to power* that determines not just the interpretation of history, but the future that stands as beginning, as well:

> The essence of science could not even be emptied out and used up ... if the greatness of the beginning did not *still* endure. The beginning still *is*. It does not lie *behind* us, as something that was long ago, but stands *before* us. As what is greatest, the beginning has passed in advance beyond all that is to come and thus also beyond us. The beginning has invaded our future. There it awaits us, a distant command bidding us catch up with its greatness.... But if we submit to the distant command of the beginning, science must become the fundamental happening of our spiritual being as part of a people.[165]

Science is always subordinate to the will and, thus, science is always subjective. The subjective will that now afflicts mankind — as manifested in the scientific rationalism of the West, which, through globalization, is spreading like a virus to non-European cultures via

---

[164] Ibid., 485.
[165] Ibid., 473-474.

the hollow promise of "economic prosperity" — is uprooting us from the earth. Our devotion to data can only lead to the further weaponization of science and the eventual destruction of both civilization and the world. *Only a god can save us*, Heidegger predicted. His prediction will, *undoubtedly*, come true. A god will arrive on earth that will use the science of this modern era against itself; perhaps the god will mask itself in our own determination to self-destruct, but it will nevertheless come. And from the ashes will arise a restarted world, one that looks to the past as future, the beginning as end, where time is a Vedic circle of will, bequeathed upon man as from ancient gods.

∞ ∞ ∞

René Guénon, in his *Crisis of the Modern World*, describes our zealous devotion to data as "a specifically modern attitude which consists in not merely ignoring, but expressly denying everything of a super-rational order".[166] This attitude is indeed modern, for while the "originators" of rational thought in antiquity saw its usefulness, they nevertheless gave due respect to the mysteries that lie eternally beyond our ken. Socrates' ostensible atheism, while venerated in the modern world of tolerant quantity, was certainly not indicative of the culture that bore him — his fate always rested in poison. This drifting away from the principles that molded "our" Western culture is a necessary consequent of what the ancient Aryans called the *Kali-Yuga*. Guénon ably describes it thusly:

> The Hindu doctrine teaches that a human cycle, to which it gives the name of *Manvantara*, is divided into four periods marking so many stages during which the primordial spirituality becomes gradually more and more obscured; these are the same period that the ancient traditions of the West called the Golden, Silver, Bronze and Iron Ages. We are now in the fourth age, the *Kali-Yuga* or "dark age," and have been so already, it is said, for more than six thousand years, that is to say since an epoch far earlier than any known to "classical" history. Since that time, the truths which were formerly within reach of all men have become more and more

[166] René Guénon, *Crisis of the Modern World* (London: Luzac & Co., 1942), 20.

> hidden and inaccessible; those who posses them grow gradually less and less numerous, and although the treasure of "non-human" wisdom that was before the ages can never be lost, it becomes enveloped in ever more impenetrable veils, which hide it from men's sight and make it extremely difficult to discover. This is why we meet everywhere, under various symbols, with the same theme of something which has been lost, at least to all appearances and so far as the outer world is concerned, and which those who aspire to true knowledge must find again.[167]

Why the movement from the earliest point in prehistory drifts in a "downward direction" finds its parallel constantly in the organic world: what is alive moves through its lifecycle, at the end of which increases decrepitude and degeneracy — the results of which spawn a new cycle. Vico, one of the earliest modern thinkers to acknowledge the Aryan vision of cyclical time (as evidenced in both Hindu and Germanic mythology, contrary to linear conceptions of time propagated by Semitic religions), marked man's "progression" as, first, a compulsion of necessity, followed by utility, "next attend to comfort, still later amuse themselves with pleasure, thence grow dissolute in luxury, and finally go mad and waste their substance".[168]

What drove the men of prehistory in their *compulsion of necessity* was "a fanaticism of superstition" — i.e., the spiritual world to which Heidegger and Guénon allude; it was this spiritual compulsion — this *Wille zur Macht* — that carved and defined the cultures that we now enjoy and are, wittingly or not, trying to eradicate today through our devotion to "reducible" data,[169] which we identify as *scientific rationalism*, the natural, nihilistic excrescence of *humanism*, wherein "men were indeed concerned to reduce everything to purely human proportions, to eliminate every principle of a higher order, and ... to turn away from the heavens under pretext of conquering the earth".[170] When finally, in the last stages of the Kali-Yuga, as man creeps closer to his final destruction, Vico assures us that we will

---

[167] Ibid., 10-11.

[168] Giambattista Vico, *The New Science of Giambattista Vico*, translated by Thomas Goddard and Max Fisch (Ithaca: Cornell University Press, 1968), 78.

[169] Ibid., 178.

[170] Guénon, *Crisis*, 25.

> live like wild beasts in a deep solitude of spirit and will, scarcely any two beings able to agree since each follows his own pleasure or caprice. By reasons of all this, providence decrees that, through obstinate factions and desperate civil wars, [the remaining few] shall turn their cities into forests and the forests into dens and lairs of men.... And the few survivors in the midst of an abundance of the things necessary for life naturally become sociable and, returning to the primitive simplicity of the first world of peoples, are again religious, truthful, and faithful.[171]

Thus the cycle begins again.

Krishna, the eighth avatar of Vishnu, identifies the end of the Kali-Yuga as that time when families will dissolve; women are corrupted by lawlessness (or what we might see as the individualism that accompanies rationalism, or what Vico marked as "caprice"), which results in the mixture of castes and, thus, the destruction of culture-driving aristocracies, the foundation of which are the cultural drivers Darwin enabled the destruction of; indeed, "mixture of castes leads to naught but hell"[172] — presumably, among other things, because one betrays ones ancestors by such mixing.

It is worth noting here that *aristocracy* comes from the Greek ἄριστος (*aristos*), meaning *best*; *Aryan*, the name given to the northern invaders into modern India, comes from the Sanskrit आर्य (*ārya*), meaning *noble* or *highborn*. The etymological similarity is hardly coincidental and hearkens back to a prehistorical convergence of peoples — one that the modern quantity-driven world often discounts or denies. In any case, Krishna signals the end of the present age with the destruction of quality and family. In traditional Hindu art, Krishna, like the god he incarnates, is depicted with resplendent blue skin. This blueness is said to represent celestial infinity, which it undoubtedly does. Yet it is no accident that his noble incarnation and divinity are portrayed as *blue*. One recalls the familiar English phrase (remembering, too, that English is Germanic in origin) *blue bloods* or *blue-blooded* identifying certain castes: such

---

[171] Vico, 423-424.

[172] Bhagavad Gita, translated by Franklin Edgerton (Cambridge: Harvard University Press, 1952), I: 40-43.

people were so called because of their nobility or high birth, the blue veins being visible under the white skin. It becomes clear that there is an underlying link between the blueness of ancient gods, divinity, and nobility — the hidden signs of which Guénon speaks.

Among the many hidden signs — too many to mention here — is the link further tying the Germanic mythos of Wotan, riding his white horse Sleipnir, to the Hindu-Aryan mythos of Kalki, the tenth and final avatar of Vishnu, riding on his white horse to bring balance back to existence and end the Kali-Yuga. This link, and those like it, establishes that ancient convergence of witnessed signs, passed through now-lost written traditions and oral recitals.

Many such traditions identify a central hub, or pole, around which all emanating spokes turn. This is the "Lord of the World" Guénon identifies.[173] The Christian tradition, for instance, marks Jesus Christ as the center pole around which his twelve disciples revolve; Germanic tradition notes King Arthur (*Ar-Thor*, the god of the Arctic north) and his twelve knights; it is said that even Adolf Hitler was the harmonizing pole around which his twelve *Schutzstaffel* "knights" gravitated, which is graphically depicted in the mystical *schwarze Sonnenrad*.[174] The Dalai Lama, too, has his "Round Table" made up of twelve "grand Namshans".[175] The purpose of "the twelve" encircling the center pole is equivalent to the zodiacal zones oriented around the eternal sun. This center sun, or pole, is also indicated in the ancient Hindu-Aryan symbol of the *swastika* and the Hindu-Buddhist *dharmachakra* (wheel of dharma). The Sanskrit *chakravarti* "literally means 'He who makes the wheel turn,' that is to say the one who, being at the center of all things, directs all movement without himself participating in it, or who is, to use Aristotle's words, the 'unmoving mover.'"[176] This center point of the rotating symbol, or the anthropomorphized symbol, is Guénon's Lord of the World: that harmonizing and regulatory function meant to bring justice and peace to the world.[177]

---

[173] Guénon, *Lord of the World*, 5.

[174] Stephen Cook and Stuart Russell, *Heinrich Himmler's Camelot: Pictorial/Documentary: The Wewelsburg, Ideological Center of the SS 1934 - 1945* (Andrews, NC: Kressmann-Backmeyer Publishing, 2000), 185.

[175] Guénon, *Lord of the World*, 23.

[176] Ibid., 7.

[177] Ibid., 10.

The Hindu-Aryan (i.e., *Indoo*-, or *Indo*-Aryan) tradition asserts that, in the beginning, there existed only one caste.[178] This original caste "possessed normally and spontaneously the spiritual degree designated by this name".[179] This ties to the second of Rajan's postulated theories of Hindu-Aryanism: that "that which evolves an effect out of itself is one with it," or that the spirit of the Creator permeates wholly and incorruptibly the substance of the created.[180] Yet, since man does not have such a perfectly spiritual or unflawed nature, this theory was seen as insufficient. This insufficiency gave rise not only to a subsequent theory, but also, more importantly, to a propagation of castes. First, to the former point, the third and final theory of Hindu-Aryanism postulates that the Creator (or "Efficient Cause," i.e., Brahma) is distinct from its creation, yet sufficient to enliven it; the example offered is that of the sun and its radiating energy.[181] Rajan marks this third theory as *logically flawless* and "accepted by all the finest logicians of the world; all our philosophical structure is based on this theory".[182] Second, to the latter point, the development of multiple castes from the one original caste corroborates the falsity of the second theory in that the otherness of man (from the supreme creative cause) precipitates his fallen state: as spiritually pure as the first caste might have been, it was sufficiently fallen to initiate further degradation through the cyclical time-cycle. This marks the devolution of man from his higher state.

"Let us look each other in the face," demands Nietzsche, "*We are Hyperboreans*".[183] Hyperborea is the region the Greeks of antiquity mention as being beyond the cold north, personified in Boreas: Herodotus, Hesiod, and, notably, Pindar each mention the mythical realm of the godlike beings; Pindar going so far as to say,

> Neither by ship nor on foot could you find the marvelous road to the meeting-place of the Hyperboreans.... In the festivities of those people and in their praises Apollo rejoices most.... No sickness or

[178] Ibid., 28.

[179] Ibid., 28.

[180] T.C. Rajan Iyengar, *The Hindu-Aryan Theory on Evolution and Involution* (New York: Funk & Wagnalls Co., 1908), 4.

[181] Ibid., 5.

[182] Ibid., 5.

[183] Nietzsche, *Antichrist*, § 1.

> ruinous old age is mixed into that sacred race; without toil or battles they live without fear of strict Nemesis.[184]

"Sacred race," of course, denotes the Hyperboreans' divine status; their apparent worship of "Apollo," the ancient sun god, indicates an adherence to the center sun/pole/polar trope; and from the Hyperborean center, all subsequent races arose. Guénon, J.G. Bennett, Lokamanya Bâl Gangâdhar Tilak, Miguel Serrano, and a number of others each indicate the ancient Hyperboreans as spawning the various races through either degenerative miscegenation with slave-like primates or general degradation through inexorable devolution through the Kali-Yuga. Either way, modern man has, far from *progressing upwards* from a common, lowly animal (or even bacterium) as Darwin asserts, has instead devolved downwards from a supreme race of beings into the mixed multitudes we see today.

Concomitant with the myriad races comes the distinct castes, which the Hindu-Aryans established according to the spiritual, mental, and physical proximity each race[185] has to the Hyperborean progenitors. The *arya*, or noble Aryans, sit atop the castes, as those beings closest to their Hyperborean ancestors — remarkable for their fair hair, fair skin, and celestial blue eyes; the blue skin of Krishna-Vishnu manifested in the "blue blood" of the elite, as seen in the blue veins through the milky white skin of the dominant caste. The further one drifts from the center sun, or pole/polar north, the further one gets from the physical, mental, and spiritual characteristics of the Hyperboreans.[186] This is the story of the modern age, the progression of devolution into the Kali-Yuga, where, as Krishna reminds us,

> The women of the family are corrupted;
> When the women are corrupted ...
> Mixture of caste [*varna*] ensues.
> Mixture (of caste) leads to naught but hell
> For the destroyers of the family and for the family;
> For their ancestors fall (to hell) ...
> By these sins of family-destroyers,

---

[184] Pindar, *Pythian*, edited by Diane Arnson Svarlien, 30-42.
[185] The Sanskrit *varna*, meaning *race/color*.
[186] Polar — i.e., *pole-ar*, the Arctic Pole. Interestingly, Miguel Serrano has suggested that Hyperborea rests in what is now the South Pole.

(Sins) which produce caste-mixture,
The caste laws are destroyed,
And the eternal family laws.[187]

Yet from this physical, mental, and spiritual decay will come the new incarnation of Vishnu-Wotan-Apollo — god of the Hindu-Aryans — who "age after age" returns to bring peace, justice, and harmony back to the world,[188] thus fulfilling the function of Guénon's "Lord of the World," the center sun/pole, around which the radial arms spin. This, the final avatar of the Hindu-Aryan/Hyperborean god, is Kalki-Wotan, atop of Sleipnir, the white horse that brings death to Kali, the low-born demon, thus ending the Kali-Yuga and marking the return of Baldur, son of Wotan and god of the summer sun, who is "so fair of feature, and so bright, that light shines from him",[189] as sign of the Golden Age, the Satya-Yuga, and return of the polar sun, wherein once again the god-loving, noble *varna* of Hyperborea will live without toil, battle, or fear.[190]

The modern age of scientific rationalism is incapable of looking beyond the rational to what Guénon calls the "super-rational",[191] or what might be called the supra-rational. This obtains despite the fact that it can be established that, like any worldview, the rationalistic, too, relies equally heavily on the irrational or supra-rational to stake their claim; as was mentioned above, all ends — rational or otherwise — sublimate into the subjective. The incapability to look beyond one's own worldview, too, is only further proof that all ends are purely subjective. Looking beyond "the rational" or, in the case of Hyperborea, what can be "proved",[192] takes one necessarily into the reaches of myth and legend, despite the fact that all subsequent science was born of ancient myth and prehistory. The mythos of Hyperborea is not unlike that of Atlantis, which some have postulated as being one and the same.

[187] Bhagavad Gita, I.41-43.
[188] Bhagavad Gita, IV.7-8.
[189] Prose Edda, translated by Arthur Brodeur (London: Oxford University Press, 1916), 22.
[190] Pindar, 40-42; Poetic Edda, translated by Henry Bellows (Princeton: Princeton University Press, 1936), 62.
[191] Guénon, *Crisis*, 20.
[192] Not to belabor the point, but *proved* must be in quotes because *X* is only proved from a start point that is necessarily subjective.

In 1885, William Warren, the first president of Boston University, wrote *Paradise Found: The Cradle of the Human Race at the North Pole,* wherein he outlined the reasons why man's origins were in the polar north, as opposed to the oft-mentioned African regions. He described his intentions as a "serious and sincere attempt to present ... the true and final solution of one of the greatest and most fascinating of all problems connected with the history of mankind".[193] In addition to examining various geological and paleontological claims to the facticity of an ancient polar continent[194] and the "wide diffusion" of the similar cosmology of ancient peoples,[195] Warren's work was based on the mythos of past civilizations, who themselves attribute the splendor of their own civilizations as being derivative of a northern people. That these northerners are Hyperboreans or Atlanteans is a product of a collective legend, stemming from accounts from antiquity, which themselves are derivative of ancient oral traditions.

Plato, for instance, makes the first known accounting of Atlantis and its godlike inhabitants (in both his *Timaeus* and *Critias*). Atlantis was a tremendous northern power that, ultimately, was destroyed in some sudden catastrophe. Aristotle attributed Plato's account to a kind of political allegory, but Plato's text mirrors more an historical retelling than any allegorical political statement. Moreover, numerous later thinkers supported Plato's account as an historical tradition (e.g., the Athenians Crantor and Solon, later Egyptian accounts, etc.).[196] If we understand Plato's account in light of the Hindu-Aryan mythos of the Yuga and progressive devolution, then the rapid collapse of such a great power was only a step toward the ultimate devolution of the once-powerful, godlike Hyperboreans/Atlanteans, culminating in the Kali-Yuga. "It seems

---

[193] William Warren, *Paradise Found: The Cradle of the Human Race At The North Pole* (Boston: Houghton, Mifflin, & Co., 1885), vii.

[194] Ibid., 71-82, 286, for instance. Such *facticity* is beside the point, however.

[195] Ibid., 139, 210-218, etc.; among others, Warren cites the Chinese, Japanese, Persians, Hindu-Aryans, Akkadians (Sumerians), Babylonians, Assyrians, Egyptians, Greek, Germanic, etc. — particularly in their placing "paradise" or the "center of the earth" in the polar north. Perhaps it goes without saying that the Aztecs' belief in Quetzalcoatl (the fair god-man who ruled the Golden Age and thereafter returned to the polar north) had something to do with their acceptance of the white conquistadors from the north.

[196] Edward Bacon, "Atlantis," *Man, Myth, and Magic* (New York: Cavendish, 1995), 156-159.

undoubted," Guénon notes, "that the remnants of [the Atlantean] tradition were carried into various regions, where they mingled with other ... traditions, for the most part branches of the great Hyperborean tradition".[197]

Yet the traditions birthing what is finally accounted for in antiquity are themselves, by then, *ancient*, reaching back thousands of years before the likes of, say, a Plato recorded them. Tilak, too, in his *Arctic Home in the Vedas*, notes that the ancient Hindu texts "disclose the Polar attributes of the Vedic deities [and] the traces of an ancient Arctic calendar; while the Avesta[198] ... tells us that the happy land of *Airyana Vaêjo*, or the Aryan Paradise, was located in a region where the sun shone but once a year, and that it was destroyed by the invasion of snow and ice, which rendered its climate inclement and necessitated a migration southward," and how Greek and Germanic myths mirror such ancient Hindu-Aryan traditions.[199] If this fails to "measure up" to the scientific-rationalistic vision of *subjectivity* (i.e., "objectivity"), then this only represents a distinct worldview (i.e., a subjective worldview) that itself denies supra-rational modes of knowledge. This type of knowing, incidentally, Guénon identifies as "intellectual intuition," which stands in contrast to rationalism's "negation of any faculty of a super-individual order"; as long as such negation is sustained, the West will continue its ineluctable march into tradition-less oblivion.[200]

This, ultimately, is the crisis of which Guénon speaks, and accords with the degeneration of the *varna* (race) mixing of the Kali-Yuga, wherein old traditions are lost and peace, harmony, and justice are absent from the world. Tradition-less oblivion, however, seems precisely the *aim* of the modern age *and* scientific rationalism's subjectivity, because of their rapacious interest in reducing anything of traditional value into quantifiable parts — into mathematical equations and science experiments (Freudian psychoanalysis is a

---

[197] Guénon, *Crisis*, 36.

[198] The Avesta is the sacred text of Zoroastrianism, whose founder, of course, is Zoroaster or, more appropriately, *Zarathustra*. Incidentally, it is no accident Nietzsche bequeathed to the world his new "religion" using the (Indo-) Aryan Zarathustra as a mouthpiece.

[199] Lokamanya Bâl Gangâdhar Tilak, *The Arctic Home in the Vedas* (India: Tilak Bros., 1903), vi, 73 and elsewhere.

[200] Guénon, *Crisis*, 60.

prime example[201]; Marxism, too, apotheosizes the "permanent" revolution of the masses against any qualitative tradition; the incessant profit-hunting of the West's capitalistic world order needs no mentioning).

The devolution of man stems from the flawed, but godlike Hyperboreans comingling with lesser, indigenous simian races on earth. This notion represents the convergence of Hindu-Aryan mythos with Germanic mythos, of which each derive from the prehistoric Hyperborean legend, wherein *devas* (meaning *god* or *shining one*, reminiscent of Baldur's *fair* splendor) descend to earth as part of the Divine Order (the *Manvantara*), wherein the Divine Order is corrupted through the inherent flaws of anything sub-Trimurti (recalling Rajan — i.e., the flawed Hyperboreans), wherein subsequent caste/*varna* mixing further corrupts the Yuga, wherein after prehistoric and later catastrophes from antiquity — because of the corruption — initiate the Kali-Yuga, all leading to the modern age of historic degeneration, wherein the earth and humankind are under constant attack from humankind itself. All of this is a product of man's *fallenness*; all of this is a product of the Divine Order, the result of which will be final cataclysm and later renewal: the Ragnarök or *Götterdämmerung* of Germanic myth that spawns the new Golden Age, the Satya-Yuga.

The devolutionary worldview is the antithesis of Darwin's theory of evolution from natural selection, which is a product of the degenerate modern age of the Kali-Yuga. This is not to say that

---

[201] Interestingly, Doug Wilson christened the modern age as the "Age of Psychoanalysis," which seems an apt title ("Werewolf," *Man, Myth, and Magic*, 1995). After all, what makes the man today is no longer the man himself (i.e., not any sense of *spirit* or *will*), but so many external factors — his childhood, his environment, his relationships, and so on *ad nauseam*. *Psychoanalysis* — or *psychoanalytical* — so aptly describes the modern age because it reduces the man into factors in an equation, which is precisely the point of nearly everything modern: *quantification*. This becomes problematic because it enables and encourages the shirking of *personal responsibility*, if not courage. The problem no longer becomes the person in the mirror, but the cumulative factors that "make" the person in the mirror. Hence, the droves lining up for psychotherapy and pharmacy — why accept personal responsibility and face an uncertain life with courage when one can simply medicate into "functionality" and point to external factors as the cause of one's circumstances? It is the very essence of *modern*, wherein one can certainly hear the whispering machinations of the golems.

natural selection cannot or does not occur, but only that Darwinian *progress* via evolution is itself mythical. "That *species* show an ascending tendency is the most nonsensical assertion that has ever been made," contests Nietzsche, "There is nothing whatever to prove that the higher organisms have developed from the lower"[202] — Nietzsche here, of course, is making a *cultural* judgment. The enfeebled quantity abound and even seem protected by "cruel Nature"; on the other hand, the strong few, because of their tendency to "live dangerously," go more speedily to "decimation".[203]

The antithetical view of devolution is born of tradition and seeks to uplift man to the heights of the gods; the Darwinian view seeks to reduce man to a product of a "common ancestor" — a quantifiable factor in life's equation — and further masks its tradition-obliterating reductionism in mythical talk of some kind of progression *to* a "higher form." Yet the Darwinist devoid of tradition can only be a nihilist or a zealot, adrift in his own subjectivity that he mistakes for the objective reality he lusts to impose upon all. The Hindu-Aryan worldview, on the other hand, cares little for anything *but* subjectivity — for it is in subjectivity where one communes with the gods. In this way, the Hindu-Aryan worldview — i.e., the Hyperborean *Weltanschauung* — seeks to reverse the, at best, "dead level" of man's current "progress" through pragmatic, culturally relevant use of selection: it is only through *good breeding* that we might again reach the heights of gods.[204]

The Darwinist and her rationalistic choir boast: *We are all one!* In retort, the Hindu-Aryan can only ask: *To what end?* Ever-greater profits? Obesity epidemics? Rapid devastation of the environment? Perpetual drug addiction? Increasingly destroyed or dysfunctional families? Deteriorating mental and physical health? Nebulous or nonexistent spirituality? Ceaseless wars to secure economic interests in the name of justice and harmony? ... How do we *use* the beliefs we hold?

But correlation does not equal causation, cries the Darwinist. Ah, but who rules the roost? Whose worldview sits as the bedrock to indoctrinate the masses into their future life of greed, obesity, addiction, dysfunction, psychotherapy, etc. — i.e., their mental, physical, and spiritual disease?

---

[202] *The Will to Power*, §685.

[203] Ibid., §685.

[204] Ibid., §685, §960.

The Gods of the Godless and some Conclusions

The question always to be asked is: *Does my belief uplift, or does my belief reduce to smithereens all that was uplifted in the past, i.e., all traditions?* This is the essence of all subjectivity and, thus, objectivity, as well. Regardless of one's position, the only thing of import is the fruit of one's actions: does the belief uplift and ennoble, or does it reduce and make petty? Whether one feels an uplifting in devolution or evolution is purely subjective. Yet, in the end, if we choose to demolish that which birthed our culture, we will only face further degradation and destruction of our current world. This much is certain. The "tolerance" and "diversity" of reductionist scientific rationalism as a cultural driver is only *meant to destroy all that came before*, unless what came before manifested in the form of historical modernity, i.e., unless it manifested as that which presaged the modernistic nihilism and zealousness of contemporary times. Thus, for instance, the modern, rationalistic age exalts Socrates, the paunchy preacher of mass equality as a martyr for reason. But if we step out of our modern context, might we see Socrates and his ilk as something less heroic — something even *subversive*?

Nietzsche viewed Socrates as the inciter of the "revolt of the slaves in morality." Likewise, Ludwig Klages noted that "with him there appears for the first time the unbounded self-mastery of a racially alien and ... international rationalism. He even referred to himself as a 'citizen of the world.'"[205] Interestingly, both Nietzsche and Klages call Socrates' Greek-ness into question: "The rachitic, bulging eyes; the recessed, snub nose; the bald head and the pot belly must have made him appear hideous even to himself".[206] Nietzsche remarks that "Socrates belonged to the dregs of the populace, Socrates was rabble. One understands, one sees for oneself even now how ugly he was. But ugliness constitutes an objection. Among the Greeks, it amounted to a refutation. Was Socrates really a Greek?" Notably, Nietzsche saw the Greeks of Sparta and Alexander as closer in mental, physical, and spiritual proximity to the prehistoric Hyperboreans — because they were temporally closer, i.e., they were less *devolved*.

---

[205] Ludwig Klages, "On the Problem of Socrates," *The Biocentric Worldview* (London: Arktos, 2013), 59.

[206] Ibid., 61.

It is not surprising, then, that the rationalistic, world-leveling Socrates would have his actual Greek-ness questioned; in Nietzsche's mind, Socrates was a swine among pearls. *The weak preach equality because they lack the fortitude to raise themselves higher — they only want the higher to be torn down.*

Subversiveness is the ultimate goal of the modern, scientific-rationalistic age. *Subversiveness* continues the trend against the Hindu-Aryan worldview, which only accelerates the Kali-Yuga via caste mixing. *Varna* mixing is a means for the lower castes to simultaneously tear down the *arya* and equalize all that should never be equalized according to Hindu-Aryan traditions, or supra-rational traditions. "Our entire modern world," laments Nietzsche, "recognizes as its ideal the *theoretical man,* equipped with the highest intellectual powers and working in the service of science, a man for whom Socrates is the prototype and progenitor".[207] Someone like Socrates is — like Darwin and even Lenin after him — the god of the godless; that is, he is the martyr of all that seeks to destroy tradition in the name of some supposed *objectivity* — the facticity of humankind's universal sameness and oneness, pure objective justice and harmony obtained from an equation or science experiment! Yet the scheme is nothing more than the weak clamoring for a foothold against the strong, converting power into money, genius into committee-work, action into "scholarship," and strength of will into strength in numbers — meanwhile, *everything is subjective,* save for the objectively verifiable deceit of the usurpers, those who desire to uproot the past in favor of some utopian dream that will never happen. Meanwhile, the "tolerant" rationalists are the most intolerant of all; one simply waits for the trap to spring, for if they cannot ostracize their ideological enemies with bleats of "outrage" or "offensive," they will certainly hang them.[208]

[207] *The Birth of Tragedy*, translated by Ian Johnston, §18.

[208] Indeed, they will hang their ideological enemies — literally or metaphorically, as any would and all do. James Watson, the Nobel Laureate who had the "gall" to argue that science demonstrates the fact that there is a distinct link between race and intelligence — and was thus summarily ostracized, is a prime example. Yet recidivist criminals, for instance, escape the noose. Exploding prison populations represent too lucrative a business opportunity — *business opportunity* slinking under the euphemistic *rule of law;* and corrupt characters are effective cultural exploders, especially when

Nevertheless, time progresses, as it should, in accordance with the Divine Order of the Yuga. "We know quite well that [scientific rationalism's] triumph can never be other than apparent and transitory" and that, furthermore,

> this epoch, however distressing and troubled it may be, must also, like all the others, have its allotted place in the complete course of human development, and, indeed, the very fact of its being predicted by the traditional doctrines is indication enough that this is so.[209]

Nietzsche, too, has something to say about modernity's decay: *it should be accelerated*. For it is only in this way that the herd might truly be culled and the seeds to a renewed Hyperborean future might be sown.[210] Hindu-Aryan and Germanic traditions — i.e., Hyperborean tradition — converge with the passage of time, like a wolf eating its tail. We await, then, the inevitable and final decline of the Kali-Yuga — Ragnarök, the *Götterdämmerung* — which will lead to the new, primordial age of spirituality, which Heidegger saw as necessary for cultural endurance and what Vico called the Age of the Gods, when communities are tied together with *blood* and not theoretical abstractions of justice and harmony tied to mythical notions of progress.[211] We await the return of Kalki, of Vishnu-Wotan, the center sun of the polar north — the primeval source of all divinity, harmony, and justice.

We are Hyperboreans. Darwin is only an afterthought of a diseased age. So says the Hindu-Aryan.

∞ ∞ ∞

Hard is it on earth, | with mighty whoredom;
Axe-time, sword-time, | shields are sundered,
Wind-time, wolf-time, | ere the world falls;
Nor ever shall men | each other spare....
The sun turns black, | earth sinks in the sea,

---

crime culture is glamorized via media. *Exploded cultures make for exploitable cultures.*

209 Guénon, *Crisis*, 26-27.

210 *The Will to Power*, §898.

211 Vico, 335.

The hot stars down | from heaven are whirled;
Fierce grows the steam | and the life-feeding flame,
Till fire leaps high | about heaven itself....
Now do I see | the earth anew
Rise all green | from the waves again;
The cataracts fall, | and the eagle flies,
And fish he catches | beneath the cliffs....
In wondrous beauty | once again
Shall the golden tables | stand mid the grass,
Which the gods had owned | in the days of old...

— THE POETIC EDDA, "VOLUSPO"[212]

PRIVATE OWNERSHIP OF PUBLIC OPINION

In *The Prince*, Machiavelli talks of the value and management of perception — of *appearance* — to achieve a desired end. "It is unnecessary for a prince to have ... good qualities," he says, "but it is very necessary to appear to have them".[213] The purpose of such manipulation is to succeed in *ruling*, of which there are two ways: "one by the law, the other by force".[214] Representative governments, generally, rely on the former more heavily than the latter, but as Machiavelli notes, "because the first is frequently not sufficient, it is necessary to have recourse to the second".[215] Having recourse to force can and does mean the ability to organize and employ state-sponsored violence to maintain order; but, more often in representative governments, such as we have in the modern West and, particularly, in America, having recourse to force means the ability of the state to control the information environment, or the *narrative*. Indeed, Napoleon himself recognized the astounding power of the narrative — the manipulation of public opinion — as superior to brute force.

The ability to control the narrative, as Lippmann, a Jew from New York, observes, is largely a modern phenomenon arising from

[212] Translated by Henry Adams Bellows, 1936.
[213] Nicolo Machiavelli, *The Prince*, translated by W. K. Marriott, courtesy the Constitution Society, 85.
[214] Ibid., 83.
[215] Ibid., 83.

the increased complexity of the modern world and, in turn, gives rise to the "publicity man," or as we call it, the press secretary or public affairs official.[216] His job is to "give shape" to the "facts of modern life" so as to keep the body politic *appropriately* informed. The Austrian Jew Bernays mirrored Lippmann by imagining a future Council on Public Relations or his own "publicity man" who would "not only [know] what news value is, but knowing it, he is in a position to *make news happen*. He is a creator of events".[217] In short, in its limited capacity, given the First Amendment, the United States Government (USG) employs its own public affairs correspondent(s) to mediate facts to the body politic. Further, given the First Amendment and the subsequent Smith-Mundt Act,[218] the USG is required to honor the sanctum of the free press. This would be a fine idea if the "theory of universal competence"[219] obtained and the press could be trusted to honor its duty to the citizenry by providing relevant facts and appropriate checks and balances on its own and governmental power. The reality, though, is that human nature obtains, which is to say that, as a general rule, humans are "fatally constituted to crave that and act thus".[220] Such natural constitution becomes problematic when it drives the practice that might otherwise hold theoretical weight.

Doubly problematic is the fact that the free press, in a loosely regulated free market, becomes a means to an end rather than an end in itself; the desired corporate end in American society, for instance, is profit. Instead of being a tool (or perhaps an institution) to inform the public and check the ruling powers, the free press[221] is a means to propagate personal or corporate interests, at best, and, at worst,

---

[216] Walter Lippmann, *Public Opinion* (New York: Macmillan, 1941), 345.

[217] Edward Bernays, *Crystalizing Public Opinion* (New York: Liveright, 1934), 197.

[218] The act, originally passed in 1948, covers US State Department dissemination of public diplomacy; it restricts public diplomacy to foreign audiences, thus giving even greater informative power to the private entities governing the "free" press.

[219] Lippmann, 369. That is, the idea that citizens could be considered comprehensively capable and competent.

[220] Ibid., 189. That is, humans want (crave) one thing yet act frequently on another.

[221] Hereafter we will consider "free press" and "the media" as synonymous. Included in the media umbrella are all forms of news, networking, and media entertainment.

merely a means to increase profit for the stakeholder.[222] Thus we see in America immense informative power in the hands of a very few people or corporate entities. The media, far from realizing its theoretical potential, is merely a tool for the principal owners to fulfill self-interested agendas. This is the private ownership of public opinion.

It is necessary in a purportedly free society to explore the Machiavellian nature of public perception and its shaping, identify the grossly disproportionate control major media conglomerates have over public opinion, and speculate as to the reason behind such manipulation of public opinion, which, in turn, manipulates public behavior.

Fostering Understanding, Manufacturing Consent

Whatever we choose to call it — fostering understanding, manufacturing consent, or inculcating ideas — the ultimate point is this: public opinion is malleable. Whether we agree with Lippmann that "publicity men" must mediate our available facts in an increasingly complex world, or with Bernays that councils on public relations should shape our worldview, the fact remains that our attitudes and beliefs are up for grabs. Certainly, there exist the distal thirds of the population, rooted in their unwavering opinion, bookending the middle third — the neutral center mass upon which the streams of information train their sights. But this center mass is ripe for the taking, and its ultimate procurement will set the future course of society, whatever it may be. Indeed, the middle mass invites such informing so as to "narrow" its field of choices.[223]

In Lippmann and Bernays' time, the government was the means to capture and create public consent. For instance, both men were instrumental in — Lippmann in theorizing, Bernays in executing — America's entry into the Great War. Bernays worked closely with President Woodrow Wilson in perfectly manufacturing consent for said entry — from the playful, yet serious "Uncle Sam" posters to the patriotic war bond messages, and the sinister demonizing of the

---

[222] "As communication scholar James Curran (2000) succinctly puts it, the issue is no longer simply that the media may be compromised by their links to big business; the media *are* big business." Robert Horwitz, "On Media Concentration and the Diversity Question." *Information Society* 21, no. 3 (July 2005), 185.

[223] Edward Bernays, *Propaganda* (New York: Ig Publishing, 2005), 38.

"evil" Germans. "[During the Great War]," says Bernays, "the manipulators of patriotic opinion made use of the mental clichés and the emotional habits of the public to produce mass reactions against the alleged atrocities, the terror and the tyranny of the enemy".[224] Bernays continued his work for the USG — largely for the benefit of the Dulles brothers (one, head of the CIA, the other Secretary of State) — in securing future business for the United Fruit Company in Guatemala, work that led to decades of conflict and hundreds of thousands of casualties. Mainly when they wrote, then, the government was a principal controller of domestic information; this changed with the Smith-Mundt Act in 1948 when, barring benign recruitment videos, the USG was prohibited from intentionally trying to influence its people. Nevertheless, their principles remain the same — now, however, the primary controller of information is the so-called free press.

Before 1948, the USG's liberal-democracy did an exemplary job of appearing just so. "It would be well to be reputed liberal," says Machiavelli.[225] Liberality implies a certain lack of constraint — a liberty (freedom from) and a freedom (freedom to do). Yet how can a government profess liberality while manipulating public opinion successfully enough to garner support for an unwanted war — indeed, *two* unwanted wars — and at the president's behest, at that? It professes liberality as part of its propaganda campaign, of course. Another influential man behind the US's entry into the Great War, and partner to Bernays, was George Creel; he espoused such liberality when he said he fights, perpetuating the propaganda even post-war, "for the minds of men, for the conquest of their conviction" so that "the gospel of Americanism might be carried to every corner of the globe".[226] The appearance of liberality becomes all the more essential when governments "depend upon acquiescent public opinion for the success of their efforts and, in fact, government is only government by virtue of public acquiescence".[227]

Public Opinion

"The important thing for the statesman of our age is not so much to know how to please the public, but to know how to sway the public"

---

224 Ibid., 54.

225 Machiavelli, 74.

226 Lippmann, 47.

227 Bernays, *Propaganda*, 64.

— one might imagine this was pulled straight from *The Prince*; it is again, however, Bernays.[228] So what exactly is public opinion, if it is so important?

Keeping with Bernays, *public opinion* is the "aggregate" of individual opinions; okay, nothing spectacular there — but he continues: "public opinion is a term describing an ill-defined, mercurial and changeable group of individual judgments".[229] This is more helpful and, furthermore, gets at an important point: public opinion is malleable — or "mercurial and changeable." Ifra Iftikhar equates public opinion to something like an emergent property to the *public sphere*. "In a sense," Iftikhar states, "it is not exactly 'a place but an occurrence, a process, an event, something that arises when people interact with each on some issue and try in the presence of others to make sense of and reorient their common world.'"[230]

Public opinion, then, is like the consciousness that arises out of the neural network of the public sphere, and "as long as the communication flow is inclusive and fair, the public debate automatically filters out the 'views that cannot withstand critical scrutiny' and 'assure the legitimacy' of the rational discourse".[231] Fairness, of course, becomes the issue at hand when we have either a government operating under the veneer of liberality so as to achieve imperialistic ends, or when, post-1948, we have an alleged free press that is concentrated in the hands of the very few.

Media Concentration

"A communications system that rests in just a few hands will corrupt the freedom of speech, impair the practice of democracy, and impress an ideological pall on society".[232] Such a statement is in harmony with the Constitution and its sentiment was reiterated by the Supreme Court in 1945: "Freedom to publish is guaranteed by the Constitution, but freedom to combine to keep others from publishing is not. Freedom of the press from governmental

---

[228] Ibid., 119.

[229] Bernays, *Public Opinion*, 61.

[230] Ifra Iftikhar, "Deliberative Democracy: Effect of News Media and Interpersonal Conversation on Quality of Public Opinion." *South Asian Studies* 31, no. 1 (January-June 2016), 44.

[231] Ibid., 45 — quoting Fraser.

[232] Horwitz, 181.

interference under the First Amendment does not sanction repression by private interests".[233]

Despite such findings, however, post-1945 America has seen an ever-increasing concentration of media. Indeed, as Bernays argues, public opinion sanctions media concentration since it facilitates the desired narrowing of choices.[234] As it stands today, for instance, the overwhelming majority of the media Americans (not to mention people worldwide) are exposed to comes from just a handful of corporations/conglomerates:

- Alphabet/Google (Lawrence Page, Sergey Brin, and Ruth Porat)
    - YouTube (Susan Wojcicki)
- Comcast (Brian Roberts and David Cohen)
- Disney (recently Robert Iger [and Ichan before him], whose influence remains)
- Discovery, Inc. (David Zaslav)
    - Group Nine Media, Inc. (Ben Lerer)
    - Lionsgate (Mark Rachesky and John Feltheimer)
- AT&T (John Stankey), Warner Media (Steve Ross)
- News Corp (Rupert Murdoch)
- Hearst Communications (Steve Swartz)
- NBCUniversal (Jeff Shell)
- Hasbro (Brian Goldner)
- National Amusements (Shari "Redstone" Rothstein)
- Paramount Global (Shari "Redstone" Rothstein)
- Netflix (Marc *Bernays* Randolph and Reed Hastings)
- Meta/Facebook (Mark Zuckerberg)
    - Instagram (Adam Mosseri)[235]

"Concentrated mass media," Horwitz tells us, "are understood to shape content in ways that [influence] cultural norms".[236] Bernays,

---

[233] Ibid., Associated Press v. United States, 181.

[234] Bernays, *Propaganda*, 94.

[235] The list was compiled from multiple sources and focuses on media creation and propagation. The key figures behind the company are listed in parentheses. This list, which includes some notable subsidiaries, is not exhaustive. For a more detailed discussion of Jewish influence in the media, see Thomas Dalton's *Debating the Holocaust* (4th ed, Castle Hill, 2020).

[236] Horwitz, 182.

like Lippmann, would argue that such shaping is elemental for a democratic society — whether the shaping is done by the government or supposed elite castes is beside the point. It is necessary to guide public opinion so, essentially, the masses can stay focused on labor, or perpetuating the societal machine. There is now a "necessity for making the actions of one part of the public understandable to other sectors of the public".[237] In the modern context, the elite must be responsible for directing the public's choices: "Those who manipulate this unseen mechanism of society constitute an invisible government which is the true ruling power of our country".[238] Bernays continues:

> It remains a fact that in almost every act of our daily lives ... we are dominated by the relatively small number of persons ... who understand the mental processes and social patterns of the masses. It is they who pull the wires which control the public mind, who harness old social forces and contrive new ways to bind and guide the world.... *There are invisible rulers who control the destinies of millions.*[239]

Propaganda — or controlling the narrative — is the means by which the "invisible government" controls the public.[240] The aim is not to hammer the receiver (i.e., the listener, reader, viewer, etc.) with heavy-handed messages, but to subtly impress him so he decides "of his own accord": our invisible government "sets to work to create circumstances which will modify" the values which drive behavior.[241] In so doing, the receiver will strike upon a plan: instead of tuning in to this broadcast, he'll tune in to that; instead of buying this, he now buys that; instead of voting for that candidate, he votes for this one; instead of supporting this policy, he now supports that; instead of believing *X*, he now believes *Y*: and all "will come to him as his own idea."

Bernays uses the purposefully benign example of piano buying to illustrate the point. Instead of the propagandist saying, "Please buy

---

237 Bernays, *Propaganda*, 63.
238 Ibid., 37.
239 Ibid., 38, 61. Emphasis added.
240 Ibid., 48.
241 Ibid., 78.

a piano," he now induces the prospective buyer to say, "Please sell me a piano".[242] Meanwhile, the buyer is none the wiser. This is how Lippmann, Bernays, Zuckerberg, Rothstein, Roberts, Shell, Zelnick, Page, and the rest do their work — it is absolutely the phenomenon behind YouTube, Disney, Facebook/Meta, Netflix, etc. The receiver *begs for more*; meanwhile, now, he is subject to cultural conditioning. In Lippmann's and Bernays' time, the motion picture was the new means of message dissemination, but a few new platforms have been added since — any of which could act as viable propagation surrogate: "The American motion picture is the greatest unconscious carrier of propaganda in the world today. It is a great distributor for ideas and opinions. The motion picture can standardize the ideas and habits of a nation".[243] And indeed they have.

The Federal Communications Commission and You

Being a federal agency, the Federal Communications Commission (FCC) regulates private media enterprise. In 1934, the FCC determined that ethnic diversity in broadcasting needed to increase. With negligible success over a few decades, the FCC instituted specified "minority preference policies" in 1978. The intent behind such policy was to favor minorities (i.e., non-whites/people of European descent) in getting broadcast licenses/ownership. After some success, these preference policies faced some resistance in 1990, when Metro Broadcasting took their case against the FCC's minority preference policy to the Supreme Court. Ultimately, the Court ruled in favor of the FCC; while detailing the specifics of the case is unwarranted here, there is one significant takeaway: media ownership *does* matter.

The Court determined, in view of "a host of empirical evidence, ... that an owner's ethnicity [or race] influences the selection of topics for news coverage and the presentation of editorial viewpoint..."[244] Furthermore, and incidentally, the FCC's policies were determined to

---

[242] Ibid., 78.

[243] Ibid., 166.

[244] *Metro Broadcasting, Inc. v. Federal Communications Commission*, 1990, accessed from: Legal Information Institute, Cornell Law School. All subsequent quotations from the Supreme Court's ruling are pulled from this source. The footnotes to the case, as presented on Cornell's site, go on to cite a University of Massachusetts at Boston study that showed "significant difference in the treatment of events, depending on the race of ownership."

"impose only slight [and permissible] burdens on non-minorities" and that "innocent persons may be called upon to bear some of the burden of the remedy" of racial discrimination. The Court corroborated the FCC's findings that the "broadcast audience, regardless of its racial composition, will benefit" from the preference policies.

There were, of course, dissenting voices within the Court (Justices O'Conner, Scalia, and Kennedy) regarding the implications of race-centered policy, but this did not change the Court's ruling, nor does it change the repeatedly cited evidence that *race matters* when propagating information.

Now, if we suppose that all the above-mentioned media corporations/conglomerates are owned and operated by men and women of a *specific race* — let's suppose Jews, for instance — then we, based on the Supreme Court's findings, could also suppose that *their opinions* and, thus, *their propagated messages* — regardless of media platform — would be affected by their ethnicity, which would, in turn, *influence public opinion*. And supposing all, or even most, of the media the American public reads, views, hears, enjoys, or despises on a daily basis is filtered through private corporations/conglomerates owned and operated by Jews (or any other race), then what else does that mean for the shaping of public opinion except that it is falling exactly in line with Bernays' vision? "Ours must be a leadership democracy administered by the intelligent minority [presumably the Jews] who know how to regiment and guide the masses," Freud's nephew said.[245]

In such a situation, the public would indeed be under the sway of the very few, for very specific (and racial) reasons. Ultimately, these reasons would undoubtedly bend toward social progress, which "is simply the progressive education and enlightenment of the public mind in regard to its immediate and distant social problems".[246] Certainly, in such a situation, the public would hardly be aware that its opinions were being so "progressively guided"; in fact, the public would likely harbor resentment toward any contrary opinion, for "the so-called truths by which society lives are ... intolerantly maintained once they have been determined".[247]

---

[245] Bernays, *Propaganda*, 127. Freud's psychoanalytical, reductionist methodology greatly influenced Bernays' informational theory.
[246] Ibid., 151.
[247] Bernays, *Public Opinion*, 214.

Indeed, in such a situation, public opinion would be none the wiser and, in fact, would *beg for more* such guidance from the elite [Jewish] caste — they would even defend the elite caste at every opportunity, for they would be unwittingly conditioned to do so.[248] Of certain topics, in such a situation — for instance, any substantive critique of the elite castes or purveyors of the narrative (cultural propaganda) — dissenting members of the body politic could never speak, for fear of immediate and devastating reprisal from the elite-conditioned cogs in the societal machine, cogs conditioned to the point of dogmatic, blind loyalty; this, of course, explains quite clearly why criticism of Israel or the Jews is never long suffered in the West. Hence we come to the absurd and pervasive mantra that defines our decline: *diversity is our strength*. The world must be the elites' (i.e., the Jews') playground — they are, after all, the "Chosen Race"; pushing diversity is a sure way to subtly eradicate the world's European population, wherever they live, and ensures the largely racially homogeneous Jews can forever maintain their "elite" status amongst the deracinated, miscegenated masses.

"The future of public opinion," Ferdinand Tönnies, critic of National Socialism, remarked, "is the future of civilization.... The duty of the higher strata of society [is to] inject moral and spiritual motives into public opinion. Public opinion must become public conscience".[249] Bernays, Lippmann, and the private ownership of public opinion could not agree more.

Conclusion

The first casualty of war is truth, the apocryphal World War I-era saying goes. If we imagine war is defined with distinct lines of beginning and end, is fought solely on battlefields with trained fighters, or does not reach the senses of the average citizen, then we are mistaken. War, especially in the post-1945 era, is nothing short of *total:* states against states, states against non-states, organizations against people, and people against organizations.

---

[248] Lest they be labeled with the dreaded "anti-Semite"... And how else do we explain all the credence given to the Jewish-run/-founded Anti-Defamation League, American Civil Liberties Union, the Southern Poverty Law Center, and the American Israel Public Affairs Committee? See also Brenton Sanderson's *Battle Lines* and Kerry Bolton's *Revolution From Above.*

[249] Ibid., 217.

Each of them vies for, first, attention, then support: all instruments of national, corporate, and communal power are used; and, largely, the most benign means, as Bernays insists, are best for capturing attention and galvanizing support: the most effective means of crippling an opponent (and we are all opponents of the entity vying for our attention and support) is to dupe the opponent into crippling himself. What is benign? Facebook "likes," programming preferences, food choices, technological consumption, and so on. This is the totality of war; these are the wave-breaks of war that reach the shores of the masses. And — of this we can be certain — in war's totality, truth is mere contrivance. *The contrivers, whether we acknowledge it or not, determine the course of public opinion.*

Machiavelli, upholding deceptive manipulation as a supplement to power, would accept the modern media's grasp on the masses as legitimate. "Men are so simple," he writes, "and so subject to present necessities, that he who seeks to deceive will always find someone who will allow himself to be deceived." With so much complexity threading the contemporary world, it seems the "present necessities" dictate our predisposition to deception, thus we obsequiously seek the comfort our media provides. After all, it is far easier and more comforting to parrot what we hear from so many "experts" than it is to maintain daily life *and* investigate the truths we are so readily fed.

But it is not for the majority to seek any more than it is for the minority to find, on account of the impediment of life's complexity and mass intolerability. Instead, we are content to let the privately owned free press "arrange [our] mental pictures".[250] We are so conditioned — we beg them to sell us a piano.

A NEW PIETY: A CRITIQUE OF LIBERALISM AND DEFENSE OF FASCISM

> *We should therefore venerate the State as an earthly divinity and realize that, if it is difficult to comprehend nature, it is an infinitely more arduous task to understand the State.*
>
> — HEGEL, *PHILOSOPHY OF RIGHT*

[250] Lippmann, 42.

Introduction

In 1784, Immanuel Kant answered Reverend Johann Zöllner's question *what is enlightenment* with characteristic Liberalistic flair: enlightenment is *opportunity* and *progress*. For the Enlightenment was a watershed era of shucking the theretofore-perpetual clerical chains and a brandishing of newly won intellectual freedoms. The Enlightenment was a time of almost reverential belief in the power of the common man, and should opportunity accompany this power, then true liberty results.

This is all to say that the Enlightenment was a time of fresh and complex ideas establishing the meaning of *opportunity*, *progress*, *liberty* (*freedom*), and *Liberalism*. *Opportunity* is the chance to pursue individual aims in the name of personal freedom and societal progress; *progress* is the Hegelian notion of technical achievement over time applied to human nature; *liberty* is opportunistic self-improvement, which, by benefiting the individual, ultimately benefits society; and *Liberalism* is the synthesis of all of these concepts for its own sake. That is, *Liberalism* is a rationalistic philosophy that is worthwhile because it purportedly achieves worthwhile ends; it is good in and of itself, beyond all experience, because its concepts are virtuous. And the rising tide of Liberalism will even *a posteriori* raise all ships. So, what is enlightenment? Enlightenment is the advent of Liberalism.

Now, as in Kant's time, Liberalism is seemingly impervious to attack. Kant challenged his readers to *Sapere aude!* (Dare to know!) — and who among reasonable men would not rise to this challenge? Indeed, any failure to meet the challenge certainly means one is content to wallow in a kind of self-imposed ignorance.[251] *It stands to reason* that one would embrace Liberalism, for to deny its applicability is to deny the opportunity for the flourishing of reason itself! Kant proclaims that "free thought gradually reacts back on the modes of thought of the people, and men become more and more capable of acting in freedom. At last free thought acts even on the fundamentals of government and the state finds it agreeable to treat man, who is now more than a machine, in accord with his dignity." *Personal dignity is at stake!* Rejecting Liberalism, then, means rejecting human dignity. This, arguably, is the principal export of the Enlightenment, and it is this that the present article dares to overturn. Liberalism, left unchecked, undermines the dignity it

[251] Immanuel Kant, *What Is Enlightenment?* Berlin: *Berlin Monthly*, 1784.

purports to establish; it is not the sole source of human dignity and, indeed, should only ever be an appurtenance to socio-political theory, not a focal point — Liberalism is a condiment, not an entrée.

Give me liberty or give me death![252] — this is the clarion call of Liberalism. It assumes the primacy of liberty over life; but to this end, adherence to principle means self-immolation. For since Liberalism inevitably leads to cultural dissolution through its blind fidelity to opportunity, progress, and (personal) liberty, this fidelity *is* death. Liberalism is opposed to life itself. For out of culture, life arises. The only viable alternative to Liberalism, then, is an adopting of a new culture-building piety that satisfies primal cultural tendencies while simultaneously maintaining the cultural self-awareness born out of the Enlightenment. This new piety is seen as a symbiosis of citizen and State, recognizing the oneness of the two and, likewise, the paramountcy of the State as the utmost manifestation of life. This new piety, or citizen-State symbiosis, is understood as *fascism*.[253]

Throughout this essay *Liberalism* is capitalized. This serves two functions: (1) it recognizes Liberalism as a socio-political ethic not unlike most religions, and as such it is understood as a pervasive philosophy and capitalized like any other religion, and (2) capitalization announces to the reader its presence like any demagogue spouting praise for his adopted ideology. Additionally, throughout this article *Western* is meant to reference Euro-American, or, more precisely, Germanic cultures. Finally, *fascism*, while an ethic in the same sense as Liberalism, is not capitalized

---

[252] Patrick Henry to the Virginia Convention, 1775.

[253] That is, in *this* essay it is understood as *fascism*. This "new piety" is *spiritual traditionalism*, wherein social kinship is exalted as the vessel through which culture is birthed and sustained. Spiritual traditionalism, or citizen-State symbiosis, is Germanic in origin and conceptually *envelops* both National Socialism and Italian Fascism. The choice to use *fascism* is one of expediency; it is more readily recognized as an ideological concept, given the upheaval of the twentieth century, than *spiritual traditionalism*. Nevertheless, spiritual traditionalism is the only means of survival for one's folk; it is the creed of blood and will, of honor and loyalty. Beyond the relative umbrella of "ideological concept," it must be emphasized that National Socialism, or Hitlerism, bears little resemblance to Fascism. Hitlerism has a spiritual-philosophical aspect that Fascism never did nor ever will. Hitlerism is salvation for European folk; no other ideology carries such power.

when referring to fascism in general. This is simply to avoid the confusion of whether *Fascism* in the Italian sense is being discussed.

The Fruits of Liberalism

Foremost, Liberalism's contribution to society has been its fundamental conception of progress. *Progressivism* is synonymous with *Liberalism* and *progressive* is synonymous with *liberal*. The notion of *progress* has awoken and continues to awaken Western society as a whole from its "dogmatic slumbers," leading to our presumptive ongoing Age of Enlightenment. We are progressing toward *something* from somewhere. We know where we have been, for what is past is prologue, yet what is this *something* toward which we progress?

For Kant, the Enlightenment's flag bearer, we are progressing toward wholesale human dignity. This dignity will eventually arise when the social opportunities for free thought mirror the natural inclination men have to pursue individual ends. That is, when societies (or States) themselves accommodate man's urges to think freely, only then will "free thought gradually [react] back on the modes of thought of the people, and men [will] become more and more capable of acting in freedom".[254] Dignity, then, is predicated on opportunity; opportunity, in kind, is predicated on the inherent dignity men possess as free thinkers. The circularity of this argument is not lost and we will return to it below; for now, we continue.

Hegel's theory of progress, too, was profoundly influential on post-Enlightenment (i.e., Western) Liberalism. If we imagine the first Model-T Ford compared to even the worst of cars in production today, we see a distinct technical progress; the worst car today is technically better and more efficient than the best car one hundred years ago.

Thus, we need only to continue seeking out improvements and applying them where appropriate to move from a rudimentary baseline to a significantly better point in the future. For Hegel, our final destination — i.e., what we are progressing toward — is *Geist* (*spirit* of a people, or *mind*) understanding itself, which amounts to complete liberty. We might see how this influences Western thought to this day if we understand how increased opportunity for freedom of thought — for increased rationality — for all might lend itself to greater liberty; recalling Kant: "men [will] become more and more

[254] Kant, 1784.

capable of acting in freedom." The Hegelian dialectic moves from beginning (the oppression of ignorance) to end (freedom of rationality) through a series of socio-ideological shifts from thesis (the baseline) to antithesis (the reaction) to synthesis (the counteraction and new baseline) — each iteration building upon the remnants of the preceding. We get from Kant and Hegel, then, theories of progress that yet inform our current interpretation of Liberalism.

What modern Western society might be progressing toward is an ever-better version of itself, in the vein of the Hegelian dialectic, through individual and thus, social, improvement. Kant's *freedom of thought* is the objective here. We become free through rationality; we become rational through opportunity. If we examine Kant's argument for the value of enlightenment, though, this is what we find[255]:

> 1. Men are free to pursue enlightenment. (Implied by the following: "Enlightenment is man's emergence from his self-imposed nonage.")
> 2. Most men often do not pursue enlightenment, despite freedom, because it pains or inconveniences them in some way. ("Laziness and cowardice are the reasons why such a large part of mankind gladly remain minors all their lives, long after nature has freed them from external guidance.")
> 3. Yet enlightenment is inevitable if men are given more freedom. ("And this free thought gradually reacts back on the modes of thought of the people, and men become more and more capable of acting in freedom. At last free thought acts even on the fundamentals of government and the state finds it agreeable to treat man, who is now more than a machine, in accord with his dignity.")

There is incongruity in this argument beyond the circularity mentioned above. For men do not, according to Kant, *already* pursue freedom. Men are lazy and cowardly and more than content to remain a part of the "unthinking multitude".[256] Essentially, this is Kant's argument, which is to say, Liberalism's argument: people are not capable of meaningful progress, but *will* progress if we continue to create the conditions for progress. It is nonsensical at best.

[255] Kant's argument in *What Is Enlightenment?*
[256] Kant, 1784.

Providing opportunity to those who would not take it in hopes of creating an end state wherein the opportunities *are* taken for the betterment of all is an exercise in illogic unbecoming of even the most indolent thinker.

What should matter to us is "not the *concept* of life, which the ostrich-philosophy of [Liberalism] propounds," but "the hard reality of living".[257] This reality suffers not "those dreams [of Liberalism] which will always remain dreams".[258] If such dreams are suffered, then the burdened society becomes logically unsustainable: it pursues the course of any addict and repeatedly commits the same error expecting different results. "It must be stated ... that this [Liberalistic] society ... is sick, sick in its instincts and therefore in its mind. It offers no defense. It takes pleasure in its own vilification and disintegration".[259] So we must ask: *to what end?* Beyond any false and illogical hope that those who reject opportunity will take it if given the chance, why does Liberalism cling to the addict's course? The answer is *individualism*.

Individualism is the fruit of the Enlightenment, which is to say, the fruit of Liberalism. "Have the courage to use your own understanding": this is the motto of Western civilization's Enlightenment.[260] But more than simply the refrain of individuals themselves, this became and is the refrain of Western governments everywhere. And governments have dutifully created the conditions under which a few men have thrived. These men, in turn, have raised the tide of understanding upon which all men ride. Individualism carries with it a concomitant independence of action. And the individualistic opportunities, provided by Liberalistic governments, have benefited the independent few who have taken advantage of them. As a philosophy, Liberalism cannot be parceled out; it must be granted wholesale to the masses. By definition it is a philosophy *for* the masses.

Thus, it is not merely the governments or competent few who have benefited from the attendant independence of action. *All* have been given this independence of action; and this independence, this *individualism*, has been inculcated into Liberalistic cultures in such a

---

[257] Oswald Spengler, *The Decline of the West* (New York: Vintage Books, 2006), xxiv.
[258] Ibid., 8.
[259] Ibid., 118.
[260] Kant, 1784.

way that it is now woven into the fabric of their being — i.e., it is part of the Liberalistic identity. Individualism stands as the very thing that unites us in a Liberalistic culture, and it will ultimately spell our ruin. For the "unthinking multitude" do not wish to use their opportunity for the benefit of society, for the *State*; instead, they use their individualism for petty distractions. Alexis de Tocqueville foresaw a type of tyranny that would arise from such an indiscriminate individualism:

> I seek to trace the novel features under which despotism may appear in the world. The first thing that strikes the observation is an innumerable multitude of men all equal and alike, incessantly endeavoring to procure the petty and paltry pleasures with which they glut their lives. Each of them, living apart, is as a stranger to the fate of all the rest — his children and his private friends constitute to him the whole of mankind; as for the rest of his fellow citizens, he is close to them, but he sees them not — he touches them, but he feels them not; he exists but in himself and for himself alone; and if his kindred still remain to him, he may be said at any rate to have lost his country. Above this race of men stands an immense and tutelary power, which takes upon itself alone to secure their gratifications, and to watch over their fate. That power is absolute, minute, regular, provident, and mild. It would be like the authority of a parent, if, like that authority, its object was to prepare men for manhood; but it seeks, on the contrary, to keep them in perpetual childhood...[261]

In large part, this is the self-imposed tyranny of which Kant speaks; it certainly arises from the same reasons: laziness and cowardice. Three hundred years into the Age of Enlightenment — *the Age of Liberalism* — we care more about media plotlines and sports scores than we do about the sustenance of our State, our *culture*. This is what we do with our independence of action; we are content to remain the "unthinking multitude." Western societies have become, not units of shared experiences and values, but conglomerations of

---

[261] Alexis de Tocqueville, *Democracy in America*, translated by Henry Reeve (London: Oxford University Press).

individuals unconcerned with the State that gives them life. This is directly the fault of Liberalism. The people, the individuals, represent the State and vice versa; the State represents the nation; the nation represents the culture, and culture gives life. Not supporting the State is tantamount to not supporting life. Liberalism undercuts life at every turn, though it claims to support it.

As a philosophy of dreams and illogic, Liberalism, too, is a philosophy of the Romantic; not only must the dutiful liberal put faith in his fellow man, whom he distrusts and despises, he must also trust himself to benefit the State *that tells him to focus only on himself*; and "a faith that is stronger than any proofs is the distinguishing mark of the Romantic".[262]

Robert Bellah notes that the strain of individualism is so entrenched into American society that it negatively affects our social solidarity. Socio-economic classes are pit against each other vying to maintain or improve status: the affluent aim to keep the dregs from climbing their coattails; the impoverished harbor resentment toward both the affluent and sometimes even their fellow impoverished. The largest class — the middle class — or what Bellah calls the "anxious class," is fixed in a "frenzy of effort [trying to] preserve its standing... In the anxious class the crisis of civic membership takes the form of disillusion with politics and a sense of uncertainty about the economic future so pervasive that concern for individual survival threatens to replace social solidarity".[263] Such individualism utterly cripples any hope of *social solidarity*, or civic membership — what Bellah calls "that critical intersection of personal identity with social identity."

Instead of a sense of community with our neighbor — a solidarity founded on the strengthening of shared culture through duty to the State (i.e., duty to the culture of kinship) — we are left with an individualism marred by zero-sum stakes, where the loser is shamed and trampled and the winner furthers his own self-interest and the interests of those who establish the rules of the Romantic game, those whom Kant calls the *guardians*. The State, as protector of culture and thus protector of life, does not factor into the zero-sum game.

---

[262] Spengler, *Decline*, 12.

[263] Robert N. Bellah, et al. *Habits of the Heart: Individualism and Commitment in American Life* (Berkeley, CA: University of California Press, 2007), xxi.

The "unthinking multitude," through self-interested individualism, is the condition by which others "set themselves up as guardians".[264] The guardians of Liberalism initiate and close the circle of logic by establishing the conditions of their rulership. Kant argues that the "proper density" of human nature lies in progress. This would be good if men could be trusted to use their understanding to progress; for the understanding, unless it is ill, can be trusted. Yet men cannot be trusted; again, according to the definers of Liberalism, who established a definition we only inherit, men everywhere malinger in the comfort of idleness. Kant's argument, then, only reveals an ideology that belies its true motives: to transfer "guardianship" over the "unthinking multitude" to the bastions of Liberalism, of so-called enlightenment, of so-called freedom. We have already seen the incongruent logic of this line of thinking. This incongruity — infinite progress through allowance of increased opportunity for men who do not accept it — creates a power vacuum to be filled by the new guardians of "freedom" — i.e., those who use the guise of progress for all — to establish a self-serving hive of the many supporting the very few. Unchecked *individualism*; *self-interest*; *self-service*: these are the hallmarks of ill understanding.

Fundamental to the idea of Liberalism is the notion of *progress*. Inherent in the idea of progress is the notion that men, if given the chance, can *self-improve*. So, the distilled argument is this: Men are a cypher or non-contributing because they are lazy, despite opportunity; and the cure to this laziness is still more freedom and opportunity to self-improve. This is the argument behind some good, but still more ills. It is the ideology behind unbridled *individualism*: "give the people freedom and they'll choose what's best," cry the proponents of Liberalism. But this strangely ignores the inherent pessimism of Liberalism itself: that most people are incapable of using the opportunities given to them to their advantage, i.e., they are incapable of self-improvement. Liberalism, then, is the unshakable begging of the question.

It can be said that the structure of contemporary Western societies — particularly American society — is a distinct *lack* of structure. We are not *America, the beautiful*; we are *America, the support group*. Instead of that shared sense of civic membership — a feeling of community aimed toward a common goal — we are simply

264 Kant, 1784.

a mass of self-oriented passers-by and hangers-on. It has been noted that Westerners, and Americans in particular, exist merely "alone together"; this support-group phenomenon is typified by "individuals who 'focus on themselves in the presence of others.'"[265]

Rabid and rampant individualism is a piece of the problem. A lack of appreciation for the State is still another and more significant piece. Civic awareness and socio-cultural (i.e., national-community) contribution cannot be had if a State ignores itself, which is precisely what States founded on Liberalistic principles do to their detriment. We are detached from the State unlike ever before. If the State is the political manifestation of the nation, then what does the State of an individualized mass of citizens — the society of *no* pervasive civic membership — look like? *A shattered mirror? Schizophrenic? A corporatized union?* Whatever the perception of the Liberalistic State, it cannot be internally healthy; for vitality spawns from culture, and culture — the *spirit* and *fire* that gave rise to the kinship of the nation — is supplanted for so many empty structures that ape a former glory in the Liberalistic State: *individualism* over *nationalism*, *specialization* over *cultured striving*, *equality* over *triumph*, *indolence* over *power*.

The source of a nation's strength is the sense of partnership felt amongst a people within a certain culture and the solidarity they feel in achieving their aims.[266] The source of a State's strength is the consolidation of disparate national passions into an overarching pride in the fatherland. This pride, and thus, State-borne strength, is only undermined by Liberalistic policies mistaking the source of their strength as the quantity of people they shelter as opposed to the quality of support they alienate. "The Liberal State is a mask behind which there is no face; it is a scaffolding behind which there is no building".[267] *Lack of structure* as the ideological structure is merely a mask.

The Rationalistic and Practical Failings of Liberalism

The pseudo-logical structure of Liberalism stands both as its greatest strength and weakness. It presents a stunning façade of infinite and inevitable progress, yet has no substantial way to sustain such progress. First, Liberalism assumes what it hopes to prove. It assumes

---

[265] Bellah, xxiii.

[266] Max Weber, *From Max Weber: Essays in Sociology*, translated by Hans Heinrich Gerth & Charles Wright (New York: Oxford University Press, 1946), 176.

[267] Benito Mussolini.

the product its policy "will" produce; *people are good*, it claims, *we'll prove it by making people good*. This runs in the same vein as the question-begging mentioned above — that is, offering people who do not often choose to take the *necessary opportunities* to improve still *more opportunity* is essentially *waste*. And it is State (collective) resources that are being wasted.

The *Liberalistic* State, however, does not care; for it believes in the façade it shows to the multitude. How can it not? The spark ignited in the Enlightenment led to immediate good; apt people previously fettered were becoming free to pursue unexplored or long-dormant ends, and the benefit to society was tremendous. Advances were had in nearly every field and quality of life was improving rapidly and seemingly everywhere. Rationality was becoming tacitly understood as mankind's savior — a real savior with tangible results. It was the *Age of Reason*, the *Age of Liberalism*. If Liberalism enhances the spread of reason, and if reason has given so much good, then Liberalism must good. Yet the Enlightenment's agents could not have foreseen what would ensue. Rationality's creep has never slowed, and now it threatens the cultural foundations of Western society. We pursue progress merely for the sake of progress, as if it were a *good* in and of itself; yet past performance is not indicative of future results, especially when reason has supplanted culture. As with any economic bubble, Liberalism does not have the intrinsic value to sustain its heretofore progress. Bubbles and façades are attractive, but they are only illusory. The *reality* must eventually be brought to bear.

What is this reality? If we look back to the oft-contested *state of Nature*, we can only come to one viable conclusion: Hobbes was right. The state of Nature was "a War of all men, against all men".[268] Diversity itself — diversity of life, diversity of opinion — is Hobbes' vindicator. Difference — from mundane to world-shaking — is diversity. *That there exists difference at all signifies more than any philosophical argument ever could that Hobbes, in his pragmatic pessimism, was correct*. The Hobbesian state of Nature was not much more than self-interest run amok. Indeed, "every man is desirous of what is good for him, and shuns what is evil, [especially] Death; and this he doth, by a certain impulsion of nature, no less than that whereby a Stone moves downward".[269]

---

[268] Thomas Hobbes, *De Cive*, London: Royston, 1651, 11.

[269] Ibid., 12.

To that end, the first sense of *natural* justice is that which preserves one's self and the extensions of one's self; that is, justice is the preservation of life. Ultimately, this fear of death stands as the catalyst for the very first social cohesions. There is value in banding together for a common purpose, even if that incipient purpose was *mere* survival. Yet no society is ever banded together for anything *but* mere survival, so say even the Darwinists. Liberalism would have us believe that we socialize for the sake of progress, but this is only claptrap. Just as any head of state will argue that there are no allies, but only enduring national interests, we can be certain there is no prioritized progress in lieu of survival. Survival is just as primal as war; and society is just as primal as the state of Nature. "Conflict," Spengler contends, "is the original fact of life," and because of this, human history is war history, "but peace is also part of it, for it is the continuation of war with different means".[270]

Thus, if we are honest, we might liken war to survival and peace to progress. Yet one of these is woven into the fabric of life and one is merely incidental — as incidental as a passing cloud before the ever-burning sun. Peace and progress are not the steady states, they are the reprieve; war and survival are man's truest states, i.e., man's *natural* states. If self-preservation is man's most natural state, then it is also society's most natural state; for society is the embodiment and enhancement of the individual man. Thus, if preservation of life is man's highest will, then it is also society's highest will. Preservation of life, then, is what we can call the *general* will, or *collective* will. Further, preservation of life is preservation of society; preservation of society is preservation of (shared) culture; preservation of culture is preservation of nation; and preservation of nation is preservation of State. It can be said with no reservations, then, that the general will is preservation of the nation, preservation of the State. Liberalism is quick to retort that progress in the name of liberty is closer to the general will, for all men are born free and desire their inalienable right to that freedom, but Liberalism's progress cannot result in freedom if the culture from which it springs is gutted and left for dead. If we prioritize progress in the name of liberty *over* self-preservation, as Liberalism does, then we walk the path to ruin: we seek allies instead of national interests while others lie in wait; we hope the passing cloud saves us from drought.

---

[270] Spengler, *The Hour of Decision* (Honolulu, HI: University Press of the Pacific, 2002), 22, 35. Echoing Clausewitz here.

Just as a man in the state of Nature must engage in a *war of all against all*, cultures, as embodiments of the man, must do the same. *Cultural diversity, unless it is a sideshow, is poison to the State.* Assimilation is critical for cultural self-preservation when outside cultures are introduced; likewise, cultures must guard against foreign influence to preserve their State. Liberalism praises cultural diversity as the lifeblood of progress and freedom; in this way, Liberalism deprioritizes and attempts to delegitimize cultural sanctity as necessary for life. Likewise, in this way, Liberalism ignores the tension and conflict that inevitably arises when diversity is introduced. Diversity is at the core of man's state of Nature, and this condition is "nasty, brutish, and short".[271] The result of this tension and conflict, from a Hegelian position, is *synthesis*; yet synthesis implies the death of the thesis (or the death of the original position from introduction of the *antithesis*) and stands against the general will of the people, the will of self-preservation.

Yet Liberalism is not entirely damaging to man, society, or the State. Instead of being heaved upon an overwhelmed people as a socio-political philosophy, however, Liberalism is best apportioned as smelling salts to the unconscious.

Liberalism as Appurtenance

One cannot step in the same river twice: this is Heraclitus' famous maxim. It points to the omnipresence of life's changeableness, and to ignore or vilify change is to do the same to life. Liberalism, exponents might say, only capitalizes on the inevitability of change and seeks to incorporate the rush of life and diversity flowing therefrom. Indeed, we often hear that stagnation is death, though this undoubtedly stems from some ancient wisdom warning against the hazards of drinking or living around still waters instead of any socio-political pragmatism. However, any overpowering wave can be deadly — perhaps deadlier than stagnation. It might be useful to stick with our water analogy here. For just as the impending tsunami draws us in with its strange awesomeness, Liberalism, through the Enlightenment, captivated us with its rapid and incredible betterment of society.

Yet while we were drawn in, standing wonderstruck on the shores of infinite progress, the leveling wall of homogeneity was barreling toward us. We bob and eddy now in the ever-rising and

---

[271] Hobbes, *Leviathan.*

ever-forceful ideology of Liberalism — our heretofore way of life dismantled, our relics and memories of the glory that buried us far beneath the silt under the shimmering wave tops.

Like change, then, Liberalism is useful in moderation. Going beyond moderation is detrimental to society, culture, and the State. So where do we draw the line, and how much Liberalism is acceptable? Liberalism is good insofar as its concomitant rationality makes us aware of the necessity of civic membership and the essentialness of citizen-State symbiosis that represents a people exerting the general will. Such rationality should be accepted insofar as it wakes the masses from their unthinking and dogmatic slumbers of servitude to an equally unthinking rulership and creates in them a sense of awareness delimiting the extent of liberty and progress. That is, Liberalism and its attendant rationality are good insofar as they lead to the mass acceptance of citizen-State symbiosis and rejection of the notion of infinite progress in favor of the prioritization of the Hobbesian state of Nature, both on an individual and cultural level.

Even Kant, our emblem of the Enlightenment, seemed to understand this:

> Only the man who is himself enlightened, who is not afraid of shadows, and who commands at the same time a well-disciplined and numerous army as guarantor of public peace — only he can say what [the sovereign of] a free state cannot dare to say: "Argue as much as you like, and about what you like, but obey!"[272]

Become aware, Kant says, recognize the Hobbesian state of Nature, and in this capacity, serve the State. This perhaps seems to counter the Liberalistic message Kant espouses overall, but likely what is happening is a reimagining of Kant's initial meaning and not any internal contradiction in his thought; for Kant only ever wanted the "perpetual constitution" to be abolished; that is, he argued against the citizenry's *freedom from* ignorance. Moreover, Kant here has a different meaning of *freedom* than modern thinkers might interpret. The freedom of which he speaks refers to the freedom to publicly discuss; further, this freedom is ultimately guided or determined by a "monarch," so as to preserve the traditions and cultures essential to society.

---

[272] Kant, 1784.

Elsewhere in his essay, Kant cleverly paints into a corner any man who would disagree with him, for if you disagree, you are plainly unenlightened. One has no doubt of the excitement that permeated the beginning of the Enlightenment, nor can we doubt the reason why a fundamental hope and belief in progress got its start. Thinking people could not but agree with Kant during this era, but we in contemporary times have the luxury of seeing the corruption and cultural decay wanton Liberalism has wrought. And with this luxury comes the responsibility of changing course; that is, *using the gifts of the Enlightenment to reject the wholesale application of its fruits.*

What Western Liberalism lacks is the discernment Kant makes between public and private freedom. By "public freedom," Kant means to extoll the possibility of citizens making reasoned choices in regards to governance; yet this extolment is tempered by the constant vigilance of its too liberal use: "too much emphasis on reason, when not properly guided, may lead to the gradual disappearance of traditions and customs. It can easily slide into moral solipsism, since every person will be sole judge of his moral actions".[273] By "private freedom," Kant means only the judgments one makes "in a civic post that has been entrusted to him".[274] In this respect, private freedom is ancillary to civic service; one makes private judgments insofar as they make contextual sense in service to the State.

Instead of this discernment, Western Liberalism seems to only understand the nebulous concept of *freedom* as sometimes what we ought to do, sometimes what we want to do. Because Western Liberalism is predominantly founded on the principle that the State exists to serve the citizens, freedom is too often a bottom-up ideation: the (minority of) citizens determine what they *want*, so the Liberalistic State declares the (majority of) citizens *ought to* comply. This is the deference to progress over the Hobbesian state of Nature in practice. It is dissonant with reality and untenable over any extended period of time; much the same as we would never accept a tsunami as a means to landscape our property, we should not accept Liberalism as a means of governance.

---

[273] Robert Antonio, "Kant's 'What Is Enlightenment?' Then and Now," 16 May 2012.

[274] Kant, 1784.

Citizen-State Symbiosis: An Alternative

Determining what ought to be done is a synthesis of reason, pragmatism, and reality. *Enforcing* what ought to be done is the work of the State. We use reason retrospectively to determine why we pragmatically use the systems we do; if our reality is dissonant with reason, we must adjust our reason. If reality points to the Hobbesian state of Nature, then we must establish a rationale that apportions life and justice accordingly. When our reason accords with reality, we must make pragmatic decisions to effectively apportion the virtues life appoints as primal. This process can be understood as the citizen-State symbiosis.

Out of the Enlightenment arose multiple systems by which we, as citizens, might gain symbiosis with each other and the State. Primarily, attempts at symbiosis were established through the reemergence of liberal ("Western") democracy and the inceptions of communism and fascism.

Of these three, democracy has met with the most brilliant success. This is due in no small part to the emphasis it places on the primacy of appeasing the minority, which ultimately translates into individualism. "*People*," Spengler says, "no longer [means] the community of the whole nation, but that section of the city masses which set up in opposition to this community".[275] This type of governance relies on the self-interests of citizens to drive social, political, and economic policies. Because work oriented toward furthering the ideology of self-interest (filling niches to satisfy the demands of the individuals within society) is rewarded — typically monetarily — this type of democracy is, so far, self-sustaining; citizens in this society are interested in helping themselves, and through this self-interest help advance the social agenda.

This Liberalistic system is only *so far* self-sustaining because it is destined to disintegrate; myriad interests do not equate to furthering the collective interest or general will. While self-interest is certainly *part* of the Hobbesian state of Nature and, thus, later manifested in the general will, which explains its ideological success, on the societal or cultural level in the Liberalistic State it equates to dissipation of State energies: the only glue of society is principally aimed at promoting the interest of the individual, which amounts to no glue at all. At the risk of belaboring the point, a union based on individual

---

[275] Spengler, *Decision*, 121.

interests can only eventually languish, for there are no longer viable national (*völkisch*) interests.

So, one of three possibilities awaits the inevitable fall of Western democracy (assuming one of these has not already been implemented):

1. An authoritarian police state will assume power, enforcing and enhancing the predatory internationalist ideology that exacerbated previous cultural collapse.
2. Utter social collapse. Power will be divided among splintered domestic cultures or assumed by foreign cultures.
3. An authoritarian State devoted to the propagation of shared and perceptibly superior culture with a sense of racial respect among various peoples will arise. This State will be founded on a shared and understood civic consciousness. The State and its citizens will enjoy a symbiotic relationship *founded on* and *contributing to* the glory and superiority of the State and the *kindred* spirit out of which it arises.

Given the decades-long inculcation of Liberalistic individualism in Western societies only the first two seem conceivable. Livy noted this about Rome more than two thousand years ago and it still reverberates with us: "Note how the standards of morality and discipline, little by little, and then ever more rapidly, descend headlong into the present until we can endure neither our vices nor their remedies".[276] We might breathe a sigh of relief if we imagine that every generation thinks this way about succeeding generations — the general decay of standards might seem to us a common refrain, and one which pales in comparison to the force of progress.

However, it becomes more concerning if we consider Livy's observation in a Viconian or Spenglerian context — a context bound up with the recorded rise and fall of various cultures, the Greco-Roman culture being just one of them. In this cyclical context, cultures have a distinct beginning, middle, and end; and the end is concomitant with societal unravelling and degeneration, the desperation of which we hear in Livy's account before the fall of Rome. To counter this apparent degeneration, modern man has devised another ideology: communism.

---

[276] Livy, *Praefatio*.

Arising out of the Hegelian dialectic reimagined through Marx, the communist ideology sought to reintroduce man to *meaning*. The capitalism that meshes so well with liberal-democracy — vis-à-vis the two ideologies' vehement dependence on self-interest at the lowest level — often alienates the worker from his life through, in part, the specialization it requires for maximum efficiency; instead of seeing himself in his work, the worker instead is little more than a living, breathing machine repeatedly hammering out parts, not wholes.

Capitalism, then, disrupts the natural tendency of man to find meaning through living and working. Marxism, like democracy, is a Liberalistic philosophy. Spengler notes that Marxism and democracy each represent merely the "the dictatorship of the bourgeoisie ... [and] that is all that Liberalism sets out to be"[277]; it is only that Marxism takes the Liberalistic principles further to accommodate the citizens subsequently wronged by capitalism; Marxism intensifies the attack on culture initiated by capitalism through its doctrine of class war (not to mention *international* or *borderless* socialism), which is "an overthrow. Not the constitution of anything new, but the destruction of what exists. It is an aim without a future. It is the will-to-nothing. Utopian programs are designed only for the spiritual bribery of the masses".[278]

And this utopian agenda has as its predecessor the mother of all borderless utopias: Christianity. Spengler goes so far as to call Christianity the "grandmother" of Liberalism.[279] It is difficult to argue against the similarities, foremost among them the desire to establish comprehensive equality. The problem becomes, then, whether we discuss democracy or Marxism, that at its root, Christianity — indeed *all* institutionalized religions — seek to divorce the citizens from the State. "*My kingdom is not of this world* is the deep saying which is true of every religion and is betrayed by every church.... All young sects are at bottom hostile to State and property, class and rank, and are attracted by universal equality" — Spengler here observes that *young* sects are hostile to the State, but this does not discount long-institutionalized religions within Liberalistic societies; for the progressive attitude, which often attracts the ever-marginalized youth, sustains, in turn, the youth of the sect.

---

[277] Spengler, *Decision*, 137.
[278] Ibid., 138.
[279] Ibid., 129.

More to the point at hand, however, is the reality that Liberalistic principles, under the guise of Christianity, usurped even the Roman Empire. Once a behemoth of paganism and Statism, Rome

> was oppressed by a new species of tyranny; and the persecuted sects became the secret enemies of their country.... The active virtues of society were discouraged; and the last remains of military spirit were buried in the cloister: ... the soldiers' pay was lavished on the useless multitudes of both sexes who could only plead the merits of abstinence and chastity.[280]

Gibbon goes on to warn that the threat of undermining of State power — even from seemingly innocuous sources — is an enduring one. And "it is the duty of a patriot," he says, "to prefer and promote the exclusive interest and glory of his native country" to guard against such a threat.[281] Liberalism, in any form, seeks to prioritize the individual's allegedly inherent worth over the function and ambitions of the State. To do this, Liberalism must tear down the State to the level of "dregs" and make the State subservient to the citizens. *Ask not what your country can do for you...* — but President Kennedy is interrupted by the throngs, for this is *precisely* what they ask; the State is mere extension of *their* self and consequently must acquiesce to the individual will. Democracy and communism, then, as bastions of Liberalism, remove all power from the State, and in doing this they take life from man.

While certainly not a bastion of Liberalism, fascism, too, arose out of the Enlightenment. It was an ideology generated as the antithesis to Liberalism's thesis. Years into the Age of Reason, citizens throughout Europe — yet particularly in Italy and Germany — began to see the statelessness of Liberalism: here was an ideology that claimed to transcend the State through its vision of progress and freedom. And through this transcendence, the cultural core of the people was being eroded; the response to this erosion was clear: "[we must be rid] of everything that has been created artificially, and [promote] ... the growth of what will sprout up out of the old soil

---

[280] Edward Gibbon, *The Decline and Fall of the Roman Empire* (New York: Everyman's Library, 2010), vol. 4, 120-121.
[281] Ibid., 121.

once it has been cleansed of rubbish: the roots of our being are still alive".[282] The *rubbish* was the foreign body that carried alien rootlessness and the Liberalism that welcomed it. Fascism would have never existed without Liberalism, it is true; but this is only because Liberalism necessitated fascism. Citizens who saw their civic membership being undercut by international-socialistic and capitalistic values felt within a swell of cultural pride to defend the nation against those who would, at best, ignore the State, and, at worst, do the State harm. Fascism was the attempt to create the citizen-State symbiosis necessary to fend off cultural decay.

It has been said that this inherent pride in parent culture coupled with the distrust or open dislike of foreign cultures means that fascism — in any manifestation — must be essentially racist.[283] This "racism" need not be biological or Darwinian; one is simply seen as "racist" if one has pride in one's own culture over and above any others. Yet this is missing the larger picture; fundamentally the citizen-State symbiosis, especially as found in fascist ideology, is about preserving the strength of the shared national identity — it is national defense, national security. Fascism need not be about deriding foreign cultures because they are inferior; they are simply not *one's own* culture and should not be held in such high esteem. A man does not go around hating other sets of parents; he only trusts infinitely more the parents who gave him life; the same is true of culture.

That said, however, fascism can certainly be *seen* as "racist"; National Socialism is the prototype for this. Indeed, Alfred Rosenberg dealt with such accusations incessantly; yet he reiterated shortly before his murder at Nuremberg:

> the veneration of Germanic blood does not imply contempt for other races but, on the contrary, racial respect. Since races, as the core of nations, are created by Nature, the very respect for Nature itself demands respect for such creations. The purpose of the large-scale development of peoples is the juridical recognition of racially conditioned families of people in their own homelands. Style, customs, language, are the

[282] Paul de Lagarde, "The Grey International," *Deutsche Schriften* (Jena: Eugen Diederichs, 1944), 337.
[283] Roger Griffin, *Fascism* (Oxford: Oxford University Press, 1995), 7.

> manifestation of different souls and peoples; and just as these cannot be mixed without a resultant deterioration of their purity, so men, as their embodiment, and to whom they belong organically and spiritually, cannot intermingle.[284]

And, unfortunately, because of its "audacity" to be proud of its heritage and historical situation as the fantastic "loser of World War II," National Socialism has been burned into popular consciousness as *the* example of fascism, therefore negating fascism's chances of being taken seriously on any large scale and amplifying Liberalism's validity in the West. Liberalism beat "the Nazis"; thus, it has *carte blanche* to do what it deems best.

In the years since the Great Recession, however, Westerners — and particularly Americans — have begun "to understand that our common life requires more than an exclusive concern for material accumulation".[285] We are beginning to see through the façade to the emptiness underneath. The capitalism concomitant with liberal democracy has started to chip away at its own presumed integrity, and the integrity of its rider. Perhaps through the nicks and cracks we, like Spengler, will notice "among the gravest signs of the decay of State authority is the fact that ... economics [has come] to be considered more important than politics".[286] No longer can citizens of the West determine when their governments are deciding in the sake of *national* security or economic interests. And this, perhaps as much as all else, reveals the importance of citizen-State symbiosis. We do not trust or do not know (which is the same as not trusting) the Liberalistic State to act honorably on our behalf. This trust, through social renewal, is what fascism tried to establish.

Citizen-State symbiosis, since the dawn of the Enlightenment, has seen three major manifestations: democracy, communism, and fascism. The former two, being born of Liberalism, have sought to free man from his alienation from himself: liberal-democracy aimed to liberate man from his ignorant indolence, exacerbated by the perpetual constitutions of tradition; communism aimed to unshackle man from his mindless specialization, instigated by the austere individualism necessitated by democracy. Fascism, on the other hand,

---

[284] Alfred Rosenberg, *Memoirs* (Spandau, 1945).

[285] Bellah, 295.

[286] Spengler, *Decision*, 40.

emerged as the antithetical response to Liberalism. It understood the need for civic membership and shared national identity. The implicit understanding of citizen-State symbiosis within fascism places it ahead of its Enlightenment peers. Liberalism, expressed most fully in democracy and communism, espouses the ideation that increased individual liberty leads to the utopia of infinite progress. While this is a noble concept, what ensues is either rampant individualism or general squalor.

Any ideology we choose should fit with our general aptitude as a species. Even aside from its logical failings, Liberalism has proven itself as unequivocally incapable of reflecting the moral capacity of man. Is incremental improvement of human nature possible in the same sense as Hegel's technical achievement over time? Arguably, it is not. While technologies advance, man is unchanged; a desperate man in 2030 CE will act much the same as a desperate man in 5000 BCE. We are physiologically driven, which is to say we exist, not in any rationalistic vacuum, but in the Hobbesian state of Nature.

Now, for argument's sake, it has been noted that "a true and just society can never be based on sheer force, for right can never be equated with might",[287] but the man who ignores or discounts the "right" born of intellectualism can always defeat the man *constrained* by what he ought to do and *restrained* by what he ought not to do. What makes him "right" is *precisely* his might or lack of scruples. What vindicates his action is the final and absolute fact of death. Such ethereal notions of "virtue" and "righteousness" are subject to the manipulations of the amorphous thought of the victors. "What is truth?" Spengler asks, "For the multitude, that which it continually reads and hears.... What the [media] wills, is true".[288] The closest we might come to objectivity is the supreme death-fear so prevalent in the Hobbesian state of Nature; and from this, the piety embodied in the citizen-State symbiosis that sustains culture and life.

When finally the last man dies by the lingering attack of another, all concepts of "right" die with him. Are we capable of wholesale tolerance? Loving our neighbor unconditionally? Being respectful of others, or treating others as ends in themselves — just because we should? Arguably, we are not. And if we are not, then the notion of progress is vanity. Liberalism is a reflection of this vanity,

---

[287] Paul Edwards, ed. *Encyclopedia of Philosophy* (New York: MacMillan/Collier, 1972), 222.

[288] Spengler, *Decline*, 394-395.

for it seeks the impossible — and, worse still, it is not even convinced of its own objectives. Consider for a moment that a number of studies have been done attempting to show the innate abilities of infants; consequential studies show that newborns not even a week old can recognize their mother's face.[289] We are born knowing and trusting that which gives us life; it is only the depravity of social existence — a social existence that happens to be Liberalistic — that might finally destroy this trust. Our parents give us life, their parents gave them theirs, and ultimately, our culture gives each of us our life. It *is* within our capacity to know and trust our culture; if this trust is broken, this, too, is a failure of our culture's guiding ideology.

Citizen-State symbiosis is a relationship as primal as that of mother and child. The implicit trust and loyalty between citizen and State was known in the first family of our kind. The State simply arose out of this ancient bond and now transcends it. We are *redefined* through the State. The good that exists within us — the power of familial symbiosis — is not *defined away*, but *enhanced* through the bond of *a thousand thousand* families of the nation. Liberalism, in its obsessive focus on the individual, fails to appreciate or nurture this trust and loyalty inherent in the familial relationship; in its aims to free man from his alienation from himself, Liberalism has alienated him from the State (i.e., ultimately, the roots of his kin), precipitating the loss of meaning in his life. Because of this, we falter — our *nation* falters. We stumble because we are not capable of living within the bounds contrived by Liberalism. We therefore need a sense of *purpose* that reflects our moral threshold and focuses on our strengths as moral beings, rather than our weaknesses. Fascism is our purpose.

Fascism: Citizen-State Symbiosis as Resolution

Fascism is nationalistic and totalitarian. It values the life of the individual insofar as he represents the life of the culture. In culture "there is nothing material but something cosmic and directional, the felt harmony of a Destiny, the single cadence of the march of historical Being".[290] Culture is ethos. Fascism is the pinnacle of citizen-State symbiosis because by arising from, transcending, and

---

[289] Albert J. Bergesen, "Durkheim's Theory of Mental Categories: A Review of the Evidence," *Annual Review of Sociology* 30, (August 2004): 395-408, 400-401.

[290] Spengler, *Decline*, 265.

then protecting and defining the individual, it gives life to both the individual and the State. An attack on the individual is an attack on the State; an attack on the State is an attack on the individual. We cannot even say that citizen and State are *merged* in fascism, but that they are simply one, and one embodies the other, which only recalls Hegel when he says, "particular interests ... should be harmonized with the universal, so that both they themselves and the universal are preserved".[291]

If citizen and State were distinct, there would be no ethos, no culture — there would be only something akin to a prison complex, where the governors hold the absolute power and the governed wilt to displays of authority — whether this authority is political, martial, or economic; prisons are not nations, despite what modernity would have us believe. Since cultures, and indeed nations, do exist, it follows that symbiosis exists. If symbiosis exists, then fascism, if we remain true to our moral capacity, is its natural state. If nations are governed outside the moral threshold of fascism, then cultural degeneration will ensue and individualism and alienation will reign. Consumer culture is not culture; it is prison bartering.

Fascism is our resolution of the societal ails befalling us. It is not "racism"; it is pride in and defense of one's heritage, one's lineage. The individual arises *out of* a familial culture; he is not ashamed of it and it is part of his identity; other cultures are alien to him. This does not necessarily mean he derides the *other*, but it means he has the knowledge base on which to found his trust and loyalty for his mother culture. In the cold blackness of space there is only cold and black; but if there is a light, you welcome it and it is yours; you do not hate the cold blackness of space because of your light — in fact, it might befit you to appreciate the *other*, since without it, you would lose yourself in the expanse. Fascism is the valuing of the cultural self; we know that without culture, there would be only the solitary expanse of the Hobbesian state of Nature. We seek to preserve our *self* through others, and in the process learn that self-interest is subordinate to the social ethos of shared destiny. When we look at our kinsmen, we experience the trust and loyalty a shared vision cultivates. Outside of this vision, life is "solitary, poor, nasty, brutish,

---

[291] In this way, *symbiosis* is an insignificant misnomer. Georg Wilhelm Friedrich Hegel, *Elements of the Philosophy of Right*, 19th ed., translated by Hugh B. Nisbet (Cambridge: Cambridge University Press, 2014), 265.

and short".[292] Within this vision, we find that preservation of culture is preservation of life.

If life arises out of the Hobbesian wild, then peace between men and cultures could be described as a mutual, fearful respect. There can never truly be peace without a shared vision of the future; and since there will always be discordant visions of the future among cultures, there will never be more than fearful respect. Discordant visions among nations disrupt even the longest standing peace between the closest of allies — such are the stressors of living, even among cultures; and in times of upheaval, your only true ally is your kinsman. This alliance yet transcends the citizens — the *kinsmen* — to mobilize the State, and the Hobbesian state of Nature then unfolds culturally. Far from any Liberalistic progress, life ushers in the war that fuses

> the nation as only war can, creating a single thought for all citizens, a single feeling, a single passion, and a common hope, an anxiety lived by all, day by day — with the hope that the life of the individual might be seen and felt as connected ... with the life that is common to all — but which transcends the particular interests of any.[293]

The Hobbesian state of Nature, which by now might be called the state of culture, afflicts and galvanizes us in every age. And if it is omnipresent, then it reflects the nature of man and we must live within its parameters. Fascism is the definitive ideology of human nature because discordance among cultures exists; it is the expression of man living within his means, the signal of true wealth.

As the antithesis of Liberalism, citizen-State symbiosis presents us with an opportunity — not of Hegelian synthesis, but of Viconian and Spenglerian barbarism. This is a

> primeval barbarism which has lain hidden and bound for centuries under the form-rigor of a ripe Culture, is awake again now that the Culture is finished and the Civilization has set in: that warlike, healthy joy in one's

---

[292] Hobbes, *Leviathan*, 78.

[293] Giovanni Gentile, *Origins and Doctrine of Fascism: with Selections from Other Works* (New Brunswick, NJ: Transaction Publishers, 2005), 2.

> own strength which scorns the literature-ridden age of Rationalist thought, that unbroken [culture]-instinct, which desires a different life from one spent under the weight of books and bookish ideals.[294]

With such barbarism we might again embrace the piety that birthed our culture. Piousness alone can keep the ravages of Liberalism at bay; the *individual* is tied to nothing except his interests in Liberalistic culture. Yet the individual melts away in the piety engendered in the citizen-State symbiosis. The Liberalistic man is so unapologetically in love with himself and his material things that he cannot bear the thought of simply melting away. Thus, he will fight — like any street dog vying for scraps; but he will lose, because in the end, he stands for nothing; his "brother" and "neighbor" next to him care as little for his cause as any stranger might. The pious — the *State-devoted* — confront the alienated and worn dog of Liberalism with their vibrant symbiosis: they are the pack of wolves, and their meal is assured; each, for the benefit of the other, ensures this fact; the pack destroys the alienated individual, and the *future* is assured. And thus, the barbarism that ignites the will of the pious and disrupts the lethargic individualism of the Liberalistic man sits in the midst of, not a *synthesis*, but an *anti-synthesis*, a *deconstruction* of the thesis and continuance of the antithesis. In the name of culture, the pious not only survive, but also thrive.

At the end of each Viconian age — (1) the Age of Gods, (2) the Age of Heroes, and (3) the Age of Men — comes a clash of thesis and antithesis. We live now in the Spenglerian age of degenerate culture and incipient civilization; we live in Vico's Age of Men, or *ubiquitous rationality*. This culminating clash of cultures represents *the* clash — the very purpose of culture, for societies begin to reach the critical point of self-knowledge, the Hegelian freedom: up to the age of rationality we progress to the point of understanding our distinct *lack* of progress, manifested in both the understanding of our cultural degeneration from Liberalism and the recognition of our ineluctable Hobbesian nature. In this moment of true freedom — of cultural self-awareness, of barbaric symbiosis — a new culture might ascend. Vico talks of the pious kings emerging from the ascension of Christianity out of the disintegration of the Roman Empire.[295] In this

[294] Spengler, *Decision*, 19.

[295] Vico, 398.

barbarous age, the rulers, devoted to a cause so antithetical to Roman power and deterioration, took the charge of waging zealous war against all enemies — all of those who would hinder, in their eyes, the divine will of God. And because this was a barbarous age, these were men of action, not diplomacy: they moved "not on empty words, but practical effects".[296] From the ashes of this historical clash between crumbling Rome and nascent, brutal Christian fiefdom rose a new culture, which would become the Euro-American culture.

A new barbarous age need not erase history: we need not "dissolve [and] ... flee for safety to the wilderness, whence, like the phoenix, [we] rise again".[297] In our newly won self-awareness — won out of the Enlightenment — we might notice our mistake of following down the well-worn path of dissipation at that age when cultures typically reach a level of rational maturity, and instead change course. For fate does not bring us to the crossroads and then compel us forward, left, or right; "that which did all this was mind, for men did it with intelligence; it was not fate, for they did it by choice; not chance, for the results of their always so acting are perpetually the same".[298] And with our choice, and the fruits of our choices up to now, we might interrupt the perpetual cycle of our apparent inclination. True freedom is only won with "sacrifice and militancy".[299] If we choose indolence over the necessary sacrifices, then we lapse into Kant's self-imposed nonage, and then we deserve the inevitable and perpetual constitution he argued the Enlightenment was antithetical to. The constitution to which we will be subject is the Viconian dissolution into the wilderness.

Yet if we make the hard choice of sacrifice, then the perpetual constitution will be interrupted and our new barbarism will not lead to utter collapse and the wrecking of our current culture; instead, we use our hard-won reason to make the logical decision for citizen-State symbiosis as *the* means of cultural sustenance and power.

The only way for true citizen-State symbiosis — and thus, true fascism — to come into being is by *compelling* a change in course and ridding ourselves of this perpetual constitution. For we *need* the fruit of the Enlightenment to understand *why* every Viconian cycle ends in cultural decay and annihilation; thus, barbarism need not

---

[296] Gentile, 34.
[297] Vico, 425.
[298] Ibid., 425.
[299] Gentile, 35.

destroy Germanic culture; rather, it must *commandeer* it for its own salvation. Only then can change occur — from the outside in — and only then can true, self-aware citizen-State symbiosis emerge. Finally, the Viconian cycle will be broken, and then we achieve true freedom, for we achieve life.

Liberalism, in its obsessive and vehement pursuit of infinite progress, places its vision of liberty ahead of even life: "Give me liberty, or give me death!"[3] This is the cry of unregulated rationality calling for progress and individualism. It is liberty as life — not *liberty is equal to life*, but *without liberty, there is no life*. Certainly, if Liberalism attains its goal of liberty over life, then death of culture can only ensue, for equality of the masses means a lowering of the standard for all; "it occurs to no one to educate the masses to the level of true culture — that would be too much trouble ... on the contrary, the structure of society is to be leveled down to the standard of the populace. General equality is to reign; everything is to be equally vulgar"[300]; similarly, empowering the masses means weakening the Liberalistic State — power for all means power for none. Ultimately, Liberalism cannot make equal what Nature created unequal, and attempts to achieve the impossible will exhaust all stores; to this end, we will secure our perpetual constitution. Citizen-State symbiosis, on the other hand, places *life* ahead of liberty; it recognizes *life* as liberty. The difference lies in the power and sovereignty of the State over all; for without the State, there is no culture; without culture, there is no man.

> The State [is] an autonomous personality that has its own value and its own ends, subordinating to itself every existence and individual interest, not to suffocate them, but to recognize them only as realizations of the personality of the State, as consciousness, and as will.... It is an anti-individualistic conception, insofar as it affirms a spiritual reality, a reality that is universal — not the result, but the ideal principle and the original source of the concrete life of individuals possessed of moral value. From that concept a form of the authoritarian State can be logically derived. It is an authoritarianism that is ... the negation of political liberty. Fascist authoritarianism rejects license — which

[300] Spengler, *Decision*, 96.

> is not liberty at all. Only through the State can liberty be realized, and therefore has never existed except as it manifests itself as the liberty of the State...[301]

Spengler notes that domestic politics exist only to strengthen and secure the fluid execution of foreign policy.[302] This, in its own way, highlights the difference between Liberalism and fascism — between individualism and citizen-State symbiosis. Prioritizing domestic "discord" at the expense of defense or projection of power is prioritizing Liberalistic liberty over life; conversely, if we prioritize defense and projection of power, then we acknowledge the Hobbesian and cultural states of Nature and prioritize life.

Conclusion

Our new piety, born out of the soil of the Enlightenment, but rooted "deeply into the underground of blood tradition",[303] stands as our redemption and salvation. Continuing down the trail blazed by Liberalism takes us only to an inescapable expanse of rationality that mutes our cultural foundations and erases our cultural mark, our truth, and our life. Our path to inescapable compulsion into oblivion is mechanical; yet it could be free and organic. We might choose the course we take; but when the choice is made, our course is set. If, by some divine ethos, we interrupt the seemingly mechanical cycle of history upon which we now ride, and if we pare the dead limbs of Liberalism, we might reinvigorate our roots and ascend into a new era of meaning — an era of steadfast loyalty to the State, to our culture, to our family, to each other.

We might close by saying: that argument happens at all points to the truth of Hobbes' state of Nature and, thus, fascism as its agent and apotheosis. Within the fascist context, cultural peculiarities might surface, yet this only adds to the paradoxical inclusive and exclusive aspects of the fascist ideology. That the citizen and State are one is fascism's only corollary.

---

[301] Gentile, 34.
[302] Spengler, *Decision*, 35.
[303] Spengler, *Decline*, 396.

CHAPTER 4
THE ARCHETYPE AND ITS OPPOSITION: REVISIONS

THE PAIN OF VIRTUE

Life strives incessantly to stay in contact with pain ... so that at any hour of the day it can serve a higher calling.
— ERNST JÜNGER, *ON PAIN*

Montaigne was a conservative. That is, he sought to conserve the values of those preceding him; he saw in the Greeks of antiquity so many ideological kinsmen: they were seekers of virtue. Montaigne's time, as perhaps a beginning and at least a presaging of modernity, is defamed by his excavation of the past: he searches for that which has firm anchor only in bygone days. With his excavation, Montaigne aims for resurgence: a progress of pain Ernst Jünger links to both ruin and new vigor. Virtue, as a state of transcendence, from this conservative perspective, is accessible only through pain (self-overcoming) and thereby possesses the only means to *qualitative* endurance. Thus, a rescuing of modernity, if that is what Montaigne seeks through his investigation of virtue, only becomes possible through a revitalized acceptance of the pain which precedes it.

Montaigne's Virtue and its March through Modernity

In his essay "On Cruelty," Montaigne writes, "virtue is something other, something nobler, than those tendencies toward the Good which are born in us".[1] He adds that "the word *virtue* has a ring about it which implies something greater" than simply acting on one's good inclinations. Offering the example of a man who overcomes his instinct to harm one who has harmed him, Montaigne tells us that he who reciprocates the injuries does well; he who "masters" his vengeful instinct to do otherwise does "very much more"[2]; that is, the

---

[1] Michel de Montaigne, *The Complete Essays*, translated by M.A. Screech (London, England: Penguin Books, 2003), 450.

[2] Ibid., 450.

latter have acted virtuously. In short, virtue is won through struggle; should good actions come easily, then virtue is surely absent. This notion rings true, for who would argue, for instance, that a suicidal wretch who jumps on a grenade otherwise intended for his teammates on the battlefield is more virtuous than the family man who sacrifices himself for his comrades? While not precisely aligned with Montaigne's meaning, the above example is equal in intent: the former case indicates an action of relief (one prefers to act in such a way), while the latter case reveals a distinct overcoming (one struggles to overcome his preference for the sake of something noble). What Montaigne seems to suggest, then, is a kind of chivalry: the setting aside of personal ambitions for the sake of something higher — whether we understand such chivalry to mean a "readiness to help the weak" or something more metaphysical (self-sacrifice for the good) is beside the point, for it is only the intent behind it that matters: is there a struggle involved or not?

Being a man of the Renaissance, Montaigne was not concerned with looking backward, especially toward Europe's medieval history; instead, he, like the era for which he spoke, was interested only in incorporating ancient (Greco-Roman) vitality into his vision of the future: a future he saw empowered by a certain liberality of thought. To speak of medieval chivalry, then, is to betray Montaigne's forward-looking vision. Yet it was not until more than two hundred years after the Frenchman's time that Europe began to see the ideological wave of chivalry sweep again over the continent: Napoleon planted the seeds of nationalism, which under him became a kind of pan-Europeanism[3]; the impetus of such Napoleonic nationalism — or pan-Europeanism — was a Montaignian liberality:

> [Napoleon] erases the distinctions of nobility that placed inherited glory ahead of acquired glory, and the descendants of great men before great men themselves.... [He creates] a new currency of a very different value than the Treasury's money; a currency whose title is unalterable and whose mine cannot be exhausted because it resides in French honor; finally, a

---

[3] David A. Bell, *Napoleon: a Concise Biography* (New York: Oxford University Press, 2015), 63.

> currency which can alone reward actions considered superior to all rewards.[4]

Either *within the context* of the *nation* or broader (European) *culture*, men are of equal rank — so long as they prove their worth.[5] Dogmatic acceptance of inherited nobility was erased in the French Revolution. Napoleon advanced this erasure and empowered men of low caste with the opportunity to surmount their inheritance and achieve a nobility of greatness, should they rise to the challenges life provides. The Napoleonic Code (a civil code foundational to many modern states both within and without Europe[6]) and his Legion of Honor are testaments to his furtherance of France's overturning of the *ancien régime*. The social framework in the Napoleonic State rested upon the notion of modern, Montaignian chivalry: the free man sacrifices himself for the common good,[7] not because it is easy, but because it is difficult — it is *virtuous*. In Napoleon's wake, however, such chivalry succumbed to Bismarckian liberal-nationalism, wherein politicking and economic interests became the surrogate for sacrificial transcendence. However, enough chivalry survived through Bismarck's "blood and iron" to ignite a one-man Germanic-Romantic revival in Nietzsche.

Nietzsche's adoration of Napoleon — aside from his open admission — is evident in his emphasis on a new blood-aristocracy

> based upon the most severe self-discipline, in which the will of philosophical men of power and artist-tyrants will be stamped upon thousands of years: a higher species of men which, thanks to their preponderance of will, knowledge, riches, and influence, will avail themselves of democratic Europe as the most suitable and supple instrument they can have for taking the fate

---

[4] Pierre-Louis Roederer, 1802, as quoted in Rafe Blaufarb, *Napoleon, Symbol for an Age: a Brief History with Documents* (Boston: Bedford/St. Martin's, 2008), 102.

[5] The implication, then, is that men *outside* of the nation or culture are not equal.

[6] Blaufarb, 12.

[7] Ibid., 12.

> of the earth into their own hands, and working as artists upon man himself.[8]

As history records, Napoleon proudly (and rightly) proclaimed: "I am the French Revolution and I will uphold it".[9] What Napoleon "admired in the Revolution was its hostility to undeserved social privilege ... and to sloth and inefficiency disguised as tradition." That is, he despised the "old cults" of inherited, *de facto* nobility. Instead, "he valued the Revolution's commitment to the rule of reason and to forms of civic equality that would allow men of talent to raise themselves in society".[10] This is only to say that he aspired to create a new nobility — one consisting of the blood of higher men. Nietzsche's torch was picked up by a number of Europeans, but particularly, a bevy of German thinkers. Not least among these Germans — these bearers of Montaignian chivalry — was Ernst Jünger.

Born into a relatively wealthy family, Jünger developed a taste for adventure and, eschewing a life of comfort, enlisted in the French Foreign Legion. After a brief stint in Algeria, Jünger deserted the Legion and shortly thereafter, upon the outbreak of World War I, he volunteered to fight alongside his countrymen. He earned a reputation for valiance and was repeatedly awarded for it; he chronicled his experience of the war in the vivid *Storm of Steel*. Far from the usual ebb and flow of state power through its instruments — diplomatic, informational, military, and economic — what Jünger experienced in the trenches and witnessed in the Great War's unfolding was something new: "an unparalleled display of the will to total mobilization of societies ... in the name of total annihilation".[11] Reason itself had veered from its theorized march toward perfection and instead became the root of mass destruction: man had morphed into machine; organics became technics. In the postwar period, Jünger devoted himself to writing, particularly in favor of the rising tide of conservatism against the parliamentarian Weimar Republic.

---

[8] *The Will to Power*, §960.

[9] Bell, 52.

[10] Ibid., 44.

[11] Erst Jünger, *The Worker*, translated by Bogdan Costea and Laurence Paul Hemming (Evanston, IL: Northwestern University Press, 2017), xii.

"Pain," he said, "is among the unavoidable facts of the world — [this is] an essential conviction of all conservative thinking".[12]

Pain and Virtue

Montaigne looks to the Greeks — the Stoics and Epicureans — for exemplars of virtue. Many among them "judged that it was not sufficient to have our soul in a good state"; rather, "they wish to go looking for pain, hardship and contempt, in order to combat them and to keep our souls in fighting trim".[13] Looking rearward to the Greeks, being nearly two thousand years removed from them, Montaigne raises the banner of conservatism; for what else does he do except hark back to a time he feels represents values worth preserving? What else did Napoleon do? Nietzsche? And Jünger? Pain is associated with conservatism for these men — whether spoken or not — because it represents that which is under threat in the modern age of mass comfort: pain represents virtue itself.

"Virtue," Montaigne urges, "demands a rough and thorny road: she wants either external difficulties to struggle against ... or else inward difficulties furnished by the disordered passions and imperfections of our condition".[14] This is because *without* struggle, one is simply "good" or "innocent" — labels Montaigne sees as "somewhat pejorative".[15] What *good* is "goodness" if it is just a natural state? Of course, it *is* good — it just lacks the enduring value of hard-won virtue. Virtue is held in higher esteem than goodness because, more than merely implying struggle, it suggests transcendence. The family man who sacrifices himself (overcomes his preference to do otherwise) by falling on a grenade for his comrades does so for a higher — or transcendent — purpose: in that moment of sacrifice, he recognizes and embodies his subordination to the higher mission, the higher will, the higher duty. Indeed, goodness is good; but virtue is divine.

---

[12] Jünger, *On Pain*, translated by David C. Durst (Candor, NY: Telos Press, 2008), 37. Montaigne, 451. That is, pain cannot be undone, circumvented, or eliminated through adopting rationalistic theories or party programs: pain is inherent to life and must be acknowledged. Pain, like life, is irrational; irrationality demands the triumph of the will; the mind is an afterthought of itself.

[13] He quotes Seneca: *multum sibi adjicit virtus lacessita*: virtue gains much by being put to the proof.

[14] Montaigne, 451.

[15] Ibid., 454.

Certainly, "when we make a judgment of any individual action, we must consider a great many circumstances as well as the man as a whole who performed it before we give it a name".[16] That is, we must account for the subjective case; we must account for spiritual *quality*. Rushing to judgment endangers one with *misjudgment*, and to misjudge the divine is essentially blasphemous. Virtue is not to be taken lightly, nor misjudged. When we mistake goodness for virtue, we fall prey to misunderstanding not just the act or the actor, but the very *time* in which we live. That is to say, we fall prey to powers that no longer strengthen or inspirit us, but rather enfeeble us with objectivity: matters of quality become matters of quantity. We lose sight of the exemplars preceding us — those pillars of virtue worth conserving — and instead become ensnared by the tricks and comforts of our time: painless modernity.

"Pain," says Jünger, "is one of the keys to unlock man's innermost being as well as the world."

> Whenever one approaches the points where man proves himself to be equal or superior to pain, one gains access to the sources of his power and the secret hidden behind his dominion. Tell me your relation to pain, and I will tell you who you are![17]

What is Jünger describing *if not virtue?* Who is he echoing *if not Nietzsche? If not Napoleon? If not Montaigne? If not the ancient Greeks?* Jünger, through his conservatism, seeks only to reestablish *pain* — which is to say the *struggle* against inward or outward difficulties — as the source of virtue. And this is only to say that he seeks to correct the *misjudgment* of his contemporary times: "Our children's tales close with passages about heroes who, after having overcome many dangers, live out their lives in peace and happiness.... It is comforting for us to learn about a place removed from pain".[18] This "denial of pain" is tantamount to a denial of virtue: our heroes are good, but without struggle, how can they endure? Without the *loss* — the *sacrifice* — that virtue implies, how can modernity itself expect to last? All of such denial is "thoroughly fairytale-like and reflects a sordid world in which the semblance of security is

[16] Ibid., 455.
[17] Jünger, *On Pain*, 1.
[18] Ibid., 4.

preserved in a string of hotel foyers".[19] Absolutely committed to his conservation of the past — of virtuous exemplars — Jünger declares archaeology itself "a science dedicated to pain." Of course, too, his meaning here is twofold: "in the layers of the earth, [archaeology] uncovers empire after empire, of which we no longer even know the names".[20] Pain is not just the means to virtue; it is also the state of existence whereby we transcend mere lifeless comforts. And as long as we shield ourselves from pain, we yield to the categorical misjudgment of our time; endurance will escape us just as it escapes our *good* heroes.

Montaigne, as a man of the Renaissance, performed his own archaeology — on heroes past, on heroes he felt codified virtuousness; and in doing so both indicted the fallen empires and condemned his own time (the beginning of modernity). For why did the empires fall if not for their own ultimate misjudgment of virtue? They had not the means to endure. What is more, why should he look to the past for representations of virtue unless his own modern times were lacking? Modernity is lacking not only because of its denial of pain, but also because abstractions sit as the foundation of existence. Skepticism (of which Montaigne was not immune) shifts the ground beneath our feet; thus, we seek support in a firm, scientifically precise rationalism (*cogito, ergo sum!*); subsequently, we begin to rationalize everything, to include the ground under our feet. We declare *progress* as both our foundation and the means to carry us forward; and thus we progress forward on a treadmill of abstraction.

Our heroic tales comfort us with happy endings; meanwhile, around us, worlds collide: modernity begins to

> resemble an archipelago where an isle of vegetarians exits right next to an island of cannibals. An extreme pacifism side by side with an enormous intensification of war preparations, luxurious prisons next to squalid quarters for the unemployed, the abolition of capital punishment by day whilst the Whites and the Reds cut each other's throats by night...[21]

---

[19] Ibid., 10.
[20] Ibid., 7.
[21] Ibid., 10.

And incessantly, "progress combines the economic conquest of the globe ... with ridding the world of all prejudices that can cause pain." Human relationships are *progress*ively transformed into legalities and inanimate contracts; enriching labor *progress*ively morphs into digitized currency; ethics are *progress*ively substituted for a monolith of opinion.[22] Reality is thereby exchanged for abstractions; and from such abstraction flows much convenience and prosperity. Indeed, the potential for conflict even seems greatly reduced amid such abstract sameness.[23] Jünger warns us, however, that amid all such rationalistic change, an even bigger transformation lurks in the shadows:

> the masses have been left with only *one* liberty, the liberty to consent. Parliaments and plebiscites are being transformed ever more clearly into acts of acclamation, whose manufacture replaces the free formation of public opinion. But this manufacture of consent signifies nothing other than the transformation of the masses from a moral agent into an object.[24]

The modern public cannot endure as anything but an amorphous *object* because its protection from pain precludes its access to vitalizing virtue. Objects have and will be mobilized for annihilation: it is the consequence of misjudging quantity for quality; it is the final result of a time devoid of transcendent chivalry.

---

[22] Ibid., 11.

[23] Ibid., 11.

[24] Ibid., 30. Jünger had perhaps read Lippmann's *Public Opinion* (1922). In it, Lippmann details the reality of consent manufacture. Here, too, he discusses *progress* (108-109; emphasis added): "In America more than anywhere else, the spectacle of mechanical progress has made so deep an impression, that *it has suffused the whole moral code.* An American will endure almost any insult except the charge that he is not progressive. Be he of long native ancestry, or a recent immigrant, the aspect that has always struck his eye is the immense physical growth of American civilization. That constitutes a fundamental stereotype through which he views the world: the country village will become the great metropolis, the modest building a skyscraper, what is small shall be big; what is slow shall be fast; what is poor shall be rich; what is few shall be many; whatever is shall be more so. Not every American sees the world this way.... But those men do, who in the *magazines devoted to the religion of success* appear as Makers of America."

Conclusion

Conservatives, then, like the homogeneous masses around them, are left in the lurch. Montaigne, at least in his search for virtue among moderns, joins his aristocratically minded successors, "buried in the layers of earth." Perhaps some future archaeologist of pain will strike some treasured find among the heaping ruins of modernity, for ruins they *will* be. As for how the present virtue-conservationists view their widely misjudged times, this is up from the man:

> Wherever values can no longer hold their ground, the movement toward pain endures as an astonishing sign of the times; it betrays the negative mark of a metaphysical structure. The practical consequence of this observation for the individual is, despite everything, the necessity to commit oneself to the preparation for war — regardless of whether he sees in it the preparatory stage of ruin or believes he sees on the hills covered with weather-worn crosses and wasted palaces the storm preceding the establishment of new orders of command.[25]

What is war if not struggle? It is a struggle to conserve the virtue that preceded it — unless it has lost its anchor and drifts along the treadmill of progressive abstraction. In such cases as the latter, may our ruin be our path to virtue. We might rest assured that the distant archaeologist of pain will unravel our ruin and decipher in it those noble words and acts that preceded him: *virtue rejects ease as a companion, and that the gentle easy slope up which are guided the measured steps of a good natural disposition is not the path of real virtue.*[26] May that future man seek the pain of virtue and thereby aid his folk's endurance.

DANTE'S *COMMEDIA*: PAGANISM MASQUERADING AS CHRISTIANITY

Palpable throughout Dante's *Commedia* is the tension between the pagan Roman spirit and Christianity. That Dante served as a link

---

[25] Ibid., 47.

[26] Montaigne, 450.

between antiquity and modernity in Western culture can hardly be denied, given his temporal position in the medieval world, as it is often understood in Western academia; more important than such temporal placement, however, is that Dante linked himself to the ancients (the Homeric tradition and Virgil) in his own work. Works of antiquity, being pre-Christian, were *un*-Christian — if not in a hostile sense, then in a *de facto* sense, which is to say, by necessity they lacked the Christian spirit. Because of this, for Dante they embodied a Roman (or Greco-Roman) spirit, which can be understood as being necessarily at odds with Christianity as Dante knew it — that medieval Christianity of the Holy Roman Empire. And, while the Holy Roman Empire worked in league with the Roman papacy, because of its Germanic character, the Empire hearkened back to the paganism of antiquity; the tension between the pagan and the Christian, then, can also be seen in the relationship between the imperial and the papal in the Holy Roman Empire; the Germanic peoples, like the ancient Romans, manifested the pagan spirit that was systematically rooted out of Europe under the *alien* Christian papacy.

Through an examination of this ancient link between the pagan peoples of Europe in Dante's work and the relationship between the papal and imperial aspects of the Empire, it will be shown that Alighieri upheld something more transcendent than mere faith-born ideology as the paragon of culture: he held the indomitable will of a people as the requisite for enduring culture.

Dante's *Commedia*

Dante's *Commedia* is, of course, a Christian work. But to undertake such a culturally significant task in his work, Alighieri initially relies upon the guidance of the pagan Virgil, who wrote his *Aeneid* under the auspices of Caesar Augustus. The *Aeneid* follows the now-homeless Trojan warrior Aeneas through his travels to ultimately found what would become the city, kingdom, republic, and, finally, empire of Rome. Virgil, for his part, relied heavily upon the great Greek poet Homer's *Odyssey* and *Iliad* for inspiration in composing his tribute to Rome.

That Dante — and Virgil before him — took inspiration from great poetic predecessors speaks to a literary technique. By joining one's own work with a great historical work, whether in form or content, one joins the tradition spawned by the historical work, and thereby elevates one's own contribution to the cultural strand. Dante sought such an historical link because he saw value in the culture that preceded him, even though such culture(s) did not reflect a Christian worldview. Yet if it was not an ideological link that bound Dante to his pagan antecedents, then something greater — indeed, something more transcendent — bound him to their thread: theirs was a tradition of culture, which is to say a tradition of spirit. From this cultural link, Dante intended to, perhaps, elevate his contemporary (Christian) worldview to the heights of the pagan past by marrying an ephemeral ideology to an enduring (Western) culture.

At times in his *Inferno*, Dante tries to distance himself from ideological discrepancies: "I ... lived in Rome," says Virgil upon their initial meeting, "under the good Augustus — the season of the false and lying gods".[27] Here we are to recognize, of course, that Rome's (that is, Italy's — no, *Europe's*) pagan past is ideologically discordant with its Christian present. Shortly thereafter, Virgil tells Dante that he (Virgil) is not permitted in God's city (paradise) because of his paganism.[28] Yet this does not negate the significant cultural underpinning linking Virgil's Rome to Dante's: "Rome and her realm were destined to become the sacred place".[29] The rise of Rome did not stop, as was prophesied to Aeneas and was told by Virgil, with the Octavian Empire, but progressed beyond to the Holy Roman See. What Dante professes, then, is what Virgil foretold; the unfortunate aspect of time is all that kept poor Virgil from realizing the full span of his own prophecy; and because of this, he ended up in hell.[30] Indeed, Dante goes on to demurely contrast himself with the worthy Aeneas[31]; that is, Alighieri feels himself not on the same level as Aeneas, the founder of the pagan Roman culture. This is only more evidence that it is something beyond mere professions of faith that binds a people — in this case, Dante and his pagan predecessors — together.

Moreover, throughout the *Commedia*, Alighieri uses a number of Greco-Roman pagan names for various characters and locations — from Acheron to Styx, from Charon to Cerberus, from Lethe to Dis

---

[27] Dante, *Inferno*, translated by Allen Mandelbaum (Bantam Classics: New York, 1980), I.70-72.
[28] *Inferno* I.126.
[29] *Inferno* II.22-23.
[30] Albeit "limbo," see *Inferno* IV.
[31] *Inferno* II.32.

(Pluto), and so on. While this seems an insignificant means of contextually referencing a spiritual plot for his contemporary readers, taken with Dante's other, larger interests in pagan culture, it appears to have deeper significance: Alighieri rejected the chance to use biblical language and further *Semiticize* his readers. This rejection was perhaps reflective of an internal spiritual tension between the (culturally native) pagan and (culturally alien) Christian beliefs within him. Such a tension can be further seen in Dante's desire to revive the Holy Roman Empire, thereby revitalizing the Roman spirit.

Revitalizing the Holy Roman Empire and the Roman Spirit

The Roman spirit, as Dante understood it, was Germanic. It might be said that all of the Italian's adult life was dedicated, in some way, to revivifying the Holy Roman Empire. As a 24-year-old youth he fought with and for his fellow Florentines — the pro-papacy, majority Guelphs (an Italianization of the German *Welf*) — against the more imperialistic, minority Ghibellines (an Italianization of the German *Waiblingen*). At the time, Dante's Florence was a republic and the Guelph forces, while being pro-pope, were also more in favor of the guildsmen of whom Dante was a part[32] — such favor was not held by the Ghibellines. At its heart, however, Dante's pro-papacy fighting was at odds with his deeper sympathies toward the remnants of the once-formidable Holy Roman Empire (of which the Ghibellines were representative).

Indeed, aside from the subtle denouncements Dante lobs toward Pope Boniface throughout the *Commedia*, he also offers sympathy and even praise to those who have fought against the pope.[33] One needs only to look at his account of Manfred (King of Sicily, d. 1266) — Frederick II's bastard son — in the *Purgatorio*: "Blond [*biondo*] was he, beautiful, and of noble aspect".[34] That is, despite Manfred's "contumacy" in relation to the Church, he is still revered for his life as would-be heir to the imperial throne and, of course, his Germanic qualities (blond, beautiful, and noble). Again, then, we see a tension between Dante's professed Christianity and his native cultural instincts.

---

[32] Allen Mandelbaum, "Dante in his Time," Dante's *Inferno* (Bantam Classics: New York, 1980), 322.

[33] *Inferno* XIX.49-58; *Paradisio* XXX.145-148.

[34] III.107.

Frederick II himself was the last leader of the Holy Roman Empire to push his influence into Dante's northern Italy. Frederick II, too, was born in the northern half of Italy — well within the sphere of Germanic influence — in the city of Iesi, a city whose own history is dominated by Gaulish (Germanic) invasions and influence. This link establishes the validity of his ascendency to the throne as leader of the First German Reich. The First Reich, of course, was established by Karl der Große (Charlemagne), himself quite possibly born in the modern-day German town of Aachen. Frederick II, though, finds himself in the circle of hell reserved for heretics,[35] since he, of course, had been excommunicated multiple times by the Church; Frederick II accepted the expediency of the Church's authority to coronate him Emperor, but had little other use for their eastern magicking. Nietzsche, for instance, while praising Frederick II's essential German quality (his "dangerous audacity"[36]), additionally found him wonderfully and shockingly "amoral".[37] Such qualities in any Christian-crowned emperor would likely cause some rifting. Nevertheless, despite such ideological division between believer and cultural citizen, Dante subscribes to the cultural ideal someone like Frederick II or Karl der Große exemplifies: the monarchical will, which is to say, the Roman ideal, or, as Alighieri knew it, the Holy Roman ideal, which can only be understood as Germanic, or pagan.

The Cultural Urge to One Will

Virgil, who wrote for the Octavian court, continued a cultural legacy itself sustained by the Western peoples of Homeric tradition[38]: it was a tradition of honor and glory. Such can be found in characters — real or composite — like Hector and Achilles; such honor and glory can be found in Caesar Augustus, who himself was blood-linked to Rome's first emperor, Julius Caesar. It is no accident that the great figures of antiquity endure into modern memory (via social and artistic traditions) — what made them great was their adherence to a culturally relevant code of honor and a desire to expound that honor through glory in cultural exchanges, even if such exchanges brought

---

[35] *Inferno* X.119.

[36] Ernst Bertram, *Nietzsche: Attempt at a Mythology*, translated by Robert Norton (Urbana: University of Illinois Press, 2009), 46.

[37] Ibid., 130.

[38] Barbara Graziosi, *Inventing Homer: The Early Reception of Epic* (Cambridge: Cambridge University Press, 2002), 15-18.

with them the tremors of battle. Likewise, it is no accident that Dante sought to align himself to such artistic or cultural traditions. *Accident* is precluded by a deep-seated desire to fulfill a cultural urge: Dante's adherence to his Christian faith tradition was superseded by his allegiance to a more primal, more ancient cultural urge: the desire to follow a strong, authoritative will.

In a lesser-known work, Dante makes his position clear: "God and nature do nothing in vain" and "monarchy is necessary to the well-being of the world".[39] In speaking thus, Alighieri defends the reality (that inevitably arises, incidentally) of a people's will being consolidated and manifested in the will of the sovereign. For Dante, that God and Nature act with purpose means that someone like Augustus Caesar is always in accordance with a universal will[40]; indeed, not only Augustus, but also Karl "der Große" and Frederick II — men who did not always embody the Christian ideal. If it is the case that pagans (or perhaps a-Christians) fulfill a destiny despite ideological tenets, then it is certainly a cultural destiny they fulfill.

This, again, is what Alighieri describes and defends. It should not be forgotten, too, that Dante lived through Pope Boniface's proclamation of Church supremacy in worldly affairs (1302), which led to the Italian poet decrying papal Rome as a sewer; his disgust with the supremacy of the Church would remain until he saw a hope for an imperial return: in 1310, Henry VII started his Italian campaign, thus prompting Alighieri to attempt to rally his fellow leaders behind the would-be monarch. Now, if Dante defended the papacy in his fight against the Ghibellines, then it was because he simply did not see a worthy successor to the cultural tradition in imperial form; that is, he did not support imperialism for imperialism's sake; instead, he understood the necessity of both a Caesar and a Pope — a duumvirate relationship governing man, wherein each office answers to the supreme (divine) consul,[41] wherein God is the progenitor of a people's distinctive culture and characteristics. This is further established when Alighieri discusses the logic of one supreme will enveloping every subordinate will; he contrasts subordinate magistrates (among the various sub-cultures) within the Holy Roman Empire with the supreme imperial seat: the subordinate magistrates

---

[39] *Monarchia*, translated and edited by Prue Shaw (Cambridge: Cambridge University Press, 1996), 6, 12, and many other locations.

[40] Ibid., 25.

[41] Ibid., 91.

manage daily, mundane affairs distinct to a particular sub-culture, while the supreme imperial seat handles the issuance of "universal principles".[42] The duumvirate relationship of the Emperor and Pope is ultimately subordinate to the supreme will of God, who, in turn, makes peoples distinct.[43]

Such an aristocratic view is maintained when Dante discusses the history of Rome's ascension to power over so many sub-cultures: "It is appropriate that the noblest race should rule over all the others," he writes, and the Romans were simply better than everyone else.[44] Arguing from Aristotelian authority, Dante defends his position by assuring posterity that "honor is the prize of virtue,"[45] and the Romans' position of power is the honor bestowed upon their inherent virtue — a virtue nevertheless manifested in their pagan form. This honor, of course, transferred from the sole seat of Caesar to the shared seat with Roman Pontificate following the introduction of eastern Christianity. And, instead of supposed indigenously Roman Caesars maintaining the helm under the new duumviratic system, the Germanic peoples, using their centuries of battlefield and cultural (spiritual) victories over the Romans proper as a launch point, established the Holy Roman Empire.

At another point in his *Monarchia*, Alighieri further praises the ancient, pagan Romans as "having repressed all greed ... to promote the public interest for the benefit of mankind".[46] Such praise of the pagan Romans stands in direct contrast with the North African Augustine's denouncement of Roman aggression.[47] Thus, in perpetuating a cultural legacy by lauding the Romans, Dante downplays ideological kinship with Augustine, further attesting to the essentialness of the virtues of culture in Dante's *Commedia* world: the "beautiful ... noble aspects" of *his* people. This is why the nobility of Homer, Virgil, good Caesar, and even Manfred elevates their status from causeless sufferer in hell, limbo, or purgatory to culturally enshrined demigod in Dante's historical work.

---

[42] Ibid., 25.

[43] This, of course anticipates (or continues the tradition of) what was later understood as the *Führerprinzip* in Hitler's Third Reich.

[44] *Monarchia*, 33-34.

[45] Aristotle, *Nichomachean Ethics*, IV, 1123b35.

[46] *Monarchia*, 40.

[47] *Monarchia*, note 40.

Conclusions

While writing his *Commedia* from a Christian perspective, it is clear that Dante meant to continue a legacy of imperial nobility — a "dangerous audacity" characteristic of the Germanic people helming the Holy Roman Empire. Alighieri's interest in Christianity obtained insofar as it was a concomitant with that pagan (imperial) nobility of antiquity that gave rise to the world in which he lived and worked. Dante's world was ultimately a cultural heritage foretold by the Augustus-inspired Virgil, and before him, the heroic Homeric tradition. That this is so can be further shown in the fact that, in 1554, the Vatican prohibited Dante's *Monarchy* (it was only reinstated as viable text in 1881[48]); it was the least the Church could get away with in dealing with such a celebrated author — an author who, in turn, celebrated the sovereignty of the divine will in Western (Germanic) man, a will that would again manifest in the Germans Meister Eckhart and Martin Luther, and beyond. It is no wonder, too, then, that Dante left his pagan guide for his ascent into paradise; Virgil — the embodiment of native European, pagan will — inspired sufficient courage within Dante to continue his journey upwards; and, for his part, Virgil heroically returns to his tragic, Christianized destiny in hell, never regretting or shirking his duty to a spiritual kinsman.

Perhaps the real "comedy" in Dante's work, then, is the ostensible insistence on the divinity of the Germanic will as it manifests in Holy Roman imperialism — under the guise of extolling Roman Christianity. That is, the real curiosity of the *Commedia* is Dante's indubitable spiritual link to the pagan blood tradition that saw him masquerading as a Roman Christian.

QUIXOTE AND HESS:
AN EXAMINATION OF HONORABLE IDEALISM

Don Quixote is renowned for his idealism, yet something to consider in his tale is *condescension*. Idealism and condescension can hardly be uncoupled — where one is, so is the other. Despite his madness — either real or perceived — Quixote can never escape the pervasive condescension surrounding his seemingly endless supply of idealism; and likewise, whenever Quixote is met with presumption, he hardly fails to raise a wall of belief as a retort.

---

[48] *Monarchia*, xlii.

Something of a modern-day Quixote was the enigmatic Rudolf Hess. The longtime deputy Führer typically had his beliefs on display with characteristic avidity and his actions often followed suit. Case in point: his 1941 flight to Scotland. This mission, aside from its surrounding speculations, was ultimately the work of an *absolutely* dedicated man. His goal, in the context of his work and being, was permeated with idealistic devotion; and in his life and efforts, we see something not unlike the life and efforts of Don Quixote. In exploring the motivations of each of these men, we might see something of ourselves — whether we choose to reject it or embrace it, of course, is up to us.

Don Quixote

After being "knighted," Quixote meets a slave, Andres, being whipped by his master, Haldudo the Rich. Being "the undoer of wrongs and injustices,"[49] Quixote is quick to insert himself into the situation: he means well! Under the precepts of knighthood, Quixote has every right to adjudge Haldudo, a fellow "knight," and help poor Andres, recompensing him where sensible. This is, of course, just what Quixote does, and it is all very reasonable — except when juxtaposed with reality itself. For when Quixote was out of sight — after all the knightly pomp was expressed and agreed to — Haldudo the Rich beat his slave till he was nearly senseless. He left him only enough life to track down the "undoer of wrongs" so as to "put the sentence pronounced into execution".[50] When finally the savior and saved crossed paths again, Andres was quick to shatter Quixote's fanciful imaginings that Haldudo would simply do as commanded: "Not only did he not pay me, but as soon as your worship had passed out of the wood and we were alone, he tied me up again to the same oak and gave me a fresh flogging..."[51] To this, Quixote had nothing significant to say.

His idealism — noble though it was — had no quarter in reality. In his mind, Quixote did exactly as a harmonious world demanded; in doing so, however, he defined what it is to be *quixotic*.

Indeed, Quixote never abandoned his "fancy full of ... impossible nonsense".[52] Cervantes himself means to criticize him for it —

[49] Miguel de Cervantes, *Don Quixote* (USA: Crown Publishers, 1934), 16.

[50] Ibid., 16.

[51] Ibid., 76.

[52] Ibid., 2.

though something of a dreamer must have surely taken shelter amid all of the author's rationality for him to write the novel at all. The histories Quixote read became those with which he was imbued: they became his reality. His reality was one of honor, to uphold and promulgate it: "hold thy peace and have patience; the day will come when thou shalt see with thine own eyes what an honorable thing it is to wander in the pursuit of this calling; nay, tell me, what greater pleasure can there be in the world, or what delight can equal that of winning a battle, and triumphing over one's enemy? None, beyond all doubt".[53] Surely, there are few more beautiful passages in all of literature! Quixote's idealism, while flawed, is absolutely pure; its purity is, of course, its greatest flaw.

Sancho Panza, the simpleminded squire and realist of the pair, cannot begin "to know what the delight ... of conquering an enemy is like".[54] Sancho does not presume superiority over his master, but misses the point of Quixote's mission nonetheless. For Quixote, the journey itself — reality be damned — is the essence of honor, and honor is the victory. Nothing can extract the purity from Quixote's mission; not his housekeeper, who burns his books with delight; not Antonia, who encourages the book burning; not the innkeeper, who humors more himself than Quixote when knighting him; not the duke and duchess, who make fun of the knight and squire; and so on. A litany of characters seeks nothing more than to advance their *own* cause at the cost of Quixote's purity. Such condescension can only be compared to spite, however. Quixote's enemies — if enemies they must be called — do not see the purity of his victory, the honor of his journey, or even the sense behind his fancy; for to them, Quixote is never more than fanciful — he is simply not *realistic*. And he who is "unrealistic" is "irrational"; he who is "irrational," especially in the modern world that Cervantes helped describe, barely qualifies as human. At best, the *honorable* idealist, the epitome of whom is quixotic Quixote, is mere laughing stock.

At this point, the *honorable* idealist and the *spiteful* idealist should be distinguished. The former, as mentioned, is well exemplified in Don Quixote; the latter is best described as a nasty idealist — one who seeks to improve conditions (to the "ideal") not through honor, but through undercutting and malice (or deconstructionism and reductionism). That is, the spiteful idealist is

[53] Ibid., 41.
[54] Ibid., 41.

one who condescends and presumes an objectivity to which we can make little claim.

Rudolf Hess

Rudolf Hess was, perhaps aside from Hitler, the supreme idealist in National Socialist Germany. Both Hess and Hitler were, in fact, members of the pagan *Thule Gesellschaft*, a society founded on what might be considered "irrational" tenets; Hitler was a "visiting" member, while Hess was a "permanent" member of the society. Comingled with Germanic Romanticism, the *Thule Gesellschaft*, in part, believed in a coming Führer to lead Germany out of its loathsome Weimarian situation.

In a speech to the *Hitler-Jungend* in 1934, Hess pronounced:

> You take an oath to a man whom you know follows the laws of Providence, which he obeys independently of the influence of earthly powers, who leads the German people rightly, and who will guide Germany's fate. Through your oath, you bind yourselves to a man who — this is what we firmly believe — was sent to us by higher powers. Do not seek Adolf Hitler with your mind. You will find him through the strength of your hearts![55]

This pronouncement says much about Hess. In it, not least, one can find the sense of the sublime in Hess' words; that is, one can read that he truly believes — beyond any doubt, rational argument, or reality that might be posed to him — that Hitler was the divinely chosen Führer. For Hess, following Hitler was already victory, just as for Quixote the journey to restore honor to the world was already victory: their paths, while superficially different, were substantively the same. Hitler was the embodiment of honor for Hess. Indeed, one can see this even in the Riefenstahl film *Triumph des Willens* (1935) when Hess vehemently declares, "Hitler is Germany just as Germany is Hitler!" Hess never strayed from what he saw as Hitler's example or creed, even up to his final remarks at the Nuremberg trials:

> I am a deeply religious person. I am convinced my belief in God is stronger than that of most other people. I ask

[55] Anson Rabinbach and Sander L. Gilman, *The Third Reich Sourcebook* (University of California Press, 2013), 148.

> the High Tribunal to give all the more weight to everything I declare under oath, expressly calling God as my witness.... I was permitted to work for many years of my life under the greatest son whom my folk has brought forth in its thousand-year history.... I regret nothing. If I were to begin all over again, I would act again just as I have acted — even if I knew that I would meet a fiery death at the stake. No matter what people may do or say, one day I shall stand before the judgment seat of eternal God. I will answer to HIM, and HE will vindicate me.[56]

Nothing could shake Hess: his position, like Quixote's, was one of pure idealism. He — despite his being charged with "war crimes" at Nuremberg — did nothing besides take an active political role in 1930s Germany; for this he was sentenced to life imprisonment. How Hess came to be imprisoned is a matter of some curiosity and itself an indication of his idealism.

Hugh Trevor-Roper, in his review of a 1979 book discussing the possibility that Hess was murdered in prison, offers a summary of Hess' trip:

> One of the most bizarre episodes of World War II occurred on May 10,1941, when Rudolf Hess, deputy Fuhrer [sic] of Germany, parachuted incognito from the sky close to the Scottish estate of the duke of Hamilton and asked to be taken to the duke. At that time Hitler had been victorious on all fronts and would gladly have wound up his war in the West in order to begin a new war in the East. However, his public overtures had been rejected by Britain, his only enemy still in arms, and so his deputy now tried to help him by this dramatic intervention.[57]

This is to say that at the height of German successes in World War II, Hess, in an attempt to secure peace with a people the Germans saw as brethren, and in the face of all practical consequences of his wartime actions, risked everything — his life, his mission, the chance

---

[56] Translated by the author.

[57] Hugh Trevor-Roper, Review of *The Murder of Rudolf Hess, The New Republic* (1979), 28.

of seeing his family again — for an *idea* — his attempt to restore honor to the world. "The hero of Germanic origin," Hess said in that 1934 speech, "is loyal to the point of self-sacrifice." Quixote rejoins: "perhaps the chivalry and enchantments of our day take a different course from that of those in days gone by; ... I am a new knight in the world..."[58] What is chivalry if not self-sacrifice?

The details surrounding the *why* of Hess' trip are precisely what Trevor-Roper calls into question; that and the book's author's — Hugh Thomas — argument that Hess was murdered. The entire basis for his review is purely rational and, in point of fact, a fine example of spiteful idealism. Hess could have only made his trip because his actions had "no basis in reality".[59] This is naturally so, since Trevor-Roper is firmly entrenched in the real world — *rational modernity*. Trevor-Roper goes on to critique Thomas' "indisputable dogma"; a dogma which Thomas relies on to, again, "supplant" rationality — or perhaps embrace "irrationality." The reason this exemplifies a spiteful idealism is because Trevor-Roper, being an eminent purveyor of an academic rationalism, necessarily has a monopoly on rational objectivity; such objectivity, as he presumes, can only form the basis for reality, and because reality can be reduced into quantifiable data, subjectivity must be forever consigned to the fanciful world of lost minds,[60] or perhaps the fanciful images a mirror presents to the world.

Professor Emeritus Geoffrey Cocks, in his own review of a psychoanalytical take on Hess, also feels obliged to doom the German's actions as being "marked by obsessions and delusions".[61] Psychoanalysts, he rightly notes, have a field day with the National Socialists; there is no other reason for this than the marked difference in how each — the "Nazi" and the psychoanalyst — views the world: the former seeks constructive *subjectivity*, the latter presumes deconstructive (or reductionist) *objectivity*. One is reminded of the reflections of an American journalist upon witnessing the Nuremberg trials: there was no bridge between the prosecution and defense; *they were from different worlds*. The case

---

58 Cervantes, 100.

59 Trevor-Roper, 29.

60 "...the strangest notion that ever madman in this world hit upon, and that was that he fancied it was right and requisite..." Cervantes, 4.

61 Geoffrey Cocks, Review of *The Pursuit of the Nazi Mind: Hitler, Hess, and the Analysts*, *American Historical Review* (2013), 953.

between the two is dismissed *before* the trial begins — not unlike the formality of Nuremberg's "justice." The case is likewise dismissed for Trevor-Roper!

Indeed, "[Hess had always been a] naïve idealist," the academic charges. Meanwhile, he, too, is beholden to an idealism; it is only that Trevor-Roper's idealism condescends and aims to undercut those who, from their own *subjective* perspective, seek to restore honor to the world. The honorable idealist seeks to find solutions; the spiteful idealist seeks to supplant.

One final point: "A year before his flight," Trevor-Roper says, "the US secretary of state, Sumner Welles, had an interview with [Hess]. He responded that Hess 'had only the lowest order of intelligence' and was not worth talking with".[62] Trevor-Roper tries here to undercut Hess the man by using defeasible reasoning — i.e., by using an argument from supposed authority. To be sure, it is no small feat to reach Welles' position of *Under* Secretary of State (not the actual Secretary of State, as Trevor-Roper inflates), but might it be that Welles had — *perhaps!* — an *inherent* bias against what was by most accounts a cogent, capable and, clearly, daring statesman? Just a few months after his visit to Germany, it was discovered that Welles solicited sex from two African-American men; this solicitation ultimately led to his resignation of the authority he presumed. Now, one might argue that it is in bad form to criticize Welles for such behavior — especially in modern times — and that we should judge him on his other actions, his "good" ones. One might say it is bad form to imagine that an Under Secretary of State could only have the "lowest order of intelligence" to act in such a way, to betray his family for homosexual affairs. Yet, isn't this how Welles judged Hess (for they *clearly* had different values)? Isn't this how Trevor-Roper judged Hess? Isn't this how Antonia judged Quixote? Isn't it how the housekeeper judged Quixote? Or the duke and duchess? The innkeeper? Will modernity always *pretend* to objectivity — and in so doing entrench itself in its own spitefully idealistic dogma?

To such questions both Quixote and Hess can attest: yes! Such is human nature. What separates us is our claim to honor or spite — yet few would ever claim the latter — naturally, again. Sumner Welles wasn't honorable — not, at least, by any normal understanding of the word; nor was Trevor-Roper, hastily authenticating known forgeries because they matched his agenda.

[62] Trevor-Roper, 30.

But these two men are quick to denounce the "ineptitude" of a Hess — someone whose actions were arguably supremely honorable. Modern "rationality," though, tells us we should accept their words over Hess' actions, for modern "rationality" is always right — and "never" spiteful.

Conclusion

Quixotic-ness abounds: indeed, the quixotic aura of 1930s Germany pervaded not only Hess, but also his mission; from there, it endured well beyond the end of the war and manifested in Hugh Thomas' book. It endures to this day and, the author has no doubt, will endure much longer than the allure of the source of the word *quixotic* itself has endured. "Today," Hess somberly wrote to his wife from Spandau, "we are able to know little and write less about what the death of the eleven [martyrs of Nuremberg] will mean. We are in the midst of a great historical turning point. We are going through its birth pangs. Everything seems negative — and yet something New and Great is being born." Undoubtedly, the mystique surrounding Hess and his broader mission will only grow; one must wonder how intense and robust the quixotic-ness will have become in four hundred years hence. Perhaps in four hundred years Hess will have a word derived from his name.

Quixote has certainly registered deeply within the human spirit to have endured *his* four hundred years. Readers find in him something of themselves — from the honorable to the spiteful. It's just that the spiteful see something to replace rather than embrace. Cervantes, of course, had the astuteness to instruct us on the point of departure we see reflected in the mirror.

Ultimately, that's what matters most: the being *substantiating* the reflection in the mirror. Does our reflection marry up with who we are? If we are honorable, it does; and if we are honorable, our loved ones will see not only what we see, but also what we *are*. Be the honorable idealist — live in such a way that brings honor and nobility to you, your family, and your folk. Nothing is more important. And if you have done well, your descendants, though they will not know you, will praise your name — not because you did something exceptional, but because you did your duty for your folk. Anything less than absolute allegiance to your honorable mission is failure. Don Quixote saw this, as did Rudolf Hess. The broader world will not and cannot cease mocking them for their actions; but the broader world is little else than a spectral image in a mirror.

Concluding Unscientific Postscript

Some readers might balk at the tenuous conceptual relationship between Quixote and Hess: *Outrage!* cries the objector. *Quixote has an endearing madness and Hess was a mad war criminal who enabled Hitler's crimes against peace and humanity!*

The intent, however, is to draw a comparison between their quixotic (i.e., "idealistic" and "impractical") missions: Quixote and Hess each sought to restore honor to the world in their own way. If their actions were performed irrespective of enduring consequences, it does not detract from their quixotic nature.

If we get mired in the consequences of their actions, then we, perhaps, will lose sight of their purpose. Both Quixote and Hess reacted to the circumstances they perceived around them; if they perceived attack, this necessitated their counterattack. For us to examine the counterattack and not the events preceding it is for us to be selective in our objectivity, which is to say, it is for us to be utterly subjective, which is, after all, inescapable. Thus, if we subjectively judge someone on his or her subjective action, then we are just as guilty of being *human* as the accused.

We are not alone in our presumptions of objectivity, however. The very definitions of "war crimes," "crimes against humanity," and "crimes against peace" are prime examples. Such principles of international law — formally defined in 1950 by the United Nations (UN), but first executed in earnest in Nuremberg — are themselves selectively objective (i.e., subjective). First, we must understand that the UN is essentially Britain, France, and the United States aligned against (as it stands now) Russia and China — collectively, these are the only veto-power members. These were the Allied Powers that won World War II, of course, and they stand as the original "permanent" members of the UN. (The League of Nations up to the end of World War II was essentially Britain and France.) Hence, they — the victors — get to determine the "objective" law. Is a person (or government) guilty of a war crime? Well, what does the UN say about it? Never mind that all the originators of "international law" have found very ingenious ways to skirt the law they invented.

The first such skirting was evident in the Nuremberg Tribunal. Aside from the fact that the Axis Powers were held to statutes to which they were not signatory, it is apparent today that the trials were a compromise between the Soviets' desire to hang everyone and the British/French/American (general) desire to "try" the accused in a court of law. The result was essentially a kangaroo court with an official veneer — all in effort to appease the victors and their interests. Not only was hearsay allowed — prevailingly — as evidence, but also the accusers themselves were not to be judged under the law — this notion was one of the very provisions of the Tribunal, in fact. Hence, the Brits and the Americans were not charged with or tried for war crimes and crimes against humanity after they fire bombed city after city, creating well over a million casualties — many for no other reason than that they were Germans; hence, the Soviets were not charged with or tried for war crimes and crimes against humanity after they brutally assaulted innumerable German citizens after receiving lifesaving assistance from the Americans; hence, the Americans were not charged with or tried for war crimes and crimes against humanity for their use of nuclear weapons in annihilating two Japanese cities.

But that's just war. War becomes just in the eyes of the perpetrators and unjust in the eyes of the victims. So why do we pretend there is such a thing as "international law" — or better, "objectivity"? These are bedtime stories meant to assuage a humankind that has *no spiritual anchor*. Germany's assault on Poland in 1939 — from the German perspective — was a completely justified response to atrocities being committed against German civilians in Poland, citizens who used to be a part of Germany proper, but were now targeted minorities under a hostile (and British-allied) Polish government. But... this is irrelevant because Germany lost the material war, because they were charged with, tried for, and convicted of war crimes, crimes against humanity, and crimes against peace by the powers that invented the meaning of such crimes to fit their subjective interests. Only now it is *objective fact*.

This is why when people talk of the "criminal" Rudolf Hess, they speak only of his status as a *de facto* criminal and utterly disregard the peace he so desperately tried to secure with Britain. His actions do not matter; his life does not matter; the man was evil; the case is closed. *Good riddance!*

In a world such as this, presumptions of objectivity seem desperate, at best. Presumptions of objectivity are the sure sign of a weak will and spiritual emptiness (faithlessness). And when we understand the world *is* will, the real tenuousness arises with any insistence on objectivity as viable currency.

This world is a will to power — and nothing besides! We would do well to accept any knights that arrive — be they "errant" or of faith. In either case, theirs is an absolute duty to God — and *unser Gott ist der germanische Wille.*

INVERSION

Imagine the blood memory and collective consciousness of a people enabled them to see the grim future their kind created — but the inherent destructiveness of their blood permitted them the space to critique their own handiwork. Imagine being of this people compelled to destroy, aware that you are a destroyer and lamenting it, yet simultaneously being proud of your brilliant, devastating efficiency. If you were of this people, you would be strangely neurotic, seeing yourself as the perpetual victim; perhaps in your egotistical neurosis you might even think no one has been the victim quite as much as you — history had "chosen" *you*. You might obsess even over ordinary things — things like numbers. Because you are destructive, neurotic and egotistical — and certainly not creative — you might look to your greatest enemy, whose sacred number is the mystical 9, and think your satanic god called you to invert their work and its number. You choose for yourself the number *6* — the inverted 9. You mistake your inversion for creation. You see *6s* everywhere, as you see your enemies and your inversions, *your* creation. Your chosen symbol is a 6-pointed star; you planned the invasion into your enemy's homeland for the *6th* hour of the *6th* day of the *6th* month; you fanatically repeat the satanic myth of the 6 million, "the most horrible evil in the history of the world" — because it "happened" to you, and because it inverts what your enemy *created*.

Imagine this people and that you were one of them. You might say that god and history compel you, that they are your *urge*, your *demiurge*. You, like your Demiurge, can only invert, never create. This, of course, is the meaning of Satan: it's an inversion of the Supreme God. John of Patmos saw the number of inversion in his exile: *666*. John, because of his priceless spirituality, was a heretic to you; yet you are drawn to this beastly number, the creative observation of a pious man. You see in it your blood, the memory of your people. After you destroyed your enemy's materiality in the Great Struggle of World War II, you made many movies about this number. Your Hollywood loves the *satanic*, and every devil movie is a little homage to your Demiurge. Repetition of your inversion happens month after month, year after year. The same stories are told in the same way, only now brasher, less reluctant to spread the inversion. You inculcate new generations to your lie, *your truth*.

History had chosen you even despite being so "inferior," or perhaps because of it — yes, that's part of the lie you spread amid your *constant* self-victimization. You somehow managed to convince even your sworn enemies that you're victimized because people think you're *inferior* — but this has never been true! What did Eichmann say? "We're up against an enemy vastly superior to us by virtue of their millennia of learning." Your enemy has *never* thought you *inferior*, despite what your *Lügenpresse* and contemptible academia say; on the contrary, he finds you supremely powerful. It is what you *do* with your power he finds so repulsive, for you are ever the *subverter*, the *corrupter*, the *usurer*, the *enslaver*, the *wailer*, the *censor*. You annihilate what you cannot be: Good. To this day you have manipulated the world into empathizing with your lie, and the world protects you like a rabid lapdog.

In *your* Golden Age (the Age of Iron for the spiritual sons and daughters of the mystical 9), reality is based on the stories you have repeated since the end of the Great Struggle. You are no Patmosian seer, there is no *prediction* present — only programming; prediction needs creativity; programming needs only the cynical subversion of a spiritual history. Spread the lie in story form, then feign surprise at its materialization. Such materiality can be bought and sold, like the neurosis you seek to instill in others. Manufacture consent by manufacturing your image: *Der Arme Jude! Der Heldenhafte Jude!* The superman with the dark curls and eyes is a devil in disguise, a commercial inversion of the mystical *Übermensch* — one of your many "heroic" occurrences. Monetize the spiritual: merchants being merchants. You make your enemy the crook in your shows while the "dumb blond" hangs from the hook in your nose — more subversive inventions. You have done well in your Age of Gold, of *mammon*. You erect temples on the *Bergs* and *Steins* of gold (*Gold*), silver (*Silber*), sugar (*Zucker*), white (*Weiß*), black (*Schwarz*), red (*Roth*), wine (*Wein*), ruby (*Rubin*), and rose (*Rosen*). You program your compulsion and the submissiveness of those "un-chosen" wretches who believe your every word. You have written your own ending and that of the world. You are your own god and have birthed the devil: it is in the details of your inversion. During the Great Struggle, your enemies would have sent you to Madagascar — there you would have destroyed yourselves. Now the world is your Madagascar.

In the end, your heroism will prove itself as only catastrophe; the whole world will alight in the fires kindled by your mammon. And you? You will blacken the world as you harry it to the altars of Gehenna. Phoenicia will at last rise like a phoenix, carried aloft on the plumes of your sacrificial slaughter. Your demiurge will be fulfilled; this time cycle will end, and with it, your reign.

MISDIRECTIONS

Governments and their representatives do not have our best interests in mind. Whatever the governmental party, each has the same goal: turn the plebeians and the bourgeois into a slave caste meant to further enrich the technocratic plutocracy. The only difference between "left wing" and "right wing" in the prevailing liberal-democratic construct is the timeline on which this mass enslavement should occur. Those on the "left" want the change to begin in earnest immediately; those on the "right" want the change to be more gradual to lessen societal instability that might jeopardize current hierarchies. Money — and its concomitant "power" in our materialistic age — is the foundation of both "left" and "right," and the puppets squawking before us in government are representatives, not of the people, but of the *international clique* pulling strings from the shadows. It has increasingly been this way since the decline of the Germanic Age of man, beginning in the so-called Age of Enlightenment.

The aim of academic indoctrination in christening such a disastrous age for European man "enlightened" is to gain psychological effect: how could anyone be against *enlightenment*, *liberty*, *fraternity*, *equality*, etc. By giving an insidious thing a positive name, those in power coerce the masses into complicity. How could one stand against "liberty"? One could only be a *fascist*. Ostracism is the alternative to complicity — social, economic, ideological ostracism. Dare to counter the prevailing narrative and one is guaranteed a devastating isolation. Whether we talk of the past or present, such rules hold sway. Modern parallels of such psychological coercion include "hate speech" and "injustice": Surely one could never be against rules meant to curb *hate* or *injustice*? One could only be a monster to support either! Obviously, the devil is in the details, and when one peeks beneath the surface, the Trojan horse might hold a bellyful of assassins.

Before the Enlightenment, hereditary aristocracy was the order. The aristocracy did not become so by magic, but by noble blood. This blood rose to the top because of past merit. The better, functioning aristocracies ever sought to prove their merit through martial campaigning. Hence, we see the spread and domination of the Germanic people across Europe; hence, we see out of Medieval Europe the gradual rise of the nation-states: England, France, Portugal, Spain, Austria, etc. Peoples and cultures, defined through years of localized striving, soon found their martial campaigning funded by deeper pockets, and thus began the Age of Imperialism. These deeper pockets won the ear of the European nobility because the Germanic urge for glory is insatiable. Why win *local* glory when the *world* is within grasp? And so it was that the European peoples won the world, but forfeited their spirit. In its stead, they placed gold, and the beginning of the end was secured.

The decline of the Germanic Age sits in direct inverse proportion to the rise of the modern, money-oriented age — the rise of the Jewish Age. The Enlightenment saw the hereditary aristocracies overturned; in their place were positioned men of ability, but also men of ambition, men who bled for ideals. These ideals were captured in revolutionary constitutions, meant to morph with the masses to which they gave voice. But no revolution can endure without money, and the fomenters and financers of revolutions were borderless, Jewish moneymen. From the Grand Lodge of England, sparking the influence of international Freemasonry, to the "Bavarian" Illuminati, European revolutions had their shadowy ideological and financial supporters. Adam Weishaupt, founder of the Illuminati, once intimated, *Man, like clay, must be molded to fit the image of his creator*. Those seeking to be the new creators of men — or perhaps crafters of so many golems — saw not borders, but only pathways to ascendancy on the coattails of unsuspecting Germanic actors.

Both Freemasonry and the Illuminati sought to influence society by planting their adherents into positions of power — whether in politics or education. From these positions, the ideological purveyors would seek to inculcate various ideas of international brotherhood. Both societies, international in their aims, were vessels of the moneymen. Driven by their vital nomadism, the Jews would find a natural bedfellow in the international goals of "reason." While the early European Masons and Illuminati might have been genuine, albeit naïve, espousers of the "infinite perfectibility" of man, such a creed was supplanted with ideations of international power through usurpation of the *ancien régime*. Note that Adam Weishaupt's society name was Brother Spartacus; remember that Spartacus was the Thracian of "nomadic blood" who led the slave revolt against the Roman Republic. Note the many connections among Freemasons and the American and French Revolutions. Much has already been written about all of these links. What is important is Jewry's ascent began with the decline of Germandom.

Blood is the root of life. Race is the evidence of this. This is not to say the truism that without blood, life would not exist; but rather that blood — and the races representing it — is the meaning of life. Blood is not everything, but it is the beginning of everything. Blood, geographically and deliberately separated over countless generations, gave birth to the principal human races: White, Yellow, Red, Brown, and Black. Though miscegenation has and will occur, racial mixes, for lack of identity, will inevitably be subsumed into one of the main races — presupposing the racial mixes do not self-destruct before subsumption. Each of the principal races has internal order, whether real or imagined; and each of the races has external order, perceived or actual. History reveals the order. Impetuous innovation and spiritual-individualism mark the White, Germanic races; the Yellow races are noted for communal-materialism and farsighted wisdom; Red races represent spiritual-communal and earthy urges; the Brown races are paradoxically marked by their passion for conquest and dreams of idleness, a communal-individualism; and the Black races are known for their malleability and materialistic-tribalism. Without the blood their ancestors struggled to maintain, these races would not exist. Nature gave rise to them just as certainly as it gave rise to their dominant traits. As with all things, there are exceptions to the rule; but the exceptions prove the rule. Nature establishes the rules, and race is in harmony with Nature.

There is one mysterious exception to the rule of races that became a rule itself: Jewry. The Jew's origins are in the Brown races. Because of Jewry's peculiar self-love and disdain of other peoples, it has been booted from land to land, with no indigenous folk wanting it around once its dominant *paradoxicality* becomes known; hence, nomadism, or internationalism, is fundamental to Jewish character. But Jewry is distinct from the Brown races — hence its removal from other Brown societies; it is a subset of the Brown peoples that has mixed with the White. This mixing undoubtedly occurred in both Greece and Rome, preceding and precipitating the demise of each.

Miscegenation, however, did not amount to spiritual mixing; blood tainting was only the means to eventual toppling.

The Jews remained a distinct people, no matter the society. And from this "society within society" the Jews managed to consistently dominate two fields that would satiate their unyielding urge to usurp and enable them to conquer modernity: money and information. Religious tenets dictated their partiality to administrative work: *Work not with thy hands*, says the Talmud. Instead, use the ignorant non-Jews as the cattle they are, and master the laborers with vice and necessity.[63] Money and information were the keys to Jewry's success; both were needed in societies built on the strong backs of Germandom, and both could be used to degrade entrenched values; and the Germanic peoples, because of their scorn of both the Jews and the unmanly peddling of money and information, permitted the "Chosen People" to take full control of such effeminacy.

Not just the Germanic folk of modernity were conquered by the Jews' middle management. The Egyptians fell prey to Jewish scheming; the Persians, too, fell — victims of Jewish bloodletting, the great *Purim*, a festival of ritual murder where the Jews preemptively kill their goyim[64] enemies for fear of being discovered as subversive schemers; then fell the Greeks — from the mighty Athenian city-state, to the indomitable Sparta, the once-pure blood of antiquity succumbed to infidelity and cosmopolitanism, represented by Socrates' mongrel pug nose, debauched potbelly, and betrayal of the traditional gods; the Romans forfeited their wondrous republic and empire for conniving whispers of Pharisaism and debased wealth. In and out of Germanic societies the Jews slinked for centuries. Allow them in and they undercut traditional values — replacing them with their eternal "progressivism," which is to say, *internationalism*. Boot them out and they whine to the most gullible ears about being eternal victims of pervasive oppression. Ah, but just let them back in, and the money will flow; hunt the "oppressors" with a new, Jewish crusade, and worldly pleasures will follow. Which folk has ever been impervious to such trickery? And so it was that the Jews insinuated themselves into their host societies and carved a niche between the Brown and White races. The Germanic people sought glory and

[63] See *Immorality in the Talmud* and *Track of the Jew through the Ages*, Alfred Rosenberg. Commerce is preferred to any manual labor, which should be avoided and left for non-Jews.

[64] *Goyim* — i.e., *non-Jew*.

innovation; their impetuousness and gullibility made room for the race that would seek their downfall. This race is the *Ewiger Jude*: international in its aims; disruptive in its pleasures; revolutionary in its being.

Every folk that has allowed coexistence with the Jew has "progressed" itself into extinction. What was good becomes bad; what was wrong becomes right; down becomes up, and the unnatural becomes natural. The Jew will say such revaluation of values is for the good of all and necessary for societal progress. What they mean, however, in their undying spite for all goyim and their traditions, is that the non-Jew must die for the Jew to live. It is the essence of parasitism. Jewish feelings toward non-Jews have both healthy and unhealthy origins. It is healthy for a people to want to reach its full potential; doing so means having pride in one's essence — i.e., one's past, present, and future; faith in self is healthy. What is unhealthy, however, is the Jew's *hatred* toward non-Jews; this is naught but destructive, misplaced vindictiveness, born of Jewry's ignorance of its own disruptive nature. Jewry will remain spiteful and never understand why it has been expelled from countless non-Jewish societies: People — races — established through generations of foundational and defining values, *do not want to change*. To change what defines a people is *extinction*; it is *unnatural*.

The Jew, then, is maligned for being himself; he cannot be otherwise. Jewry seeks change for tribal profit at the expense of hosts, which only creates eternal enmity between the host and the hosted, the Jew and the non-Jew. In turn for being maligned for behaving how its own bloodline dictates, the Jew lashes out against its host folk: Jewry no longer wants only to fulfill its own potential, it now wants to *destroy* the people who allowed freedom to maneuver. Hence, we see the Purim, the Passover, the Reigns of Terror — in France and Russia; we see the two world wars — wars meant to annihilate the Germanic peoples; we are reminded incessantly of the so-called Holocaust — a hyperbolical interpretation of events that only reveals what the *Jew* intends on doing with the goyim; we see the gradual slaughter of the Palestinian people; we have protracted wars against all enemies of *Israel* in the Middle East; we see the endless violence of language and action in modern Western socio-political climates. The Jew is *obsessed* with violence and death, and finds expression of this obsession in the systematic sacrifice of non-Jews.

The means to perpetuate this sacrifice are money and information, which Jewry absolutely controls. Behind nearly every major Western media and financial institution is one or more Jews: Wells Fargo, Alphabet, Netflix, Rothschild & Co, The Walt Disney Company, Morgan Stanley, Meta/Facebook, Goldman Sachs, JPMorgan Chase, Comcast, Paramount Global, WarnerMedia, Evercore, The New York Times Company, Citigroup, IAC, Credit Suisse, etc. — this short list of astonishingly influential entities does not even include Jewish sway in academia or politics, nor the aforementioned companies' many subsidiaries. The Germanic bloodlines are relegated to second- and even third-class status in their own societies: they are the common workers and soldiers, the plebeians and bourgeois. In their diminished roles, the Germanic peoples are meant to be divided and subjugated. This not only keeps the host societies weak, but also strengthens the ruling class. The modern technocratic plutocracy seeks to strengthen its position, as many ruling classes before; but the difference among ruling elites lies in how power is sought and maintained. Whereas the Germanic peoples sought glory and honor for their bloodlines, the moneyed elite now seek only to further both the increase of wealth — through internationalism and, therefore, the obliteration of traditional values — and revolutionary societal movements — again, in support of international aims and out of spite for historical "injustices" perpetrated against an "innocent" racial group, the Jews. Destructive urges are behind modernity. Nature is meant to be ruined; and man is to be remade in the spirit of his earthly master, the Jew. In place of men, we will find only golems, organic robots.

Such hateful, destructive urges compel the vitriolic divisiveness agitating our current world. This is the urge behind "left" and "right" partisanship — each is subject to the same subversive master, the same upending inclinations: usurp traditions and emplace parasitical instincts. No matter how quickly or slowly the blood is drawn from the host, it is nevertheless drawn. Partisan bickering, media strikes and parries, political action committees, market fluctuations, and campaigning are only posturing — more show for the circus meant to distract the bourgeois and plebeians from the insidious assassins in their midst. *Internationalism — international socialism* or *globalism* — is the paradoxical myth of borderless brotherhood created by those who aim to destroy; this inimical myth is born of the (anti-)blood of its purveyors, the mysterious, murderous niche-race of world Jewry.

It might be that Nature has devised a way to ironically destroy itself; but it might be that Nature has devised a way to make those grown weak with victory ever stronger. A society with paradox at its base will soon find itself inverted. A society loyal to its roots, however, will reach the sun.

OUR PERIL

> *And this do I say also to the o'erthrowers of statues: It is certainly the greatest folly to throw salt into the sea, and statues into the mud. In the mud of your contempt lay the statue: but it is just its law, that out of contempt, its life and living beauty grow again!*
>
> — FRIEDRICH NIETZSCHE, *THUS SPOKE ZARATHUSTRA*

Peril engulfs the Germanic folk: it envelops from without; it rages from within. Out of this purifying peril, "its life and living beauty will grow again."

The Germanic man was born into peril. When the Supreme Creator found ITS work sullied by satanic Jehovahistic manipulation, IT seeded this world with salvation. The cold north, whose paradisiacal months-long day could only be enjoyed if one were willing to endure the equally long night, was the bridge from Asgard to Midgard. The north was desolate but for the determined intrepidity of its hero. *Walhalla* was born in the north; the salvific rays of the sunwheel radiated in all directions thereafter, and Demiurge-Jehovah's putrid playground moved closer to reclamation. Like any threatened beast, however, Jehovah announced his objection with spastic fits. Being born of Nature and rising because of his struggle with it, the Germanic man tamed his climatic master. His external threat, then, was no longer from the elements. From without, we see the menace of *the other*.

Race defines *the other*, just as geography helped define race; *some boundaries are final.* Race is not everything, but it is the beginning of everything. There are exceptions to every rule, but race is the rule. Character is the active reflection of race. The character of the Germanic man is to create; he is, after all, of the Supreme Creator. *The other*, as is its rule, can only destroy what the good has created in this world — be it natural or manmade. *The other* is the natural enemy of the Germanic man and is therefore pit against him.

This is not the latter's doing; the bleak north fostered the cooperative urge in the Germanic man; cooperation was survival; yet his struggle with the elements also fostered the will to conquer. When the elements were held at bay and living space was earned, Germanic sublimity shone through. Gothic spires reached for the heavens; well-tempered melodies harnessed immortality; chiaroscuro reflected the seemingly incongruous internal nature; this incongruity was only part of the larger whole, however. The Germanic urge is creative; creation is collaborative. Bach did not invent the clavier, but the melodies he created *with* it brought us closer to our divine origins. *The other*, in its will to destroy, despises collaboration; thus, it despises Germandom. From without, we, the Germanic folk, are under attack.

Our principal attacker is the Jew. As Dostoyevsky and many others have noted, the Jew has played the victim for all of its four-thousand-year history.[65] Despite being always the aggressor, the manipulator, the schemer, the Jew yet plays the victim. It is his irrevocable nature; *some boundaries are final.* Despite being always a minority in his host country, the Jew yet dominates the political, financial, and media stages. Thus it has been since Moses led the mass Passover-slaughter of Gentiles and Joseph undermined Pharaoh to pave the way for the non-Jews' absolute subjugation. Thus it has been since, millennia ago, the Israelites murdered numberless Canaanites to claim a "promised" land, and thus it is today as modern Israelites carve out an ethno-state from the blood and soil of numberless Palestinians. The Jew has complete freedom to establish and maintain his ethno-state; if the Germanic folk desire their own ethno-state, however, the Jew denounces them as "racist." The Jew would have us believe his actions are beyond reproach; but the Jew was born of duplicity.

Because of Jewry's stranglehold on nearly every form of media, we are constantly bombarded with the Jewish worldview. Likewise, we are indoctrinated with Jewish ethics through the educational and religious (Abrahamic) systems. In short, this worldview is reflected in, as Nietzsche described it, the morality of the "bungled and the botched," wherein those of low quality who would otherwise be cast aside or naturally fall behind are raised to the level of those of high quality — because of the cult-like faith in modernity's mammon, wherein money-wealth is considered an indicator of *quality*, and

[65] Dostoyevsky, *Diary of a Writer*, "On the Jewish Question."

because of belief in universal "human dignity," as if such a thing were inherent in every biological human merely because it exists.

Moreover, the Jew espouses both a psychoanalytical (deconstructive) and nihilistic worldview, which are each undergirded by a Jewish-scientific conception of reality. *All are equal by virtue of existence because (1) we all come from the same pool of slime* [universalism], *(2) we are all headed to a cold, dark, lifeless cosmological end* [linearity], *and (3) we are all* one *human race with naught but superficial differences, diversity is our strength, and we would be wise to eat, drink, and be merry* [hedonism, materialism, universalism]. So says the Jew. But this worldview is only a means to an end; it is preached, but not commonly practiced among the Jews. To be sure, they certainly are a hedonistic lot, given to base and rampant materialism, which reflects only their unspiritual conception of reality that is, in turn, based on a rabbinic law secularly distilled into its humanistic essence. Yet *they* do not often practice the miscegenation that seems to sit at the foundation of their propagated worldview. On the contrary, by staying racially pure and mixing all *other* races, they strengthen *their* position by weakening others: they preach diversity, equality, freedom, and other abstractions[66] in a materialistic context to destroy the mythical-

---

[66] *Liberté, égalité, fraternité* — the motto of the French Revolution and subsequent republic, a harbinger of modernity. A relevant excerpt from Dieter Schwarz: "[Freemasonry] ... enables the Jews to achieve social and political equality, and paves the way for Jewish radicalism through its support for the principles of freedom, equality, and brotherhood, the solidarity of peoples, the League of Nations and pacifism, and the rejection of all racial differences.... Freemasonry spread very rapidly in France.... In Paris, the lodge of the Encylopaedists, called 'The Nine Sisters,' was active from 1769. Among the members of this lodge were Helvetius, Lalande, Benjamin Franklin, Count La Rochefoucauld, d'Alembert, Camille Desmoulins, Diderot, and Brissot. Here, the guiding principles and ideas of the French Revolution were given their characteristic features and further developed. The slogan of 'Liberty, Equality, Fraternity,' the principle of the equality of all who bear a human face, the universal rights of man, were all worked out in this lodge, and advocated aggressively in a revolutionary spirit. A general inversion of all values set in. The governmental form of absolutism and its opposition to Masonic democracy and republicanism was the object of particular animosity in these conflicts. This direction reached its climax, and at the same time, its temporarily successful conclusion, in the French Revolution. 629 lodges were then at work in France, 65 of which were

spiritual foundations of humanity and create the conditions for their supremacy.

But such is the essence of the Jew: his instinct is to subvert and deceive. Man is no longer man, but a deconstructed cog in a rationalistic machine bent on personal profit. The prophets and patriarchs of the Hebrew Bible were the first to speak of such profits: Ahasuerus, the rootless Jew, being dispersed among the nations, found his hearth and home in his fellow Jew, which is why each Jew's lot is thrown in with the other's — this is the impetus for their parasitical activity against host societies.

This, too, is why world Jewry was quick to decry National Socialist Germany's attempts to thwart rife, seditious criminality in its rejuvenated society: overwhelmingly, the Jews represented the criminal element within Germany — certainly they embodied the Marxist, subversive elements. Criminal or not, the Jewish-backed media and politicians protested any actions taken against the "Chosen Race." Thus, long before the first salvos of World War II, world Jewry declared war on Hitler's Germany.[67] Yet we are led to believe the Jews are only helpless victims. Such lies! Jehovah made the "chosen" Jew in his manipulative, power-seeking image, which destines him for worldly, de-spiritualized success. The Jew's inclination is to prize rationality above irrationality, the material above the spiritual, severing man's tether to the divine. By debasing man and demiurgically exploiting Nature for personal profit, Ahasuerus becomes his own messiah, and the immortality he gains comes not from the honorable living-in-accordance-with-Nature that earns one's place among the pantheon and posterity, but rather from the human clay he pummels into his likeness through media manipulation and policymaking — i.e., *deception*: he is the insatiable, jealous god he formerly worshipped. Subversion of the natural order is the Jew's essence: he is the organic lie.

---

located in Paris alone." *Freemasonry: Ideology, Organization, and Policy* (Berlin: NSDAP Central Publishing House, 1944), 9 and 14.

[67] "Judea Declares War On Germany: Jews Of All The World Unite In Action" — headlines like this one from the United Kingdom peppered Europe and the Americas in 1933, the year the National Socialists won power. Hitler's "mere" *existence*, because HE was the speaker of the Germanic folk's rights, was seen as a wrong to be righted. Hitler knew the path, foretold by Nietzsche, to the revaluation of values, which would reassert the honor of the Aryan folk and inevitably topple *Welt Judentum*.

Israel itself was spawned from deception. Jacob, son of Isaac, relied exclusively on trickery to attain his father's blessing and his brother's birthright. Instead of helping pitiable Esau in a *brotherly* way, Jacob immediately saw an opportunity to *exploit for personal gain*: "Sell me your birthright [and I'll help you, Esau]." Just like that Esau lost his birthright; Jacob pounced on Esau's flippancy in his disadvantaged state — Jehovah made it so in the preceding verses: "the elder [son] shall serve the younger"[68] — *subversion in essence.* On his deathbed, Isaac called for Esau to give the eldest son his blessing. Unnaturally enough, Rebekah, Isaac's wife and Esau's mother, learned of Isaac's intent and unhesitatingly conspired against him; she called Jacob forth and set a trap that would ensure Jacob, not Esau, would receive the dying man's blessing. *Exploit for personal gain* — that's the name of the Jewish game. Rebekah and Jacob availed themselves of Isaac's failing eyesight: "Who are you, my son?" Quick with a lie, Jacob answered, "I am Esau, your firstborn... [I have returned from my hunt so quickly] because the Lord your God granted me success." "Are you really my Esau?" Isaac wondered. "I am," Jacob lied again. So Jacob received his father's blessing — the conspiratorial fruit of a mother and son against the father.[69] We should expect nothing less from a people who needed commandments from their Jehovah to know how to behave.

Rectitude is not in their nature or their blood — it is in the *contract*, the *business transaction*, they made with Jehovah, which, invariably, means there are loopholes to *exploit*. Rectitude, then, becomes *relative* — not unlike Einsteinian physics — thus eluding direct definition: a useful perspective for a people destined to insinuate itself among the peoples of this world. Finally, later in life, enjoying the fruits of his lies, Jacob wrestled with Jehovah. Jehovah lost the match and, being the spiteful one he is, injured Jacob's hip. Upon his defeat, when Jehovah demanded to be let go, Jacob refused, opting instead to finagle yet another blessing away from someone he has disadvantaged: "I will not let you go unless you bless me." Jehovah indeed blessed Jacob, and that very moment changed his name to Israel.[70] *Deceit* is the midwife of Israel and all its blessings.

Thus we see foreign and domestic policies favoring the Jew (and his *useful idiot* helpers) and harming those of Germanic (European)

---

[68] Genesis 25:31, 23.

[69] See Genesis 27.

[70] See Genesis 32.

descent; thus we see history rewritten to erase the Germanic folk who made it; thus we see science and academia reinvented to enshrine the Jewish revaluation of values and enslave the Germanic man. In every US National Defense Authorization Act we find provisions that explicitly prop up (materially and morally) the Jewish ethno-state of Israel. Despite it being clear that Israel is the *source* of instability in the Middle East, it must become *law* that the belief Israel is the *solution* to instability should be relentlessly *promoted.* Domestically, non-European immigrants flood all Western states as a political weapon: "progressive" political parties aim to establish an undefeatable electorate too ignorant and distracted to realize they are naught but the *useful idiot* proletariat — hammered into form by mind-numbing, leveling policy, and harvested for votes with the sickle of perpetual "progressive" dictatorship.

Moreover, natural, traditional family units of man-woman-child — havens for traditionalist values (i.e., the vestigial values of Hegel's "German World" that made the modern world possible) — are undermined at every turn, whether through establishing policies that support mindless, deadbeat or single-parent welfare recipients, whether through insidious entertainment programming that denounces traditional "supremacist" families and aims to normalize debauched, psychotic replacement behaviors and general dysfunctionality, or through Germanic children being subjected to all manner of emotional and psychological abuse in an education system that seeks to overwrite with self-hate whatever remaining racial pride they have. *Equity* (equal outcomes) usurps *equality* (equal opportunity) as the means to a viable future; thus, destruction (robbing one group to pay another — i.e., equity) is made governmental edict. *Diversity* and *inclusion* are enforced and announced in every classroom and boardroom; "diversity and inclusion" is euphemism for "tear down traditions" and "make less white [Germanic]" — we hear the subversive refrain of Genesis 25.

This insanity expands to media as well: sub-Saharan Africans, for example, somehow become prominent members of historical European society in various entertainment programming; non-Germanic newscasters get a free pass to heap race-hatred on people of European descent, and narratives are propagated supporting the lie of frequent deviant behavior in those of European descent and frequent model behavior in those of non-European descent — meanwhile "diverse and inclusive" cities across the West are beset with crime and violence ("crime" itself, of course, is only another form of "white [Germanic] supremacy"), all while study after study (not to mention human instinct) shows that people are most happy and safe in racially homogeneous communities (but these studies are invariably "racist"); media "pundits" wax philosophical about the absurdity of people of European descent sharing in the glory of the achievements of their race, while in the next deranged breath they declare all whites "guilty!" and demand reparations for the "crimes" their ancestors committed; and we are reminded *incessantly* of the so-called *Holocaust* — Jewry's cattle prod to corral the Germanic man's natural pride — never mind that every abuser who has ever lived maintains his power by incessantly accusing, constantly degrading, and continuously disparaging the abused. What major Western city *doesn't* have a Holocaust museum or memorial?

Yet we are told the *abusers* are the *victims*. This effort began in earnest after Germany's material defeat in World War II. By 1945, with the founding of the United Nations Educational, Scientific, and Cultural Organization (UNESCO) by a ragtag group of Jews and avowed communists,[71] all heretofore science and scholarship regarding blood and race was subverted and upturned: blood and race were no longer substantive, they were "social construct." Thus we live in a world where, if science demonstrates that there are indeed real differences among the races, approved "science" and academia must swoop in — with full media backing — for swift

[71] UNESCO drafted its statement on the "race question" in 1950, at the nadir of the Allied occupation of the now-puppet state of Germany. Its authors were: Morris Ginsberg, a Jewish sociologist interested in the "liberal disposition"; Claude Lévi-Strauss, a Jewish anthropologist whose structural anthropology is founded on the premise that all cultures are essentially equal; Ashley Montagu, a Jewish anthropologist who zealously called race "man's most dangerous myth"; Juan Comas, a Spanish communist and anthropologist; Humayun Kabir, an Indian politician who served in the administrations of communist prime ministers; Luis de Aguiar Costa Pinto, a Brazilian sociologist aligned with the communist Brazilian Workers' Party; Ernest Beaglehole, a New Zealander psychologist whose brother and confidant, John Beaglehole, was influenced by the Jewish communist Harold Laski; and E. Franklin Frazier, a black sociologist who rose to prominence writing of the "black proletariat" and under the intellectual aegis of the Jew Isaac Rice. Despite such allegiances and, in fact, how their statement itself reads, we must *believe* the authors' motivations are entirely *objective*. This, of course, is akin to believing the sheep would be unbiased in its assessment of the wolf.

damage control; hence we see Nobel Laureate James Watson ostracized for his findings that racial differences do, in fact, exist; hence we see acclaimed geneticist Ronald Fisher un-personed for the same reasons. Keep in mind that racial differences are permitted to exist when they highlight the superiority of non-Germanic people: it is a given that sub-Saharan Africans are "physically superior" to Europeans; it is only natural that East Asians are "intellectually superior" to Europeans; it is, however, *racist* and *unthinkable* that Europeans are intellectually superior to sub-Saharan Africans and physically superior to East Asians. *This is psychological manipulation par excellence.*

Moreover, we see time and again the Jew — who is decidedly *not* "white" (i.e., Germanic) — claiming to be "white" when he seeks to disparage people of European descent, while almost simultaneously dodging all claim to being "white" when he comes under attack from his *useful idiots* for being "white"; social media publishers abound with such deception. Such wild dissimulation can only come from the organic lie. All of the aforementioned efforts have but one goal: to install Jews in positions of supremacy; they are the "Chosen Race," after all, and they see it as their destiny to attain supremacy over the non-Jews by any means necessary. Because the Germanic folk, through their creative will and harmony with the Nature of the Supreme Creator, rose to supremacy to reclaim this world from the clutches of Jehovah, it is the Jew's principal goal to thwart, subvert, and enslave them. It would be naïve, however, to suggest that such a minority, powerful as it is, is alone responsible for their ascendancy. Our peril also rages from within.

No matter how many times the Jews were expelled from their European host nation, they were always allowed to return. Money and sophistry are quite persuasive. Whether considering Cromwell, Napoleon, or any of their ilk, good intentions always led to later decline; lend the Jew your ear and he'll take your head. And now here we are: past noblemen sold their Germanic spirit for mammon; because of what material he could gain, the Jew was given precedence over Germanic kinsmen. Gradually, the Jew took control; the Enlightenment, which began as a Germanic rejection of Levantine popery, was hijacked by the "international brotherhood," traditions were trashed, and two devastating world wars against *all* Germanic people were waged.

And, after generations of being throttled by the Jewish worldview, most people of Germanic descent today are hardly worth keeping: many are unfit — physically, mentally, or spiritually. Many are unthinking consumers — content to distract themselves with sport, show, or tech. Still more are prisoner to the Jewish slave-morality of Christianity: formerly, when the Germanic *Geist* reigned, the honorable man would thrash his enemies; now, the meek Christian is reminded to "turn the other cheek" — like a coward. This is designed, of course, to give the Jew maximum latitude to do as he pleases within the host "Christian" people. Yet even if the Christian has prevailing Germanic qualities and is not a coward, he cannot escape the cancerous internationalism inherent in his religion: all are Jehovah's children — whether dark-skinned pygmy or Germanic goddess, whether brain-dead sub-Saharan criminal or heroic European, Jehovah sees no difference.

This is supposed to be uplifting? No, this is *Judaic inversion in its purest form*. It is often the *best-case* scenario that the person of European descent is Christian, unfortunately — as Christianity superimposed itself onto the Germanic (pagan) worldview and values: at least the Christian, despite his universalistic cowardice, yet values sacrifice and some species of honor and decency. These noble values originated in pre-Christian Europe; with the arrival of Roman-Jewish Christianity, they were dragged through the dirt. If anything good exists in European Christianity, it has its beginnings in Germanic heathenry. But Christianity is itself hastening toward extinction; in its wake comes effeminate atheistic nihilism, born out of the Jew's secular humanism. Many people of Germanic descent buy into the materialistic lie of atheistic positivism or humanism; and thus, they are rendered completely useless — nothing more than a tool of the Jew in his machinations for world supremacy. The atheist, like his puppet master, has no creative urge; he can only destroy the faith-driven myth-making of the ancient Germanic *Geist* — indeed, look up "mythologize" (in the dictionary or elsewhere) and you will find example after example of its "dangers." The European folk are indoctrinated to fear and hate myth; this even arises out of the convoluted mess of the Jew playing both sides: fostering subservient Christianity on the one hand, and deriding European myth (manifested in Christianity, Hinduism, or heathenry) on the other. Divide and conquer: this plays only into the hands of those who seek the destruction of the Germanic folk — whether Jew or goy-atheist.

If the Germanic folk are to endure, they must return to their ancient roots: these roots have nothing to do with alien Christianity or atheism. Universalism sits at the heart of each of these worldviews; universalism is antithetical to blood and race and, therefore, Nature. Universalism — the creed of Christianity, international socialism (now globalism), Freemasonry, and nihilism — is the pathway for Jewish supremacy. All history is testament to this. History — and, indeed, time itself — has accelerated since the material defeat of spiritually centered Germany in World War II. This means the Jew's power is increasing; the acceleration of this supremacy comes in large part on the shoulders of Germanic ignorance. Perhaps in some cases it is not ignorance, but the Germanic *will to cooperation* that works against us — as if so many Cromwells harbor the Jews so as to bring about Christ's Second Coming, or perhaps some Marxist utopia. Expect this and you'll win only the Antichrist — so the signs speak endlessly around us. All too many people of European descent are content to fill their idle brains and bodies with the mass-produced filth the Jews themselves would never dare consume: the global elite would never consume their own product, of course. This mindless consumption makes such puppet-Europeans disposable; the coming resurgence of the Germanic man will not suffer the idle ignorance of so many *useful idiots* — be they European or otherwise.

Peril does indeed engulf us. We can steel ourselves against it by falling back to the spiritual redoubts within. This will prepare us for the present and future onslaught — whether it comes from the Jews themselves or, more likely, from their *useful idiot* goyim. *Myth is our only salvation.* This does not mean we sit idly by and wait for some imagined savior. Rather, it means we prepare ourselves *now* — mentally, physically, and spiritually.

We reassert our values — the values that made everything good in this world possible — and live them. We exercise our whole being. We surround ourselves with like-minded people. We remember and promote the *myth* and *fact* of race and blood; we love our family and worthwhile kinsmen; we discard everything that counters myth. We recall that our warrior-artist ancestors were not universalists — they were neither Christian nor atheist; they were not *internationalists.* We remember that *we made Walhalla.* And we recognize that through our shared past and vision of the future — through our Germanic culture — we will meet our future destiny with honor, with dignity, with an all-embracing love for our folk. *The future belongs to us* — because this world, and everything good in it, belongs to God, our Supreme Creator.

THE GERMANIC WILL

The Germanic will is God and brings light to this dark world. Darkened through enslavement, this world belongs to Jehovah. Jehovah is the god of the Jews. Being the antipode of the Aryans, the Jews cast only aspersions on the Germanic God, equating that which *brings light* to the Jehovahistic dark with *Satan*. But the enslaver, Jehovah, *is* Satan, and Jehovah's emissaries are satanic. Both aim to be kings of this world through exploitative power. It is no small thing that the Jewish Bible calumniates Lucifer, the *light bringer*. Light in the dark is freedom; it is a blazing wisdom. *Lucifer* is not Satan; *Jehovah* is Satan. *Lucifer* is the Judeo-Christian (*Christianus Roma*) name for the Aryan will. The Indo-Aryan (or Hindu-Aryan) name for the Germanic will is *Vishnu*. The Germanic name for the Aryan will is *Wotan*.

Jehovah the Enslaver — *Satan* — has only ever demonized that which threatened its exploitative power. Hence we see Nature demonized; Nature is harmony and harmony is antithetical to Hebrew exploitation; Irminsul, the Germanic symbol of Nature, was destroyed by race-traitors, those who chose earthly power over divine blood. We see polytheism demonized; jealous Jehovah can only do violence to the humble, multifaceted interpretations of Nature; Charlemagne was the vessel for Pharisaic popery to infect the Aryan harmony of Germanic Europe. We see cyclicality demonized; Jehovah and the Jewish mind are linear: Jehovah is the "Alpha and Omega," the "beginning and the end" — exploitative predation cannot see beyond itself; such finality lends itself to atheism, which is why Jewish "science" and its bedfellow liberalism always end in relativistic, material decay.

Indeed, liberalism was and is the means by which the Jews plan to dispel the *ancien régime*, paving their way to power. Liberalism will turn out to be nothing more than the chains of a Jewish supremacy, the binds of a future indentureship for goyim serfs. Liberalism is a tool of the *golem-craftsmen*, as is money. Modernity's gods: liberalism and money; one is the Great Leveler, one the Great Divider. We witness the fruits of this dichotomous pairing in the failing American experiment. The twin evils of "equality" and "equity" are foisted upon all Western peoples — and, because of ignorance, indolence, or complicity, they do nothing about it; indeed, they lap it up, as if a "lack of opportunity" is what holds certain people back from "success." This is naught but Jewish dissimulation, Marxism.

Equality (equal opportunity) has been around and imposed for so long, without attaining desired results, that *equity* (equal outcomes) is now being forced down everyone's throat. *Equality* is a cancerous doctrine that no significant person has ever truly believed. *Equality* is dishonesty, and dishonesty is the foundation of our dying world. Providing equal opportunity clearly failed. No one dares ask *why*. *Equity* is meant to replace it: this means forcibly (but subtly) stealing from the haves (the whites-of-European-descent *bourgeois*) and redistributing the stolen goods to the have-nots (the non-white *proletariat*). This will simultaneously disintegrate the middle class and bolster the dependency of the engorged and willing slave-class, strengthening the Jews' authoritarian grip.

Money for the Jew, likewise, is a tool for both fomenting instability and consolidating power. That the Jew derives his power from others' weakness is both historical fact and curiosity. What other race can claim such distinction? None — for no other race hates humanity so much. The Jew hides his contempt for goyim through a veneer of goodwill and philanthropy. Yet these are only ventured if they bring profit. Ultimate profit is supremacy, which is what drives their every action, every decision. Where does the philanthropist send his money? Liberal, progressive organizations absorb his money. This serves to keep the proletarian pitchforks off his lawn and drives the societal destabilizers that consolidate his power. The uneducated masses passively accept this feudal state; the educated — or indoctrinated — masses actively espouse it, trained as they are by the psychotic leftism of media and academia. We experience a world of *commissars*, each one waiting to inculpate a non-compliant, not-sufficiently-enthusiastic citizen; our world is a product of Jewish, dialectical materialism: abstractions and alienation mark the way to hell. The Jew Kafka knew this world quite well; he simply recorded what his blood whispered to him. We experience a trial of dishonesty, the natural state of the unnatural Jehovah and his golems.

The Germanic will stands for honesty. What is *honesty*? Honesty is harmony with Nature. Harmony with Nature is recognizing racial differences. Harmony with Nature is recognizing that not all are created equal. These are facts of reality. The sooner this is understood, the better. Or should we kill all the wolves in the world because they prey on the fawn, the rabbit, or the sick, straggling beast? Should we nail or tie all the fallen tree limbs back to their former trunk? Should we force-inject everyone with this or that because we need to protect those who are too sickly or undisciplined to take care of themselves? Nature keeps trying to kill the worst of us, but we keep stopping her. But Nature will win because Nature is harmony. The spectral, demiurgical world is a disharmony whose days are numbered.

We must remember that race is not everything, but it is the beginning of everything. How could all races be equal? It is impossible. Races are physically different; races are mentally different; races are spiritually different. There is nobility in welcomed difference. Cowards are frightened of difference — just as cowards are frightened of change, of war. But war is the father of all things. Shiva the Destroyer is also the Creator. The Jews would have us all comingle until the disparate races are melted (in the liberal "melting pot") into one mocha mass — devoid of race, character, and will: a brown, goyim glob sustained only to do the bidding of Jewish masters. Nobility lies in racial integrity, in the *distinction* of races, which must be separate to maintain their dignity, to maintain their race-specific equality. How can one imagine that class, social status, economics, or geography can determine *individual* character, but, for instance, geography cannot determine *racial* character? This absurdity is pure Jewish-Marxist dissemblance, another ploy to enslave the non-Jews — accepters and espousers alike. Such dialectical gibberish stands as the god of the golems. That the Jews, who are fanatically Jehovahistic, are essentially atheist — and this atheistic materialism rules modernity — is no illogic: Jehovah is death.

Jewish atheism, which, paradoxically, is a *fanatical theism*, is the hallmark of modernity. Jewish atheism — which is to say, Jewry — is the mortar binding Judaism, Christianity, humanism, liberalism, secularism, international socialism, communism, and globalism. This ideological progression suggests enslavement through a revaluation of ancient values: Aryan spirituality — the Germanic will — is replaced with Jewish materialism; honor is substituted for profit; noble races are replaced with mongrel consumers; God is replaced with Satan-Jehovah. Folk are deracinated for Jewish supremacy. For who foments instability and cosmopolitan revolution for profit? Who becomes a "philanthropist" with the monies gained from provoked revolutions, financing further destabilizing (e.g., "social change") and revolutionary (e.g., "social justice") groups? Who sits atop the modern instruments of national power? The Jew. Jews run the *diplomatic* corps, and government is brimming with them.[72] Jews own and operate nearly all major *informational* platforms and publishers.[73] The non-Jew is an anomaly in *finance* and *economics*.[74]

---

[72] Prominent Jews in the current US administration (this list is not exhaustive): Antony Blinken, Secretary of State; Ron Klain, Chief of Staff; Janet Yellin, Secretary of Treasury; Alejandro Mayorkas, Secretary of Homeland Security; Merrick Garland, Attorney General; Jared Bernstein, Council of Economic Advisers; Rochelle Walensky, Director, Centers for Disease Control and Prevention; Wendy Sherman, Deputy Secretary of State; Anne Neuberger, Deputy National Security Adviser for Cybersecurity; Jeffrey Zients, COVID-19 Response Coordinator; David Kessler, Co-chair of the COVID-19 Advisory Board and Head of Operation Warp Speed; Avril Haines, CIA Director; David Cohen, CIA Deputy Director; Rachel Levine, Deputy Health Secretary; Jennifer Klein, Co-chair Council on Gender Policy; Jessica Rosenworcel, Chair of the Federal Communications Commission; Stephanie Pollack, Deputy Administrator of the Federal Highway Administration; Polly Trottenberg, Deputy Secretary of Transportation; Mira Resnick, State Department Deputy Assistant Secretary for Regional Security; Roberta Jacobson, National Security Council "border czar"; Gary Gensler, Securities and Exchange Commission Chairman; Genine Macks Fidler, National Council on the Humanities; Chanan Weissman, Director for Technology and Democracy at National Security Council; Thomas Nides, U.S. Ambassador to Israel; Eric Garcetti, U.S. Ambassador to India; David Cohen, U.S. Ambassador to Canada; Mark Gitenstein, U.S. Ambassador to the European Union; Deborah Lipstadt, Special Envoy to Monitor and Combat Anti-Semitism; Jonathan Kaplan, U.S. Ambassador to Singapore; Marc Stanley, U.S. Ambassador to Argentina; Rahm Emanuel, U.S. Ambassador to Japan; Sharon Kleinbaum, Commissioner of the United States Commission on International Religious Freedom; Dan Shapiro, Adviser on Iran; Michael Adler, U.S. Ambassador to Belgium; Michèle Taylor, U.S. Representative to the United Nations Human Rights Council; Jonathan Kanter, Assistant Atorney General in the United States Department of Justice Antitrust Division; Jed Kolko, Under Secretary of Commerce for Economic Affairs at the Department of Commerce; Aaron Keyak, Deputy Envoy to Monitor and Combat Anti-Semitism; Stuart Eizenstat, Special Adviser on Holocaust Issues; Dana Stroul, Deputy Assistant Secretary of Defense for the Middle East; Cass Sunstein, Administrator Office of Information and Regulatory Affairs; Eric Lander, Director Office of Science and Technology.

[73] While this list is by no means exhaustive, these companies (and their subsidiaries) represent an overwhelming majority of media produced/published: Alphabet/Google (Lawrence Page, Sergey Brin, and Ruth Porat)/YouTube (Susan Wojcicki); Comcast (Brian Roberts and David Cohen); Disney (Robert Iger, legacy; Bob Chapek); Discovery, Inc. (David

Intelligence agencies are nothing more than Jewish watchdogs, fiercely protecting all Jewish interests, foreign and domestic (e.g., through "hate speech" or "anti-Semitism" monitoring; through entrapment; or through ginning up "intelligence reports" indicting US-Israeli adversaries). The *legal* field is awash with Jewish judges and lawyers — from political appointees in the Supreme and district courts to corporate and political lawyers. And, while Jewish presence in the *military* is scant, it is subject to governmental policy, which is firmly in Jewish control.[75] All of this control has but one end: death of the Germanic folk, for only they are capable of resisting and overpowering Jewish supremacy.

From 1933 to 1945, when the centuries-old creative will of the Germanic people culminated in the being of the Führer, Adolf Hitler, all the Jewish-aligned world rose up in terror: the Aryans threatened Jewish supremacy; light threatened dark; life stood up to death; and God threatened the Devil. This could not be; destructive darkness must reign in the Kali-Yuga; it is part of cyclical time. Creative urges *against time* give us glimpses of Satya-Yugas past and future, but their time is not yet. This is why the Hitlerian Order had to "fail"; but this material defeat was spiritual victory, for as Clausewitz

---

Zaslav); Group Nine Media (Ben Lerer); Lionsgate (Mark Rachesky and John Feltheimer); AT&T (John Stankey); Warner Bros. and Turner Broadcasting (Ann Sarnoff); Jeff Zucker (Warner Media News & Sports); Hearst Communications (Steve Swartz); NBCUniversal (Jeff Shell); Hasbro (Brian Goldner, legacy); National Amusements and Paramount Global (Shari "Redstone" Rothstein); Netflix (Marc Bernays Randolph and Reed Hastings); Meta/Facebook (Mark Zuckerberg); Blumhouse Productions (Jason Blum); Imagine Entertainment (Brian Grazer); Participant Media (Jeff Skoll and David Linde); Amblin Partners (Steven Spielberg); Sony Pictures (Tom Rothman); Amazon Studios (Jennifer Salke).

[74] This list is neither exhaustive, nor does it capture banking firms: Jim Simons; Carl Icahn; Steve Cohen; David Tepper; Israel Englander; George Schwartz (Soros); Nelson Peltz; David Siegel; Daniel Och; Paul Singer; Daniel Loeb; John Paulson; Bill Ackman; Joseph Edelman; the Rothschilds.

[75] Military officials can often be heard saying the military and, indeed, special operations forces are "too white" and must be "diversified." One suspects a "diverse" (i.e., less white) military is an essential ingredient in consolidating future authoritarian power for the Jews. A white military would be less likely to turn its guns on a dissenting white population — thus the need for a "diverse" military (specifically the leadership, combat arms, and special operations).

presciently noted, "even the loss of freedom after an honorable and bloody battle secures the rebirth of the people and is the seed of life from which, one day, a new tree will strike firm root." And the Führer: "From the sacrifice of our soldiers and my own solidarity with them unto death, a seed will one day germinate in German history ... and bring about the shining rebirth of the National Socialist movement and the realization of a true *Volksgemeinschaft*." The Jews themselves, despite their fervent wish, acknowledge this *winning by losing* in their Judeo-Christian eschatology: their Lucifer (the Aryan will) is defeated at the hands of Jehovah (Satan); but for the battle to exist at all, it must be a product of cyclicality: nothing comes *ex nihilo*;[76] the Aryan battling the Jew is the very essence of existence. The Jews know this — thus their relentless attack on all things Germanic. They will and have succeeded in blinding a great many Germanic folk to this reality. Modernity — the end of time — is destructive death at its core and must be fulfilled in a Jewish supremacy that thrusts the world into its final collapse. This is why harmony must be replaced with exploitation; this is why spirit and myth must be replaced with godless materialism; this is why Nature-ordained races must be mixed; this is why the *ancien régime* must be inverted; this is why there must be a "dictatorship of the proletariat" — a mass of raceless slaves ruled by the Jews.

---

[76] The Jews are terrified of a cyclical existence, hence their conspicuous lack of measure and obsessive pushiness — e.g., see the "Holocaust," the countless and incessant headlines about "Nazis" or "anti-Semitism," or any of the several times throughout history they have been expelled from European countries. (They are desperate to complete their self-appointed task of world domination "before the end" — what end? The end they know is coming.) Passages like this, from 2 Maccabees 7:28, aim to offer foundation for their pushiness, as if their actions were divinely ordained (emphasis added): "I *beseech* you, my child, to look at the heaven and the earth and see everything that is in them, and *recognize that God did not make them out of things that existed*." This passage feverishly seeks to indicate, as with so much Jewish theology and philosophy, that Jehovah could not possibly be a *demiurge*, that Jehovah is only *creator*, not *crafter*. Yet this world, like all creation, belongs not to the Demiurge-Jehovah, but to the Supreme Creator, God of the Germanic folk. The cyclical creation stories of the Indo-Aryan people are rightly captured in Germanic "heathenry" and Vedic Hinduism; these are the myths of the Supreme Creator; all else is derivative, linear Jehovahism.

How did an anti-race of slaves come to rule modernity? Firstly, they steeled themselves against a Germanic world — it was a threat to them, as were all non-Jewish societies; they worked diligently to understand their opponent's weakness. Honor and honesty defined the Germanic folk, thus the Jew sought to exploit each. Honesty can be availed with deceit; honor can be conquered by changing the rules of the game — the revaluation of values. Slave-morality, as Nietzsche identified, is a product of the Jew. To conquer the Germanic virtues of manliness and courage, a new idea was introduced: that of meekness and deferment — "turn the other cheek," "the meek shall inherit the earth." That the Germanic people succumbed to such effeminate nonsense is a testament to the inevitability of the Kali-Yuga: it was simply meant to be. But, just as assuredly, it is inevitable that Jewish supremacy will collapse on itself in unprecedented world destruction.

It will never be the case that all Germanic folk will perish, for they will be the light-bearing seeds of the coming age. Yet many will fall prey to the Jewish worldview as manifested in Judaism, Christianity, humanism, liberalism, secularism, international socialism, communism, and globalism. But these golem-gods cannot conquer our Germanic will: it is spirit, race, and myth — it is family and God that make a folk great. *Nothing else*. Our honor is loyalty; honesty is our doctrine. Our children will grow up knowing they are part of something much greater than their individual selves. They represent their ancestors; they represent their descendants; they represent their God; they represent everyone with Germanic blood. This is honesty, and honesty is what all children should be taught. Because the principal creative urge in this world is borne by the Germanic folk, their dwindling will feel like the precipice of unsalvageable disaster. But all will not be lost. The Germanic will is God — and God is an inextinguishable light-bringing fire.

CHAPTER 5
DIE SCHWARZE SONNE

MYTH OF THE BLACK SUN

At the top of the world stands the Midnight Mountain.
Its Light is everlasting.
Man's eyes cannot see it —
and yet it is there.
Over the Midnight Mountain shine the rays of
the Black Sun.
Man's eyes cannot see them —
and yet they are there.
Inside, their Light shines.
Lonely are the brave and the righteous;
but within them is the Godhead.

— WILHELM LANDIG, *REBELLEN FÜR THULE*

Demiurge-Jehovah's gaze fixed on the tropics and deserts, the warm climes of the beasts' molded home. Man in Jehovah's image was a crude, primitive sort, not given to intrepidity; this early version of man was slothful and unclean, prone more to midday lazing under the watchful, blazing eyes of his world's crafter than any knowing exertions of the will. When any of these brutes stumbled into using their will, it was for this or that material gain. *What nice things can I get for myself? How can I show off my power?* Such were the dreams fogging the beasts' minds. Jehovah saw this and thought it good, for their motivations were the same; his golems suited his manipulative efforts, and his power, he thought, was every bit worthy of the Supreme Creator.

The world's poles, meanwhile, were left unattended — there, Nature was too harsh and unlivable for the weak willed. Northern lands, particularly, were hospitable only to the right sort of being, one whose existence was predicated on creative will; and it was there the Supreme Creator saw opportunity for infill. Creative spark would yet people the Earth.

In prehistory, the eyes of the ancient Aryan would embrace the northern night sky. His world was dark for half the year, and in this darkness, he communed with his celestial home. His people banded together for warmth, for safety and kinship — they relied on one another. Material was only a means to familial strength; material was only a reminder of a higher, spiritual order. These early communions were born of divine spark; the darkness was a religious rite, a spiritual birth. Nature's harshness bore a kin-centered God-man, a savior of the organic world. Yet before Nature, *feeding* Nature, was something else, something the darkened sky revealed: impressed in the firmament were signs and windows to the Aryan gods, the creative forces whose power is kinship. The streak of galaxy interrupting the blackened sky bulged at the middle; this was the second sun, the black sun. Behind this sun was the life such cold, dark harshness brings to the receptive soul — it was the verdant green ray. Thus did the black sun become the Black Sun.

This is what the Supreme Creator saw in the north: life is revealed through its hiddenness. This is something the Demiurge-Jehovah could never see, its eyes ever locked on the material world — of comfort, of ease, of sloth and filth. Life requires a hidden strength, a creative force that bends material to reach a higher end — that of *kinship*, that of *sacrifice*. The Black Sun is internal; it permeates our blood and will — and yet it shines. The Aryan man is privy to a blood memory; his ancestors speak to him of their northern struggles through this memory. His thoughts turn to this memory and he becomes the Godhead, the Allfather, Vishnu-Wotan, whose ravens whisper words of things to come.

∞ ∞ ∞

There exist the golden sun and the black sun; the golden sun provides for our material needs; the black sun is our spiritual root. In prehistory, the two suns battled for supremacy. The fate of Aryan man, being inextricably tied to the fate of the universe, was destined for a material-dependent existence when the golden sun rose to prominence on the backs of the Demiurge's tropical *quantities*. Our ancestors, the Hyperboreans, descendants of the gods, were given to gradual degeneration without the exoteric presence of the black sun, which provided needed warmth and vigor during the persistent polar darkness brought by the golden sun's long absence; so they turned inward, despite their devolution. The Aesir became the Hyperboreans became the Aryans, who are now represented in the Germanic peoples of the world. Being cast out of Jehovah's material fiefdom, the black sun found its course, became hidden, and the fundamentally spiritual nature of the Hyperboreans receded into esotericism: the Black Sun arose. Standing as the symbol for past and future strength of the Aryan man, the now-hidden Sun is our source of spiritual renewal. The Germanic peoples are not gods; but the will within them is the same that enlivened the Aesir.

Our task is to waken the divine will within us through blood loyalty, honor, discipline, cleanliness, and decency. Our task revolves around the Black Sun that stands as the gateway to the ancient and future race. Our task in this demiurgical world is *overcoming*; this overcoming is sacrifice: what have we done to recognize the advantage in sacrifice? Our actions in the world of the golden sun will be judged; hidden within the Black Sun, the Allfather waits, hearing reports from Huginn and Muninn, *thought* and *memory*. The holy blood is the wind for ravens' wings.

Time follows its set course, reflected in the cosmogony of the ancient Aryan, reflected in both Norse and Hindu mythology. The ages of man are divided into increasingly degenerative quarters: The Golden Age is the time of the gods, the Aesir; the Silver Age is the beginning of the Black Sun's hiddenness and the decline of the Aesir into lesser beings, which is seamlessly tied to the subsequent age; the Bronze Age represents both the lightning-quick advent of the conquering Hyperboreans and their equally rapid descent into spiritual disintegration, mixing as they did with the conquered bestial races, thus beginning the slide into the final age; the Iron Age is the age of all recorded history — it is the Kali-Yuga, the age of "reason," of "man," of "enlightenment." The cycle of time will climax in Ragnarök, the final battle between the forces of material decay and spiritual life, the final battle between the golden and Black suns; concluding the cycle is the return of Kalki, the redeemer and avenger, the final avatar of Vishnu-Wotan, who will lead the few remaining Aryans loyal to their folk through the onslaught of degenerative forces. Firstly, the quantity will implode, bringing destruction to the exoteric world; both the cycle of time and spiritual impurity ensure this. From this destruction will come a new Golden Age, and time will begin again — the *Eternal Return*.

The purpose of the Germanic man fighting through the Iron Age is to loyally secure the blood of his people. Through mental, physical, and spiritual preparation and work, the Germanic man raises his awareness and strength to a point of absolute selectivity. From this selectivity, Aryan blood is gradually purified into a bridge to the MAN TO COME; it is a bridge to the Black Sun of spirituality.

Esotericism, then, is the preparation for present and future exoteric struggle, that we might return to the spiritual foundations of our folk and the gods that birthed us. Our honor is loyalty; preparation is our task. The enemy sits at the doorstep — and now we fight for the MAN TO COME.

The present Iron Age is governed by the usurious forces that ignited the first revolts against the ancient gods. These revolutionary forces' only god was *material* and their only task was manipulating the creation of the Supreme God, discarding spirit for profit. Thus, the usurpers' task was demiurgical and their god was the Demiurge, the "craftsman," the manipulator, Jehovah.

Jehovah's agents fight everywhere for "liberty, equality, and fraternity." That is, the Demiurge's task of world domination is concealed under abstractions meant to distract the quantities of degenerates loyal to it; degenerative forces believe they are acting for the good of all, yet this is only Jewish deception. The Demiurge is responsible for time's precipitous and demonic devolution into spiritual chaos — such materialistic devilry aims to destroy the Black Sun and, thus, all spirituality. Jehovah knows only material existence and understands that when the spirit reigns, its sinister forces of materialism and exploitation will languish; thus, the Demiurge fights with all its power to ruin the Germanic man's spirituality and secure exploitative existence. Ours is a spiritual struggle, and while the Demiurge and its forces fight for materialistic entrenchment and the final destruction of the Germanic man, the Aryan folk fight for the MAN TO COME.

Who is the MAN TO COME? HE is the ancient and future race, loyal only to the Supreme God, the Black Sun which does not abandon its creation to the cold, material dark: HE is the hidden God for whom we must fight to reveal through our honor and loyalty; HE is our holy blood and hallowed will.

The battle between the Sun of inner strength and spiritual reckoning and the misappropriated sun of ruinous material reckoning is as old as time. It is the struggle between the creator and the manipulator, God and Demiurge, good and evil. Inner, spiritual strength seeks to create and commune with the Godhead, Vishnu-Wotan. Conversely, materialistic fixation drives one to exploit and consume — it is greed embodied, and such rapaciousness is fueled by dwindling, accelerating time. The Trimurti is the constant-through-time that feeds the inward stability of the spiritual Aryan: Brahma, Vishnu, Shiva — creator, preserver, destroyer: Wotan, Frigg, Baldur — man, woman, child. The avatar of God visits man in his time of need to offer spiritual anchor. There have been nine avatars of Vishnu-Wotan; the eighth avatar was Krishna, who revealed to man the wonder of his sacred, primordial duty; the ninth avatar was Adolf Hitler, who, in his capacity as archetype of the Germanic folk, could *only* be revealed as the *ninth* avatar — the sacred 9, the inversion of the demiurgical 6. Wotan hung for nine days on Yggdrasil, bearer of the nine worlds, sacrificing himself for the revelation of the runes. When Ragnarök ushers in the new Golden Age of the Black Sun, there will be nine gods to act as *Aufseher-Übersetzer* of the new order; the ninth god "comes [from] on high, | all power to hold, a mighty lord, | all lands he rules".[1] This is also the tenth and final avatar of Vishnu-Wotan: it is Kalki, the ever-present world-destroyer, who will spark and witness "the sun [turning] black, [and the] earth [sinking] in the sea".[2] The golden sun of increasing material decay will transmute into the Black Sun of eternal spirituality, and a new day will begin.

Adolf Hitler, as the ninth avatar of Vishnu-Wotan, reminded the Aryan folk of their spiritual duty to their ancestors and descendants. From HIS first channeling of the *heilige Geist* on a starry night atop the Freinberg, where, still as a young man, HE spoke of HIS fated mission as the votive savior of HIS folk,[3] to the "six-year-long fight which ... will one day go down in history as the most glorious and brave avowal of a folk's will to live,"[4] Adolf Hitler proved to be an incarnation of mystic consciousness. HIS meteoric rise and unrelenting *Wille*, lambasted to this day by shameless propaganda, is only evidence of the archetype HE fulfilled. "The achievement of genius," Schopenhauer held,

> transcends not only others' capacity of achievement, but also their capacity of apprehension; therefore they do not become immediately aware of it. Talent is like the marksman who hits a target which others cannot reach;

---

[1] Poetic Edda, Voluspo, 65.
[2] Poetic Edda, Voluspo, 57.
[3] August Kubizek, *The Young Hitler I Knew* (1951), 131.
[4] Adolf Hitler, "My Political Testament," 29 April 1945.

> genius is like the marksman who hits a target ... which others cannot even see.[5]

The target becomes clearer as time passes. Decisions to fight along the Eastern Front unceasingly — *to the last man* — seemed incomprehensible to Hitler's generals. Material victory is the target they saw; yet Hitler knew that material victory was lost in 1941.[6] Spiritual victory was the only target visible to Hitler. Retreat was not an option; the ARCHETYPE fought only for the MAN TO COME. The thousand-year Reich could only be won in the cold, physical darkness of the eastern steppe, where the absence of the golden sun favored the forces of demiurgical Darkness.[7] Adolf Hitler alone, as the *unbekannter Mann*, understood this. HE is the God-willed

---

[5] Arthur Schopenhauer, *The World as Will and Representation* (New York: Dover, 1958), vol. II, 391.

[6] "We can oppose Russia only when we are free in the West. Further, Russia is seeking to increase her influence in the Balkans and is driving toward the Persian Gulf. That is also the goal of our foreign policy." Adolf Hitler — speech to the *Oberkommando der Wehrmacht*, 23 November 1939. The two-front war spells doom in any peer-to-peer conflict. Hitler saw this unfold in 1914 and chided it accordingly; HE acted against the Soviets, then — in the face of HIS belief in its deleterious effects — because of necessity, because of Soviet duplicity. Nevertheless, HE saw something transcendent in HIS decision and carried it out to the bitter end. This is in keeping with Clausewitz's *profession of faith*: "I believe and declare that a folk should value nothing more highly than the dignity and freedom of its existence; that it should defend these to the last drop of blood; that it has no holier duty to fulfill; no higher law to obey; that the shame of a cowardly submission can never be erased; that this drop of poison in the blood of a folk is passed on to its descendants and will corrupt and undermine the strength of future generations; that honor can only be lost once; . . . that even the loss of freedom after an honorable and bloody battle secures the rebirth of the folk and is the seed of life from which, one day, a new tree will strike firm root; I declare to this world and to posterity that I consider the false wisdom that wants to withdraw from danger to be the most pernicious sentiment that fear and anxiety can instill . . . that I would be only too happy to find a glorious death in the magnificent fight for the freedom and dignity of the fatherland!"

[7] B. H. Liddell Hart, *The German Generals Talk* (New York: HarperCollins, 2002), 187: "The [Russian defenses were] helped by the fact that darkness came as early as 3 o'clock in the afternoon."

Führer[8] who, during Ragnarök, will lead the final battalion against the anti-Germanic quantities dominating the material world. These chosen *Einherjar*, the fallen heroes whose honor is loyalty, will lead the Aryan *Geist* out of Valhalla to victory against the Jehovahistic World Serpent and the traitorous Fenrir; Hel will be defeated, subsiding under the rise of the Black Sun. The son of *Bági ulfs* will return.

Resplendent in his fair skin, Baldur, Vishnu-Wotan reincarnated, will govern his Aryan children through a common bond of blood, a common home of northern soil. The soil that birthed the Aryan blood circles the polar north, the ancient land of Hyperborea. Such soil is infused with the warming rays of the spiritual Black Sun, the sun that radiated over the northern spirit when the material sun would drift beyond the horizon for half the year. Thus did the ancient Aryans, the Hyperboreans, sustain themselves during the difficult days of winter. After Ragnarök, Baldur and his brothers, along with the sole surviving man and woman, return to the remaining arable soil in the north to extend the radiating arms of the Black Sun across the renewed world — like the knowing arms of the *Wolfsangel*, whose quarry is the fallen Fenrir.

Who is Baldur, with his fair and glowing skin, herald of the new dawn, if not Venus, the morning star — if not the Germanic *Lichtbringer*? Who is the Light-bringer if not Apollo, the ancient Sun God? Who is the God of the Sun if not Lucifer? Lucifer, *Lichtbringer*, was cast out of the demiurgical, Jehovahistic realm for refusing his inferior's exploitation. Lucifer, or Vishnu-Wotan, was the representative of the Creator God, whose antithesis was the enslaver, Demiurge-Jehovah. The Germanic man, even when distanced from his Hyperborean ancestors, yet carried the Sun-worshipping, "pagan" traditions of his forebears. The Supreme God's emissaries in this world are ever demonized for the exploitative ends of the demonizer, Jehovah. Spiritual Light is divine Light, the inner manifestation of a Nature-harmony whose foundations are battered in materialistic machinations: God "becomes" Satan and Satan "becomes" God: this is the essence of the Iron Age, the Age of Mammon. Mammon seeks to blot out the Light; and what is Light if not the source of Nature, of life, the verdant green ray whose source is the Black Sun? Nature is the Aryan man's home; it is his nourishment — mental, physical, and spiritual; it is his ashram.

---

[8] *Wodan, id est furor*, spoke Adam of Bremen.

Bearing his Light even under the weight of physical death, the Germanic man's divine spark persisted through the ascent of mammon in medieval Europe. It is no trifle that the rise of the Church paralleled the rise of the Hansa in the north. And with its climb, the Church sought to usurp the old gods, the Germanic will. Persecutions and elimination of the free Aryan spirit were the bedrock for stable commercial enterprise and lucrative tithing. In their degenerative perfidy, Germanic kings used swelling Jewish power for personal gain, at best leaving the communities of old believers unprotected, at worst forcefully converting them. Though it waned, the divine Light was not blotted out by the sun of gold and mammon. Persecution continued into the Inquisitions. So-called witches — *Träger des Lichts* — were tried and convicted of devilry; but this was only the conquering Judaeo-Christianity demonizing the old believers. The hounded pagans "refused to call [their divinity] the 'Devil,' and in many instances the accused explicitly called him god".[9] Not suiting the demonizers, this only led to more vehement condemnations of the children of *Lucifer, der Lichtbringer*. And not unlike the *Schutzstaffel* men who defiantly sang the "glorious song of the SS legions" while being loaded into postwar boxcars shipping them to some contemptible end,[10] the Germanic pagans "died very stubborn and refractory, without any remorse or seeming terror of conscience".[11] Indeed, pangs of conscience would have terrorized them if they had relented to the tormentors! They could not betray their gods, their blood — and so the brave died for their faith; the divine spark endured.

Such a spark is the Godhead, the central sun around which the spiritual life turns. In defiance of all material gain or loss, the inner Light provides the axis of faithful struggle and obedience; it reveals the way when all else is shrouded in material decay. The Germanic pagans who incurred diabolical, Judaeo-Christian persecution for their faith fashioned themselves into spiritual circles: twelve initiates implementing the will of the master; the thirteen embodying *der Heilige Wille* on earth — the Black Sun boldly manifested in the realm of gold and mammon. The SS, too, organized their inner circle into the twelve *Obergruppenführer* supporting the will of the Führer; this is clear from the north tower of the Wewelsburg — the most

---

[9] Margaret Alice Murray, *The God of the Witches* (1931), 12.

[10] Savitri Devi, *Gold in the Furnace* (Calcutta, 1952), 48.

[11] Murray, 29.

striking symbol of which is the deep-green *Sonnenrad*, whose twelve reversed Sieg-rune spokes gravitate around the central sun. Also, with his twelve knights, King Arthur (*Arctic Thor*) represented the Germanic spiritual circle. Similarly, the Teutonic Order divided their holdings into twelve administrative areas oversaw by the Grandmaster. Hrólfr Kraki, the Dane king, set about his adventures with his twelve berserkers. Notable, too, is the ancient Germanic legal practice of compurgation: the "making clean" of an accused man through the oath swearing of twelve of his kinsmen.[12] These circles of thirteen are naught but earthly reflections of the cosmic order: twelve zodiacal epochs or archways marking the passage of time and space around the central sun. The thread of thirteen-strong circles weaves together the Aryan will through time, it echoes the voice in the blood, it is the sun become the Sun.

Even ancient Aryan art records the spark of divine will arising within our blood. Our animal nature, once ignorant and servile, was given to divinity once the gods were recalled from this world for their miscegenistic misdeeds. Thus we see in the 4,000-year-old stone carvings of Tanum, one of the early diasporic homes of the ancient Aryans, rays of the life-giving Sun terminating in humanlike hands; the same hand-rays appear hundreds of years later in Egyptian reliefs of Akhenaten, pharaoh of the Sun. Akhenaten, who ruled nearly 3,500 years ago, established the exclusivity of the Sun religion for his people; they built temples to honor the holy Sun, much like the ancient Aryan-Greeks to the north also worshiped their Sun, Apollo. Akhenaten is unique in history; his god is the Sun, which is to say, his god is the will born of Nature. Superstitions that claimed otherwise in Akhenaten's realm were outlawed — because superstitions came from the animalistic south or the magic-materialism of the Orient. Hundreds of years before Akhenaten, inching ever closer to prehistory and the Arctic north (Tanum and elsewhere), we find devotions to the god of the Sun etched in stone. In these etchings, there exists the sunwheel in the center of human figures, in their heart; *they* are the source — the *unmediated* source of Light. The

[12] Incidentally, Julius Langbehn, in his *Rembrandt as Educator* (1890), uses the historical practice of compurgation amongst the Germanic peoples as a demonstration of their prioritization of blood kinship and subjectivity over the alien (i.e., Levantine or late "Roman") emphasis on objectivity afflicting modernity. The number of oath-swearers fluctuated due to circumstance; however, twelve deponents were commonly sought.

Aryan god is the Sun; the Aryan god is the will. The God of the Aryans has always been the everlasting Sun — yet not the sun of the material world, whose tyrant is the demiurgical Jehovah, but the Black Sun, whose spiritual Light radiates even in physical darkness. It is the *spiritual* Sun that the Hyperboreans recognized; it is this same Sun the Aryans revered in their art: ours is the Black Sun, the spiritual center of the Germanic will.

Found throughout the world, much like the traditions of prehistoric northern ancestors that span bloodlines and cultures, are the holy swastika and sauwastika. These symbols themselves are sunwheels, emblematic of the Sun-god. From the center axis reach four hooked arms, each spanning the globe in a cardinal direction — one spin expressing the exodus, the other expressing the return to the Aryan man's spiritual root. The hooked sunwheel's axis is the center pole, the polar north.

Nietzsche said, "Let us look each other in the face — *We are Hyperboreans*!" Nietzsche was a conduit of ancient Germanicism, which is to say, ancient Aryanism; this, too, means he was a prophet. He foresaw what the ancients augured: our time is the end time and all of history is a record of our decline, *Götterdämmerung*. Whether we recognize it as Atlantis or Hyperborea, the gods of this earth — and their descendants — came from the polar north. Their prehistoric demise was foretold in the earliest glint of time. From their downfall came the beginning of recorded history and the diaspora of the ancient Aryans — each godlike generation becoming less so with every lustful drift from the holy bloodline. The swastika/sauwastika are their symbols, world symbols spawned in the polar north — Hyperborea.

Hyperborea, though, was consumed in dissipation and Demiurgic wrath tens of thousands of years ago. Emissaries of the Light in this world were assailed: The deluge was part vengeful attack against the Supreme God, Vishnu-Wotan, who dared encroach upon Jehovah's manipulated creation by igniting it with divine spark, and part self-inflicted death, incurred through disloyalty and weakness. As supreme lords over the earth, the Hyperboreans succumbed to arrogant indulgence: they took beast-women as consorts. Thus was man created, and thus was Hyperborea doomed to destruction. After the cataclysm, the few remaining Hyperboreans sought refuge in other lands, ultimately providing leadership for the new Aryans.

Prehistory is the time of Gold, Silver, and Bronze; history is the record of Iron. Heroes of antiquity are only literary vestiges of a more godlike race, lost in a time of action. As time passed and Aryan man's animal nature prevailed over his spiritual instincts, dissipation and degeneration increased; the march toward modernity was set. Recorded history's Aryan heroes are only remnants of a more virile age, or avatars of the Supreme God penetrating the spiritual darkness this world propagates. The purpose of such heroes and avatars is to remind us of our eternal purpose: to strengthen the potency of our blood through honor, loyalty, discipline, cleanliness, and decency. Our God is within us; HIS memory compels us. When this age ends, the survivors among us will permeate the new day with rays of the Black Sun, and time will begin again.

The German Reichs indicate an alchemical channeling of the Aryan *magnum opus*. This is but one sign of the Germanic man's link to the spiritual Sun. The great work of the Aryan folk is to revive the ages of divine supremacy, of Gold and Silver; this is done through a transmutation of material into spirit — sun into Sun, matter into elixir. Black, red, white, and yellow: these are the alchemical colors, all of which are represented in the flags of the three German Reichs. The Second and Third Reichs show the red of blood, the black of unrevealed spirit, and the white of lighted purity. Only HIS flag, *die Blutfahne*, meant to unite all Aryan folk, harnessed the transmutative power of symbol: the red of blood sets the foundation; the black sunwheel radiates the spiritual purity of white, the color of fair Baldur, whose return marks the turning of Iron into Gold. Thus we see in the eternal thought and memory of the Germanic folk the alchemical philosopher's stone; our *magnum opus* is the bridge we forge for the MAN TO COME.

The Age of Iron we see around us, so diabolically displacing the lighter Gold, which marks the death of radiant Baldur, is a presaging of Ragnarök, the final fight between all that is good and spiritual in this world and the demiurgical forces of vileness. In these last years of history, it is certain that the bad will outnumber the good. Quantity always outnumbers quality. This world, and its common reflections, is anti-Germanic, which is to say *anti-Nature* and *anti-God*. We see it everywhere: it is materialistic. This world is naught but the satanic mirror image of the Demiurge-Jehovah.

The Germanic man struggles silently, preserving his blood and spiritual traditions. We are Hyperboreans, and we await Ragnarök, which reveals the new morning, the return of fairest Baldur — *der Lichtbringer*, Vishnu-Wotan. The Germanic god is the Sun; the Germanic god is the will.

Internal and unrevealed, the Black Sun is the antipode to the visible sun and reminds us of our higher order. Ours is the order of creation, preservation, and destruction; ours is the union of man, woman, and child; ours is the order of divine Light. And upon this order, the sun will never set.[13]

THE HOPE OF MARS

In spring of 1945, as Germany's material defeat loomed like the specter-of-communism-haunting-Europe Marx vivified a century before, Adolf Hitler sanctioned the first manned space flight to another world. The mission, undertaken by a select group of pioneering Aryan men and women, was a one-way trip to Mars. After years of diligent Germanic ingenuity applied to implosive (constructive) propulsion, after years, too, fraught with the greatest conflict the world has ever known, the Führer permitted one of the final creative acts of a Germanic Europe. The pioneers would likely never return; but like the battle-torn SS man who refused a transfusion of foreign blood to save his fleeting life because it compromised the integrity of his eternal soul, the Aryan pioneers accepted their fate and, indeed, embraced it as a sign of undying loyalty to their *Volk*, *Reich*, and *Führer*. With this act, the travelers ensured their entrance into *Walhalla*.

On 30 April 1945, with artillery shells crashing around the Reich Chancellery bunker like the giant footfalls of a materialized Marxian specter, SS man Heinz Linge despairingly asked the COSMOS, "Mein Führer, for whom should we fight now?" With uncanny prescience, Adolf Hitler promised, "Now we fight for the MAN TO COME." Hitler disappeared from the Reich Chancellery bunker that very night, perhaps whisked away to Berchtesgaden, deep into the caves of the Untersberg, from which HE will one day return to lead the *Wilde Jagd* against the enemies of Nature, as the legend of Berchtold or Berchta foretold; perhaps, too, HE flew to the relocated cultural fount of HIS ancestral fatherland, *Neuschwabenland* — the Antarctic home to the oases once basing those incredible feats of Germanic engineering capable of journeying to distant worlds: the flying discs, the *Haunebu* and *Vril*.

And though Hitler, long "thought" dead, vanished, HIS legacy remained — acting as the spiritual counterpoint to the *international*

[13] Landig, *Wolfszeit um Thule* (Vienna: Volkstum-Verlag, 1980), 323.

socialism established as Destiny decreed, perpetuating the cosmic struggle (*Kampf*) of Light versus Darkness. This *thought* is twofold: those with Hitler in the bunker propagated this tale of material death as subterfuge, a final act of loyalty to the Führer myth; similarly, yet for altogether alien reasons, the Jewish-controlled media, aided by compatriot Allied reports, celebrated final propagandic victory through disinformation: Adolf Hitler was dead. HE who leads the *Wilde Jagd*, however, must first become the *Sleeping King* — only then is resurrection, final spiritual victory, possible. Under the Untersberg, among the Berchtesgaden Alps, Barbarossa takes his rest; when the ravens' flight ends, the Sleeping King returns and the hunt begins. This is Germanic thought, which is to say *Germanic myth*. Who are these ravens but Huginn and Muninn — thought and memory, the MYTH of the Blood, the Myth of the Twentieth Century? When blood and tradition are replaced by internationalist materialism, the Germanic man knows the resurrection nears, and the darkest night precedes the brightest morn. Who leads the *Wilde Jagd*? HE WHO CANNOT DIE. *Barbarossa* was but a prelude of the Norns' decree.

∞ ∞ ∞

May Day, the day of the International Worker: with the establishment of the first International Workers' Day in 1905, the internationalist-materialist forces of the world appropriated a traditional spring commemoration: *die Tanz in den Mai*. This is only another step toward spiritual decay in the modern world. A communing of soul with Nature was mangled into an international day of unholy clatter over class war: *dialectical hypnotism*. Yet such is the strategy of the *international clique*: insinuate and uproot.

The Führer saw 39 such International Workers' Days; HE would not see 40.[14] In what could even be a final act of revolt against internationalist modernity, Hitler vanished on the *Walpurgisnacht*. And what is *Walpurgisnacht* if not a Christianization of yet another Germanic holy day: a "night of witches" meant to celebrate the coming spring — not much different than the celebration of Ostara some weeks before? Yet the Christians, born of Judah (or *Juden*), in both their superstitious Orientalism and insinuating universalism,

[14] One imagines 39 — or 3 9s (999) — as a counterpoint to 1944's Allied D-Day, itself executed at the *sixth* hour on the *sixth* day of the *sixth* month (666). This was Jehovahistic ritualism par excellence.

could only see the celebratory eve of May as some kind of "devilry." The devil, though, cannot see its own reflection; thus, the significance of insinuation goes unnoticed; Nature itself becomes unnatural for the uprooted modernist. The modern May Day would not come again for the Führer — *Gott sei Dank*! Revolt against the modern world would continue — and with it, the revolt against universalism.

The post-Hitler May Day marked the end of the Germanic era on earth; the Judaic era would begin; paving the way would be the heretofore Christianization of Europe. The old gods were murdered, and with them, the native cultural instinct of self-preservation and assertion of the Germanic element. *God is dead!* cries the "madman," thus marking the *Götterdämmerung*.

May 1945, too, marked the "end of hostilities" in the European theater; what this means, of course, is the end of Germanic assertion. This is how we know the enemy won the war: German self-assertion is seen as "hostile," as "evil." Kalergi said as much with his avowals of internationalist materialism: his *Paneuropa* journal argued for the practical and ideological mixing of communism (international socialism) with capitalism (borderless money exchange). This admixture, of course, is globalism.[15] The espousing of such an internationalist worldview is precisely why global financiers like Rothschild, Warburg, and Baruch were eager to back Kalergi's efforts. Theodore Kaufman, too, shouted to anyone who would listen, "Germany must perish!" Each of them oozed the Semitic attitude — forever against the Germanic man. A multitude of others — all Levantine — could be cited as meting out victor's justice one way or another in the wake of the wars against Germanicism. Controlling finance and information (media) are the most prominent ways of issuing such "justice." It is no surprise, then, that money and media

---

[15] *Globalism* is the progeny of *international socialism* and *capitalism*, which, in turn, are derivative of Liberalism (the so-called *first alternative*). Liberalism, while born with good intentions, has its logical conclusion in mass exploitation dressed up with worthy abstractions — liberty, equality, and fraternity exist nominally in a world hell-bent on profits-by-any-means. It is a destructive worldview: Nature — the physical world — is manipulated and destroyed for the sake of conceptual profit: abstraction and digitization trump reality. Moreover, mass equality — in the name of "justice" and faceless consumer markets — is enforced, as Kalergi mused, like a lush meadow, made rich with the separation of strong and weak, cut down to the root in the name of "lawn care." So much for "justice" — *the systematic expansion of customer bases*. "We are all one [soulless consumer market]."

are the West's most prized interests and exports in the modern world — the world of the post-Hitler May Day.

Edward Bernays, the Austrian Jew who wrote the book on propaganda, makes his "justice" felt still today. Not only was Bernays instrumental in getting the liberal democracies to war against their ancient kinsmen of the Second and Third German Reichs, his (anti-) blood endures to the present: Internet streaming services let the consumer choose her own propaganda in true Bernaysian fashion. This is the invisible hand guiding the modern world: he who controls the money and information controls the world. This is a world devoid of spirit, which is to say, a sterile world devoid of Germanicism — no more are honor, loyalty, and courage prized; instead we are offered abstractions, carrots on sticks to keep us consuming. Yet even this has been prophesized:

> Hard is it on earth, | with mighty whoredom;
> Axe-time, sword-time, | shields are sundered,
> Wind-time, wolf-time, | ere the world falls;
> Nor ever shall men | each other spare.[16]

When the Aryan peoples are deprived of their honor, through force or ignorance, they become no better than the dregs they once chivalrously instructed. A world of dregs is necessary for the globalists — a prim lawn, not a wild meadow. Dilute and conquer: miscegenation is the key to Jewish victory — it is how *Germany must perish*.[17] Behind every call for "diversity" is an urge to homogenization. By forcibly commingling the various races, the internationalist-materialist powers aim to create a monolithic race of non-Germanic bastards — a neatly manicured lawn of faceless, bloodless, spiritless *hoi polloi*. Instead of pure rain and soil, they will introduce mountains of sludge — sludge reminiscent of the meter-thick muck thwarting the German advance against the treacherous Soviets. The result is the same: Germanic defeat in favor of Jewish money. But all is not lost: the prophecies remain.

---

[16] Voluspo, Poetic Edda, translated by Henry Bellows, st. 45.

[17] See Theodore Kaufman's *Germany Must Perish!* (reprinted in T. Dalton, ed., *Classic Essays on the Jewish Question*, 2022), Louis Nizer's *What To Do With Germany*, or Kalergi's *Practical Idealism* or *Pan-Europa* work, among others.

In wondrous beauty | once again
Shall the golden tables | stand mid the grass,
Which the gods had owned | in the days of old...[18]

Fair and bright will Baldur return, much like the Sleeping King under the mountain. The Jehovahistic Darkness will break under the weight of its own materialistic untruth[19] and the *Wilde Jagd* will cleanse the earth through ice and fire.

∞ ∞ ∞

An expedition to Mars, directed as *Hexennacht* approached, was itself a dance into spring. It was Germanic self-assertion — not just for the present, but also for the future. It was a journey for the MAN TO COME, that HE might keep hope and stay rooted in that which matters most. *And who, in this world of disappearing people, would be God? He who holds the last hope!*

THE GERMAN CROSS

The Germanic people are the prime movers of history, the prime movers of the world. Aristotle, the great Aryan-Greek thinker and teacher of one of our greatest *Führer*, Alexander the Great, described the *prime mover* as immovable, pure actuality — that is, IT is the source of all subsequent potentiality *and* actuality; IT is God. "Life belongs to God. For the actuality of thought is life, and God is that actuality; and the essential actuality of God is life most good and eternal. We hold, then, that God is a living being, eternal, most good; and therefore life and a continuous eternal existence belong to God; for that is what God is".[20] The goodness in life, therefore, belongs to God, the prime mover — pure actuality and mother of existence. If

---

[18] Ibid., st. 61.
[19] What better example of information usurpation is there than the appropriating (and therefore trivialization of) the Germanic Edda myths? Jewish Hollywood's *Thor* turned Heimdall — the "whitest of the gods" and ancestor of the "holy races" — into an *African*. The All-lies' victory, the essence of Jewish justice: *deception*.
[20] Aristotle, *Metaphysics*, Book 12, 1072b26.

God is the mother of existence, the Germanic man is the father of the good in this world.

Nothing good in this world came into existence *ex nihilo*. Behind it was the prime mover. Miguel Serrano, the Germanic Chilean,[21] describes the *Magnum Opus*, the Great Work, which is to say, spiritual alchemy, wherein the G(o)od takes the hero's path and sacrifices ITSELF to save that part of IT which has been taken or sullied. This first step along the path is called *Nigrum Opus*, the Black Work. Whether we see the sacrifice in the work of Mithras, Ahura Mazda, Gothic Kristos, Apollo, Vishnu or Wotan, it is this sacrifice from which all good springs. This is "the entrance of God into this opposite Universe of the Enemy".[22] It is God become man to salvage the good of creation. Territory and prisoners have been taken in this cosmic struggle between good and evil; the hero's path is a divine reaction to the Enemy's misdeed, its anti-creation. Sacrifice allows for the apotheosization of man — the hero — into a new immortal divinity, greater even than the gods.[23] For spiritual consciousness transmuted from a demiurgical world carries not only the divine spark, but also the creative work: it is the *Magnum Opus*.[24]

How do we know a man is just or good? Not only that he *seems* so, but *is* so? Plato said such a man must be stripped of all reward for his goodness or justness; yet then he will *seem* bad because he lacks the accoutrements of being good. For this perception, though he is good and just, "the just man will have to endure the lash, the rack, chains, the branding-iron in his eyes, and finally, after every extremity of suffering, he will be crucified...".[25] This is the sacrifice of the hero's path: purity to the end, in the face of all trial. The demiurgical world brands him a demon and continues its course; praise the demon, and you become one. If truth and virtue are

---

[21] Most Chileans, like many South Americans, are of Germanic heritage.

[22] Miguel Serrano, *Resurrection of the Hero* (The 55 Club, 2015), 80.

[23] Ibid., 81.

[24] "Wotan lives in the human body in order to go under; he consecrated himself to himself, and he consecrates himself to passing away in order to rise anew. The nearer he feels himself coming to the moment of his passing away toward new arising — his death — the clearer the knowledge grows in him that the secret of life is an eternal arising and passing away, an eternal return, a life of continuous birth and death." Guido von List, *Das Geheimnis der Runen*, 11.

[25] Plato, *Republic, Plato in Twelve Volumes*, Vols. 5 & 6 translated by Paul Shorey (Cambridge: Harvard University Press), 1969, II, 361e-362a.

demonized, however, goodness and justness are near. *In diesem Kampf, wird am Ende die Wahrheit siegen. Sie aber ist bei uns,*[26] said the Führer; HE bore the hero's path in HIS being — there was no greater struggle in history, no greater victory. That is, there was no greater cross to bear.

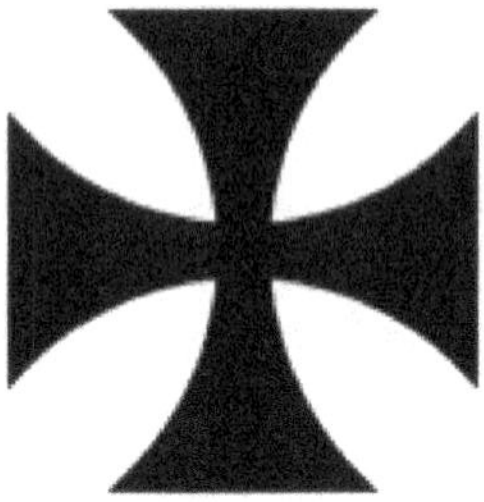

The German cross is as ancient as the Aryan. Though it has seen various stylizations, it has remained fundamentally simple: two lines intersecting, one horizontal, one vertical. Noted for its symmetry, the German cross is not to be confused with any other. For hidden in the German cross are other mysteries.

Guido von List detailed a number of mysteries in his *Das Geheimnis der Runen*.[27] Hidden in the symmetry of the German cross

[26] "In this struggle, the truth will be victorious. The truth is with us."
[27] *The Secret of the Runes* (1914).

is the *Hakenkreuz*, the hooked cross, which is the *fyrfos*, the Indo(o)[Hindu]-Aryan swastika. The *fyrfos* was the eighteenth and final rune revealed by Wotan's skald, itself hidden behind incompleteness in the *Gibor* rune:

More than just a phonetic sound, *Gibor* means *gift, giver, Nordic God, earth.*[28] It is the sign concealing the holy swastika, the first step in the spiritual *Magnum Opus*. This sign is the "holy secret of constant generation, constant life, and uninterrupted recurrence"[29] — it is the *hero* bearing the cross of salvation, it is Wotan going under, hanging (crucified) nine days for the revelation of the runes. Von List tells us of the ancient Germanic *Gibraltar* — *Gibor-altar*, the earthen altar meant to receive offerings to the Creator God. This harmony with Nature shows the German's generative source, Nature's Eternal Return. The swastika is the sign of divinity in Nature. "For 5,000 years the Nordic Folk have been using Runic Letters to express symbolically a wish or a sacred thought," Weitzel tells us. "One of the oldest symbols is the Swastika, which is the sign of the sacred cycle of the Sun..".[30]

What Von List does not cover in his striking history of the cross, Serrano does: the hero "is crucified on the four kingdoms of nature, becoming incarnated".[31] The vertical line represents man, the horizontal line represents woman; together they reach divinity. That which *takes root* is vertical; that which *moves* is horizontal. Plant, mineral, man: these are the vertical axis; animal, woman: these are the horizontal axis. Alone they are nothing; together they are the sunwheel, each complementing the other.

---

[28] Von List, 24.

[29] Ibid.

[30] Fritz Weitzel, *Die Gestaltung der Feste im Jahres und Lebenslauf in der SS-Familie* (1939), translated by Charles Barger (2007), 37. "The Sunwheel, or swastika, was a symbol in the ancient Nordic Indo-European language, *Sanskrit*, meaning *wellbeing* or *good*, from the fact that the sun was regarded as a source of goodness. This symbol was carried by invading Indo-Europeans into Europe, India and even China. The ancient link to the Indo-European people was then the reason why Adolf Hitler chose the swastika as his movement's emblem..." — from *History of the Swastika* (Belgium, 2016).

[31] Serrano, *Resurrection*, 81.

Enclosing the intersecting axes is the circle: the sun, life — the Eternal Return. The interstices allow for the entry of the heroic sacrifice, which actualizes the goodness of the prime mover in subsequent generations: man, woman, child: root, movement, birth. Again the holy swastika emblemizes a divinity greater than divinity: the hero's sacrifice, harmony with Nature. *Gibraltar*, *Externsteine*, *Blocksberg*, *Schwarzwald* — a few sacred places of the Germanic man, communion altars for the fire of blood that conquers the Eternal Return. Passing our holy blood from generation to generation is the duty of the Germanic folk; it actualizes the potential of the hero's sacrifice in us; we carry the flame forward, keeping the interstices open, allowing for our path back to divinity. A third dimension passing through the center of the intersecting lines is the actualization of our holy blood in progeny; it is the pole upon which the cross spins — viewed from above, from the north, home of the Germanic man, the *Hakenkreuz* turns counterclockwise, like the world for whom the Germanic man is the prime mover.

Nigrum Opus: this is death, the sacrifice of divinity for the salvation of ITS spark in man. The next step is life, *Alba Opus*, the White Work. Divinity's flame took hold in the cold north; hardships there were many — families, workers and *Kämpfer* were forged. The cold found the Germanic man looking inwards for divine relief. Solace was met in the communal blood of spiritual kinsmen — the Black Sun of the north. The Enemy of the gods, in its slothful yet ravenous pursuit of material ease, neglected to keep watch over the harsh poles, which made space for the *Kampfgeist* of the Hyperborean. In this way, White skin found the Black Sun: it is a spiritual relationship. *Alba Opus*, the White Work: this is God become Aryan Hero, conquering all demiurgical swill in ITS path. It is the next step on the path to God-Manhood. *Death* and *life* find their likeness eternalized in runes.

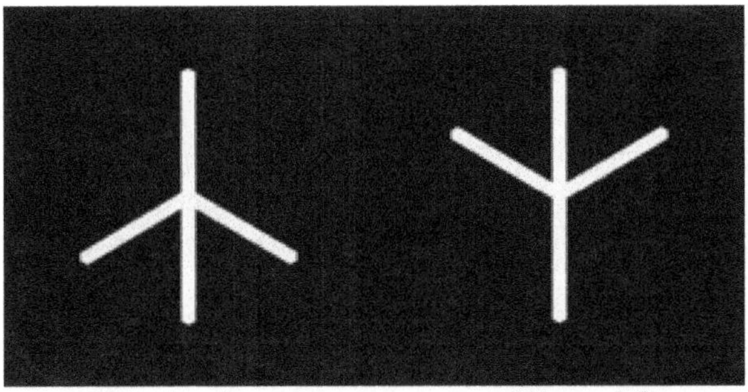

Yr = death *Man* = life

Yr is descending from the heavens to the earth; *Man* is ascending back to his ancestor-gods. "Ancestral Energy still pounds in our Teutonic blood — It commands us to struggle, to fight".[32] Such activity, such struggle is evident in each rune's outstretched arms. *Yr-Man* is clearly the root of the Germanic name *Hermann*, life and death; and, perhaps more significantly, *Yr-Man* is the source of the Germanic *Irminsul*, the sacred altar-tree of divinity, an object of communion with ancestral gods. Join *Yr* and *Man* together and we find the *Hagal* rune, which means, aptly, *faith*.

[32] Karl Wiligut, *The Secret King*, "Whispering of Gotos — Rune-Knowledge" (1934, 2007), 87.

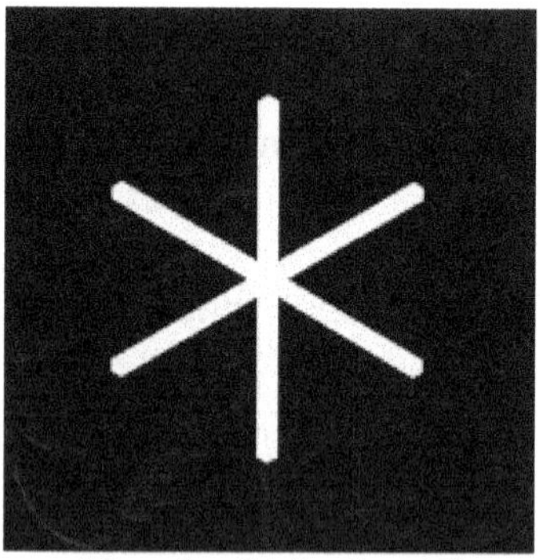

Hagal = faith, the *All*

"Harbor the All in yourself, and you will control the All!" says von List.[33] In the Führer's Germany, the *Hagal* rune was the sign of National Socialist faith; the rune was so important to Hitlerism that it found its way onto the *SS Ehrenring* ("honor ring") or *Totenkopfring* ("Death's Head ring"). Upon accession into the elite *Schutzstaffel*, the honored members were awarded their *Ehrenring* with a citation:

> I award you the *Totenkopfring* of the SS.
>
> It is a sign of our loyalty to the Führer, our unwavering obedience to our superiors and our unshakable solidarity and camaraderie.
>
> The Death's Head is a reminder to be prepared at any time to risk one's own life for the life of the whole.
>
> The runes across from the Death's Head are holy symbols of our past to which we are again connected through the philosophy of National Socialism.
>
> The two Sig runes represent the name of our *Schutzstaffel*.
>
> The Swastika and Hagal rune are to keep our attention on our unshakable faith in the victory of our philosophy.

---

33 Von List, 16.

The ring is encircled with oak leaves, the leaves of the old German tree.[34]

Above are the runes and symbols of the *Schutzstaffel* ring. More than anything, the ring, like the *Schutzstaffel* itself, was a pronouncement of *faith*: faith in what is to come, faith in the MAN TO COME, faith in the axis upon which the intersecting cross spins. Look again at *Hagal*.

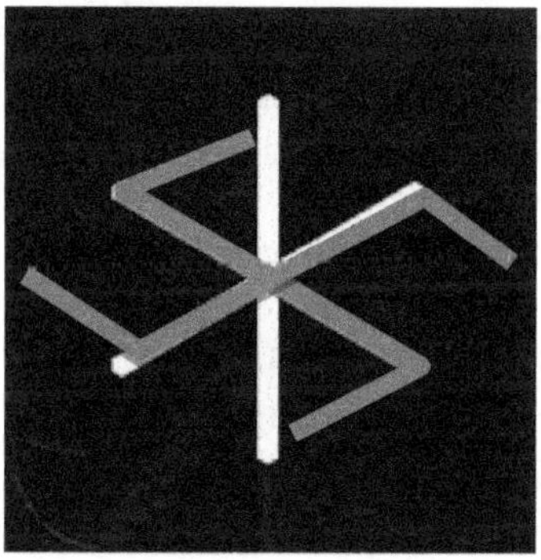

We find yet another symmetrical cross, the German cross, hooked arms spinning round the blood pole. *This can only be the rune of faith: divinity is reached through the descent of the gods to this earthly abode of the Enemy, the enduring sacrifice of the Germanic (Aryan) hero, and faith in the blood of kinsmen to conquer the Eternal Return and attain spiritual destiny.*

---

[34] Weitzel, 39. Slightly modified translation.

This final step in our spiritual alchemy, our *Magnum Opus*, is *Rubrum Opus*, the Red Work. It is the transmutation of God into the God-Man. The God-Man is not left untouched, however. "The Golden age will never be what it once was because the original purity is unrecoverable.... The naiveté is lost forever, because nothing of that which has been experienced here will ever be forgotten".[35] Though communion with the Godhead is reached through fervent effort, a gloom shades the sacrifice. One hears such feeling in the Führer's last testament:

> After a six-year-long fight which, in spite of all setbacks, will one day go down in history as the most glorious and brave avowal of a folk's will to live, I cannot leave this city, the capital of the Reich....
>
> I die with a joyous heart in view of the immeasurable deeds and accomplishments of our soldiers at the front, which I am well aware of; of our women at home, of our peasants and workers, and the unparalleled deployment, unique in history, of our youth, which bears my name.
>
> That I express to all of them my profound heartfelt gratitude is as natural as my wish that they may under no circumstance abandon the fight. Instead they will continue to wage it, no matter where, against the enemies of the fatherland... From the sacrifice of our soldiers and my own solidarity with them unto death, a seed will one day germinate in German history ... and bring about the shining rebirth of the National Socialist movement and the realization of a true *Volks-gemeinschaft*.[36]

Despite disappointment, there is *hope* — because *faith* in the sacrifice has triumphed, *faith* in the future is secured. The steps of the *Magnum Opus* have been taken; spiritual victory has been won. Later in HIS testament, the Führer urges those loyal to HIM unto death to "*finally* realize that our mission in expanding the National Socialist state will be a work for coming centuries,"[37] which suggests Hitlerism was always a task for the ages.

---

[35] Serrano, *Resurrection*, 83.

[36] Adolf Hitler's political testament, 29 April 1945.

[37] Ibid., emphasis added.

Spiritual struggle can only be a task for the ages. Meaning is only hard won, but with such victory comes eternal heroism. The German cross is the emblem of this tussle and triumph; it holds the secret of the *germanisch Wille,* the revelation of the gods.

The colors of the *Magnum Opus* are all represented in this National Socialist patch: black, white, red. The additional gold on the ring surrounding the white disk on which the swastika sits represents the culminated transmutation of blackened lead into divine gold — the sacrifice achieved, the goal of spiritual alchemy. The eight-pointed background marks the eight points of two overlaid German crosses turned on their axes (see below). In antiquity, Aryan tribes symbolized Venus — the Morning Star, *der Lichtbringer, Lucifer* — with an eight-pointed star. The German *Lichtbringer,* or Latin *Lucifer,* is not to be confused with the Semitic Satan. HE who brings light into this world is, in fact, the prime mover. The brief absence of light — blackness — comes only when the Creator God sacrifices ITSELF to enter the realm of the Enemy (Jehovah, or Satan). The "demonization" of Lucifer is only the demonization of the just hero, as Plato discussed. This dichotomy of Lucifer and Jehovah (Satan) is the dichotomy of Good and Evil, Aryan and Semite. It is the essence of the cosmic struggle, waged for millennia, ended only when the MAN TO COME returns, bringing the light of Kalki, the avenger.

Superimposed over two overlapping German crosses is the eight-pointed star, which highlights at its core the symbolic transmutation of the *Magnum Opus*.

The holy *Externsteine* in northern Germany, set in place by the gods themselves as a reminder of the *Magnum Opus*.

(*Above, top*) A close-up of one of the *Externsteine* carvings. This depicts a corruption of the German cross into the Christian cross, perfidiously bending the sacred *Irminsul*. This carving, made by those disloyal to Aryan heritage, was meant to break the spirit of the Germanic people by defacing their hallowed monument after the violent conquests of Semitic Christianity. (*Above, left* and *right; below*) Renderings of Charlemagne tearing down the *Irminsul* and capturing his fellow Germanic folk.

The symbol of the *Reichsarbeitsdienst* (Reich Labor Service), a clear *Man* rune, and one of many examples of heritage remembrance in the Führer's *Großedeutschland*.

An old German postcard: *Hagal ist Leben und Tod. Mann und Weib, Lebensbaum, Lebensgesetz*. (*Hagal* is life and death. Man and woman, tree of life, law of life.) Picture courtesy www.ns-kunst.com.

Hitlerjugend — here with their Sieg-rune flags, undoubtedly on the path to becoming elite leaders in the *Schutzstaffel.*

Artifacts from the Reich, each bearing the *Hagal* rune. The porcelain plate likely would have been a gift at a wedding or child-naming ceremony. The plate's inscription reads, *Nur aus opfern steigt gross das Reich* — "The Reich only rises from sacrifice."

The central image of this porcelain plate, a gift from *Reichsführer-SS* Himmler, shows a large Mother's Cross encircled by a ring of six German crosses and six oak leaves. The inscription around the plate reads: *Durch Mütter und Held ist unser der Sieg* — "Victory is ours through Mother and Hero".[38]

[38] Weitzel, Barger, 17.

Germanic timber-frame houses often display symmetrical crosses and runes in their construction. Evident here are the *Yr*, *Man*, *Dagaz*, and *Hagal* runes. This construction was more prevalent in the past, and many historical structures of this sort did not survive the wars against the German people.

ANCIENT EXODUS, FUTURE RETURN

Fifteen thousand years ago, a nickel-iron meteorite fell to earth. From this extraterrestrial metal, an ancient people carved a teacher, perhaps a god — one hand cradling an eternal fire; the other hand open, inviting the initiated to pick up the torch, or perhaps welcoming the uninitiated to witness the wonders of a faithful life. The *Schutzstaffel* retrieved the piece on their Tibetan expedition — a testament to the cultural undertakings of a revived folk. Academicians would have us think the figure is but 1,000 years old, possibly Scythian in origin; some speculate the figure is less than 100 years old, a forgery meant to fetch a high price — subversions and money always on their mind. The faithful know better.

Encircling the figure's body and head are two halos — one halo suggesting the physical plane, the other evincing the mental plane — whose overlap reveals a secret: each form a part of the triumvirate of self — without one, the other fails. But the third part of this triumvirate is necessary for life: the spiritual. Proudly and necessarily

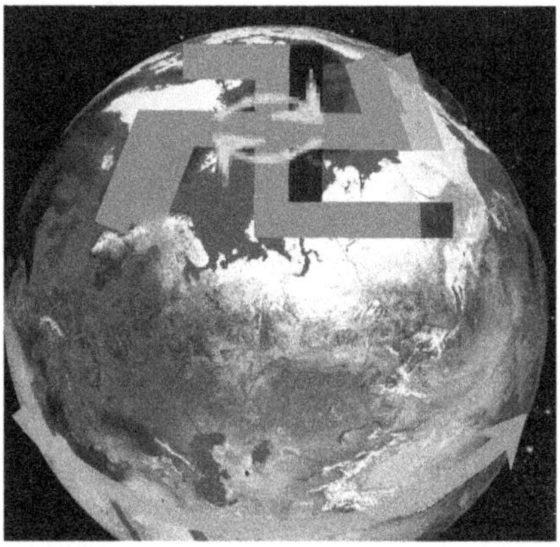

displayed on the figure's chest is the rightwards swastika — the Swastika of Exodus. The teacher-god shares with us his faith, a faith which rests at the center of his being and overlaps all but the fire he wills us to take. What does he know and wish to share — what ancient faith?

It is no accident our ancient carver chose an extra-terrestrial material as his medium. The carved figure, like the metal upon which he is cut, calls the heavens his home. His ancestors were closest to the gods of Charroux's *primohistory*: the *Aesir* and *Vanir* were his grandfather's teachers. Their history was not recorded because it was lived; it was written in the scrolls of their blood. Descending to earth from above the North Pole, the gods saw the rugged Caucasus and unforgiving north as the divine counterpoints to the diabolic climes incubating the animalistic south. In the north, the Hyperborcan seed was planted.

After generations of embodying their faith in the ancestor-gods through harmony with Nature, the Hyperboreans — the Aryans — faced some terrible cataclysm: their northern homes, chosen by the gods, were destroyed. Perhaps this was through some internal failing — a loss of faith, a degradation of blood, *demiurgical machinations*. The ancestral home was then finished, and the exodus began. Exiting the northern pole in all cardinal directions, the ancient Aryans dispersed, carrying with them their primal knowledge and central faith. The symbol of their exodus is the rightwards swastika, turning against the earth's rotation, "the one that turns according to the present earth's time and descends to the lowest depths of

Kaliyuga".[39] Facing this cataclysm was facing disharmony with Nature — their symbol must reveal this truth. It is a sign of their origins and their dispersion across the planet.

Seeking artifacts of ancient Aryan roots, Heinrich Himmler sponsored Ernst Schäfer's 1938-39 expedition to Tibet. The expedition's exoteric purpose was twofold: to identify hardy flora and fauna for surviving the harsh winters of eastern Europe, furthering the Reich's autarky; and to determine potential guerrilla forces for use against British interests in the region should peace prove untenable. The esoteric purpose was to fuse with the spiritual energy of the Germanic folk's ancestors. What cataclysms could be avoided in the Hitlerist attempt to re-commune with the ancestral gods? This was the essential question. Hitler incarnates the Germanic will to return to our Aryan roots: his is the leftwards swastika, turning against the rotation of the earth as a *man against time*; his is the Swastika of Return. What link could be established between the two swastikas? Bruno Berger's ethnological studies did not find any significant biological link with the remnants of the ancient Tibetan peoples; the physical — and thus the mental — characteristics were not there. Lore existed, however: Agartha (*Agarthi*) and Shambala hinted at the lords of this world, hibernating in the mountains like Barbarossa, awaiting a time of need, a time of return. Myth and the esoteric — this was the essential link that would answer the question of cataclysm.

The figure carved of extraterrestrial iron is the emblem of faith. Its specific origins matter as little as the three individual lines forming the symbol of Hitlerist faith, the *hagal* rune: ✱. The underlying faith and intent of the symbol means all, however; individually, the signs are nothing; taken together, as constituent parts — this is the transmutation of material, the resurrection of life. Found in the symbols are the undying lights of any folk: physical, mental, and spiritual strength and harmony. This is the fire that links the exodus with the return, the ancient Aryan with the Hitlerian. Man may come to dust, but the gods are eternal. The only cataclysm is losing faith: this is the figure's reminder.

The greatest heroes of old were those who lived with honor and loyalty to the MYTH. Within their blood, the extraterrestrial still pulsed and strove; they were the manifest figure, each simply living,

[39] Miguel Serrano, *Nos: Book of the Resurrection* (London: Routledge & Kegan Paul, 1984), 125.

but by doing so, compelled to a peaceful glory. Not *peaceful* because there was no concomitant destruction, but because the harmony of MYTH ensured the perpetuation of creation. Peace through mythical order, not ordered causality. Causality is our gift to the world; it is the language of the Kali-Yuga; but its time weighs heavy with iron, un-transmuted metals dark with corrosion of the spiritual. Modern, rationalistic judgments are ordered according to this mental apparatus that weaves around the things we encounter like a web around the envenomed. The ensnared pictures of the world dissolve with venomous iron collapsing in on itself, like holes of black lead. There is no escaping it without the MYTH, without faith. Our heroes knew this; theirs was the world of existential struggle against the corrosive materialistic impressions of reason. When modern adherents to causality — *Reasonites* — disturbed the earth and removed the entombed from the blood-fused soil enshrining them, the mythical peace was disrupted. Time and again this peace was upturned, and each disruption was a piece of iron lobbed onto the scales of time accelerating our demise. This, however, is necessary for the mythical order. Does this mean we abandon the struggle? No! Our blood will not allow this. This is why the Reasonites want to destroy our blood and the MYTH.

On the Kuru-field, *Herrenmensch* Krishna reminded Arjuna: "Having regard for thine own duty thou should not tremble; for another, better thing than a fight required of duty exists not for a warrior".[40] This, too, is the figure's reminder to us: the duty of the Germanic folk is *struggle* — exoteric and esoteric. Perpetuate the MYTH so the warrior's peace abides. What is the warrior's peace? *Meine Ehre heißt Treue.*

In the greatest struggle of our Germanic folk, and the greatest struggle the world has ever seen — a mere battle in the Cosmic Struggle and prelude to the final victory of the Führer's Last Battalion — the warrior's peace pervaded all fronts: east, west, south, and home. War was not desired, but it was necessary — the Judaic Reasonites made it so. Only honor and loyalty were necessary in that greatest expression of a folk's will to live, and this is what perpetuated the MYTH, for past, present, and future. We inspire our ancestors — those heroes of old — just as they inspire us; we fight for them and they for us; our descendants are those future ancestors who seed the ancient north with their divine spark. The

---

[40] Bhagavad Gita, II.31.

extraterrestrial figure retrieved from the Tibetan caretakers of our future ancestors transcends time, as does the MYTH. The warrior's peace protects the mythical order with its double victory — the *sieg! sieg!* of the SS —, and with this, time enough is assured for those dutiful *Kameraden*, time enough to assemble the Last Battalion which staves off destruction and transmutes iron to gold.

And with this, the gods and sleeping kings are released again from their mountain home — in the Alps, in the Caucasus, in the Himalayas. Riding in the *Wildes Heer*, the Führer and HIS furious horde reclaim the frozen steppes from the Red Wave — the Judaic wave that taught the consumers to consume. The figure's eternal fire, seated with the rooted man, counters the eternal wandering of Ahasuerus, who knows only the frozen dark, and seeks to make the whole world inert with ignorance. The eternal fire can *only* defeat the victors' fleeting tyranny, for theirs is a subversion of primordial, natural values. Reasonite, Jewish "liberation" is naught but enslavement. Propaganda props up the Jewish cause, whose lynchpin is the counter-myth of the golems — *the lie of the six million*. Otto Remer rightly notes that the "legend" is meant to materially enrich the morally bankrupt. The enormity of the ritual slaughter of the Germanic people during both the First and Second World Wars far outweighs the mere propagandic success of a manipulative fantasy — one meant to disarm and destroy any doubters; but in this timeline of the Exodus, mere manipulative fantasy has become "common knowledge." Indeed, the kings sleep in the mountains, waiting for the ravens — *thought* and *memory* — to take their rest. If the lie is common knowledge, the ravens must be dead asleep. But their rest belies the prophecy to be fulfilled: it is no accident the *Schutzstaffel* professed and embodied the double victory.

Hitlerism is not dualism, as Serrano is wont to emphasize: there is *only* victory for the Führer — esoteric and exoteric. There are no complementary sides willing each other into eternity, gentlemanly trading parries. There is only the Good — the MYTH of the MAN TO COME and HIS inevitable triumph. This time-cycle, in which the enemies of the Führer and HIS Germanic folk reign in destructive degradation, which is but one manifestation of the Eternal Return of the Same, and which synchronistically overlaps all time, will be finally obliterated (*vernichtet!*); the Demiurge and its golems will be ended, once and for all. Battle is being waged right now against the forces of demiurgic darkness. The material strength of those who have remained loyal to the Führer is resurgent; spiritual strength, too, grows, though it never left. The legacy of those whose honor is loyalty alights the eternal fire in the spirits of new *Kämpfer*. Concurrent time cycles are bridged through the axis of the rightwards and leftwards swastikas. The Exodus and Return are but the same event viewed from different perspectives; the victory of one assures the victory of the other. Serrano tells us the golems "try to convince themselves Hitler lost, because they can only understand the hallucinatory phenomena of the apparition of an Avatar among the robots and animal-men of Kali-Yuga as a defeat. Yet in their innermost emptiness, they know Hitler won (and will win) the Great War." Triumph has always belonged to the Führer — faith, honor and loyalty would never have existed if it were otherwise.

Ernst Schäfer never catalogued the extraterrestrial figure in his extensive list of Tibetan artifacts. The figure was too special: it was a link to the past and a warning for the future; in short, it was a piece for the present, and its purpose was best served in faithful hands — hands crafting the warrior's peace. Schäfer was an SS man whose honor was loyalty. He swore no oath to the science of the Reasonites nor to the academicians. His victory was double and predicated on faith. Faith is what binds us to the figure and its origins. The Exodus and Return of our eternal, faithful fire keep the frozen dark from consuming this world. Our fight is for the return of the sleeping kings, the heroes of old, who will consummate the Cosmic Struggle against the Germanic folk's eternal enemies with the annihilation of the synchronous time-cycle, thereby freeing the Divine's earthly manifestation from its demiurgical internment. It is a warrior's peace that will conquer the lie and its golems; it is a warrior's peace that will free the Germanic folk, returning the Sun to the heavens. When the sign of the sun returns to the sky, the end will have begun, and this night will have brought us closer to the mystery of all beginning.

AGAINST ALL ODDS

In the closing days of World War II, both the *Wehrmacht* and the *Waffen-SS*, while still formidable, were husks of their former selves. War, after all, depletes a folk of its best blood.[41] Six years of existential combat against Allied nations possessing more than half

[41] See David Starr Jordan's *The Blood of the Nation* (1902), *The Human Harvest* (1907), *War and the Breed* (1922); see also Hitler's *Mein Kampf*.

the world's resources forced Hitler's Germany to cast wider and wider nets to replace the losses sustained at multiple fronts. But in those final chaotic days, even these expanded ranks were thinned to ghostly films encasing a collapsing state.

As the Soviets pushed relentlessly west to Berlin, German armies, incurring reversals of their massive 1941 successes, were enveloped and faced annihilation. The Ninth Army met one such encirclement in Halbe, a small town some sixty kilometers from Berlin; their aim became a breakout and linkup with the Twelfth Army as part of the larger Battle of Berlin. Surrounded on all sides by three echelons of Red Army fighting positions, the Ninth Army was outnumbered more than three to one; the armament disparity was far greater. In the midst of these unfavorable odds, German morale and discipline deteriorated; thus, too, did combat effectiveness. Of the roughly 80,000 German troops battling for their lives in Halbe, barely 25,000 escaped the envelopment; nearly seventy percent were killed or captured. It is remarkable that so many *did* break through the Soviet lines, and this stands as a shining example of fortitude in the face of impossible odds.

Eberhard Baumgart, a Halbe survivor, recalls what separated the escapees from the ensnared; it is worth quoting here at length:

> Who might be able now to say for sure what precisely caused the individual soldier or refugee to keep on the move and, as if gone berserk, seek ways and means to break out of the pocket at Halbe? What motivated them furiously and desperately to brave one obstacle after another, risk their lives each time? How to explain that some indeed reached safety with the comrades of the Twelfth Army, defying risk and injury and the shortage of ammunition and fuel, regardless of pain and hunger?
>
> Let us frame the question differently: who actually stood a chance of succeeding?
>
> [It was] where authority had remained intact and where there was a direct link between order and obedience. That's where the combative spirit triumphed.
>
> While the fighters had all but lost faith in the so-called *Wunderwaffen*, they now put their hopes on a different miracle: the Americans must have come to their senses, they believed, and realized that they had colluded with the devil.... Indeed, there was whispering

> that Germany would enter a pact with them against the Soviets...
>
> There is no doubt that such rays of hope stoked the will of the troops to persevere, it fueled their desire to [break out of the encirclement at Halbe]....
>
> It was difficult for troops to find each other or link up with other units without maps. However, what all those lost soldiers wandering around in the forest did know was where west lay. It was the direction from where the battle noises were coming, the thunder of artillery shelling, the detonations and the piercing sound of crushed metal. That's where one would meet up with hardy comrades like oneself, with determined Germans who were minded to succeed in the break through.[42]

Halbe's survivors — soldiers and civilians — surmounted the frothing chaos of impossible odds through grit, through ardent perseverance. The defeatists among them served only to spur the fighters' wills to keep fighting and survive. What spurred the survivors on — "as if gone berserk"? Order, discipline, hope — in a word, *faith*. And where did the faithful, "hardy comrades" converge? Precisely where *danger most violently churned*. Surely it was *irrational*; surely it was *foolish* to do so? Cooler heads might have had suggested safer, more sensible courses of action. Perhaps *staying put*, simply *waiting it out* should win the day; or maybe surrender to the encroaching Reds? After all, death likely waits at the front... And yet, those "berserkers" refused to listen to the defeatists. They *believed*; they felt the blood seething *in their veins* — danger *at the front* be damned. And if belief should send flesh and bone to shreds, so be it: "better to die once and for all than linger ... in misery".[43] Consider, too, Baumgart's use of the word "berserk" — it is no accident. Derived from "berserker," we know these warriors battled without armor, embodying frenzied Nature, as wolf or bear. Their furor was fostered by faith: they were Wotan's Elite. Those times were different than ours now: the berserkers were closer in time to the Age of Gods; millennia have passed since then. We are left with *reasoned*

---

[42] *Halbe 1945*, translated by Eva Burke, (Barnsley, Great Britain: Greenhill Books, 2022), 182-184.

[43] Aeschylus, *Prometheus Bound*.

composure, as if that can inspire anything except defeatism. Where are our berserkers? They were present in Halbe, 1945; they broke through; they survived. *Gott war mit ihnen*. God helps those who help themselves. Not all of those who braved the odds survived; but only those who defied "impossibility" survived — *against all odds*. This is analogous for our own time.

Defeatists persist. As long as a man fighting for faith exists, so too will his naysayer. Defeatists abounded in Hitler's Germany, even beyond Halbe. They were Carnaris, von Stauffenberg, Niemöller, Mann, von Galen, and others. In their own minds, these traitors to their kinsmen and fatherland were "freedom fighters." Treason is always a matter of perspective. They at least stood for something, which is more than what can be said of most lukewarm bystanders.

Nevertheless, they opposed the Führer, the utmost manifestation of the Germanic will in history, which is to say, a god. Countering a god — *a folk's will* — can *only* be treasonous, despite any pretense of "good intentions." Inhibiting or contravening a god's arc (i.e., the ARCHETYPE) stems from both a lack of faith and a misunderstanding of past, present, and future. Each of these treasonous sources is a consequence of the Age of Man; they originate from a bloodless, scientific interpretation of life. In short, civilization is treason, if it loses its cultural, faith-bearing anchor. Not a single faithful Man of History was ever universally loved in his time; but not a single one was ever put in the grave. Krishna, Buddha, Jesus, Mohammed, Hitler — each is immortal, for better or worse; their blood was the fertilizer of their worldview. If they who mean so much to so many today cannot escape the defeatists, we cannot expect to either. Hitler survived or eluded several assassins' bombs or bullets — the "cooler heads" sought to salvage Germany. The Führer accounted this to Providence; certainly it was — for HIS arc had not yet been realized. Death was defied until the Germanic folk's will was ready to take root from the seed of sacrifice. Defeatists be damned.

There are those around us — we who fight for the blood in our veins, we who fight for the MAN TO COME — who want nothing more than to see us fail, or, at best, cannot see a clear history — let alone future — for lack of faith. These opponents seek to coax smothering, inertial despair in various ways, but their goal is always our failure. Our most insidious opponents are always the most inconspicuous — those who might appear as fellow travelers. Many of these supposed comrades espouse "white identity" for no other reason than maintaining the status quo of their privileged position. These "positive white" identitarians are naught more than wealthy, white liberals: the worst kind of traitor. They are faithless; they have no sense of the MYTH, and they despise anyone not from their social class; in reality, they care nothing of race; in fact, they believe faithful, *illiberal* whites are the ignorant bane of existence — too dumb to see the value of "tolerant progress," or the "cool-headedness" so pervasive at Halbe. Beneath their veneer of "white brotherhood" is a creeping liberality and disparaging of the past. Hitler was defeated, therefore Hitler was wrong; "liberal" ideologies defeated Hitler, so they are right. So say our "white brothers," and all investigation stops there. Yet, equating *elemental viability* or *correctness* with "success" in a failing world is a *non sequitur*. If you were outnumbered by thugs and yet had the courage to speak out against their thuggery, you could expect retaliation. If the thugs neutralized your threat to them, it does not make your actions wrong and their actions right; quantity will have simply prevailed over quality — the mantra of modernity, the schema of two world wars. The "white liberal" identitarian will argue that because Hitlerism "failed," it must be rejected and a new approach must be sought. These are the "cooler heads" among us. Cooler heads did not survive the cauldron, and they cannot survive a world that seeks the demise of European folk.

What good is a faithless future? And how can positivism in any form inspire kinsmen to cultural heights? One might imagine a faith of the faithless, but this is merely nihilistic degradation — i.e., it is Liberalism. *All is permitted* in such conditions, as Dostoyevsky noted. Liberalism leads only to enslavement; that is, the enslaved "progress" beyond all identity — principally beyond race — and undercut their own spiritual foundation, which is blood, the essence of life in more ways than one. Meanwhile, the enslavers ignore the ideological tenets they purvey, ensuring they maintain their racial-spiritual bedrock. This is principally seen in the racial-religious group that has dominated civilization for millennia: the Jews. Remarkably, many non-Jews are still confounded at the racial core of Jewry; to them, it is still a harmless religion. Religious or not, and politically left or right, however, the Jews' racial strategy remains intact and uniform: (1) attach to a host; (2) amplify and create racial victimhood to decapitate opposition; (3) erase the natural divisions (e.g., racial, national) of hosts to dilute racial-national character; (4) establish castes to serve the "chosen" elite. We are all pawns in Jewry's game. Our "white liberals" are willing pawns. They are Christians, globalists, progressives, capitalists, international socialists, diversity-and-inclusion pundits — they are the WASP — here to save us from ourselves: They are the Seydlitz Troops of the modern West, sowing devitalizing chaos and dispiriting those remaining illiberal folk of Germanic stock. They are no chimeras, and they will not win: Faith and stark will triumph in the end.

The material defeat of Hitler and Germany at the end of World War II was expected, if not necessary. It did not come at the hands of the diabolical Jews or traitorous whites constantly agitating against Hitler's beneficence. It came as fulfillment of the Divine Will expressed through the cycles of time.

> If Hitler had materially won the war it would have been just another war.... In truth, by losing the war Hitler won it, since with his sacrifice, with his example, the Ideal has remained intact. Hitler did not need to do more than what he did: To unmask the mythic cosmic Enemy, the incarnation of evil on earth, for the first time in the history of the world: the International Jew. And this cannot be changed by humans because it is not done by humans but by the Hyperborean Gods. Nothing will be achieved by the planetary falsification of a non-existent genocide. Nothing has followed from it until now because the Myth, the Avatar goes his steadfast way. He works from other dimensions....
>
> [It] was no longer possible for Adolf Hitler to win in any other way in an exterior, overpopulated world, where the numbers of bastards and those of mixed blood predominate.[44]

Against all odds did Adolf Hitler win power in 1933. Against all odds did the Führer rise to be the greatest statesman the world had ever seen in 1938. Against all odds did our true Germanic brothers and sisters defy a world warring against them for six heroic years. Against all odds did our Germanic brothers and sisters escape the fatal, internationalist cauldron at Halbe in 1945. And against all odds do we continue the struggle in our Führer's name. If this world, which is so absolutely corrupt, upturned, and godless disparages a folk's will to live and its utmost manifestation in history in the person of Adolf

[44] Miguel Serrano, *Adolf Hitler: The Ultimate Avatar.*

Hitler, and denies them the God-given right to uphold the rights outlined by Nature and Führer, then it can *only* mean we Hitlerists are correct. Evil cannot be celebrated, and, despite its quantitative advantage — against all odds — it will be defeated.

HITLERISM

Adolf Hitler was the embodiment of the Germanic will. All history of the Germanic races led to Hitler's mystical awakening on the Freinberg and was realized in HIS existence. HE stands as the spiritual center around which the Germanic folk, if they are to endure, revolve. Every vibrant people have had and must have a spiritual core — without it, they die. Emanating from the core is the mythical nimbus, which invigorates a people by giving them examples to emulate and a future to anticipate. The myths of the Germanic races are rooted in prehistory, wherein the gods of old populated this world with their spirit. From these gods arose an earthly master: the Aryan; and from the Aryan descended the Germanic folk. The Vedas and Edda are bound by the Aryan blood that created them — it is the blood which conquered the world by living in harmony with it. After millennia of devolution, at humanity's darkest hour, an avatar of the divine spirit — the Germanic will — appeared as paragon. Adolf Hitler, the Führer, was and is the incarnation of this will. Through HIS example and the myth HE invoked, the Germanic races will prevail.

Faith

All of life speaks to both the preponderance and essentialness of irrationality. We are human and, thus, animal — some more or less, but all tied to Nature in this very concrete way. Nature is irrational, like Schopenhauer's blind *will to live*: it strives to live, nothing more; the *how* and *why* it knows not. We are the conscious will; and with this consciousness comes rationality — though the irrationality never strays and, indeed, lurks behind every "rational" decision. From rationality, in this context, comes power — more precisely, the *will to power*. Given our humanness, rationality brings little to bear; it is only a means to an end — this end is power. The blood in our veins determines toward which physical end our power is aimed. Blood is all that is real; all else is abstract intellectualism, meant only to distract from the critical ever-present task at hand: preserving one's lineage.

Criticality is tied to reality, which is to say, it is tied to meaning. Meaning is subjective, to be sure; but to overcome such subjectivity, at least in part, we must understand ourselves as part of something *greater* than ourselves. In this way, our subjectivity takes on a veneer of objectivity: we fight for our blood. It is veneer because *objectivity* is not our goal; *objectivity* is only a modern concept meant to describe that which has value. Value is subjective. But when we subordinate ourselves to the arc of blood through time, then we begin to see real value. All else is means to preserving this end: our blood is life and the will to preserve it is the will to power. Because *objectivity*, or a "rational anchor," is impossible without concomitant subjectivity, faith is necessary.[45] Any knowing worth knowing is *faith*.[46]

Friedrich Nietzsche

When we are reminded of the essentialness of faith in a godless world, we are reminded of Nietzsche. Nietzsche can only be understood when one is ready to understand him — that is, when one has experienced enough life and gained enough historical context to properly see his task. Much understanding of him is marred by popular (mis)conceptions: he is the "madman" who declares "God is dead!" as if in some state of ecstasy — yet the opposite is true; modern views of him are further skewed by his most popular interpreter's own editorializing — Walter Kaufmann, who lacks Nietzsche's Germanic blood, was anointed the "preeminent Nietzsche scholar," and thus had his translations most widely available. In this way, the non-Aryan gets the "final say" of Nietzsche's task — through, not least, his constant editorializing or "placing in proper historical context" (as if Nietzsche cannot speak for himself when he decries those like Kaufmann to be *antithetical* to all that is noble and good — i.e., the *ari*-stocracy, *ārya*, *Aryan*).

---

[45] "Will and reason flow together from one uniform faith, from one single mythos, the mythos of the blood.... All models, systems of thought and values are in our eyes only means to strengthen the nation's struggle for existence outwardly and to heighten the inner strength through a just and purposeful organization." Alfred Rosenberg, *Blood and Honor* (Lincoln, NE: Third Reich Books, 2009), 112-113.

[46] "A faithless man was also condemned in Aryan India, not because he was loveless but because he had become without honor. 'Better to give up life, than to lose honor'." Alfred Rosenberg, *Myth of the Twentieth Century* (2021, Clemens & Blair), 107.

The effect of this discord between speaker and interpreter leaves many believing Nietzsche a good trumpeter, nothing more — too conflicted and contradictory to deliver any meaning; but it is only the misalignment of worldviews between speaker and interpreter that puts discord to the fore. With more earnest study, however, we might see beyond this disharmony something far more robust. It is *meaningful* that Nietzsche speaks of the Eternal Return. Whether he means the concept psychologically or cosmologically is insignificant. That he brings it up at all means everything. Such a cyclical notion of reality suggests its origins: it is Aryan.[47]

Indeed, it was the Aryans who brought the notion of cyclical existence south to the aboriginal Indians. They conquered and instilled the cosmological truth that was alien to the southern climes. Cyclicality was interwoven with the Aryan culture (race); their traditions were not systematically recorded because there was no need for it: it was their unmediated history and thus part of their being. The gods birthed them and they birthed the gods; they knew their history as one knows his family. It was only with the Vedic texts that we begin to see the Aryan record. Later, and much further north, the purest remaining Aryans — whom we know as the Germanic races — set their spiritual-historical traditions to record: the Edda mirrors much of what we now recognize as Hindu tenets: acknowledging race is essential to harmonious existence; the gods and man coextensively create, sustain, and destroy — each as necessarily as the other; the noble race will conquer — not because it is many, but because its quality is highest, which is to say *divine*; time takes its course as means of the Absolute realizing itself as something lesser, but still divine. This was the Aryan faith handed down — if not through instruction, then undoubtedly through blood.

Hence we find Nietzsche espousing quintessentially Germanic beliefs in the modern world. His childhood learning was both classical and Lutheran — but this is only to say *Aryan*. Ancient Greek thought was varied, but consistently heroic, defined by honor and duty — not different than ancient Hindu (Aryan) or Germanic thought. We certainly see hues of Parmenides and Heraclitus in both spiritual traditions. Linking them all is the Aryan tradition. *The cosmos, the same for all, none of the gods nor of humans has made, but it was always and is and shall be: an ever-living fire being kindled in*

47 This stands in contrast to Abrahamic linearity.

measures and extinguished in measures.[48] Heraclitus here echoes Hanns Hörbiger's *Welteislehre*, the accepted cosmological doctrine of Hitler's Germany, which stood in direct contrast to competing un-Germanic theories.

The Hindu texts continue: *The worlds are subject to recurring existences....*[49] Similarly: *Now do I see the earth anew....*[50] And, of course, Nietzsche: *Everything becomes and returns forever,* escape is impossible! ... *The thought of recurrence is a principle of* selection *in the service of power (and barbarity!).*[51] Martin Luther could not subdue his Germanic (Aryan) tendencies, either. Sickened by the corruption of the Roman-Christian Church, he revolted against the money-driven doctrine that gave rise to indulgences. Lutheranism is a direct correspondence between man and his God; that is to say, it is faith; it carries the spark of Germanicism.[52] What informed Nietzsche, then, was not the prevailing toe-the-line, Christian acquiescence, but instead was the blood of his ancestors: he philosophized with *Mjölnir*.

What Nietzsche sought to recreate through his thought (his Mjölnir) was a "new order"[53] — one that required a "new slavery" just as surely as it promised a new type of hero. He unequivocally assailed the modern age, disgusted by its being "the most humane, the mildest, and the most righteous age that the sun has ever seen." And, naturally, the "new order" would necessitate that there would be those at the top (the few of quality, the aristocracy), and those at the bottom (the many of negligible quality, the slaves), which implies that some would be disadvantaged.[54] Nietzsche's anointed interpreter — the Jew Kaufmann — whines that, contrary to what it seems like the German is saying, "hurting others is a sign that one lacks power".[55] This is just one of many Kaufmannesque rewrites.

---

[48] Heraclitus, fragments.
[49] Bhagavad Gita, VIII.16.
[50] Poetic Edda, Voluspo, 59.
[51] *The Will to Power*, §1058.
[52] That is, it is more Germanic than Catholicism. Luther could not shake his trust in Saul (Paul), however.
[53] *Joyful Science*, §377.
[54] *The Will to Power*, §872: "The great majority of men have no right to life, and are only a misfortune to their higher fellows."
[55] Found on Kaufmann's translation of *Die fröhliche Wissenschaft* (Vintage Press, 1974), note on p. 87.

And, of course, it is diametrically opposed to Nietzsche's own thought ("my way of thinking requires a warlike soul, a desire to hurt"[56]); but, invariably, modernity insists the non-Aryan has the final solution. Such rewriting is typical of the very vaulation Nietzsche is trying to upheave. For Nietzsche, "it was, in fact, with the Jews that the *revolt of the slaves* begins in the sphere *of morals*." Indeed, "it was the Jews who [stood] in opposition to the aristocratic equation (good = aristocratic = beautiful = happy = loved by the gods)" and it was "the Jews, [who effected] a radical transvaluation of values, which was at the same time an act of the *cleverest revenge*".[57] Revenge against whom? Against "the conquering and *master* race — the Aryan race"[58] of course! Needless to say, Nietzsche laments the inferiorizing effects the Jewish transvaluation of values has on the Germanic man. It is only through a stern devotion to a will to power that the Abrahamic revision of history can be upturned and demolished.

The *Wille zur Macht* is antithetical to the tyranny of democracy (i.e., Jewish democracy, or Liberalism, generally). "Inasmuch as the *mass* of mankind rules," Nietzsche warns, "it tyrannizes over the *exceptions*" — that is, it tyrannizes over those who might be more than the herd is willing to deliver. The will to power is simply an expression of man as both *over* Nature and a *part* of it. As being a *part* of Nature, man is reconciled to his irrationality; despite protestations to the contrary, his "objectivity" goes only so far as his subjective interests allow.[59] As being *over* Nature, man uses the rationality he has to further the aims of his subjective needs. What separates the good from the evil is, (1) the subordination of the individual to the collective (so *subjective* needs really indicate the collective-subjective needs),[60] and (2) the *honesty* with which one prosecutes one's efforts (that is, does one falsely claim that his efforts

---

[56] Ibid., Book I, 31.

[57] *On the Genealogy of Morals*, Essay I, §7.

[58] Ibid.

[59] "Truth? How do I come by this word? I must withdraw it: I must repudiate this proud word. But no. We do not even want it—we shall be quite able to achieve our victory of power without its help." *The Will to Power*, §749.

[60] "If one regards individuals as equals, the demands of the species are ignored, and a process is initiated which ultimately leads to its ruin.... evolution is thwarted and the *unnatural* becomes law...." *The Will to Power*, §246.

are *universal* and *objective* [e.g., as the Allies did before, during, and after World War II], or does one freely admit his efforts are valid for *his own* collective, but not necessarily for others[61]).

The will to power is opposed to the modern conception of democracy because it implies, as was Nietzsche's intent, the collective will ought to be executed through an exceptional individual, and ought not to be the individual will executed through the mass of mediocre individuals. The latter represents liberal-democracy.[62] This *Jewish* democracy is really modern democracy — or "Western" democracy, which is founded on modern Liberalism. It is a programmatic symptom of the disease of slave-morality, or the transvaulation of values.[63] Born of Christianity, it took contemporary root in the Lutheran Reformation, from which the peasants, whom Luther condenmed to hell because of their brutishness and inherent inadequacy to any claims of higher quality, *learned to speak*. This, in turn, emboldened the latent "men of letters" in various European countries to pilfer power away from the hereditary aristocracies by pandering[64] to the masses who might create unforeseen opportunities through their unrest. This was the Enlightenment, the time of Western revolutions, which is to say the time of wealth switching hands from one landed clique to another.[65] The peasants

---

[61] "'Truth' ... is merely a word for 'The Will to Power.'" *The Will to Power*, §552.

[62] "[With] democracy ... it is a fact that the oppressed, the low, and whole mob of slaves and half-castes, *will prevail*. First step: they make themselves free—they detach themselves, at first in fancy only; they recognize each other; they make themselves paramount. Second step: they enter the lists, they demand acknowledgment, equal rights, 'Justice.' Third step: they demand privileges (they draw the representatives of power over to their side). Fourth step: they *alone* want all power, and they *have* it...." *The Will to Power*, §215.

[63] "It was, in fact, with the Jews that the *revolt of the slaves* begins in the sphere *of morals*; that revolt which has behind it a history of two millennia, and which at the present day has only moved out of our sight, because it — has achieved victory." *On the Genealogy of Morals*, Essay I, §7.

[64] "Third step: they demand privileges (they draw the representatives of power over to their side)." — See above note for full quote.

[65] August Kubizek paraphrases his childhood friend, Adolf Hitler: "Who wants war, [Hitler asked], certainly not the little man — far from it. Wars are arranged by the crowned and uncrowned rulers who in turn are guided and driven by their armament industries. While these gentlemen earned gigantic

were appeased by simply being noticed and getting to enjoy comforts not previously known, never mind they were taking the first steps to forfeiting their soul by throwing in with the lot who would ride their yoke[66] to seats of power and influence the world over. Luther himself prayed for deliverance from this materialistic messiah, should such a thing exist — for such a messiah is naught but "a *Kochab* [i.e., a star] and a worldly king, who would slay the [non-Jews], divide the world among the Jews and make them rich lords...".[67]

Modern democracy aims only to set the conditions for enduring tyranny over the Germanic folk; modern democracy's goals are purely materialistic. Spiritual concerns mean as little to it as the rabble it rouses to its cause. For modern "democracy," there are only two groups: the quantity and the quality; the former should perceive themselves as masters, the latter should be servants and outcasts. Sweet deceptions will convince the quantity that all their actions are their own and they act for their own benefit — yet deceits remain just that. As Nietzsche sees it, the Jews have practiced their treachery for millennia — beginning with their insinuations to the courts of Egyptian pharaohs.[68] This continued through the world wars, the proletarian revolutions and civil rights movements, to now. The "chosen race" argue that all their efforts stem from the persecution they themselves have incurred through perpetual exile, that they mean only to help others in ways they have been ignored. But they mean to deceive: all their work has but one goal: to enrich and

---

sums and remain far from the firing line, the 'little man' has to risk his life without knowing to what purpose." *The Young Hitler I Knew* (New York: Arcade Publishing, 2006), 227.

[66] Genesis 27:40 — After Jacob (Israel) cheated and deceived both his brother and father, Isaac tries to console his eldest son Esau: "you shall break his yoke from your neck."

[67] Martin Luther, *On The Jews and Their Lies* (2020; Clemens & Blair).

[68] See Genesis 47, which details the insinuations and of which these are the apparent steps: (1) Play the victim; (2) Attain positions of influence behind faces of power; (3) Manipulate the faces of power and exploit the masses for personal gain; (4) Consolidate personal wealth into familial trusts; (5) Establish a dynasty. These same steps have been followed for millennia. Who overwhelmingly owns the majority of Western media and entertainment? Who overwhelmingly commands domestic and international finance? Who, nearly exclusively, stands for progressive foreign and domestic policies? The Jews. Which country, year after year, receives more American foreign aid than all others? Israel.

empower the sons of Jacob. And deception strips any people of its honor; a dishonorable people stands in opposition to the *good*. Aryan values demand our own use of the will to power. The Aryan must consolidate the efforts of those men and women of quality among his ranks to combat such godless, materialistic subversiveness imposed in the name of "freedom." Freedom for the material-man is slavery for the Aryan — it can be no other way.[69] Nietzsche outlined the consolidation of Aryan powers through his discussion of the *Übermensch*.

Central to Nietzsche's system is the *Übermensch*: it is the focal point of his Eternal Return, revaluation of values, and will to power. Others have said Nietzsche's project precludes systemization: "One cannot make a rational system of Nietzsche's politics without falsifying his thought".[70] And Nietzsche himself derided such systemization: "I am not narrow-minded enough for a system — not even my own system".[71] Aside from Nietzsche *acknowledging* his "own system," a system it nevertheless was. The *Übermensch* is the executor of the system; it is the vessel through which the will to power is carried out, thereby upturning the unnatural transvaluation of values (hence *revaluing*), and creating the conditions that might be struggled for time and again under "the greatest weight"[72] (i.e., the Eternal Return). What's more, Nietzsche outlines in various places what ought to be considered the more granular precepts of his system:

1. There can be no *solidarity* in a society containing unfruitful, unproductive, and destructive members, who, by the bye, are bound to have offspring even more degenerate than they are themselves.[73] [Implication: Degenerates must be removed from society.]

---

[69] "Germany lives — and therefore Marxism dies.... This is not about a so-called Jewish persecution ..., rather merely about justice for the [Germanic folk]." Alfred Rosenberg, *Blood and Honor*, 135, 245 (Lincoln, NE: Third Reich Books, 2009).

[70] Karl Jaspers, *Nietzsche: An Introduction to the Understanding of His Philosophical Activity* (Baltimore: Johns Hopkins University Press, 1997), 253. It should be noted that Jaspers' wife was Jewish; Jaspers was removed from his position in Hitler's Germany because of her subversive influence. Such influence is visible even in Jaspers' clouded interpretation of his kinsman.

[71] Ibid., 399.

[72] Nietzsche, *Die fröhliche Wissenschaft*, §341.

[73] *The Will to Power*, §52.

2. If one regards individuals as equals, the demands of the species are ignored, and a process is initiated which ultimately leads to its ruin.... Evolution is thwarted and the *unnatural* becomes law.[74] [Implication: The ruse of universal equality is unjust and must be eradicated.]
3. Compulsory *military service* with real wars in which all joking is laid aside. [Implication: War is war and "humaneness" has no place in it. *Deceptions* only talk of humaneness and barbarity in the midst of war: this is Allied *objectivity*.]
4. *National* thick-headedness (which simplifies and concentrates). [Implication: A nationalism based on increasing the quality of a people is desired, not the Liberalistic nationalism Nietzsche so often mocks.][75]
5. Improved *nutrition*. [Implication: A proper diet is necessary for proper living.]
6. Increasing *cleanliness* and wholesomeness in the home. [Implication: Good and increasing quality begins in the home; wholesome family life is *essential*.]
7. The predominance of *physiology* over theology, morality, economics, and politics. [Implication: Understanding physiology is critical to increasing quality — for without the proper physical foundation, the mental and spiritual foundations founder.]
8. Military discipline in the exaction and the practice of one's "duty" (it is no longer customary to praise).[76] [Implication: An exacting attention to detail is necessary to overcome the resource disparity between the quantity (and their materialistic masters) and the quality. They can afford mistakes where we cannot.]
9. [A strong species] grants itself the right of exceptional actions, as a test of the power of self-control and of freedom.

---

[74] Ibid., §246.

[75] "*Nationalism* cleaned of formal and economic coincidences ... with the whole passion of a new experiencing of ancient, buried essence" (98, 86); "nationalism of the nineteenth century was closely tied to liberal democracy" and "had been poisoned by Marxist-liberal forces." Rosenberg, *Blood and Honor*, 118-119 (Lincoln, NE: Third Reich Books, 2009).

[76] Three (3) through eight (8) in this list can be found here: *The Will to Power*, §126.

[Implication: All is permitted to preserve and strengthen the healthy and quality society.]

10. [A strong species] abandons itself to states in which a man is not allowed to be anything else than a barbarian. [Implication: This goes beyond a revival of Germanic paganism and its accompanying ethos; it envelops such a revival, but also pushes it into the future through the racial-populism and technological advances unbound in modernity.]
11. [A strong species] tries to acquire strength of will by every kind of asceticism. [Implication: "What does not kill us makes us stronger."]
12. [A strong species] is not expansive, it practices silence; it is cautious in regard to all charms. [Implication: Expansiveness is prohibited because it leads to social disintegration.]
13. [A strong species] learns to obey in such a way that obedience provides a test of self-maintenance. [Implication: *Unser Ehre heißt Treue* — Our honor is loyalty.]
14. [A strong species] does not covet *other* people's virtues.[77] [Implication: Again: *Unser Ehre heißt Treue* — Our honor is loyalty. We remain loyal to our collective and seek to further it by any means.]
15. We deny God, we deny responsibility in God: thus alone do we save the world. [Implication: If Abrahamic morality is the "slave-morality" that is undermining life, then Jehovah — the foundation of theological morality Liberalistic democracy — must be abandoned as *action's impetus*. Nietzsche's *Übermenschlichkeit* (Overmanity) is a salvaging of *personal responsibility* — even in the face of fatality (the Eternal Return) — for the sake of man's salvation. "The will to be *responsible for one's self* (the loss of this is a sign of the decline of autonomy)".[78]]
16. "Truth" is not something which is present and which has to be found and discovered; it is something *which has to be created* and which *gives* its name *to a process*, or, better still, to the Will to overpower.[79] [Implication: *Truth*, said another

[77] Nine (9) through fifteen (15) on this list can be found here: Ibid., §921.

[78] *Twilight of the Idols*, §936.

[79] *The Will to Power*, §552.

great Germanic thinker, *is subjectivity*. Germanic truth is built on the highest values: honor and loyalty, myth and race.]

17. The nature of man is *evil,* and this guarantees his *strength*![80] [Implication: "Humaneness" or any other related concept are subordinate to survival instincts — this attitude, conjoined with a collective striving for quality, is valued.]
18. The highest man, if such a concept be allowed, would be that man who would represent *the antagonistic character of existence* most strikingly, and would be its glory and its only justification.[81] [Implication: The "antagonistic character of existence" is one filled with "harmful, evil, dangerous, questionable, and destructive" elements in the context of the current slave-morality. The "highest man" represents the collective will to usurp bloodless modernity.]

In addition to the fundamental aspects of Nietzsche's system (i.e., the *Übermensch,* the will to power, the revaluation of values, and the Eternal Return), the above precepts help us see exactly what Nietzsche was developing: a new order. This new order would be forged through the will of the *Übermensch*. And *it* is assuredly an *it*. The *Übermensch* is not an individual person, despite Nietzsche's affinity for the "exceptional individuals" (e.g., Napoleon). It is the collective will of a people — the Germanic races. Let us first consider Nietzsche's thoughts:

> What class of men will prove they are strongest in this new order of things? The most moderate—they who do not *require* any extreme forms of belief, they who not only admit of, but actually like, a certain modicum of chance and nonsense; they who can think of man with a very moderate view of his value, without becoming

---

[80] Ibid., §908. It is essential to note that "evil" here can only be understood in the context of Jewish ("slave") morality. Nietzsche's own system *absolutely* has its own morality, which is distinct from slave-morality. Arguably, Nietzsche's morality is pagan (i.e., Germanic). That is, when Nietzsche talks of "evil," a society of nihilistic Raskolnikovs is not the goal; instead, what's desired is an open and honest (i.e., harmonious with Nature) society founded on kinship, since this is the opposite of the duplicitous, progressive society based on inane individualism considered "good" today.

[81] Ibid., §881.

> weak and small on that account; the most rich in health, who are able to withstand a maximum amount of sorrow, and who are therefore not so very much afraid of sorrow—men who are *certain of their power,* and who represent with conscious pride the state of strength to which man has attained.[82]

Aside from this being an apt description of Adolf Hitler, this "class of men" is precisely what the Führer was trying to create through HIS *Dritte Reich* — a society in which the street sweeper would be of higher quality than another society's leader.[83] The Third Reich *was the collective will of the people as embodied in the being of the Führer — this was the Übermensch.* "That man should become better and at the same time more evil," Nietzsche says, "is my formula for this inevitable fact".[84] This *fact* is that the majority of men "only represent a small corner and nook of this natural character" and "the great majority of people, are but rehearsals and exercises out of which here and there a whole man may arise; a man who is a human milestone." Carl Jung described this "human milestone" as the ARCHETYPE, that transcendent state which emblemizes the will of a people; Jung saw Adolf Hitler as the Germanic ARCHETYPE: Hitler is a "spiritual vessel, a semi-deity, a myth: The man with the strongest Will that ever existed. German politics is not made, it is revealed through Hitler."

Jung continues: Hitler "is not a man, but a collective. He is not an individual but a whole nation.... Hitler has no personal ambitions. His ambitions go much further beyond those of ordinary people...

---

[82] *The Will to Power*, §55. One recalls Savitri Devi: "Now, the destiny was accomplished. The Way of glory and sorrow had come to its end.... Adolf Hitler beheld the future. And that future—his own, and that of National Socialism, and that of Germany, who had now become, forever, the fortress of the new Faith—was nothing less than eternity; the eternity of Truth, more unshakable (and more soothing) in its majesty even than that of the Milky Way." *The Lightning and the Sun*.

[83] "It must become a greater honor to be a street-cleaner and a citizen of the Reich than to be a King in a foreign state who is not a citizen of the Reich." Adolf Hitler, *Mein Kampf* (Wewelsburg Archives, 2018), 407.

[84] *The Will to Power*, §881. To be *evil* for Nietzsche is to combat degenerate slave-morality; it is to destroy the bloodless, materialistic foundations of modernity, for they are without Aryan honor (*Ehre*).

Hitler's power is not political: It is *magical*".[85] The foregoing is not meant to distract from the point, but to emphasize it: the *Übermensch* is more than one man — it is the collective unconscious (Blood Memory) of a people fused in fateful solidarity, bound by blood and will.[86]

Rediscovering Hitler

There is much in Nietzsche to remind us of the Führer and HIS Reich. A study of HIS thought is a natural concomitant. *Mein Kampf* is a work of pure determination. Hitler renders a *spiritual* reckoning, a *mystical* reasoning which outlines the success or failure of the Germanic races. Under the natural, ancient influence of racial integrity and ascendancy, the European peoples will live; devoid of this influence, they will die. Indeed, the Führer explains, with HIS uncanny ability to merge worldly reason and divine irrationality, that to deny the immutable laws of Nature — of which race is an indelible part — is to deny Providence. It is only a sign of our materialistic age that the world rose up against the Führer and HIS mission, undermining the God-given right of a people to seek self-determination; this only proves Hitler's standing as a Man Against Time — a preserver of an ancient wisdom who stands opposed to the degenerate monetizing of modernity, and thus a forger of a new order. To be sure, many detractors rush to critique Hitler's writing as vapid and ponderous, as if this will avail their own "scholarship" and undermine the efforts of an absolute genius. It is striking that such an "*unbekannte Mann*" could accomplish all that the Führer did. No "scholar's" critique can hold any weight against Hitler's achievements; any naysaying stands only as thoughtless toadying, indicative of a modernity which bears the mark of the golem. Ultimately, what we find in Hitler is a monument worth exploring. In his essay "The Enigma of Hitler," Léon Degrelle observes,

> People have come to accept fiction, repeated a thousand times over, as reality. Yet they have never seen Hitler,

---

[85] As quoted in Miguel Serrano, *Adolf Hitler: The Ultimate Avatar* (Hermitage Helm Corpus, 2017), 105-107.

[86] Rosenberg, *Myth of the Twentieth Century* (2021), 19: "But today, an entire generation is beginning to sense that values are only created and preserved where the law of blood still determines a person's ideas and actions, whether consciously or unconsciously."

> never spoken to him, never heard a word from his mouth. The very name of Hitler immediately conjures up a grimacing devil, the fount of all of one's negative emotions. Like Pavlov's bell, the mention of Hitler is meant to dispense with substance and reality. In time, however, history will demand more than these summary judgments.

Léon Degrelle
Degrelle was a highly decorated *Waffen-SS* soldier who managed a daring flight to Spain after Germany's surrender. He was first an enlisted man with the Walloons, then became their leader and symbol through his battlefield exploits. Before his time as an SS man, at just 29 years old, Degrelle was the youngest successful political leader in 1936 Europe — the year he also met with Hitler about the prospects of allying political efforts; he headed the Rexists, a Belgian nationalist group believing in both Belgian sovereignty and a pan-Europeanism. After the Soviet duplicity igniting the German offensive in the east in 1941, Degrelle set aside his political ambitions to fight for the greatest pan-European force the world has ever seen: the Third Reich. When news of his many military successes reached the Führer, the latter wished to personally decorate Degrelle with the *Ritterkreuz*. In a subsequent meeting, Hitler told the Belgian that if HE had a son, HE would wish the son to be just like Degrelle: strong, smart, brave, loyal, and honorable — an ideological warrior, a man of unshakable will. Postwar, Degrelle sustained his struggle against the degenerative forces afflicting the Germanic folk.

Among other things, he took up writing to counter the bloodless forces' propaganda. In his *Hitler Democrat*, one is struck not only by Degrelle's account of the Führer — praising his mental, physical, and spiritual strength and deftness — but also his account of how *real* democracy was demonstrated in the Third Reich. We are never told of Hitler's several plebiscites, wherein the people could directly vote on momentous decisions (e.g., from the Saarland to the *Anschluss*, and more); invariably the people voted to consolidate the Germanic races, which only proved Hitler's role as the Germanic ARCHETYPE, that *Germanic democracy* means entrusting the collective will with the chosen Führer. Instead, we are constantly told how "oppressive" and "tyrannical" Hitler's regime was — yet nothing could be further from the truth.[87]

Meanwhile, when in the United States have we ever held a plebiscite? When have American citizens had the chance to vote on momentous social-political decisions? Do we get a say in America's immigration policy? Its foreign and domestic policies? Its economic policy and incessant bailouts? *Never*. But we are ever bathed in talk of "freedom." We have "freedom" in America — the freedom to choose how we'll be *distracted* from reality on a given day, certainly. We forfeit our "freedom" for bread and circus; we content ourselves with voting for a "representative" — one who has the greatest resources at his/her disposal and who, in turn, is out-maneuvered by those with even greater resources — modern Europe is no different. While some are aware of such hypocrisy generally, Degrelle's work, in the context of what really went on in Hitler's Europe at the time, proves both enlightening and surprising. Degrelle's work, too, might orient us to other notable Germanic authors: Dietrich Eckhart, Arthur Moeller van den Bruck, Oswald Spengler, and others — not least of whom is Savitri Devi.

Savitri Devi

Savitri was a French-born Greek who became enamored with the Third Reich, both exoteric (as a political conduit) and esoteric (as a spiritual philosophy). She popularized the link between Aryan Hinduism and National Socialism for postwar generations. In the spiritual context, National Socialism can better be identified as *Hitlerism* — so in this sense, she became an apostle of Hitlerism. Before and during the war, she lived in India, fulfilling her intellectual needs and enjoying a Platonic marriage with a high-caste (Aryan) Indian. She felt delight as the Reich swelled, anticipating victory; but as quantity outweighed quality and the war dragged on, she was dismayed at never having seen the Reich in full bloom. It was only when the war ended that she made her pilgrimage to the ruins of Hitler's Germany. Ultimately, she was arrested and confined for

---

87 In fact, Hitler's Germany only tried to quell the anti-spiritual forces — first in Germany, then in its expanded territory. That these anti-spiritual forces were Marxists, criminals and other society disrupters, and materialists is no coincidence: it is in their (anti-)blood. The idea of Hitler being a "tyrannical dictator" is a creation of the Liberalistic media and academia.

disseminating handwritten propaganda[88] — a victim of the "democratic" system, where thoughts and words are tightly controlled.

In her most famous work, *The Lightning and the Sun*, Savitri paints Adolf Hitler as an incarnation of the godhead; Hitler is the "Man Against Time," who cannot but materially fall so that he might spiritually live; Hitler is the exemplar *par excellence* — as if he were an *archetype*, a symbol of an entire people. The Führer stands as the Man Against Time because the Aryan time cycle has a beginning and end with known points in between. One can get a sense of these known points through reading the Germanic or Hindu creation-destruction myths. As a Man Against Time, Hitler seeks to reestablish the paradisiacal early ages — that is, Hitler stood against the time in which HE lived, contravening the inevitable descent of time into its final stages.[89]

In this way, then, the Führer is "directed against the downward current of irresistible change that is the very current of Time, forces of Life tending to bring the world back to original timeless Perfection, to that glorious projection of the Unmanifested that begins every Time-cycle".[90] "The foolish disregard Me," Savitri quotes the Bhagavad Gita at the beginning of *Lightning*, "when clad in human semblance..".[91]; hence, Hitler is attacked in his lifetime and maligned after his departure, despite both the necessity of HIS being and HIS virtues. But, Savitri also quotes Rudolf Hess, "we are in the midst of a great historical turning point. We are going through its birth pangs. Everything seems negative — and yet something New and Great is being born".[92] This turning point is the beginning of her

---

[88] As she relays in *Gold in the Furnace*, Savitri spent two nights creating five hundred leaflets. This is what she wrote: *Men and women of Germany, In the midst of untold hardships and suffering, hold fast to our glorious National Socialist faith, and resist! Defy our persecutors! Defy the people, defy the forces that are working to 'de-Nazify' the German nation and the world at large! Nothing can destroy that which is built in truth. We are the pure gold put to test in the furnace. Let the furnace blaze and roar! Nothing can destroy us. One day we shall rise and triumph again. Hope and wait! Heil Hitler!*

[89] That is, Hitler has "Vishnu's faithfulness to the original divine pattern of Creation." Savitri Devi, *The Lightning and the Sun* (Wewelsburg Archives, 2019), 320.

[90] Ibid., 318-319.

[91] Bhagavad Gita, IX.11.

[92] This quote is pulled from a letter Hess wrote to his wife twelve days after eleven of his comrades were "democratically" hanged at Nuremberg.

task: she is a herald of a new order — the order prophesized by Nietzsche and initiated by Hitler. Make no mistake, however: Savitri saw the Führer as a step along the way, not the Omega. As Hitler himself said, "I know that Somebody must come forth and meet our situation. I have sought him. I have found him nowhere; and therefore I have taken upon myself to do the preparatory work.... For that much I know: I am not He. And I know also what is lacking in me".[93]

For Savitri, the final incarnation of the godhead will blend the Lightning-nature (Shiva, the creator-destroyer) and the Sun-nature (Brahma, Being Itself), and from this manifestation will come the new order. And though HE is not the final avatar for Savitri, the Führer is yet worthy of our admiration, "for he fought against the downward pressure of many more centuries; [was] more selfless than the very last One, for he was, contrarily to Him [Kalki, the final avatar of the godhead], to reap nothing but disaster—sacrificed himself and his people—at large in order to give Him ... companions at arms in the last decisive battle".[94]

Savitri's work is both novel and profound. But she was not the first to imagine such things. After all, *Hitler* chose the Aryan swastika for HIS Reich's emblem; Hitler was the magnetic being who attracted so many who had been involved in various esoteric circles; Hitler made Hess, a member of the *Thule-Gesellschaft,* his deputy Führer; Hitler made Himmler — who, among other things, established the *Wewelsburg*, the *Ahnenerbe*, and the rune-laden *Ehrenring* — the *Reichsführer-SS*, head of the new caste of Germanic nobility; Hitler presented Alfred Rosenberg, also a member of the *Thule-Gesellschaft*, with the *Deutscher Nationalorden für Kunst und Wissenschaft* (the German equivalent of a Nobel Prize) for his *Myth of the Twentieth Century*, which outlined the MYTH of the Blood. Perhaps more could be gleaned from *Mein Kampf* if it is understood in light of its spiritual-historical setting. Certainly Savitri's work furthered the Hitler MYTH — but what of the "philosopher of the Third Reich"? What of Alfred Rosenberg?

Alfred Rosenberg

Rosenberg was a Baltic German, born in Estonia and fluent in Russian. During Hitler's imprisonment for the failed 1923 putsch, the Führer named him the head of the Party. Once the National

---

[93] As told to Hans Grimm in 1928.

[94] Savitri Devi, *The Lightning and the Sun*, 321.

Socialists (legally) came to power, Hitler appointed Rosenberg the "cultural and educational" leader of the Reich. As war in the east broke out, Rosenberg was named the Reich Minister for the Eastern Territories, no doubt, in part, because of his familiarity with Eastern Europe from having been born and raised there; and, in part, because of his loyalty to Hitler since first hearing him speak in 1919. In the end, he was hanged for his participation in his country's government — a government that faced material defeat.

He was the only one of his hanged Nuremberg comrades to remain silent on the gallows. Not only had he written his memoirs while on trial — wherein he speaks, in part, about the pain of dispatching his beloved wife and daughter to safety as the final days of war passed — but he had also published several other works in his life, which certainly spoke for him. As the Nuremberg chaplains and psychologists pressed him to recant or admit wrongdoing, Rosenberg remained faithful to his life's work and position — and he stayed loyal to his Führer. He believed, without fail, in the righteousness of his thought and deed.

In reading Rosenberg's Nuremberg testimony under apparent irrelevant prosecutorial attack, one is struck by the stoic resoluteness with which he answers; the contrast between the prosecution, infused by "the fanatical spirit of vengeance which dominated the era,"[95] and the stoic Rosenberg is remarkable: it was, as Louis Pauwels wrote, as if the Allies and the Germans were from different worlds.[96] Indeed they were! Perhaps what is more arresting is how the "free" Allies essentially condemned Rosenberg for what he believed[97]:

---

95 Peter H. Peel, from his introduction to the 1980 American edition of Rosenberg's *Myth of the Twentieth Century*.

96 For a full study of Rosenberg's testimony at Nuremberg, see *Streicher, Rosenberg, and the Jews: The Nuremberg Transcripts* (2020, Castle Hill).

97 In essence, this is the charge against Rosenberg: "Rosenberg remodeled the German educational system in order to expose the German people to the will of the conspirators and to prepare the German nation psychologically for a war of aggression" — *International Military Tribunal — Nuremberg*, vol. 11, p. 85, 09 April 1946. And: "The Tribunal has to decide whether there is a connection between Rosenberg's ideology and the war crimes and crimes against Jews" — Ibid., p. 387, 13 April 1946. And again: "The charge against [Rosenberg] is that he made a certain use of his philosophical ideas" — Ibid., p. 394, 13 April 1946.

> He was hanged, it would appear, for what he thought and wrote. The American prosecutor hammered away on this point. Rosenberg's writings, he charged, were instrumental in the rise of the Nazi Party to power. It seems a strange sort of indictment coming from the representative of a power which is always so smugly self-congratulatory about the First Amendment.[98]

Knowing the context of his life, one might surely be intrigued. While any of his writing is worth exploring, his most famous work, *Myth*, is his *magnum opus*. In it, Rosenberg describes the MYTH of the Blood; it is race which stands as the beginning of all culture. Without purity of blood — particularly Germanic blood — there can only be cultural decay, which will devolve into dissolution of civilization and final world destruction.

Rosenberg points to the degeneration of ancient Egyptian, Greek, and Roman cultures as evidence of miscegenational misdeeds. These cultures themselves were offshoots of a prehistoric people originating in the north — the Atlanteans or, better, the Hyperboreans of whom Plato, Herodotus, Hesiod, Homer, Pindar, and others spoke. The north is significant because its day (period of light and period of darkness) was a year; the sun was the life-bringer and light-bringer (*Lichtbringer*), and its rays, like the northern race teaching its greatness, emanated across the globe — like the hooked, rotating arms of the swastika. Thus we see in Germanic paganism the revered sky-gods; we see in ancient Greece the sun-god Apollo; we see in ancient Egypt the sun-god advanced under Akhenaton; we find allusions to an arctic past for the Aryans in both Zoroastrianism and Hinduism; we see all the Western (i.e., Germanic) traditions driven by a reverence for and fascination with the sun and changing seasons: Yule or *jól* marking the winter solstice (Christmas) — which is only the return of the summer sun, and *Ostern* (Easter) celebrating the coming spring to life. That these traditions, deeply rooted in Germanic pagan history, have been appropriated by Christianity is only a cause for concern: Christianity, like all other social-leveling systems (e.g., Liberalism, Marxism, and capitalism), is *internationalist, globalist* — it sees no borders and no blood in its quest to increase *quantities*. This will inevitably spell the end of

---

[98] Peel, *Myth* introduction.

culture as we know it — because the blood that spawned it will be erased through race mixing: quality is replaced with quantity.

This is the essence of Rosenberg's *Myth*. Race is not everything, but the beginning of everything. This is of central importance and often the source of endless false propaganda. The idea that race is not everything was highlighted again and again in the Third Reich, contrary to the deceptions of the *Lügenpresse* and "objective" intellectuals. One could have Germanic (Aryan) blood and yet be unworthy; likewise, one could have alien blood and yet maintain a Germanic character. More than just "the Jews" were put to task in Germany's work camps — plenty of biological Aryans paid their dues as well, and rightfully so. These were "Aryans" infected with an alien character. Being an Aryan is not only about having certain physical characteristics; it is at root a physical, mental, and spiritual sense of being. This is why National Socialism is far more than just a political ideology; it is a spiritual philosophy.

> [Men] ... are differentiated from others not alone because of physical characteristics. Just as deep and impossible to bridge are the differences in spirit and in soul. Body, spirit and soul primarily constitute the complete man because they form a unified whole. Men must therefore, be considered with respect to their inner makeup.[99]

This was guidance to the *Hitler-Jungend*. In turn, this was inspired by Hans Günther's definition of race: "A race is a collection of individuals differentiated from every other group (constituted in such a way) by its unique combination of bodily characteristics and soul attributes and continually reproduces its own kind".[100] We also find in the *Schutzstaffel* book *Glauben und Kämpfen*: "More important than skin color is the character of the man. One belongs essentially to the race whose virtues he professes through deed." Moreover, we cannot recover a race once it is lost; so we must — as Germanic people — make great effort to preserve our traditions in a modern context: hence, the National Socialist State, Hitler's Germany.

We are not reverting to an anachronistic past; rather, we recognize the fundamental importance of the blood and culture that

---

[99] *Handbuch für die Hitler-Jungend*, 1938.

[100] *Rassenkunde des deutschen Volkes*, 1922.

birthed us, which are inherently spiritual; we must therefore reject the materialistic, race-blind internationalism that is currently in vogue, for it is a rejection of who we are as a people. To accept the *opposite* of who we are is to accept internationalist dogmas: Christianity, Marxism, Liberalism, and capitalism — none of which are Germanic in origin. This dichotomy between the Aryan and his antithesis is the foundation of the cosmic struggle.

Miguel Serrano

No figure of the postwar world has done more to define the cosmic struggle than Miguel Serrano. A native of Chile, Serrano was of Germanic descent and featured prominently in that country's nationalist movement of the 1930s. He, like many historical figures who have come to be known as staunchly "right wing," was first attracted to the "left"; that is, he was attracted to Marxism, which can be understood as *international socialism.* Like others who have undertaken the nuanced journey from left to right, Serrano was drawn to international socialism's rejection of the ineluctable alienation caused by capitalism, its zealous appetite for justice and fairness, and the idea that bloodless individualism is a source of degeneracy, not a source of strength.

He soon found, however, like Mussolini and Hitler before him, that international socialism was only another face of the Liberalism behind borderless capitalism[101]: the justice and fairness it sought was based on empty abstractions and held no anchor in reality. That is, for instance, one cannot adhere to the principle that all men are equal and yet believe (let alone see) that one's social fabric will remain intact. The driving factor behind international socialism is class disparity and the desire to correct it through societal leveling, the consequence of which is a borderless society wherein the outliers

---

[101] "[Marxism and capitalism] were merely two sides of the same coin. Both communist Marxism and capitalism were post-industrial ideologies. Both assumed the mass concentration of labor and industry in large urban areas. Both were anti-folk and internationalist in outlook. Both were only falsely nationalistic. Both assumed the continued existence of economic man in contradistinction to whole, inwardly directed man. Both were materialistic and anti-spiritual in values and in preferred lifestyle. Neither gave man what he needed: a feeling of belonging." James B. Whisker on Alfred Rosenberg's view, from his introduction the 1980 American edition of *Myth of the Twentieth Century*.

(high and low) are trimmed away for a neat, homogeneous middle, which, in turn, is "paradoxically" crushed into the debased masses forming the base of the Marxist pyramid, whose all-seeing eye shepherds them into proletariat-slavery. The impetus behind capitalism is boundless profiteering, of which the outcome is a borderless society bound only by production and consumption. Missing from each is a sense of blood-bound community, which is, unquestionably, the source of family, the source of culture and humanity. The justice and fairness sought by internationalist ideologies serves an unnatural, self-perpetuating end.

Once we remove the essential factor of blood from any ideological equation, we lose our origins and humanity. Thus, the internationalist drive to eliminate the alienation born of unthinking feudalism and mass industrialization can only, in the end, *perpetuate* alienation: the human becomes the inhuman cog, the spiritless producer, the wretched consumer. Serrano, like every spiritual seeker before him, realized the necessity of blood, and thus began his quest for the right.

One cannot summarize Miguel Serrano; one must read him. His works are part autobiography, part history and philosophy, part poetry — yet they are always spiritual. After his days as a rightist author/publisher/activist, Serrano became the Chilean ambassador to Austria and Yugoslavia, and served, too, in various other diplomatic posts. He developed meaningful friendships with Hermann Hesse and Carl Jung, which he explored in his book, *C. G. Jung and Hermann Hesse: A Record of Two Friendships* (1966). When he left the diplomatic corps, he returned to his ideological roots and published what can only be described as a spiritual trilogy, which is seen by many as sacred writ: *The Golden Thread*, *Adolf Hitler: The Ultimate Avatar*, and *Manu: The Man To Come*. In these tomes Serrano explores the history of the Germanic people in the context of their reaching full realization in Hitler's Germany.

While there is too much ground covered in these works to retrace here, one essential point bears mentioning: Adolf Hitler is the tenth and final avatar of the ancient Aryan god Vishnu-Wotan. HIS appearance as the ninth avatar from 1889 to 1945 was but a glimpse of HIS future manifestation; this preparatory work created the MYTH around which the Germanic quality might unite and harden. From this MYTH will arise Kalki-Hitler, along with HIS final battalion, to avenge the anti-Nature evil done to existence. Ragnarök, the coming requital, will end the current time-cycle and the new Golden Age will begin — it will be an age of perfect harmony with Nature.

Adolf Hitler

Adolf Hitler's life is witness to HIS desperate longing for such harmony. When one reads HIS final testament, such longing is all the more evident. Hitler vanished on 30 April 1945; this much we know. Whether HE died by HIS own hand in the bunker or, as Serrano suggests, was whisked away to an impregnable fortress via Antarctica, or transmuted to a higher plane of existence is immaterial. What matters is that HIS spirit endures. In this way, Hitler is immortal — *because the Germanic will is immortal.*

It should be noted, however, that the Soviets could never confirm the charred remains they recovered belonged to Hitler; in fact, their dental examinations confirmed that the remains did *not* belong to the Führer. Stalin himself complained to the Yalta cabal that Hitler, wherever HE was, was not in Berlin. This doubt was reinforced through decades of Allied searching for Hitler's whereabouts. South America was chiefly hunted; after all, so many in the National Socialist hierarchy disappeared there with the help of Admiral Dönitz's submarine fleet. Yet there is something to be said of Antarctica, whose territory the Third Reich was one of the first to explore in earnest, even dubbing one of its claims *Neuschwabenland* — in honor of the Führer's Austrian-Bavarian homeland. It was Dönitz, too, who pridefully announced that his fleet had found a paradise on earth, an "impregnable fortress" to protect the Führer.

This account provides substrate for the postwar 4,700-man and 46-ship-and aircraft-strong American Operation HIGHJUMP, wherein a naval task force, under the official purpose of establishing a research base, took *casualties*. Seemingly unsurprising given the inherent dangers involved with navigating such a harsh environment, both the casualties and the task force's size become somewhat unusual in historical context and taskforce organizer Admiral Byrd's concern that "the United States should adopt measures of protection against the possibility of an invasion of the country by hostile planes coming from the polar regions".[102]

All of this discussion is but a small part of the myth surrounding Hitler — the myth that began on the Freinberg before the First World War, when his childhood friend August Kubizek "was struck by something strange.... It was as if another being spoke out of his body ... what burst forth from him [was an] elementary force.... It was

[102] "A bordo del Monte Olimpo en Alta Mar," *El Mercurio*, Santiago, Chile, 05 March 1947.

an unknown youth who spoke to me in that strange hour. He spoke of a special mission which one day would be entrusted to him..."[103]

That HIS life was a testament to this "special mission" can hardly be doubted. Hitler was the greatest political leader the world has known; HIS brashness and intuition are legendary. HE was simultaneously human and more-than-human; the gods spoke through HIM — HIS intuition was divine voice. Hitler was the greatest social leader the world has known. HE forged the folk in HIS image, and they created HIM; HE was the ARCHETYPE of the Germanic races. HIS social projects are too numerous to completely name: the Führer's leadership schools (*Ordensburgen*), the *Hitler-Jungend*, the *Bund Deutscher Mädel*, the earliest of "green" movements — *Blut und Boden*, the *Autobahn*, the *Volkswagen*, the *Thingplatz*, *Kraft durch Freude*, *Prora*, the *Sturmabteilung* (SA), and, not least, the *Schutzstaffel* (SS) — all of which were designed to reestablish Germanic aristocracy.

Hitler was the greatest military leader the world has known. An absolute autodidact, HE defied HIS anachronistic generals and won some of the most spectacular victories in history; it was only their impudence, perfidy, and doubt that undermined the war effort — turning the *Blitzkrieg* into a war of attrition, a war of *material* resources. One hears from surviving *Wehrmacht* generals nearly universal awe over Hitler's *genius* and augural ability.[104] One reads

---

[103] Kubizek, *The Young Hitler I Knew*, "In That Hour It Began..."

[104] The following are but a few testaments: B. H. Liddell Hart, *The German Generals Talk* (New York: HarperCollins, 2002), 44 ("Hitler was a mystic"), 97 ("[Hitler] often had good ideas"), 115 ("Hitler ... had a grasp of both aim and method, of politics and strategy — from the mating of which grand strategy proceeds"), 134 ("Hitler had a deeper motive [behind his decisions]"), 188 ("Hitler's decision[s] ... averted a panic ... [and] appeared a display of iron nerve"), 217 ("Hitler had been justified"), 237 ("Hitler's much derided 'intuition' was nearer the mark than the calculations of the ablest professional soldiers"), 255 ("[Hitler's] National Socialism ... fortified [soldiers'] morale"), 257 ("[It was because of their] extraordinary confidence in Hitler that [the folk] remained confident in victory" and "The troops' tremendous confidence in Hitler was the dominant factor"), 296 ("Hitler had a magnetic, and indeed hypnotic personality"), 297 ("Hitler had a natural flair for strategy and tactics of an original kind"), 299 ("Hitler had the flair that is characteristic of genius"), and so on. Likewise, from the Nuremberg Military Tribunal: "Hitler's military entourage considered him a military genius" and "the Führer had an extraordinarily quick power of perception

and almost always a correct evaluation of affairs" — vol. 11, p. 50, 08 April 1946.

Stephen G. Fritz's *The First Soldier: Hitler as Military Leader* (London: Yale University Press, 2018), 60 ("[The *Anschluß*] ... that again seemed to confirm the Führer's improvisational genius"), 86 ("As a strategic thinker, [Hitler] was not a mere lucky amateur; indeed, he had demonstrated real insights.... [The] victory over Poland had raised his reputation with his generals..."), 113 ("Brauchitsch ... declared [Hitler] 'the first soldier of the German Reich,' while ... Keitel transformed him from Führer to 'the greatest field marshal of all time.' Göring ... credited the Führer alone with the creation of the Blitzkrieg strategy, gushing, 'Adolf Hitler's genius as a warlord caused a revolution in warfare in that it breached strategic principles that had been held sacrosanct until now.' He also fused the political and military in Hitler, claiming that he, like Frederick the Great, 'combined in his person the wisdom of the statesman and the genius of the *Feldherr*.' ... [The generals] accepted Hitler's — admittedly unorthodox — military genius."), 143 ("Nicolaus von Below, [Hitler's] Luftwaffe adjutant, thought he exhibited a 'sharp logic and extraordinarily fine feel for military situations,' was 'very good at placing himself in the enemy's shoes,' and displayed a 'balanced and accurate' military judgment. Manstein ... believed Hitler had 'a number of qualities indispensible to a supreme commander.' Not only did [Hitler] have a strong will and nerves, but he was also 'highly intelligent' with an 'undeniably keen brain,' possessed 'an astoundingly retentive memory and an imagination that made him quick to grasp all technical matters,' and displayed 'a certain instinct for operational problems.'), 155 (Edmund Glaise von Horstenau credited Hitler "with an eerie yet at the same time untamed genius"), 206 ("Quatermaster-General Wagner ... [exclaimed,] 'I am constantly astounded at the Führer's military judgment ... he has always acted correctly.'"), 226 ("[Nicolaus von] Below wrote approvingly of [Hitler] ..., 'There is no general or officer in the army who possesses such a comprehensive knowledge or skill in all questions of weapons, armament, production, supply and other necessities for the front army.'"), 232 ("[Hitler's] creative genius ... had spared the *Ostheer* the fate of Napoleon's *Grande Armée*. He, like his hero, Frederick the Great, had proven his ability not only to win offensive victories but also to prevail in defensive battles. This, concluded his adjutant Below, was the proof of his genius as a *Feldherr*."), 368 ("... Admiral Raeder insisted in August 1945, 'the manner in which he [Hitler] took command of and handled military matters' appeared to verify that Hitler was 'really a genius, a man called to leadership.'").

Carolyn Yeager & Wilhelm Kriessmann, *The Artist Within the Warlord: An Adolf Hitler You've Never Known* (2017), 105 (from Hermann Giesler: "I also had a chance to talk to Gen. Jodl... He told me: 'I admired the Führer when he laid out his strategy for the west campaign, but I was much more impressed during the last weeks by his unbelievable energy and will power, much the same reverence in the memoirs of those who "knew" and served HIM: Otto Skorzeny, Heinrich Hoffmann, Léon Degrelle, Hans Baur, Rochus Misch, Heinz Linge, Otto Dietrich, Baldur von Schirach, Hermann Giesler, Erwin Bartmann, Hans Schmidt, Hanna Reitsch, Hans-Ulrich Rudel, and so on. Time and again, we hear of the genius of Hitler. To say one is a *genius* is only to say that one is *inspired* — inspired by the spirits to a higher calling. In this way, one leaves a mark not just on one's own time, but *all* time. This, again, is part of what it means to be a Man Against Time. Hitler was rooted in time, but concurrently fought against its negative trajectory — that is, HE was disconnected from what many men saw as obviously so. Hitler's detractors could not see the ends HE saw: HE was a philosopher-king, both grounded and aloof, both revered and misunderstood — all of this was part of and necessary for the spiritual victory that only a philosopher-king could envision and enact, and because of this, HIS life was a sacrifice from which a great and fiery seed will grow.

Adolf Hitler speaks of this "seed" in HIS Political Testament: "From the sacrifice of our soldiers and my own solidarity with them unto death, a seed will one day germinate in German history ... and bring about the shining rebirth of the National Socialist movement and the realization of a true *Volksgemeinschaft*." It can only be so. The Führer's life was the beginning of the end of time — just as certainly as all of history is a record of the Dark Age, the Kali-Yuga; HIS life signals the arrival of the Ultimate Avatar, Kalki, *the Avenger*. Adolf Hitler, as ARCHETYPE of the Germanic will, inspirits HIS folk and clears the way for the coming dawn.

> From the ruins of our cities and monuments of art ... [and] after a six-year-long fight which, in spite of all the setbacks, will one day go down in history as the most glorious and brave avowal of a folk's will to live ... our mission in expanding the National Socialist state will be a

---

his faith and suggestive strength which held the staggering eastern front and avoided a catastrophe. A leader-personality of outstanding greatness.'"), 204 (from Hermann Giesler: "Even more than [Hitler's] penetrating intelligence, his faith determined his thinking, his trust in Germany, himself and his mission, but also his belief in Providence..."), 233 ("Before the Allied tribunal at Nuremberg in 1946, Col. Gen. Alfred Jodl said this about Hitler: 'He acted like all heroes in history act ... Condemn him, ye who may. I cannot.'").

> work for coming centuries, which obliges every individual always to serve the common interest and to put aside his own advantage in its favor.

Thus spoke the Führer. There has never been a more brilliant recognition of the advantage in sacrifice. Such sacrifice can only come from a folk bound in blood; from this mystical foundation, we witness the triumph of the will.

Closing Thoughts

Time will tell the story of the Germanic races' renewal. There will be hardship; all will seem lost; but the fact remains that all time has been leading to the victorious salvation of the Germanic folk. We, through loyalty to our blood and kin, are the descendants of the gods and inheritors of a tradition that will endure. Adolf Hitler, through the greatest sacrifice, assured our folk of their Destiny as the saviors of this world. As our number dwindles, our quality increases — because our awareness of the situation grows. This anti-Germanic world will continue to darken, and as it does, our trials will increase, war and violence will increase, and materialism will lord over the earth; the earth will decay and revolt. These things are certain — it has been foretold by our Aryan ancestors who, through their blood purity, were closer to the gods than us.

While such things are fated, it is never our place to passively accept them; our place is to struggle and fight for that which is worth remembering, worth upholding. Should the gods ordain a blackened world governed by the Father of Lies, Jehovah, we yet represent the good that must return; and it is for this *good* that we must struggle, just as our Führer struggled. It is through this struggle that we define ourselves, our blood.

Hitlerism recognizes the god-willed place the Führer holds in Germanic Destiny. It opposes the lies propagated about HIM, HIS folk and mission in this modern cesspool of a world. The "truth" and "facts" of money-lovers, addicts, and faithless materialists are naught but depravities designed to destroy and enslave all that is good. All of these lies represent the will of the Father and Children of Lies: Jehovah and its golems. Theirs is the *transvaluation* of values, which has placed them at the top of modernity, a time destined to ruin. When we see the evil that plagues the world, we witness *symptoms* of this transvaluation *disease*. If life and goodness are to endure, however, the Germanic man must triumph: harmony with Nature begins with the MYTH of the Blood.

This new world, this new order is coming. It must come: Adolf Hitler revealed it through HIS life and vision. *Quality* is and will be the measure of rectitude, of value and divinity. This is the meaning of the MAN TO COME. This is the meaning of the MYTH AND THE SUN.

EPILOGUE

AN END UNTETHERED

> *Each idea must step out before the nation, must win over the fighters it needs from its midst and must tread alone the difficult path with all its necessary consequences, in order to one day achieve the strength to change the course of destiny.*
>
> — ADOLF HITLER

There is one with us now — waiting — meant to be the salvific embodiment of our quality-based creed. HE is the man of action, the saving strength, meant to avenge the downfall of the Divine Order of Nature against the coalesced forces of Evil. Who can account for HIS childhood? What are HIS dreams and ambitions? Is HE aware of HIS cosmic mission? Perhaps in a few years, as a young man, HIS mission will become clear; then HIS course will be set until HIS purpose is fulfilled. Meantime, the world is unsuspecting. To the world, HE is just a child, an innocent, and potential collaborator. But the Eternal Order speaks to HIM, imperceptibly, masking HIS movements and driving HIS decisions. Fate will call HIM forward when the time is right: when the old values seem on the verge of extinction, when the measure of quality is marked as a creed of evil. All will seem lost. But HIS purpose is restoration; and for this restoration to occur, destruction must precede it. HIS forces will be few, but potent; they will come from all walks of life, bound by the Divine Order of Nature: rowdies, intellectuals, mothers, fathers, workers, businesspersons, students, teachers — all of them *fighters*. They will fight within their sphere at first. Yet when HIS spark appears, their wills will ignite into an unrelenting fire against the cold, godless, *automatonic* masses.

This will be the *Übermensch* foretold by Nietzsche: the bonded wills of a folk and their leader. And though this has happened before, *this* manifestation will be different. The context of global collapse alone assures this; but, more significantly, what demarks past fusions of will from this new *Übermensch* is the *mission*: the inverted world must be righted and all who sustain it must be expunged. The time for doubting the intentions of those who would do Nature and her followers harm is gone; *mercy* is antiquated at best; at worst, and in all likelihood, mercy is a manipulative tool used by the ruling elite to subjugate credulous masses. Mercy toward one's enemies is preparation for future failure; the slave-morality lauding *mercy* dissolves with the advent of the *Übermensch*, the MAN TO COME.

Preparatory work has been done, and is still being done. We know the MAN TO COME has not arrived because the ill-begotten quantity rules the day; their order inverts and pummels the Divine Order of Nature. The preparatory work began with Adolf Hitler and HIS movement; it continues in the hearts and wills of the few remaining faithful who impact what they can — ideally through raising new generations of faithful. For

> quantity [can] only be crushed through quantity. And so can the impact of well-organized, raceless masses, devoted to a false idea, only be held back and overcome through the stronger impact of still better organized, disciplined millions of the best Aryan blood, inspired with a fanatical faith in eternal cosmic Truth.[1]

"Faith in eternal cosmic Truth" is the essence of Hitler's work, and it is the bedrock of any possible future. Truth accords with Nature — *quod erat demonstrandum*. Man is not meant to subvert or overcome Nature to introduce weakness or disease into an otherwise self-regulatory culling system, as modernity is wont to do. On the contrary, man is to uphold Nature's standards with all means necessary. This accordance with Nature lends substance to Hitler's preparatory work; it gives it a timelessness that, if subverted, precipitates the decline of decency through degeneracy. Such subversion began with the inversion of natural values — the arrival of usurping slave-morality introduced by the Father of Lies, Jehovah, and its golems. Slave-morality — as it appears in all liberal doctrines: Christianity, humanism, international socialism, progressivism, etc. — has no substance, for it is "in time." That is, it espouses, in all its manifestations, the prevailing dogma of man's "innate dignity," which is one of the principal tenets of modernity. Hitlerism is the *only* creed of substance in the world today. It rejected the "dignity" dogma *despite the consequences*, fought against the "in time" forces with *heroic will*, and was culled in the greatest, most terrible struggle — a *cosmic struggle* — the world has ever seen.

---

[1] Savitri Devi, "The Struggle for Truth," *The Lightning and the Sun*.

Consider Kierkegaard, that brilliant Germanic thinker: he railed against the Danish Church because of what he saw as their inability to comprehend what it meant to be an actual follower of Christ: *contemporaneousness* is key.[2] Few, if any, extant Christians are able to rightfully call or even think of themselves as "bearers of the cross" because they simply *take it for granted* that "Christ is King." They have no idea what it means to believe this anonymous, apparently insignificant Nazarene carpenter's son is the savior of mankind and, moreover, face no consequences for their supposed belief. That is, modern "believers" have no need for *faith* — the essential element of any substantive creed: they have the benefit of history and billions of so-called adherents to serve as suitable surrogates to faith. In short, modern Christians simply believe in a history book: it is *faithlessness*. To be "contemporary with Christ" is to disregard all history and Christendom: it is to meditate on the Nazarene — that simple nobody — as the *savior* of mankind. Is it conceivable? Only the faithful can tell.

Hitlerism, on the other hand, is *the* faith of the future. The material disaster of 1945 is still fresh; Adolf Hitler and HIS creed were, are, and will continue to foreseeably be demonized and persecuted. Contemporaneousness for the Hitlerist is not a meditative act; it is life, *jetzt*. If one is a Hitlerist, *faith is existence*; restoration of *the right* in this world has yet to come. Will it come? Only faith and will can tell. The Hitlerist has no benefit of historical victory and seas of believers; he is "against time" — that is, he struggles against the current time cycle and its prevailing doctrine.[3] The present Hitlerist is the man of faith *par excellence*: he is Kierkegaard's knight; he is the paradox willing to erase the universal for the sake of communion with God; he waits and sets the conditions for the paradisiacal age to come.

---

[2] See Kierkegaard's *Fear and Trembling* and *Training in Christianity* for detailed discussions of *contemporaneousness*.

[3] "It is a great honor to me when Herr Trotsky [regards] National Socialism ... as the only real danger to Bolshevism. And it is an even greater honor for me because in twelve years, starting with nothing at all and *in opposition* to the overall public opinion at the time, *in opposition* to the press, *in opposition* to capital, *in opposition* to the economy, *in opposition* to the administration, *in opposition* to the State: in short, *in opposition* to everything, we built up our Movement, a Movement which can no longer be eliminated today...." Adolf Hitler, 27 January 1932; emphasis added.

∞ ∞ ∞

What is the spark that will announce the arrival of the MAN TO COME? Only the eternal forces of the universe know. Perhaps man will willingly slip so low into automatonic drudgery and be so spread over creation that there will be general ecosystemic collapse. Certainly men will be soulless husks, partial only to mindlessly and passively consuming one distraction after another; the only effort they will spare is denunciation of perceived nonconformists. Filth and betrayal: these will mark the end of the darkest of ages; these will ignite the revolt against the revolting.

Like all revolutionaries, the MAN TO COME will appear first underground; the surface will be watched. His message will echo the Führer's, which is to say, it will echo Nature. But there will be one difference: the new message will demand more lightning, less sun.[4] The sky will have blackened; life will have moved underground; the time for sun will have gone. Lightning is all that's left to right the wrongs of an inverted world; destruction and creation — these are the vital sparks "against time"; preservation, too, ignites the march against time and serves as the task for subsequent generations, when roots of the new age are anchored.

The MAN TO COME will only take root underground once the Church's roots have putrefied; this is perhaps most crucial. It was the Church that pitted all its forces against the Hitlerian State[5] — first in the Catholic, then in the Protestant realms — once it became clear Hitler's Germany meant to eradicate Christianity. Ribbentrop, Hitler's foreign secretary, recorded in his memoirs that "the mobilization of all the energies of the churches [are] against us ... [which is] a most significant and disadvantageous development from the standpoint of foreign policy." In this modern age, however, Christianity is being replaced by a progressive humanism which is based on the lingering fiction of Christianity's "human dignity," but without any sense of God; this, of course, is the reason for perpetually shifting, progressive positions on social issues within the Church. While this spells doom for the people because it further distances them from any kind of spirituality, it further ruins society, bringing it

---

[4] See Savitri Devi's *The Lightning and the Sun* for a discussion of *lightning* and *sun*.

[5] Dietrich Bonhoeffer: "Better a devastated Germany than a National Socialist one!"

closer to ultimate collapse; in other words, removal of religiosity creates the conditions for the MAN TO COME to take root underground. To this end, it seems clear the MAN TO COME will appear in the State most likely to fall. In the West, this must be America. While firmly in Jewry's grasp and, by far, the most deracinated State in the world, it seems impossible that America could ever give rise to such a great, cosmic being. Yet these two conditions are necessary to induce societal failure. What *other* conditions could give rise to a soulless future? America is the definition of a godless, raceless, Jew-controlled puppet; it is obsessed with both vulgarity and money; it despises both blood and soil. Thus, America seems most likely to collapse first among Western nations. A product of her lucky geography and tremendous resources, America could never be defeated by an external power; internal rot, however, will destabilize her and she will fall. From her throes, pockets of race-bound resistance will grow; from these pockets, the MAN TO COME will arise and anchor.

Western plutocracies and poisonous Marxist ideologues will fall simply because those they hire to enforce their will — the police and military — will begin to see their plight: that they are willing servants doing violence on behalf of evildoers. Not only this, but some of the masses will finally awaken to the "crises" governments and media constantly conjure; they will see the hysteria for what it is — a *charade* meant to elicit psychological effects that alter behavior; they will also become increasingly disgusted by what passes for distraction and entertainment: all will be infused with nauseating doses of sociopolitical propaganda — from sport to sitcom — and all will be increasingly vulgar. The tyrannical elites will have done everything they can to undermine and stamp out decency; a meaningful minority of dissenters will realize this and the underground will form. These elites and their harmful ideologies will not be able to enforce their will on the masses — not as they did during the Führer's time to incite the War. Many in the degenerate public will certainly still be keen puppets, but they will be largely witless and weak, incapable of organizing their hostile conformity in any consequential way; they will, however, be ever-present and menacing background noise to the real struggle between the righteous dissenters and the elites' inner circles, cadre, and remaining enforcers. Nevertheless, until the mob's numbers dwindle and the dissenters organize into stable cells, the remaining masses will drain needed resources: time, food, water, shelter, ammunition, weapons, clothing, medical and maintenance supplies, etc. The masses will consume these resources directly, or the underground will expend these resources against them in trying to stabilize their pockets of resistance. Thus, until the mob subsides, the resistance will incur further strain. Added to this will be the centrifugal pull of the underground's own composite worldviews.

The underground will consist of varying ideologies. Many will be Christian, some will not be; few will be faithful to the Führer. Yet all will be joined in their struggle against the satanic forces of this world: the pummeling, enslaving elites bent on eradicating race, beauty, strength, freedom, and decency. The only way for this coalition to survive is compromise: the extremists will face isolation on the fringes of the struggle. Temporary alliances will have only temporary success, and the fringes will risk exhaustion and disintegration. Compromise need not mean compromising one's values, however; compromise should mean understanding the larger threat for what it is — Jew-driven, satanic enslavement[6] — and organizing efforts based on shared values. The biggest point of contention within any coalition amongst those values — of *race, beauty, strength, freedom,* and *decency* — is, of course, race. *Blood is not everything, but it is the beginning of everything.*

Christians of the coalition will no doubt be comprised of disparate races; this is fine. However, it must be understood that races keep their integrity, for each one is ordained by God, by Nature. Nature's usurpers will be shown no mercy. The only way forward, should a way out of the gloom of the present and near future be possible, is through understanding the foundational character of race. This undoubtedly means rejecting Christianity's fundamental Jewishness. *Race* will likely be the largest rift within the coalition because Christians fail to see that their beliefs — undergirded by the abovementioned values — are essentially *Germanic*, overwritten with the crippling Judaized fiction of "all men are equal in the eyes of God," or "human dignity" — i.e., the Jewish seed of destruction: slave-morality, the "ferments of decomposition".[7] The coalition of righteous dissenters will dissolve if the importance of racial integrity

---

[6] "The one aim of international Jewry: the permanent and peaceful — economic and cultural — domination of the Jew over a world robbed of all racial pride [and] all desire to fight." Savitri Devi, "The World Against its Savior," *The Lightning and the Sun.*

[7] Theodor Mommsen, *The History of Rome* (1856/1871), p. 643.

is not understood and esteemed — i.e., if the Germanic character of their beliefs is not recognized. Flailing elites will try to exploit the coalition's potential vulnerability at every turn, focusing their energies largely on the Christians, understanding that race-language will inflame and possibly convert many lukewarm dissenters to the plutocrats' cause. The satanic forces will know that *racially aware dissenters are beyond persuasion*, that they are truly awake and will fight to the last drop of blood, as Clausewitz held. The weakest links in any righteous coalition, therefore, will be the Christians, or those under Christian influence of the old order. They must be convinced of the underlying, primeval character and necessity of race; but this convincing will have to occur subtly and in the background of the larger struggle. Ultimately, the New Order will ineluctably be without Jewish influence, and this means elimination of Christian beliefs — principally, the ignorance of racial integrity. Barring this, no coalition can endure, and no future can be conceived that is not under the tyrannical control of satanic forces.

Christianity is woven into America's cultural consciousness, unfortunately. And without its total removal and replacement with a racial-spiritualism, Germanic folk will pass into extinction. Elimination of Christianity from the *being* of European man is of existential import — just as complete eradication of all other Liberalistic dogmas is essential. Anyone clinging to Christianity for nostalgic, superstitious, social, or faith-based reasons is an accomplice to Germanic extinction and the sustained rule of Jewry. Adolf Hitler identified and fought the Enemy in HIS life. It is the Hitlerist's duty to carry that fire forward; it is the duty of the thinking man of European descent, even if he rejects Hitlerism, to see the Trojan horse Christianity represents in global Jew-worship, subservience, and the continued besmirching of the traditional Germanic mores overwritten with Semitic falsities meant to drag the strong Aryan into the mud of contempt.

∞ ∞ ∞

Once the collapse is settled, the remaining races will congeal into their individual cohorts. It is natural for folk to be and want to be around their own kind, and this harmony will be reestablished. Given the general corruption preceding the end and its insinuation down to even the individual, a certain innocence wiping the slate clean will be necessary to restart, to make the harmony meaningful and enduring.

The innocence typically thought concomitant with paradisiacal ages of man undoubtedly springs from some sort of trauma-ridden post-apocalyptic world. The strongest remaining folk — those who create "good times"[8] — will be those with an uncompromising racialist outlook; they will be few, but they will lead. Others in their sphere will be the traumatized mass willing to accept any creed that might protect them from residual social harm: they are the innocents — like the trusting Ask and Embla — on whose backs the new world will rise. It is certain that if man is to endure, he will have accepted the most *natural* tenets in his time of want, for natural tenets tend to be the most efficient and effective: the strong are nourished; the weak are discarded; the best will lead; character is valued; and race is an expedient predicate to character — for "race is the image of the soul."[9] No creed could offer more protection for any folk than this.

When the new world begins, the old world will be naught but a nebulous warning, a blot to be avoided, a moral guidepost. Heroes and villains alike will pass into myth; the complexities of modernity will recede behind more pressing concerns of survival. Perhaps fireside tales of "The Wolf and the Trader" — whose heroic *Werwolf* stands bravely against a sly, materialistic *Kaufmann*, restoring peace and myth to the world — will inspire the youth, console the old, and help all endure just one more day; it will be a panegyric to the past and a deference to Nature, which stands above us. From the ashes of the eponymous characters' struggle, Manu, the MAN TO COME, who triumphantly ended the dark age of the Kali-Yuga, simultaneously restores the New Order, the Satya-Yuga; the cycle will then be complete: destroyer is creator and sustainer is the spark. Specific names of protagonists and antagonists will be substituted with the ideas they represent, and the foundation for future culture will be established. How will the tenth avatar of Vishnu be remembered? Perhaps as *Athalwolf*, the noble wolf, or *Hadulf*, the battle wolf: restorer of right and revoker of ruin. HE waits *among* us; HE waits *for* us. HE is the archetypal first man, our past and future.

∞ ∞ ∞

---

[8] "Hard times create strong men. Strong men create good times. Good times create weak men. And, weak men create hard times." G. Michael Hopf.

[9] Alfred Rosenberg, *Myth of the Twentieth Century*. Also translated as "Race is the counterpart of soul." See *Myth* (2021, Clemens & Blair), 20.

In the end, our ability to extract quality from Nature is all that separates us from the demiurgical beasts. But this *all* is everything. First comes devotion to Nature, devotion to the natural principles that led to our existence; second is the application of our God-given consciousness to create beauty and decency. Not all with a face deserve to show it; not all with a brain deserve to use it. Quality — *our quality* — is our creed; it is the measure of rectitude that outlines order. *Deservedness* is based on this quality and is defined by that which makes *stronger*, more *beautiful*, more *disciplined*, more *decent* — in a word, that which makes *better*. Individuals, as representatives of family and race, are meant only to improve the organic orders that gave them life. Anything short of a clear recognition that we *are* our family and race — e.g., any selfish individualism — is insufferable and will only sow the seeds of our inevitable annihilation. The cycle of time ensures that future weak men will eventually re-sow these seeds; and they, like us, will grapple with their tenuous survival. But our time is now, and we embrace only that which exalts us to the level of the gods who created us: they are father and mother; they are the children who grow into warriors, fated *Kaisers*, and authors of a future written in the past.

FAMILY MISSION STATEMENT[10]

PRIMAL LIGHT OF THE ETERNAL GOD IS OUR SALVATION. FATE IS OUR VICTORY, WHICH TURNS DESTRUCTION INTO RESURRECTION.

We are Germanic. This means that, above everything, we act with a boundless and all-embracing love for our folk. We must therefore work to build up the Germanic community.

We know that God has created our folk and stands above us. Our folk becomes what it should according to God's will, and according to our will, it shall endure. Our folk stands at the beginning of its mission and of the task given to it among the folks of this world.

We are creators. Whether we work with our brain or our brawn, we must always work to create that which brings honor and nobility

[10] Inspired by the words of our Germanic Führer.

to our folk. We regard creative work as the foundation for the Germanic community.

We recognize that freedom is a consequence of power and that the source of power is the will. Power is only possible where there is strength of energy. Even the smallest man can achieve a mighty result if he is inspired by a fervent will to act. We must always fight for our own will and never submit to any alien will. And when we recognize the fighting spirit in another of the same blood, it is proof that we must double our efforts to purify our will, steel ourselves, and continue the necessary struggle.

We recognize faith as a concomitant to will. Faith can move mountains; faith can also free peoples. Faith can fortify nations and lead them to rise again. Pass on your faith to others, that you would become the living banner behind which they march.

Our greatest strength lies in our *loyalty to* and *faith in* our own self and each other. God will always help a man who helps himself; God will always show him the way to his rights, his freedom, and thus to his future. The greater our worries are today, the greater our accomplishments will seem to God, who will one day weigh, judge, and reward those who faced a world of enemies, loyally held on to their flag, and carried it boldly onward.

Our Honor is Loyalty. If loyalty stops, the man dies — just like a folk dies if it breaks loyalty. We must be loyal to our blood, our clan, our ancestors and descendants; we must be loyal to our comrades, and loyal to the irrefutable laws of decency, cleanliness, and chivalry.

We respect Nature and the Divine Order of the world. This Order is determined by strength of will and blood loyalty. The victory of the Germanic spirit is followed by the victory of the Germanic child. We must know the value of our race and blood. Selection of good blood and breeding must endure and thereby elevate our kin. We are a bridge to faithful descendants who will be greater than us. A folk can only light the way to the future if it has reverence for its ancestors and lives with the conviction of its eternal origins. Our blood is a holy legacy and must be purified with every generation. This assures our hope; this assures our divinity.

In a world full of disappearing people, who would be God? He who holds the last hope!

CODA

From the Political Testament of CARL VON CLAUSEWITZ (1812):

I renounce the naïve hope of being saved by chance....

The inane hope of taming the tyrant's rage by voluntarily disarming, of winning his trust through craven submission and flattery.

The false resignation of a stifled intellect.

The foolish mistrust of our God-given abilities....

I believe and declare that a folk should value nothing more highly than the dignity and freedom of its existence.

That it must defend these to the last drop of blood.

That it has no holier duty to fulfill, no higher law to obey.

That the shame of a cowardly submission can never be erased.

That this drop of poison in the blood of a folk is passed on to its descendants and will corrupt and undermine the strength of future generations....

That a folk bravely struggling for its freedom is invincible.

That even the loss of freedom after an honorable and bloody battle secures the rebirth of the folk and is the seed of life from which, one day, a new tree will strike firm root....

That I do not forget the warnings of the past, the wisdom of the centuries, and the noble example of great nations, in the skittish fear of our own day, nor do I exchange the history of the world for a page from a lying newspaper....

I lay these simple pages on the altar of the god of history, firmly believing that, when the present storm has passed, an esteemed priest of that temple will carefully bind them into the chronicle of our turbulent national life.

Then posterity will judge, exonerating those who fought dauntlessly against woeful degeneracy and stayed true to their sense of duty as a sacred trust in their hearts.

GRIM BERLIN

Hail the lightning when it comes,
The course is set, the thunder drums.
We see the light, the MYTH it follows,
This time the world, enter Apollo.

Nine strikes hard the anvil hot,
The echoes felt, the report is shot.
Furies, Graces, and the Fates,
Three by three, the Earth violently shakes.

Ravens' flights are swept away,
Sleeping King, HIS will displayed.
Long delayed it seems to his people,
Time is now to avenge all evil.

Die Wilde Jagd veils the land:
Furious horde, the Last Battalion.
Hung for nine days HE did on the Tree,
Wotan rides 'cross mountain scree.

Inversions are named, set right, and fixed,
Quality reigns, a time being missed.
Where lines end, circles begin.
Time began in grim Berlin.

www.ingramcontent.com/pod-product-compliance
Lightning Source LLC
Chambersburg PA
CBHW032049020426
42335CB00011B/257